Homes Away from Home

STANFORD STUDIES IN JEWISH HISTORY AND CULTURE

Edited by David Biale and Sarah Abrevaya Stein

Homes Away from Home

JEWISH BELONGING IN TWENTIETH-CENTURY PARIS, BERLIN, AND ST. PETERSBURG

Sarah Wobick-Segev

STANFORD UNIVERSITY PRESS

STANFORD, CALIFORNIA

Stanford University Press
Stanford, California

© 2018 by Sarah E. Wobick-Segev. All rights reserved.

No part of this book may be reproduced or transmitted in any form or by any means, electronic or mechanical, including photocopying and recording, or in any information storage or retrieval system without the prior written permission of Stanford University Press.

Printed in the United States of America on acid-free, archival-quality paper

Library of Congress Cataloging-in-Publication Data

Names: Wobick-Segev, Sarah, author.
Title: Homes away from home : Jewish belonging in twentieth-century Berlin, Paris, and St. Petersburg / Sarah Wobick-Segev.
Description: Stanford, California : Stanford University Press, 2018. | Series: Stanford studies in Jewish history and culture | Includes bibliographical references and index.
Identifiers: LCCN 2017052515 (print) | LCCN 2017053531 (ebook) | ISBN 9781503605145 (cloth :alk. paper) | ISBN 9781503606548 (ebook)
Subjects: LCSH: Jews—Europe—Social life and customs—20th century. | Judaism and secularism—Europe—History—20th century. | Community life—Europe—History—20th century. | Public spaces—Europe—History—20th century. | Individualism—Europe—History—20th century. | Leisure—Europe—History—20th century.
Classification: LCC DS135.E83 (ebook) | LCC DS135.E83 W63 2018 (print) | DDC 305.892/404—dc23
LC record available at https://lccn.loc.gov/2017052515]

Cover design: Angela Moody
Cover painting: Lesser Ury, "Lady in black evening dress with green scarf" (1908). Wikimedia Commons
Typeset by Bruce Lundquist in 11/14 Adobe Garamond Pro

To Ran,

For a journey that began many years ago.

וְתַגִּיעֵנוּ לִמְחוֹז חֶפְצֵנוּ לְחַיִּים וּלְשִׂמְחָה וּלְשָׁלוֹם

And to our children, Hodaia, Aviad, and Alma

וְהָיָה כְּעֵץ שָׁתוּל עַל פַּלְגֵי מָיִם אֲשֶׁר פִּרְיוֹ יִתֵּן בְּעִתּוֹ וְעָלֵהוּ לֹא יִבּוֹל
וְכֹל אֲשֶׁר יַעֲשֶׂה יַצְלִיחַ.

Psalms 1:3

Contents

Acknowledgments

Historical writing is a lonely task, or so we are frequently reminded. Yet, from the very first days of graduate school to the last stages of putting together this monograph, I have been surrounded by dedicated, supportive, and generous people. I am so very pleased now to be able to thank them here.

This book had its origins in a series of seminars at the University of Wisconsin–Madison, which turned my attention to consumerism, space, religion, and comparative European history. During this time, I had the good fortune to learn from and work with Rudy Koshar, David McDonald, and Mary Louise Roberts. Their careful reading, feedback, and guidance helped me not only to begin this project but also to turn it into a book. I owe a great debt of gratitude to Tony Michels. I thank him for his time and mentorship and for the many engaging conversations, which helped me formulate some of the essential arguments of this book. It is impossible to imagine this book having come into fruition without the support and advice of my adviser, David Sorkin. David has guided me through many stages of this project and my early career. I have benefited profoundly from his intellect and erudition, and no less from his faith in my work and in this book. I am deeply grateful for his continued help and support.

During graduate school, I had the immense fortune to meet a series of engaged and driven young scholars, including a number who came from Israel every year as part of the George L. Mosse exchange program. I am so very thankful to Sean Gillen and Stacy Milacek for helping me survive graduate school and to Na'ama Cohen-Hanegbi, Arie Dubnov, Gil Ribak, Adi Gordon and Vanessa Walker, and Scott Ury for their support, friendship, and guidance. As well, Ethan Katz has unhesitatingly and repeatedly offered sound advice and kindly read through parts of the manuscript. Gideon Reuveni has been a friend, collaborator, and early champion of my work. I am grateful for his support and the time he spent reading parts of this monograph. And Ofer and Jen Ashkenazi have long earned my deepest and most profound gratitude; colleagues and dear friends, they have been nothing less than lifelines in interesting times.

Since leaving Madison, I have had the pleasure of working with and getting to know a number of other scholars who have taken the time to read parts or all of my work, speak about my project, and offer advice and encouragement. Marion Kaplan has been enormously generous with her knowledge and experience, time, and help over the years. She has read many parts of this book, always offering excellent feedback and words of insight. Her work and example have been inspirations for me, and her support has given me well-needed motivation. I am also particularly grateful to Derek Penslar, who read the entire dissertation and made incisive and helpful comments. His feedback helped me restructure the very foundations of this book. I thank him for his long-standing and continued support, solid judgment, and scholarly example. Michael Brenner read several chapters of this book and offered important observations and criticisms, helping to make the project clearer and more focused.

Dan Diner posed challenging questions while I was a fellow at the Simon Dubnow Institute and pushed me in fruitful directions. Yvonne Kleinmann shared her knowledge about St. Petersburg and Jewish culture there and helped me locate sources at an early stage in my research. I am grateful to Israel Bartal and Shaul Stampfer for being encouraging mentors while I was at the Hebrew University of Jerusalem as a graduate research fellow. Michael Beizer's vast knowledge of Jewish life in St. Petersburg and Leningrad has illuminated more than one mystery about spaces of Jewish life in St. Petersburg. I have continued to enjoy conversations with Joachim Schlör, who has been an insightful interlocutor and has consistently pointed me to unexplored sources and directions over the years. And engaging conversations with Eliyana Adler, Steven Aschheim, Benjamin Baader, Jay Berkovitz, Boaz Cohen, Mary Gluck, Heidi Knörzer, Simone Lässig, Paul Lerner, Maud Mandel, Michael A. Meyer, Guy Miron, Steven Nadler, Inbal Ofer, Shachar Pinsker, Till van Rahden, Nils Roemer, Jonathan Sarna, David Shneer, Yfaat Weiss, and Marcin Wodziński helped me fine-tune arguments made in this book. Now in Israel again, I feel privileged to be working with Richard I. Cohen. I thank him for his support and mentorship.

The scope of this book required no small amount of archival research across three continents. I was very fortunate to encounter dedicated and energetic archivists and librarians at all turns who helped me locate essential materials and shared with me their insights. Diane Afoumado, Jenny Eckert, Katy Hazan, Peter Honigmann, Benyamin Lukin, Laure Politis, and Barbara Welker are but a few of the many archivists who made researching this book possible and enjoyable.

I also owe many thanks to the anonymous readers who read the manuscript thoroughly and asked difficult but necessary questions, helping me make the final and necessary changes to this monograph. I would further like to express my deep gratitude to the series editors, Sarah Abrevaya Stein and David Biale, and to the editors and staff at Stanford University Press for their diligent work, support, and patience in making this book possible.

This book would have been impossible to research, write, and publish if it were not for the generosity of the Mazursky and Weinstein families in Madison as well as funding from the Simon Dubnow Institute in Leipzig, the Foundation for Jewish Culture, the Jim Joseph Foundation, the Richard Koebner Minerva Center for German History at the Hebrew University of Jerusalem, the World Union for Jewish Studies, and, last but certainly not least, the George L. Mosse Program at the University of Wisconsin–Madison. Like many former Mosse fellows, I owe both a professional and a personal debt of gratitude to John Tortorice, who oversaw the Mosse Program with much energy and dedication and encouraged a generation of young scholars to build bridges between two continents.

Finally, my deepest gratitude goes to my family. To my father, Wayne, who loved and raised us on his own, and to my brothers, David and Jason, who have always been there. To my children, I hope that they will someday understand what this project meant to me and how this book in its own strange way accompanied our young family as we sought our own place in the world. And to my husband, Ran: To him I owe a debt that I will never be able to repay. He has been my strongest ally, most ardent supporter, and also most critical reader. He has remained steadfast by my side on a journey that has taken us across countries and oceans, and he provided a great playlist along the way. It is to him and our family that I dedicate this book.

To be sure, all mistakes in this book are my own.

Notes on Transliteration and Dates

For sources originating in Russian, Hebrew, and Yiddish, I have followed a modified version of the Library of Congress transliteration rules, eliminating most diacritical marks (save for the soft sign in Russian). Nevertheless, in the case of well-known figures, I have opted to use the YIVO Institute for Jewish Research's standardized spelling (e.g., Simon Dubnow and not Dubnov). Finally, for foreign words that have made their way into English (e.g., bar mitzvah), I have used the standardized dictionary spelling and not transliterated them anew according to the Library of Congress rules.

All dates from Russian sources before the calendar reform in 1918 follow the Julian calendar and are thus twelve days behind the Gregorian calendar.

Homes Away from Home

Introduction

In late August 1819, during the anti-Jewish Hep! Hep! riots that spread across German-speaking lands, a young Jewish man was accosted in a popular Hamburg café. In the police report that recorded the details of the altercation, the young man complained that an assailant had ripped the "Prussian medal that I wore on my breast," a medal that he had been awarded while serving in the Prussian army during the anti-Napoleonic campaigns.[1] It was neither random that the young man chose to wear his medal during the early days of the anti-Jewish riots in Hamburg, nor was it coincidental that he was accosted in, of all places, a coffeehouse. Rather, the violence, the prominent cafés where the anti-Jewish riots in Hamburg began, and the man's military service medal all played symbolic parts in the larger debate, begun in the previous century, on the place of Jews in German and, in fact, European society.

Even though the Hep! Hep! riots were particular to Central Europe (spreading eventually to Denmark and Poland), a heated and *emplaced* discourse of the Jewish question was not. By the early nineteenth century, the place of Jews in the public had become a matter of both internal and external contentious debate, which sometimes would erupt into violence between rival factions. The presence of Jews in relatively new social spaces functioned as a synecdoche to their status in European society. The Christian refusal to accept the participation of Jews in sites of leisure and sociability often reflected anxieties about Jews' place as would-be fellow citizens in the political sphere.

Russia also struggled with the question of the place of Jews in its empire, a question the government initially resolved by restricting Jewish settlement to the Pale of Settlement, thereby preventing Jews from residing in the central Russian provinces and two historic capitals. In France, despite emancipation, Napoleon's "infamous decrees" challenged Jews' very ability to integrate and become good French citizens. Napoleon created institutions to monitor the integration of the Jews and to coordinate with non-Jewish authorities. One such institution was the Consistoire (Consistory), which became the official space for a French Judaism defined exclusively on theological grounds. In this sense, the debate over the "Jewish question" was already always a question of space, and an emotionally charged one at that.

The story of Jews' evolving place in European society has largely been seen and studied as a legal struggle over the abstract status of Jews as a group living in European society. Yet, in effect, Jews' changing relationship with and to the state—based, first, on their status as a corporate body entitled to legal rights bequeathed to them as individual citizens—was at the core of that same emancipation process. In this book I show that the late nineteenth to early twentieth century was a key moment in the creation of the Jewish individual—a moment when forms and structures of religious, familial, and communal authority were replaced by and subsumed under the needs and concerns of the individual.[2] By the end of the nineteenth century most European governments had enacted emancipation legislation or had at least significantly eased legal restrictions on Jews, permitting, though not guaranteeing, greater integration into non-Jewish society. New state laws in Germany and France permitted intermarriage without conversion, allowed Jews to leave the Jewish community *without* joining another religious group, thereby radically altering the definition and composition of the community.[3]

Jews at the fin de siècle were in an unprecedented position to determine for themselves the level and nature of their involvement in Jewish life and religious observance.[4] For many European Jews, Halacha (or Jewish law) had ceased to serve as a normative set of guidelines and no longer governed everyday conduct. Personal desire increasingly defined the limits and scope of Jewishness, resulting in the creation of voluntary Jewish communities. As Shulamit Volkov reminds us, the ensuing "search for community" was, like emancipation itself, dependent on and "directed—primarily and fundamentally—at the individual Jew."[5] This individualized nature of the Jewish community was essential for the various reformulations of Jewish life that took place in the years that followed.

The emergence and evolution of the Jewish individual occurred roughly at the same time as another pivotal social and cultural development: Leisure sites were gaining increased popularity in European society as available free time increased. The number of cafés grew; restaurants became fixtures in major cities; hotels offered large meeting rooms and halls to gather and celebrate; children's vacation camps proliferated; and associations flourished. In the context of a growing market of largely, though not exclusively, capitalist consumer spaces, Europeans of all stripes and confessions had new and greater opportunities to meet and socialize publicly and informally. At the same time, leisure and sociable spaces were not neutral sites, even if they were increasingly open to different members of the larger public.

As Lucette Valensi has noted about the Jews of North Africa under quite different political circumstances, modern states, including new colonial regimes, witnessed an opening of "places for socializing independent of religious differences, whether these were schools, outdoor cafés, theaters, or athletic clubs." Although these new spaces for socializing did not dissolve the barriers between various ethnic and religious communities, they did lower them. Importantly, the same places "permitted a certain freeing of individuals from the constraints of their group and their religion."[6] In this sense, it is important to recall that the individuation of Jewish communities was not exclusive to Western European "assimilated" Jews. Across Europe and even beyond, Jews came to have multiple loyalties, as fissures became increasingly apparent in their once purportedly unified identities.[7] Self-selection and exclusion played important roles for the various would-be participants of any site of leisure, be it on religious, economic, or political grounds.

These were momentous changes and ones that elicited often profound emotional responses. Some contemporaries greeted the new spaces with enthusiasm and curiosity. Nostalgia colored other individuals' perceptions of the past. Still others were anxious about the clear alterations made to communal and private life; they looked with uncertainty at the world around them and the future in front of them. Numerous European Jews debated the morality and properness of entering leisure establishments and participating in the various social activities found within their walls. As Shmuel Feiner has noted, already by the late eighteenth century *maskilim* "preached against the pleasure-seekers, wine-drinkers, and merry makers who neglected their souls" and warned against the changes wrought to Jewish society with the "total abandonment of tradition."[8] Numerous nineteenth-century rabbis wrote against the pernicious effects of wasting time, which was instead supposed to be spent on the performance of religious duties.

One of the leading voices of the burgeoning neo-Orthodox movement, Rabbi Samson Raphael Hirsch, argued in his essay "Religion Allied to Progress" that "since the beginning of the century the ancient religion had been to them—ancient; it no longer fitted into the society of the sons and daughters of the new age with their frock coats and evening dresses. In club and fraternity, at the ball and supper party, at concerts and salons—everywhere the old Judaism was out of place."[9] These often younger Jewish Europeans who participated in the religiously and socially mixed environment of cafés and operas could thus find themselves transgressing communal expectations and challenging the authority of (older) religious and intellectual elites. These changes only accelerated as emancipation became a legal reality. In this increasingly porous social environment, a Jewish population in transformation was faced with its *own* Jewish question—what did it mean to be Jewish?—and many of the younger generation turned to many of these same social and leisure spaces to fashion an answer for themselves.

These public and semipublic spaces opened new ways for Jews to associate, congregate, and educate (both formally and informally) as a group and provided opportunities to celebrate Jewish holidays and rites of passage differently. Jews in Paris, Berlin, and St. Petersburg turned to many of these sites to create new forms of community. Moreover, as individual Jews began to make these spaces into Jewish sites according to their own fashion, the leadership of authoritative Jewish spaces, such as the synagogue, had to respond to these new needs and reposition itself. This is not to say that what we might assume to be "traditional" Jewish spaces had remained untouched over the modern era; the synagogue itself underwent an important transition in the nineteenth century from a "house of gathering" to a sanctified "house of God," "a place of holiness separate from the secular world and a place of refuge from it."[10] In short, Jewish space and the Jewish use of space were in significant transition.

Too often the story of emancipation and of the historical development of Jewish society in its aftermath has focused on the questions of integration and assimilation (or the failure of both). As a result, these histories have been frequently inscribed into a quick and ready crisis narrative. I am less concerned with the successes or failures of such integration and more interested in exploring how Jews *felt* about these changes and how they sought to maintain senses of difference by harnessing new spatial solutions.

This book, then, is a story about the changing expressions of self-identification that took place as leisure time grew for those living across the continent. Although many of the sites were capitalist in nature and organization (e.g., cafés, restaurants, and hotels), others were philanthropic or not-for-profit institutions. The story that unfolds in the following pages therefore joins a nascent scholarship exploring the intersection of Jewish history and the histories of consumer culture, consumerism, and capitalism, but it pushes the questions animating that scholarship in new directions as well.[11] As much as I can and do suggest that the demise of capitalist leisure and consumer spaces would have critical repercussions for Jews in such cities as Leningrad, more important was the simple variety and choice of spaces for Jewish interaction, not necessarily or simply their funding scheme.[12]

In this book I explore how Jews reconciled their growing inclusion into general European society with a desire to maintain an exclusive sense of belonging that marked them distinctly as Jews. The nature of Jewish self-identification, its limits and its boundaries, was of critical importance to Jews who lived in European urban centers. Jews might have spoken the vernacular and often dressed like other non-Jews, but they desired to maintain and transmit a sense of Jewish fraternity regardless of whether they kept the mitzvot (commandments). Faced with emancipation and the rise of nationalism and living in a significantly more open and porous society, Jews had to negotiate their place in society and, in so doing, were compelled to redefine what it meant to be Jewish in the modern era on an individual, familial, and communal level.

The redefinition of Jewish belonging did not happen primarily in synagogues or other religious spaces, though they have a part in this story. Rather, new Jewish spaces served as central sites for the expression of modern Jewish identity. In these sites European Jews sought to create social and cultural environments that would respond to their individualized needs *as* Jews. The relatively open and malleable nature of these sites further allowed

Jews to gather and express their belonging to a community and to form an identity out of a sense of Jewishness that was not merely religious in nature. These places facilitated the option of secular Jewish self-identification, marking a distinction between Judaism and Jewishness that would have been next to impossible on a large scale in the pre-emancipation era.

The social, religious, and political changes of the nineteenth century helped provoke a search for new formulas and novel spatial solutions for Jewish self-identification. I argue here that the early twentieth century witnessed no less than a *spatial revolution* for European Jews. Zionists looked to Palestine, where they worked to build a macrospatial solution, whereas most European Jews looked to solutions within Europe and sought to build a microspatial Jewish environment in restaurants, cafés, and children's camps and on sports fields. Alongside traditional-religious spaces—and, for some Jews, instead of them—leisure and consumer sites served as oases of Jewish life. This was not merely an "imaginary community" but one that existed in and through physical spaces.

Nevertheless, this story has remained largely invisible. Until recently, much of the historical literature on twentieth-century European Jewry did not talk about how Jews sought to create a Jewish home on European soil; rather, it focused on its destruction (for many good reasons). Yet this tendency conceals an important story. Even though the twentieth century did witness unparalleled persecution and violence against the Jews of Europe, it was also a vibrant and dynamic period of rebuilding and construction. Building on the recent scholarly move away from teleological narratives of persecution, I assess and uncover various renaissances of Jewish culture that began in the late nineteenth century and climaxed in the 1920s and 1930s.[13]

During this transformative period, changes occurred that would determine the face of Jewish life as we see it today. Patterns of leisure, celebration, and fraternity that continue today first evolved in the late nineteenth and early twentieth centuries. Moreover, these patterns became vital to the reconstruction of Western and Central European Jewish communities after the Holocaust. I therefore seek to uncover how European Jews confronted both the positive and the negative aspects of modernity, without viewing early-twentieth-century Jewish history as a prelude to a predestined set of tragedies. Urban European Jewish society was certainly in a state of flux, but it was not always in a state of *crisis*. For most participants the early twentieth century did not mark a crisis of identity—they knew they were Jews (and, to be sure, all individuals discussed in the following pages self-identified as Jews). Although a vocal minority experienced a crisis of *meaning* and sought to find and propagate alternative significance to their Jewish self-awareness, most did not experience an *identity* crisis.

A Tale of Three Cities

My choice to compare Paris, Berlin, and St. Petersburg (later Leningrad) has provoked curiosity, surprise, and even deep skepticism. It was long assumed in the annals of Jewish history that Jewish life in Western and Eastern Europe had little in common; comparative analysis would only confirm what we already knew: that the communities were vastly different and in effect incomparable. Fortunately, these impressions have begun to change, and scholars are more willing to consider the possible similarities and points of contact between East and West, just as they are increasingly interested in carrying out comparative studies of Jewish communities.[14] Yet, until now, no scholar has examined a Western, Central, and Eastern European Jewish community. On the basic level, Paris, Berlin, and St. Petersburg serve as clear and prominent examples of Jewish communities from those three geographic regions.[15]

The purported dichotomy between Eastern and Western European Jewish communities centers on perceived political and ethnoreligious distinctions, just as it relies on statements made by contemporary Jews themselves. We must consider these statements cautiously, however, because they frequently hinge on the imaginations of Eastern and Western Jews who imagined and popularized a distinction between the Jews of the "East," whom they portrayed as being seemingly more religious and spoke Yiddish, and the purportedly more "secular" Jews of the "West," who spoke the vernacular of the society and adopted "European" manners.

In the past scholars frequently echoed these stereotypes without considering several important factors. First, many of the Eastern Jews coming to major Central and Western European cities were not only migrating from one part of the continent to the other but also undergoing a process of urbanization. What we have long assumed to be differences between East and West are just as likely (if not more so) to have resulted from the migration from rural to urban spaces. Second, the Jews who left the Pale of Settlement in the late nineteenth and early twentieth centuries were not necessarily significantly more "traditional" than those Jews who had come to Paris and Berlin from the rural hinterland of France and Germany a generation before. Indeed, the Jewish community of Paris at the beginning of the nineteenth century was insignificant, amounting to "a tiny unauthorized settlement of several hundred Jews."[16] Throughout the nineteenth century, the Jewish population of Paris rose, largely thanks to migration from the provinces of Alsace and Lorraine. Similarly, before 1823, the Jewish community of Berlin rarely numbered more than 3,500. The Jewish population grew only after the 1820s, as Jewish migrants from Brandenburg and Pomerania moved to the city, joined a decade later by Jews from West Prussia, Posen, and Silesia.[17] Linguistically these migrants often differed only in their dialect of Yiddish, not in their use of the language. The Eastern Jew, as historian Solvejg Höppner once pithily suggested, was simply the one who came "after me."[18]

Politics has been another major contributing factor to the perception of an East-West divide. The popularity of distinctly (and ethnically) *Jewish* political movements, such as Zionism and Bundism, in the East seems to suggest a radically different sense of political selfhood and collective identity than the liberal or left-wing integrationist politics more common to Jews in Central and Western Europe. On the one hand, this difference cannot be overlooked and bears an important truth. On the other hand, Bundism, for example, was quite popular in early-twentieth-century Paris among the working class. And in St. Petersburg, many Jews, especially among the elites, were committed to a liberal, integrationist political vision.[19] Jewish communities in major cities across Europe were politically diverse, and their members voiced political positions that spanned a wide spectrum.

The perception that ethnic politics dominated the Eastern Jewish political landscape and that integrationist politics dominated in the West is an outgrowth of assumptions made about the severity and pervasiveness of antisemitism in different parts of the continent and Jewish responses to it. By the 1880s and 1890s positive as well as negative interactions with non-Jews in all three countries had provoked changes in the politicization and political methods of the Jewish population, leading to discussions, debates, and practical work toward a new Jewish future.[20] Nationalist, Bundist, and Zionist responses are well known and again are typically viewed as particularly Eastern European responses to antisemitism and antisemitic violence (even if we know that Bundist and Zionist voices could be heard across the continent).

Yet there were liberal Jewish responses as well, and they too spanned the continent. The Dreyfusard Republicans in France and the leading voices in the Obshchestvo dlia rasprostraneniia prosveshcheniia mezhdu evreiami v Rossii (Society for the Spread of Enlightenment Among the Jews of Russia, or OPE) in Russia[21] and the Centralverein deutscher Staatsbürger jüdischen Glaubens (Central Association of German Citizens of Jewish Faith, or CV) in Germany offered liberal, integrationist responses to the growing hostility from non-Jews. Moreover, these same organizations, rather than rejecting Jewish collective identity, came to express a closing of ranks among Jews and voiced strong Jewish pride just as they asserted the worthiness of Jews as fellow Europeans.[22] Jewish collective consciousness was therefore not just the purview of nationalists; by the end of the nineteenth century liberals had also come to recognize the importance of strong Jewish identity and self-defense.

Furthermore, the long and bloody Great War influenced attitudes toward integration and the ways in which Jews felt attached to their Jewish roots. This led to a stark encounter with Jews from across the continent, one that would inform and alter self-perception greatly on all sides.[23] If the activities of Jewish groups and organizations sought to respond to the new Jewish question, the interwar years witnessed an even more significant process of pushing at the boundaries of identity and community and, in so doing, redefined the status quo. Even for the outwardly acculturated Jews in the communities, the desire to create or give voice to a "new Jewish culture" was of growing import.

Structurally as well, by the end of the nineteenth century the three capital cities of the leading European empires—Paris, Berlin, and St. Petersburg—served as the primary centers of Jewish life in their respective countries. Demographically, Paris was the undisputed center of French Jewry and was predominantly, though not exclusively, Ashkenazi in character. Berlin, too, had the largest Jewish population in Germany, even if other cities, including Frankfurt and Hamburg, had historically important and demographically significant populations.

St. Petersburg's growing Jewish population was smaller than that of Paris or Berlin and also smaller than the overall Jewish population in the Pale of Settlement. Only in the middle of the nineteenth century, during the era of the Great Reforms under Tsar Alexander II, were certain professional categories of Jews permitted to settle in St. Petersburg (first-guild merchants in 1859; those with university degrees in 1861; guild-registered artisans in 1865;

and Jews who had completed their military service in 1867). Despite these restrictions, the Jewish population of the city grew substantially. By 1897 the *guberniia* (province) of St. Petersburg had an official Jewish population of 21,122 (most of whom lived in the city itself). Unofficial estimates place the Jewish population at roughly double the official figure.[24] Although the population in absolute numbers was smaller and although gaining residence privileges was more complicated in St. Petersburg, the Russian capital, like Paris and Berlin, was home to the intellectual and business elites and both symbolically and institutionally served as the center for the most significant Jewish organizations, including the thriving Jewish press.

Moreover, the Jewish communities of Paris, Berlin, and St. Petersburg were well versed in the experiences, practices, and even histories of each other. The cultural world that many middle-class Jews of St. Petersburg established and inhabited resembled that of other bourgeois urban Jews across Europe. This was no accident, because they frequently strove to imitate their coreligionists in Western Europe, and Western European Jews also adopted practices and attitudes that had foundations further to the east.[25]

Finally, we must consider the sheer number of Jewish individuals and institutions that traveled between these cities. The histories of the three cities and the Jewish individuals and institutions residing in them were deeply intertwined. On the most obvious level, the pogroms of 1881–1884 catalyzed a massive wave of immigration to the West that continued well into the 1920s. These migrations brought members of the communities together and radically changed the demographic composition of the Jewish communities of Paris and Berlin. Thus, by the eve of World War II, France was home to the third largest Jewish community in the world, and the Jewish population of Paris was split nearly 50–50 into those who were born in France and those who were born in Eastern Europe.[26] In 1890 Berlin had a Jewish population of 108,044 individuals. Yet by 1925 the population had risen to 173,000 people, thanks largely to immigration from Eastern Europe. This immigration wave meant that the Eastern European Jews living in Berlin accounted for a little more than one-fourth of the Jewish community.[27]

Organizations and newspapers also made this westward journey. The Society for the Protection of the Health of the Jewish Population (Obshchestvo okhraneniia zdorov'ia evreiskogo naseleniia, or OZE), founded in St. Petersburg in 1912, developed into an international organization that by December 1923, three years after the closing of its Petrograd office, had its headquarters in Berlin. Later, the head office relocated to Paris, where the organization was renamed OSE: l'Oeuvre de secours aux enfants.[28] The Russian-language Zionist newspaper *Razsviet* (The Dawn) made a similar journey. The successor to *Evreiskaia Zhizn'* created in 1904, *Razsviet*, formally came into being in St. Petersburg in 1907.[29] In 1922 its central office moved to Berlin, under the editorial direction of Zeev Jabotinsky, and then to Paris several years later.

Although this book is a comparative work, it was never my intention simply to point out the similarities between the three cities and ignore the differences. Inasmuch as we can and should note certain commonalities between the three cities, the general political distinctions between the three countries are responsible for many of the differences that emerged during the period under discussion and were pivotal for the ultimate differences between them in the 1920s and 1930s (as well as after the Shoah). National, state, and local politics played a key role in delineating the parameters of what was possible or impossible for Jewish communities and their expressions of belonging.

A New History of Jewish Space

Philosophers and theoreticians have long reminded us that we live in an "era of space."[30] Although the geographic turn has actively redirected our attention to narratives of place, much of Jewish history has long been concerned with place—from religious and institutional spaces to cultural and associational spaces. Indeed, a spatial narrative about the transformation of European Jewish communities had already emerged by the 1990s, at the latest, suggesting that Jews altered their patterns of affiliation and solidarity in response to processes of political, cultural, and social modernization.[31] At the same time, many historians and scholars of Jewish studies have made only indirect or tangential reference to space and place without placing them at the heart of their intellectual mission.[32] Only more recently can we discern a growing body of literature that foregrounds place in historical analysis.[33] This academic development is linked to a growing awareness that place truly matters and does not merely provide a colorful backdrop to the "real" story.[34] Yet all scholars of place recognize that places without people—without people talking about them, thinking about them, or interacting in them—do not really matter.[35] This book, then, is not an architectural guide of Jewish Paris, a history of Jewish institutions in St. Petersburg, or even the story of the Jewish café in Berlin. Rather, I seek in the following pages to offer a history of individualized Jewish being through a spatial analysis, taking the three cities as case studies and settings for these developments.[36]

As such, I find resonance, perhaps unexpectedly or even ironically, in Martin Heidegger's discussion of place and the search for authenticity. His famous essay "Building, Dwelling, Thinking" explores the imbricated search for home and a unified identity that can be located in the individual's quest for harmony with her surroundings in a time of displacement. Heidegger wrote his article after World War II, in a period of significant housing shortages in Germany. His text seeks to connect building, being, and dwelling in space. Thus Heidegger reflects a desire, if not to turn back time, then to re-emplace the displaced. He offers a bridge between spatial and emotional understandings, reminding us of the modern challenge of fractured identities and urban displacements.[37]

The search for rootedness in the face of fracturing and fractured identities reflected a basic reality of many European Jews across the twentieth century. As Mary Gluck has noted in the case of the Jews of Hungary—an observation that holds true for communities across Europe—"Jews had become unalterably modern selves, who inhabited a fractured world, in which religious and national identities, private and public loyalties; economic and civic activities no longer formed a harmonious whole."[38] Facing this fundamental alteration, Jews frequently harnessed retrograde imaginations of a harmonious past to create a sense of stability and belonging.

The search for authenticity and home is a recurring motif in the modern Jewish experience. Historian Richard I. Cohen has noted how for some "the rapid move from the relatively slow-moving Jewish community to the pulsating life of Europe's capitals and cities tended to produce feelings of disorientation and emptiness, which certain Jews tried to counteract by re-establishing an attachment to that 'ghetto' world which they or their parents had abandoned."[39] Klaus Hödl has noted a similar search for an authentic but ultimately invented past among the founders of the Jewish museum in Vienna.[40] This practice reflects essentially modern experiences and the creation of modern values (like authenticity) as resulting from a dislocation from previous communities and spaces.[41]

These examples also highlight how the theoretical study of space and place can implicate our emotional senses.[42] Places are social processes, concrete in their physicality but extended through discursive representation and through human imagination.[43] Yet materiality, representation, and imagination are not distinct fields. They overlap: "It is only in the social practices of daily life that the ultimate significance of all forms of activity is registered."[44] They come together because we do not just live in spaces; we think about them and we represent them. They are the spaces of our "fantasies, desires, fears and longings" and "are expressed in actual behavior."[45] And although "emotions are inevitably personal and individual," groups and communities "can, and do, influence and coordinate how and what their members feel and how they may express their feelings. They can encourage and discourage them to feel shame, pride or honour; they can support them to show or withhold rage, hatred, and compassion."[46] Emotions are thus a window into motivations and collective attitudes.[47]

However, the study of emotions can pose obvious challenges to academic expectations of cool and rational objectivity. I have tried not to take emotional statements at face value; instead, I have sought to explore what personal statements reveal about expectations, hopes, and beliefs. For instance, statements about love frequently tell us more about the individualization of the community and the growing expectations of self-fulfillment and personal growth than they do about the actual love felt or perhaps feigned. Other challenges emerge in studying the emotional registers and expectations of cultures that highly resemble our own. The anthropologist of distant cultures will quickly notice the radical differences in the emotional vocabulary or manners of that culture, even if it might take her longer to explain those same differences. This is not our challenge. The Jews of Europe in the late nineteenth and early twentieth centuries frequently experienced and voiced emotions that resonated and made sense to other Europeans at the time and, importantly, continue to do so today. Our challenge is to pay attention to their emotional expressions and not take them for granted because of their sameness; in fact, it is their sameness that we should appreciate.

Thanks to memoirs, autobiographies, personal archives, and the Jewish press—which account for the majority of primary sources used in this book—we know that individual European Jews valued personal satisfaction, self-fulfillment, and autonomy. They expected that their encounters with Jewish religion and culture would be entertaining and varied—both for themselves and their children—and not simply educational or instructional. They expressed the desire to find personally fulfilling companionship and a sense of togetherness and meaning with like-minded individuals.

Religious and lay leaders often voiced anxiety and fear in the face of social and cultural changes. They wrote and spoke of their wish not only to encourage good religious behavior and norms but also to instill pride, love, and belonging to Judaism and the Jewish community. Even though we can argue that these statements, especially those made in the Jewish press, were proscriptive in nature and intended to direct and alter patterns of behavior, I try through these different sources and texts to offer a broader picture of the emotional messages and expressions conveyed. Where possible, I note the agendas behind them, highlighting the motivations behind the creation of certain spaces and practices.

It is also important to recall that it was not always up to individual Jews to determine the market of available spaces. Political regimes would rise to power across Europe that, for different reasons, would close down or prevent access to spaces that hitherto had been useful for creating and maintaining Jewish solidarity. Returning to theories of space and place, many of the places discussed in this book can be understood as what Michel Foucault dubbed heterotopias: spaces that are "in relation with all the other sites, but in such a way as to suspect, neutralize, or invert the set of relations that they happen to designate, mirror, or reflect."[48] Cafés, hotel halls, summer camps, and other sites of leisure in effect "juxtapos[e] in a single real place several spaces, several sites that are in themselves incompatible."[49] Summer camps took children away from the family home and the community with the aim of reinforcing communal identities, in the hope that the children would take this identity back into the community and continue their allegiance to it. Cafés, as Hermann Kesten long ago observed, functioned as "home and country, church and parliament, desert and battlefield, cradle of illusions and cemetery. . . . In exile the café becomes a single, continuous place."[50]

These sites invited the possibility of inverting or destabilizing relations, suggesting the subversive (and thus socially beneficial) role of heterotopias. In other words, the openness of these spaces to multiplicity and diversity could potentially destabilize the aims of nefarious, homogenizing regimes. As Foucault succinctly opined, "The ship is the heterotopia par excellence. In civilizations without boats, dreams dry up, espionage takes the place of adventure, and the police take the place of pirates."[51] Open, flexible, and creative places of dreams—spaces determined by individuals and the relations between them—have been necessary for Jewish life to flourish and continue in the modern era. In cities (and countries) where "police take the place of pirates," spaces for the practical expression of Jewish life close and Jewish life caves in on itself in the process.

Structure of This Book

In Chapter 1, I explore how Jews integrated into European society but used leisure and consumer places to maintain a sense of group cohesion and collective identity. In aiming to preserve but also in effect re-create a sense of collectivity, an increasing number of Jewish individuals turned to new social spaces to make and nurture friendships and solidify networks. The chapter is thus about boundaries: those between Jews and non-Jews and those between different Jewish groups as they were expressed in social spaces. I explore how writers, intellectuals, artists, immigrants, and the working classes used cafés to create friendship and fraternity and how they used hotels and restaurants for new forms of conviviality and community building.

In the second chapter I examine the transition from arranged to companionship marriages among Ashkenazi Jews in the three cities; in particular, I look at this transition as a reaction to the expanding market of leisure spaces. The formation of the contemporary Jewish family dramatically shifted as the notions of individual autonomy came to supersede the predominant influence of the extended family. In the process the changing needs and expectations of the Jewish family imposed new expectations on the community as a whole regarding how and where the Jewish family was to be formed.

In Chapter 3, I look at how, by the late nineteenth century, growing anxiety over the future of Judaism and Jewishness expressed itself in a redirection of efforts toward children and youth. Vacation camps and youth movements were seen as ideal venues for formal and informal education, and their creators and organizers hoped that such spaces would create bonds between Jewish children and instill in them a sense of Jewish belonging. Yet social and cultural anxiety was only one part of the story. Just as parents had come to use leisure and social spaces to solidify belonging with other Jews and to find a spouse, the hope was that children and youth would also use such social and leisure practices to develop a sense of Jewish self-identification. This growing demand created a new market for social and leisure programs that responded to the rapid change in family life and the structure of the community.

I explore how the largely Ashkenazi Jewish community began to alter the ways in which it celebrated holy days, weddings, and bar mitzvahs in

Chapter 4. In the chapter I examine the ways in which Jewish celebration patterns were changed as they were moved out of traditional Jewish spaces and into consumer and leisure spaces. Through an examination of the bar mitzvah ceremony and newer initiation rites, I reveal debates between religious authorities and lay members of the community. Religious leaders sought both to infuse older rituals with new meaning and to create new rituals that would appeal to children. Families, for their part, brought the celebrations out of the synagogue, often making rites of passage into family affairs. A similar story is revealed when I examine the changing patterns of wedding celebrations, changes that also included moving the services out of religious spaces. Finally, I explore how different Jewish groups began to change the celebration of Jewish holidays. In particular, I note the popularization of holiday balls as a new means to celebrate Jewish holidays, including Hanukkah balls and even anarchist Yom Kippur balls.

In the final chapter of the book I explore how pre–World War II models for creating Jewish solidarity were used to reestablish togetherness for Jewish adults and children after the Holocaust. This last chapter demonstrates that the patterns developed before World War II were vital to the reconstruction of Jewish communities after the Shoah, especially in Paris and Berlin. By this time, the Jewish public had come to expect wider social and cultural programs that would cater to different guises of Jewish belonging beyond strict religious definitions. I also assess the vast and critical changes wrought by the Holocaust, exploring its repercussions in the postwar communities and why these social patterns were not replicated in Leningrad, despite periodic attempts to re-create public Jewish sociability in the former capital along similar models.

This book is thus the story of how a religious and ethnic community sought to establish spiritual and physical homes alongside their primarily Christian neighbors by using new social outlets, which were becoming increasingly fashionable in the late nineteenth century. Yet leisure and consumer spaces did not just offer sites for entertainment and diversion. They afforded the opportunity to refashion Jewish solidarity, religious and cultural identity, and community at a grassroots level. The forms of sociability and patterns of community building that emerged between the 1890s and the 1930s would lay the foundations for a legacy that can still be felt across much of Europe and the Americas today.

CHAPTER I

A Room of Their Own
Friendship, Fellowship, and Fraternity

S. Y. Agnon's short story "Yedidut" (Friendship) follows an anonymous man in an unnamed city. The protagonist moves from one encounter to another, increasingly irritated by those he meets. His purposeful excursion—to call on friends now that his wife has returned from a long journey—devolves into aimless and confused wandering through an urban landscape as his wife, sad and weary, carries on without him. Once separated from her, he loses his way home, unable to remember the name of the street on which he lives. Moving from one symbol of the city to another (shops, a streetcar, the post office), deliverance and direction finally come through an old friend, whom the main character meets by happenstance in a local café. Yet the first moments of their reunion are uncertain. Our protagonist is overjoyed to see his friend after twenty long years since their last meeting, and he rushes "into the coffeehouse and grip[s] both his [friend's] arms from behind, clinging to them joyfully and calling him by name." The friend turns toward the main character but remains unmoved. Confused, the protagonist wonders "why he was silent and showed me no sign of friendship. Didn't he see how much I liked him, how much I loved him?" And then the reason for the friend's cold response is made clear: The friend has gone blind. Their brief conversation refreshes the man's memory, and he tells his son, "This gentleman was my friend." Reunited, the old friend bids his son to help the protagonist find his way home. Yet the son is reluctant to leave his father alone in the café. The blind friend turns to the main character and gazes deeply into his eyes. Seeing his friend's eyes now suddenly shining (symbolizing a moment of mutual recognition and renewed friendship), the disoriented protagonist realizes that he is, in fact, far from lost and is actually "standing beside my home."[1]

The urban European metropolis of the late nineteenth and early twentieth centuries was by all accounts a marvelous, enchanting, and yet potentially overwhelming place. It was an environment where one could easily get lost, both literally and metaphorically. Not surprisingly, numerous contemporary scholars spent countless hours and pages analyzing urban space.[2] In fiction the city takes the role of backdrop and sometimes protagonist, and certain literary works even suggest that the bewildering nature of the city could pose a danger to one's very soul.[3] Agnon's short story does not go so far. Yet it reflects both the disorienting nature of the modern urban landscape and the pressing need to find one's place within the city walls. A story that could in many ways resonate with both Jews and non-Jews of the time, the tale has particular significance for a Jewish audience; it hints at the challenges faced by European Jews as they attempted both to integrate into European society and to maintain group cohesion during a time of significant social and cultural alterations and disruptions. As Agnon's story stresses, friends and companions are essential if one wants to navigate the confusion of the city and find one's way home.

Yet the turn of the twentieth century was not only remarkable for the fast-paced nature of urban development and cultural change (especially in the realms of consumerism and leisure); the increasingly common yet often jarring process of migration meant that individuals had to create new networks and social resources far from home, a socially and even emotionally complicated process for those who came from rural areas to Europe's cities and metropolises. Furthermore, the last decades of the nineteenth century ushered in momentous political changes for Jews, with various civic developments and political movements pushing and pulling at Jewish self-definition. Civic emancipation and selective integration had altered the status of Jews, even if social integration frequently lagged behind. In Republican France most French Jews affiliated with the Republican camp, identifying their status as citizens with the French Revolution and the values that had made emancipation possible.[4]

Yet French society was far from united in its appreciation of secular Republicanism. Although French Jews enjoyed a relatively higher degree of professional integration in fields such as the officer corps and civil service than their coreligionists in Berlin (and especially in St. Petersburg),[5] any sense of full acceptance was shattered when Captain Alfred Dreyfus was accused, tried, and then sentenced to life in prison for treason in 1894. The ensuing Dreyfus affair (which began in 1894, gained significant political attention in and after 1898, and finally ended in 1906)[6] highlighted the sharp divide between secularist Republicans on the one hand and conservatives, Catholic traditionalists, and monarchists on the other. It also brought to the fore political antisemitism in a way that shocked Jews and non-Jews in France and across the continent. Importantly, antisemitism in France was not just popular in right-wing conservative circles. There were notable and vocal antisemites on the left. For example, Édouard Drumont, author of *La France juive* (Jewish France), blamed Jews for the various ills of "modern, urban capitalist economy," including railways, industrial factories, and the department store.[7]

The Dreyfus affair did not discourage most French Jews from supporting the Republic and Republican values, but it did serve as an impetus for a number of them to re-identify with and take renewed pride in their Judaism and Jewish roots.[8] The larger process of migration influenced France and French Jewry as well. Yet the growing population of Eastern European Jews in Paris were doubly if not triply outsiders. Foreign by birth, nationality, and language, they were not always welcomed by or accepted into the existing French Jewish community; socially, they were members of the working class; and politically, they found voice in trade unionism and, to a lesser extent, at least before World War I, in radical politics, including socialism, anarchism, and Bundism.[9]

Like the "native" French Jews who had identified politically with the movement and ideals that had led to their emancipation during the French Revolution, most German Jews supported liberal political parties, guarantors of full civic emancipation for Jews.[10] The German Jewish population in Berlin was successful and overwhelmingly middle class. However, the professional glass ceiling in Germany was lower than that in France, and Jews were excluded from the civil service and officer corps and in many cases even faced difficulties obtaining positions as university professors.[11] In addition, a new political movement emerged that attempted to revoke Jewish emancipation and also suggested that Jews were not a religious group but a race. Antisemitism, a term coined in 1879 by Wilhelm Marr, was not only an ideology of intolerance and hate but also a political program that aimed to strip Jews of their equal legal status.

The growing acceptance and popularity of antisemitism on the political right in Germany, even in the more mainstream Conservative Party, had repercussions for center and center-left parties. More and more political parties refused to run Jewish candidates on their lists for fear of alienating their non-Jewish voter base. When the German Social Democratic Party (Sozialdemokratische Partei Deutschlands, SPD), outlawed in 1878, returned to the Reichstag in 1890, it rejected the growing antisemitic atmosphere and ran Jewish parliamentary candidates on their list. Over time, larger portions of the Jewish population recognized the party as a strong and vocal opponent to political antisemitism.[12] Despite this obvious political ostracism, most German Jews in the Kaiserreich remained optimistic about their ability to overcome these challenges and believed in the overall progressive path of German society.

Politically, the position of Jews in Imperial Russia was even more unstable. Russia remained an absolutist monarchy until 1905. Jews were not emancipated, but some sectors of the Jewish population gained selective access to the two capital cities beginning in 1859, during the era of the Great Reforms under Tsar Alexander II. Wealthy and elite Jews in St. Petersburg, despite their economic fortunes, did not and could not gain access to the same levels of political power and social acceptance as Jews in Berlin or Paris did. Jews remained religious outsiders, despite efforts at partial integration, and over time were seen as a distinct national group. Moreover, the precarious nature of Jewish residency in the two capitals was made painfully clear when an imperial edict ordered the expulsion of numerous Jews from Moscow, first artisans in 1891 and then descendants of Jewish soldiers who had served during the time of Nicholas I in 1892. In addition, religious anti-Judaism was popular and highly influential, including in the highest offices.[13] Repeated waves of pogroms broke out in 1881–1884, and with even greater brutality between 1903–1906,[14] especially during the revolutionary year of 1905.

Jewish life in Imperial Russia could be precarious, and the Jews lived at the mercy of the tsar. Yet in many ways one could say much the same thing about all Russian subjects. Russian society was still based on estates (*sosloviia*) and thus on a series of complicated laws that defined each group's set of privileges and duties in relation to the autocratic state and tsar. The movement for political representation in Russia was multidimensional and ideologically broad, with activists espousing socialism, anarchism, various forms and expressions of nationalism, and liberalism.[15] Elite and intellectual Jews in St. Petersburg were no exception, though we can detect a strong interest in both liberalism and nationalism and, in the case of members of the influential OPE, an evolving combination thereof.[16]

The Revolution of 1905 and the resulting October Manifesto led to the creation of the first Duma (parliament) and the introduction of limited representative government: "Jewish liberals and socialists enthusiastically formed a coalition with centrist and left-wing Russian parties, convinced that a revolutionary front would bring justice and equality to all the peoples of the empire."[17] The Revolution of 1905 also brought with it a degree of freedom of assembly, precipitating the creation and expansion of social groups and movements in the city and of voluntary associations.[18] But the long-term political successes of the 1905 revolution were few, and by 1907 the revolution had clearly failed. Russian liberals, socialists, anarchists, and nationalists, Jews included, nevertheless remained committed to a different political vision for the still autocratic state. The Great War and the political, social, and economic crisis it would engender occasioned a more decisive wave of revolutions in 1917.

The wider turn toward representative government across much of Europe marked a sea change that affected the ways in which citizens and potential citizens understood their relationship to political institutions and seats of power. Yet, just as many Jews across Europe found political voice through parties that sought to represent more than one religious group or social class, others sought out political representation that would speak to their needs as Jews. Linguistic, religious, and cultural difference served as centripetal justifications for the creation of specifically Jewish parties; new antisemitism and older forms of anti-Judaism both further reinforced this sense of difference and justified a need for explicitly and programmatically Jewish political representation.[19]

As the nineteenth century closed, the first Zionist Congress in Basel, held in late August 1897, marked the political beginnings of the Zionist movement (though not its practical inception), and roughly five weeks later the General Jewish Labor Bund in Lithuania, Poland, and Russia (Algemeyner

Yidisher Arbeter Bund in Lite, Poyln un Rusland) was formed in Vilna. In the historiography both parties are identified with Eastern Europe, where they shared wide popular support. The Bund, created in and by the Jews of Imperial Russia, not surprisingly focused its political and practical attention on those lands, organizing strikes and in its early years politically working within the framework of the Marxist Russian Social Democratic Workers Party. Moreover, after World War I the Bund made its most significant political gains on the Jewish street in the newly created state of Poland.

Yet, to suggest that Eastern Europe had a monopoly on Jewish socialism would be to overlook the clear importance of the Jewish labor movement more broadly across Europe, including in interwar Paris, where the Bund became the most important socialist movement among immigrant Jews.[20] Zionism also enjoyed greater popularity among Jews of Eastern Europe, but this is not to say that Jewish nationalism generally and Zionism specifically were not influential across Europe; German-speaking Jews played a key role in the development of Zionist ideologies, far beyond what one might expect, given the general disinterest in Zionism among German Jews.[21]

Although the two parties aimed to represent the Jewish voter, albeit the Bund through class struggle and the Zionists through national awakening, the women's movement and the Jewish women's movement in particular agitated for legal-political personhood for women, economic and social rights, educational access, and women's right to political voice and representation. The women's movement challenged the status quo on a profound level. At stake was the potential reversal of the entire social, cultural, educational, and legal order and a radical overturning of the status of women. Although often associated with the suffragette call for women's right to a political voice, the broader women's movement sought to find answers to much larger questions, including but certainly not limited to where women could study, what they could study, which professions they could practice and how much they would earn, whether they could travel or work without the permission of male relatives, and what property rights they could enjoy. The changing legal, political, and social attitudes regarding the place of women in society served as one of the most important and central transformations in European society at the dawn of the twentieth century.[22]

And at the heart of all these changes and the site of fascinating responses to them stood the European metropolis, home to leisure and consumer spaces that would allow European Jews to create new networks of solidarity and confront the challenges of self-definition in the late nineteenth and early twentieth centuries.[23] Jews used cafés to create or strengthen personal, business, and political networks; they held balls in lavish halls for Jewish philanthropy; and they organized lectures and concerts on Jewish themes, highlighting in the process the growing distance from "traditional" Judaism while cataloguing the past and offering lessons for the present and future.[24] These practices allowed them to address a deep emotional need for connection and rootedness at a time when religious belief and halachic observance were waning among large segments of the population. This novel use of space highlights processes of secularization, new political and national identities, and changing attitudes toward leisure time and gender roles.[25]

Despite certain similarities between the three cities at the turn of the twentieth century, the influences of World War I, the Russian Revolution, and the rise of Nazism resulted in significant differences in the sociable practices and options available to the Jews (and often to other groups) living in the three metropolises. Even though these cities (and countries) became progressively distinct from one another, the political movements that prompted the changes also provoked major migration waves, bringing members of the communities together in a real and concrete fashion.

Jewish Fellowship and the Modern Café

By the late nineteenth century the leisure world of the inhabitants of Paris, Berlin, and St. Petersburg had expanded dramatically, and increasing numbers of individuals had both the time and the means to enjoy it. The Jewish desire for conviviality, comfort, and a space to meet with friends and associates echoed similar interests among non-Jews. For example, Anna Pavlovna Vygodskaia, a student enrolled in the Bestuzhevskie Courses[26] in St. Petersburg in the late 1880s, wrote in her memoirs about the leisure activities that the Russian capital offered. A fun-loving young woman who enjoyed dancing and the company of others, Vygodskaia noted with enthusiasm the delights of the impressive city. She wrote about her love of the opera and musical concerts and noted her good fortune that the financial means of her suitor and later husband, a medical doctor, allowed them to get good tickets without waiting in long lines.[27] She also noted her pleasure in going to cafés, such as the Konditerskaia Andreev on Nevskii Prospekt. Again, class and means were important in this choice. Cafés,[28] restaurants, and hotels were relatively new in St. Petersburg and therefore relatively expensive.[29] For most of the Jewish population of St. Petersburg who lived in and close to the Pod'iacheskii neighborhood,[30] despite their geographic proximity to Nevskii Prospekt (only several blocks to the north), their meager incomes prevented them from enjoying most of the cafés and restaurants there.[31]

The European café and café culture have received a significant amount of scholarly attention.[32] Jewish coffeehouse culture is no exception, and the image of the Jewish coffeehouse regular had already gained the status of a well-worn stereotype by the early twentieth century. Why did the coffeehouse become such a well-loved and popular space in the late nineteenth and early twentieth centuries? On a simple level, cafés offered warmth, shelter, and even electric lighting (a relatively recent luxury), all for the price of a cup of coffee or perhaps something stronger, depending on one's taste and budget.[33] The coffeehouse was also quite famously a space of sociability and discourse, a site where one could ideally purchase access to social networks or create one's own.

In practice, the café was never a truly open or democratic space. Instead, different cafés catered to particular socioeconomic or ethnoreligious groups, allowing for distinctions to be drawn between the clientele of one or another café. At the same time, by the late nineteenth century it had become common and acceptable for women to visit certain cafés, even alone, and a number of cafés were known for being family-friendly establishments. But the reputation of an establishment mattered greatly. After all, certain cafés (and restaurants) catered to a male clientele seeking a particular kind of female companionship; women who entered these venues risked having assumptions made about their virtue.[34] Geography, reputation, amenities, and politics were factors that influenced the choice of one café over another among Jewish guests. The same factors also highlight the overlapping functions that cafés played.

For Eastern European immigrant Jews living in Paris, geography, socioeconomics, and political persuasion played key roles in the choice of a café and could lead to the repurposing of cafés into institutions of mutual aid. In the early 1870s most of the small Jewish community lived in the 3rd and 4th arrondissements in an area known as the Marais (or "swamp"), where many centuries earlier the first Jewish community of the city had lived.[35] The Franco-Prussian war of 1870–1871 and the resulting German annexation of the Alsace and Lorraine provinces increased the migration of Jews to Paris, continuing a process that had begun in the early nineteenth century.[36] By the 1880s, in response to worsening socioeconomic conditions and the pogroms of 1881–1884, the number of immigrant Jews from Eastern Europe began to change the overall demographic composition of the Marais and it gained a new appellation, the *pletzl* (Yiddish for "little square"). Thus by the early twentieth century the Marais emerged as a neighborhood predominantly composed of working-class immigrant Jews,[37] and it became the home of a number of mutual aid societies (or *landsmanshaftn*), soup kitchens, cafés, and restaurants.[38] And it was in the Marais in the late nineteenth century that Café Trésor[39] came to serve as the head office for the Chambre syndicale des casquettiers (Cap Makers Trade Union).[40] This café, and others, served as a place for both food and drink and political and professional activism.

As the immigrant population grew, the well-to-do French Jewish population began a progressive migration to "better" areas. First, this meant moving within the Marais itself to a more desirable street, such as the rue des Francs-Bourgeois. From there, they moved to the 9th arrondissement (north and west of the Marais), not far from the central consistorial synagogue, the Temple de la Victoire.[41] As these Jews climbed the social ladder, they moved into either the wealthier 8th, 16th, and 17th arrondissements or the western suburbs.[42] Just as the bourgeoisie moved progressively westward, the working class also began to leave the Marais. Blue-collar immigrant Jews settled in the 18th arrondissement neighborhood of Clignancourt and at the foot of Montmartre.[43] As they moved, they frequented other Parisian cafés, institutions that remained important to the social and political world of the local proletariat, Jewish and non-Jewish.[44]

Gilbert Michlin, whose family emigrated in the mid-1920s from Poland, noted that his uncle would regularly meet after work with a circle of friends at the Café du Commerce. His uncle, Albert, came to the café, where he would "find his friends, who were from Russia or Poland, and they would play cards."[45] Here again, class and the immigrant background of his parents' generation were reflected in the spaces in which they chose to meet. Still in business today, the Café du Commerce opened in 1921 and initially catered to the working class of the 15th arrondissement, particularly those in the automobile industry.[46] It offered affordable meals and a social space that was welcoming to those of lesser means, such as the Jewish immigrants of whom Albert was just one example. The sociable nature of the coffeehouse helped support and build networks, bringing together people of a similar background. These meeting spaces facilitated sociability among members of specific socioeconomic and immigrant groups.[47]

Solidarity could also lead to the creation of other institutions, producing webs of interaction. Bundists in Paris would meet at a café on 50, rue des Francs-Bourgeois (in the Marais) during the 1920s. It was in the same space that the group decided to create the Medem Club (later the Medem Library).[48] The Bund member Marc B., who arrived in Paris in 1925 seeking work, later recounted that, to create the library, "they organized a memorial evening; the greatest writers—Sholem Ash [sic], Schneour—came to that evening. They said: 'We'll charge a fee, and whatever we take in will be used to create a library.' We collected a certain sum and created that library, which was in that café."[49] In this case the café served as an initial platform for the creation of an additional Jewish space, the Medem Library, which still exists today. The example further demonstrates how Jewish literary figures participated in creating Jewish popular culture and cemented Jewish belonging.

Jewish literary cafés in Berlin reveal similar patterns. Beginning in the early nineteenth century, the small but growing Jewish community of the city tended to live in the central district, despite having residential freedom. The Scheunenviertel (literally, "Barn District") in Berlin-Mitte[50] was the location of numerous synagogues, including the Neue Synagoge on Oranienburgerstrasse (the main synagogue of the Jewish community and the largest in Germany at the time of its construction) and the separate Orthodox synagogue (Austrittsgemeinde), Adass Jisroel. The Scheunenviertel was home to numerous kosher restaurants and shops but was also relatively close to Friedrichstrasse, a large boulevard nearly synonymous with consumerism and leisure in late-nineteenth-century Berlin. Not far from the Imperial Palace, Friedrichstrasse featured many restaurants (kosher and nonkosher),[51] cafés, and hotels as well as a major train station just north of Unter den Linden (another major artery that intersects Friedrichstrasse).

It was on Friedrichstrasse in early-twentieth-century Berlin that the large and lavish Café Monopol, with its marble tables and orientalist design, served as a meeting place for Jewish intellectuals, actors, literati, Zionists, and even doctors.[52] Itamar Ben-Ami, son of the Hebrew-language revivalist Eliezer ben Yehuda, quipped that the Monopol was home to "German-Jewry in its entirety" and to Jews from various cities across Europe. The cost of a coffee and "a single pastry on the side," he continued, "permitted you to be in their company for hours on end."[53] Geography could explain in part the reasons for the café's popularity and diversity of clientele: It was at once in the heart of Berlin, opposite the bustling Friedrichstrasse train station, but also close to the poor, largely Eastern European Jewish immigrant neighborhood, the Scheunenviertel.

Owned by a non-Jew, Café Monopol became a center for Hebrew literati and Zionists and home to an "*Eretz Israeli* [Land of Israel] corner," where participants spoke Hebrew. Even the non-Jewish waiters were known to greet the Zionists with *shalom*. The café also hosted a Yiddish table—home to a quite different political and linguistic vision of the future of European Jews—whose denizens gathered in plain sight of the Hebrew speakers.[54] Together, the various coffeehouse guests put their political and linguistic nationalist self-identification on regular display each time they met in the café. For many Jews Café Monopol was not only a place to enjoy a beverage but also a dynamic social space where they could express themselves as part of a series of subcommunities. The social space reinforced and sustained Jewish groups and networks, allowing for public self-identification and communal solidarity.

Sometimes the appeal of a specific café rested not only on the other visitors one could meet but also on the number and type of additional amenities a café provided to its customers, including billiard tables, writing paper, and newspaper subscriptions. Berlin's bourgeois and family-friendly Café Bauer,[55] on the corner of Friedrichstrasse and Unter den Linden, had one of the most impressive collections of journals and newspapers on the continent.[56] Its selection of reading materials was so vast that the café printed a separate menu listing the more than 300 periodicals available to paying guests.[57]

In the late nineteenth and early twentieth centuries, Hirsch Hildesheimer, son of the Orthodox rabbi Esriel Hildesheimer of the separate community Adass Jisroel, was a regular to Café Bauer. Every morning Hildesheimer would visit the café, drafting articles for his newspaper, the pro-Zionist, Orthodox *Jüdische Presse*. There he sat "surrounded by a giant mountain of all the authoritative newspapers that came out in Germany in order to write down or cut out all that could interest his readership." His daughter, Henriette Hirsch, later noted in her memoirs that

> everyone knew him there, of course; often he was the focal point of a large circle, since everyone knew that one could meet him up on the second floor, to the right, at his particular table in the late morning, around 12 p.m. How often he would be sought out, badgered, bothered by one person or another, distracted from his work, which was so important to him.[58]

This last statement is misleading, however. If quiet was what Hildesheimer so yearned, he could have worked at home or at the *Rabbinerseminar* where he taught, or he even could have rented a separate office space. He could have also taken advantage of the library collections at the University of Berlin, where he had once been a student. Yet the advantages of Café Bauer

Café Bauer   Abb. 42   1888

Figure 1. "Café Bauer," drawing by Lesser Ury, 1888. Source: Adolph Donath, *Lesser Ury: Seine Stellung in der Modernen Deutschen Malerei* (Berlin: Verlag Max Perl, 1921), 87. Courtesy of the National Library of Israel.

were hard to match; cheaper than a private office space with unparalleled materials for his work, the café allowed Hildesheimer to buy access to information in a comfortable setting. The coffeehouse also gave him the space to meet with friends and acquaintances at his regular table, where he sat each day at the same time. In this sense, Café Bauer helped Hildesheimer create and reproduce a Jewish community of colleagues and friends and, through his newspaper, a virtual community of readers. He sat in the same space at the same time because he wanted to be "sought out" and "bothered." The café made it possible to build networks, take a prominent role in his community (a position he enjoyed, as we will see later in this chapter), and create community through his writings and publications.

By 1915, after the closure of the bohemian haunt the Café des Westens, the Romanisches Café[59] emerged as another central meeting place for modernist German and German Jewish writers, bohemians of all stripes, and Hebrew and Yiddish authors. The café was infamous for its threadbare state and numerous tables (more than 100).[60] Nachum Goldmann, who frequented the café with his friend Jakob Klatzkin (founders of the *Encyclopaedia Judaica*), suggested grandiosely that "each group had its own table; there were the 'Yiddishists,' 'Zionists,' 'Bundists' and so on, all arguing among themselves from table to table."[61] The list of regulars to the Romanisches Café included some of the leading figures in Jewish literature in the 1920s, such as the lyrical poet Else Lasker-Schüler, authors Arnold and Stefan Zweig, Yiddish writer Dovid Bergelson, Russian author and poet Ilya Ehrenburg, and novelists Joseph Roth, Hermann Kesten, and Alfred Döblin.[62]

The literary aspect of the Romanisches Café is an iconic story, well recounted elsewhere.[63] It serves our purposes here to note that much of these writers' literary output became important expressions of Jewish culture that the increasingly secular communities turned to as a source of pride and self-identification. The literati's examples also help focus our attention on the café's role in helping coalesce belonging. The Romanisches Café's size and reputation meant that the many regulars came not just to nurture their creative muses; the café helped them forge friendships and build networks. Lasker-Schüler mingled from time to time with Yiddishists, having befriended fellow poet Abraham Nokhum Stenzel.[64] And Dovid Bergelson[65] was essentially able to recreate his former Yiddish sphere (the Kiever Kulturlige) in the same space.[66] His son later wrote that Bergelson "often spent his evenings in the Romanisches Café at the Memorial Church, which was the meeting place for the Berlin bohemian scene. . . . The atmosphere of the café held a great attraction for him. Its regulars included many artists and well-known Berlin figures and he also met friends from his Kiev days there."[67] Beyond his Yiddish-speaking circles, Bergelson met and befriended German Jews, including Alfred Döblin.[68] The Romanisches Café's role in creating and consolidating friendships was a fact that only enhanced its popularity.

Alexander Spiegel, a medical doctor and Red Cross employee,[69] was friends with several leading Jewish personalities (including the Hebrew poet Shaul Tchernichovsky, Revisionist Zionist leader and author Vladimir Jabotinsky, and Yiddish writer Sholem Asch), and in his memoirs he recounts how the Romanisches Café could at times function as a second living room, especially after the guests had spent sufficient time in his own. Spiegel recounts how late one afternoon, as his home filled with guests, including Tchernichovsky and the Hebrew and Yiddish poet and author Zalman Shneour, his "wife brought out bottles of French cognac, Russian vodka, and other drinks. Drinking whets the appetite," he continued, "and I knew that Tchernichovsky was hungry in any case, so I nodded to my wife, and soon all sorts of dishes started appearing on the table. The bottles and the plates were emptied. . . . At about midnight we finished and the guests prepared to leave [though not for home]. I told my wife that we must accompany our distinguished guests to the Rumanian [*sic*] Café on the Kurfurstendam [*sic*]."[70]

And it was to that destination that they headed. As they approached the café, they met with café *Stammgast* and acquaintance Dovid Bergelson, who asked Spiegel for his help in obtaining visas for two other authors who wanted to return to the Soviet Union. This was a task that Spiegel had repeatedly undertaken both in Germany and earlier in the Soviet Union; and it was how he had initially met many of these figures.[71] The experience of hurried and at times desperate emigration had helped to forge important friendships and had made the need for fraternity immediately obvious. The café again helped to bring together friends and acquaintances and served as an easy meeting place to arrange all sorts of business.

Several literary cafés in Paris would play a similar role. By the 1920s Parisian cafés had already become popular among literary figures. In addition, after 1933 a number of the same thinkers and writers who had frequented Berlin cafés in the 1920s fled into exile and found homes in Parisian cafés. Hermann Kesten quipped that he had sat in a dozen "exile cafés" and "it was as always the same café, on the sea, in the mountains, in London, in Paris. . . . I sat in the coffeehouse of exile and wrote."[72] And there in the Parisian cafés of exile, Kesten met with his many, many friends: "from Asch to Zweig" in the Café Régence and with Joseph Roth and Alfred Döblin in the Café des Deux Magots.[73] The pages of Kesten's writings read like a who's who of Jewish and modernist literature, just as they read like a tourist guide on European cafés. Yet the importance of the sociability cannot be overlooked, and his friendships, formed and nurtured in these spaces, were critical in tumultuous times. The café allowed Kesten to overcome the strangeness of a new city: "I only needed to sit down in a café, and already I felt at home."[74]

Yet not everyone found a home within the café's walls and access to its sympathetic sociability. For those with few or no friends, the café could be as sad and lonely as the city outside its doors. The Hebrew author David Vogel frequented Paris's literary café during the 1920s and 1930s. Vogel struggled financially and had trouble making friends. Yeshurun Keshet, another Hebrew author, in one instance made a conscious decision to join Vogel and his wife. He wrote, "I began a conversation with them. I did this deliberately: I simply could not bear the sight of the isolation and sadness that enveloped them like a kind of fine mist, like a sort of transparent, vague imprint."[75] Tensions resulting from the search for a place and a vocation in modern Europe were not always easily resolved, and the city (and its institutions) remained for many a hostile place.

The More We Get Together

Moyshe Grayvis . . . was an old and very pious Jew, whose children had recently brought him to Berlin from a little Ukrainian ghost town.

Old Grayvis couldn't sleep. His children had gone to some ball, leaving him all alone in the apartment, and they wouldn't be back until daybreak. Some three hours ago, when Moyshe Grayvis had said his bedtime prayers, put out the light, and sighed the sigh of a pious Jew as he got into bed, he mused that Berlin, where he'd been living for three weeks now, was a very big and blasphemous city; Berlin was like Nineveh, which in the days of the prophet Jonah, had angered God, and God had wanted to destroy it and wipe it out, just as he had wiped out Sodom.[76]

Toward the end of the nineteenth century, as they began to increasingly adopt popular and widespread activities, Jewish organizations in Paris, Berlin, and St. Petersburg started to use hotel halls, restaurants, and cultural institutions to host lavish balls and musical concerts and to organize public educational lectures. Such gatherings reflected both the growing perception that Jewish belonging needed to be encouraged through leisure and entertainment and the conviction that this belonging needed to be grounded in new lessons. Balls and concerts raised funds and brought together individuals through the latest popular forms of sociability with new (frequently political) messages; public lectures taught novel lessons from Jewish history and traditional culture and lauded Jewish writers and poets for giving expression to concerns of the time. In the context of a broader process of secularization, history and literature served as "the building blocks of a new Jewish identity."[77]

Among Jews and non-Jews across Europe, balls and concerts (sometimes at the same event) had become fashionable means of entertainment and fundraising by the end of the nineteenth century.[78] Rather than merely appealing to a community's sense of charity or social justice,[79] organizers hoped to elicit participation and charitable giving through extravagance and entertainment. Balls were not simply upscale bourgeois events organized by men's and women's groups; students, the working classes, and different political and religious movements held balls and organized concerts for different causes and to different ends.

Nonetheless, by holding balls, Jewish groups not only adopted a widespread practice but also engaged in new social practices and decisively challenged changing religious sensitivities (including those that had, over time, come to forbid men and women, even married couples, from touching in public, let alone dancing together).[80] Musical concerts, which frequently featured female singers and soloists, posed yet another halachically problematic matter—transgressing an injunction that forbids Jewish men from hearing a woman sing.[81] As we will see, these tensions remained despite the fact that balls and musical concerts became popular events.[82] The following examples highlight how new uses of leisure and social space along with shifting gender norms transformed social practices.

By 1889 the Société de la bienfaisante israélite (Israelite Benevolent Society) in Paris organized its third annual ball at the exclusive Hotel Continental in Paris.[83] Billed as a family affair, the charity ball aimed to raise money for the poor.[84] The event was declared a resounding success. It was held on a Saturday night, and nearly 1,000 people attended, including members of high finance, the rabbinate, and prominent businessmen. The evening featured a kosher dinner and live musical entertainment. The music was provided by, among other acts, "the Gypsies," whose "entertaining rhythm of their foreign [or 'strange,' *étrange*] music" caught the attention of the dancers and the author of a report in the *Univers Israélite*.[85]

Beyond its success, this ball was socially accepted both in form and content. Intended for families, attended by financial and religious elites, and held at a posh hotel, the Société de la bienfaisante israélite's annual ball was an event of the establishment, not those who sought to overturn it. The kosher meal and presence of members of the Consistoire further suggests that rather than challenging religious authority, religious leaders participated in part or in full in the event and, by so doing, sanctioned it. How can we account for both the success and the acceptance of public mixed-gender dancing among Jews, especially the elites and authority figures?

A contributing factor in the tolerance and approval of balls appears to lie in their obvious success in raising money for charitable causes. Also, some religious elites, including consistorial authorities, saw the benefits of overseeing such balls instead of opposing them. Because each ball was prefaced by at least one speech, typically given by a prominent community member (the text of which was frequently reprinted in part or in whole in the Jewish press), this platform was often used by these same elites to spread their own message. Accepting balls and using the platform they offered meant that one could spread an idea or promote a specific agenda. In an era of declining synagogue attendance, an audience of 1,000 individuals, as was the case for the ball of the Société de la bienfaisante israélite, was a significant enticement for religious and communal authorities to participate.

In Berlin, too, balls became popular and enjoyed widespread acceptance, including among leading members of the modern Orthodox community. For instance, the Frauen- und Jungfrauen-Wohltätigkeitsverein "Mathilde" (the Ladies and Young Ladies Charitable Association "Mathilde") held its fourth anniversary meeting at the Königstadt-Casino in 1896. The numerous and "illustrious" attendees were treated to a speech by Rabbi Dr. Lipschütz (rabbi of the Lippmann-Tausz Synagoge). The rest of the festivities "mingled dance, humorous and elocutionary speeches, so that old and young" were properly entertained.[86]

Henriette Hirsch similarly recounted in her memoirs that her parents regularly participated in charity balls in Berlin. Her father, journalist Hirsch Hildesheimer, often gave speeches and even led the dancing: "Father would give a celebratory speech [*Festrede*], which was at times funny and humorous, other times serious, full of sagacity and dignity. Almost always his speech would end with an admonition to donate for this or that charitable cause." Her parents, she reminisced, enjoyed the occasion and dressed the part: "My father loved to go to balls, which were regularly organized in the winter by various associations. My father in tails, my mother in one of her elegant evening gowns, they made a sensational pair." Perhaps most strikingly, Henriette's parents participated in the actual dancing, something Henriette knew firsthand, because her parents took the children along with them. Thus Henriette could explain:

> In those days it was common to begin a ball with a Polonaise. Mother and father, to the excitement of those present, would "lead.". . . Sometimes they would participate in another dance, the contra-dance or the Quadrille à la Cour. . . . My father took great joy in leading the dances. I still hear his beautiful, deep, sonorous Bass voice calling through the hall: "En avant."[87]

The example of Hirsch Hildesheimer and his wife's participation in charity balls reminds us of the degree to which codes concerning personal relations were in a state of modification. The family's leading presence and involvement in all activities gave further legitimacy to the events themselves and to their role in Jewish life. Finally, the fact that Hirsch Hildesheimer was given the opportunity to speak in front of various groups and for varying causes also reminds us of the advantages that such publicity could serve for those who chose to take advantage of it.[88]

In St. Petersburg, too, balls became common means to raise funds for charitable causes.[89] The society Poal' Tsedek/Chestnyi Truzhenik (Worker of Justice/Honest Worker) held an entertaining evening and ball in 1914 to raise funds for the education of poor Jewish children. The event took place on the evening of March 2 at 8:30 p.m. at the hall of the Blagorodnoe Sobranie (the Noble Assembly) on Moika Road 59.[90] The entertainment included readings from the works of M. S. Rivesman and Sholem Aleichem and a concert featuring operatic performances by male and female singers. After the concert, the dancing began. Other philanthropic events in the city also featured musical performances. For instance, in 1910 a benefit concert was held in the stylish *Dvorianskoe Sobranie* (the Assembly of the Nobility, at Italianskaia 9/ Mikhailovskaia 2)[91] for the Jewish orphans' home and the prominent OPE.[92]

Yet, despite this widespread use of balls for charitable ends, not everyone accepted the changes in social patterns and especially in gender norms. Others registered significant fear and anxiety about the social and normative-behavioral changes that were visible through these new activities. One anonymous article published in 1892 in *Der Israelit* (the most important Orthodox journal in Germany) maligned the damaging influence of attending "the theatre and concerts, balls and festivities," even for "charitable causes," and saw these actions as the sign of and contributing factors to scandalous moral decay.[93] And although mixed-gender dancing and balls had become increasingly popular, the question of whether men and women should dance together did not go away. A concerned member of the Orthodox youth movement Mizrahi, for example, asked Yeshayahu Leibowitz in the 1920s whether young men and women were permitted to dance the hora together. Leibowitz pointed to the many changes in social interactions between men and women at the time and did not see any reason to prohibit hora dancing.[94] Even though Leibowitz responded positively, we can see that the question of mixed-gender dancing remained an issue for certain segments of the observant community, creating a division between those who accepted these practices and those who did not.

From these examples it is clear that Jewish youth were at the heart of a debate about the propriety of new modes of sociability, in no small part because they represented a significant number of the organizers and participants of such events. Student groups were among the various organizations to hold annual balls.[95] Groups of Russian Jewish students in the West,[96] far from home, created associations that offered camaraderie, entertainment, and self-help. These student organizations gathered together and raised funds much along the lines of other Jewish organizations in Paris and Berlin. The Association parisienne des Étudiants israélites russes (Parisian Association of Russian Jewish Students), for example, held a musical and literary evening and an annual ball a week after Purim in 1895.[97] In November of the same year, the group organized a musical and literary evening followed by a ball on Saturday, November 30, at the Salon de la Marine. Proceeds were to be donated to the Cuisine des étudiants (Students' Kitchen) that had recently opened on 12, rue Flatters (a short walk south from the École normale supérieure).[98]

In some cases these events were organized as conscious attempts to resist and challenge the old order, but mostly they sought to appeal to the growing desire for entertainment, companionship, and Jewish togetherness.

Entertaining sociability was thus a way to create new forms of Jewish belonging according to new rationales. New political ideologies, in addition to country of origin (as was the case with Russian Jewish students), were central to these emerging notions of Jewishness.

Among the many groups to hold a ball in Berlin in the winter season of 1895–1896 was the Vereinigung Monbijou (Monbijou Association), which held its second anniversary celebrations at the Hotel "Zu den vier Jahreszeiten" on March 21, 1896. Like many other such celebrations, the event included a ball. Yet, of equal importance to the entertainment it provided was the very reason for its inception. The Vereinigung Monbijou was founded in the mid-1890s as a response to growing antisemitism in German society and politics and out of a desire to strengthen solidarity among Jews.[99] Believing that Jews were different from their German neighbors "because of our race and ancestry [*Abstammung*]," the association recognized the decline in religiosity and noted as a result the need to awaken the interest of the younger generation in Jewish history and literature, thereby promoting a love for *Judentum*.[100] With "over 100 members, all of whom came from the best Jewish families of Berlin," the association suggested that it served as a respectable space for forging new friendships and relationships. The desire to enliven Jewish belonging was a key component of their activities; dances and balls were part of their social strategy. The organization thus arranged weekly meetings with "interesting lectures and lively discussions," recognizing that sociability and conviviality (*Geselligkeit*) were necessary components for young men and women from all streams of Judaism.

Figure 2. Advertisement for the anniversary celebration of the Vereinigung Monbijou association. Source: *Berliner Vereinsbote* (March 13, 1896): front page. Courtesy of the Universitätsbibliothek Frankfurt am Main/Digitale Sammlungen Judaica. Reprinted with permission.

In light of secularization and changing Jewish self-definition and faced with new political challenges from antisemites, the Vereinigung Monbijou, like many others, had to look to different sources of Jewish solidarity. History and literature became key sources of Jewish pride and self-awareness, and the group proudly established a library to help disseminate and teach these subjects to the city's young Jews.[101] In addition, in the context of an expanding market of leisure and entertainment, the process of identity building and Jewish education had to be done with an eye to entertainment. The serious job of being Jewish had to be fun, especially for youth.[102] It was hoped that sociability would serve as the basis for lifelong friendships with other Jews.

Similarly, organizations in Paris used fashionable balls as a means to create new venues for community construction. Building on their institutional success, many of the same organizations were then able to create wider social and spatial networks. The Union Scolaire, for example, began in 1882 as a mutual aid society of former pupils of Jewish communal and consistorial schools of Paris, most of whom came from predominantly working-class families.[103] Annually, the organization held balls, which typically included dancing, a banquet, and a raffle.[104]

Yet, by 1897 and with the philanthropic help of Mrs. Baron de Hirsch, the group had changed its mandate to cater to young Jews of differing backgrounds across the city. In the words of Louis Lévy, who wrote for the *Univers Israélite*, the association aimed to "give to the Republic citizens conscious of their duties and capable of fulfilling them and to Judaism Jews proud of their religion and in the position to defend it."[105] The emphasis on Republicanism and Jewish pride was a clear reflection of the political position taken by leading members of the Jewish community during the throes of the Dreyfus affair, a position that emphasized both strong Jewish self-identification and a dedication to Republican values. Stressing that Jews could be like other Frenchmen and women, Lévy pointed to the larger context wherein Catholics and Protestants sought to "cultivate the character" of youths through lectures, activities, circles, and even games, all in the hopes of connecting young individuals to their traditions and values. Lévy praised German Jews for taking such necessary action and offered examples of Jewish reading rooms from Berlin and other German cities. In an expanding world of seemingly immoral or at least amoral leisure and entertainment, Lévy cited not only the need to protect Jews between the ages of 14 and 30 from antisemitism but also the obligation not "to lose them to café-concerts and gambling." Lévy's article ended on a positive note and cited the Union's major and recent innovation: the opening of a social space on Beranger 19 that had conference and reading rooms, a library, and a small room for games.

Three years later, a speech by Adolphe Caen, the president of the Union Scolaire, was reprinted in part in the *Univers Israélite*. Caen suggested that camaraderie was the basis of the house (on Beranger) and of the association itself: "It is camaraderie that must guide all our actions . . . and in camaraderie . . . another emotion will flourish to unite us all, closer and more precious again, the most beautiful, the most noble of existence, the flower which delightfully perfumes it: friendship."[106]

As in Berlin, friendships and fun (respectable and responsible, of course), were the ideal foundations of Jewish belonging. Yet this same Jewish belonging needed a strong message and a firm basis. A significant number of groups in the three cities sought to provide their audiences with a new set of heroes and role models, turning to modern literary and political figures to these ends. Episodes from Jewish history were chosen to offer a path for the present and the future, and a once living culture seemed to serve as artifacts for collective remembrance.

In early 1910 the Petersburg Jewish Folk Music Society held a "grandiose concert of spiritual and folk music" that included Hasidic music in the hall of the Dvorianskoe Sobranie, an event that caught the attention of a couple of Jewish newspapers in the city.[107] One article, written by M. Nagen in the journal *Razsviet*, began with an assessment of the audience and by extension the highly acculturated nature of the local St. Petersburg Jewish community. Nagen was deliberate in noting the community's supposed preference of Russian theater and concerts over "our folk music." Nagen suggested, however, that "even the half-assimilated soul of the Petersburg Jew, which usually remains little affected by all that is Jewish, cannot resist the charm of the spontaneous folk spirit."[108] This evaluation of the event and its purported effects on its Jewish audience, however, ignores the distance between the everyday cultural reality of both spectators and performers and the culture on display in the show. Jewish folk music was not part of the audience's daily life but an object of detached and mediated cultural appreciation, something experienced passively, not engaged in actively or on a regular basis. As Mikhail Beizer has noted, by the 1890s Jewish scholars in St. Petersburg were already urgently calling for the collection of ethnographic records of Jewish folk music, because, as they noted at the time, "this living material . . . is in danger of being lost irretrievably unless it is registered in good time."[109]

Jewish culture—music, literature, and history—was therefore presented to early-twentieth-century audiences in St. Petersburg, Berlin, and Paris to confirm and reinforce the gap between secular and religious, past and present. When Simon Dubnow gave talks about Jewish history, including one titled "What Is Hasidism," at the hall of the technical college in St. Petersburg, he did so to explain a religious movement that was not known to its audience through firsthand experience.[110] In the face of an obvious decline in religious observance and the dislocation concomitant with widespread migration and urbanization, a new basis for Jewish belonging was required, a fact widely recognized by the members of the three communities.

To bridge the gap between past and present and to create a new set of role models, the Jewish community emphasized and esteemed literary, intellectual, and political figures and the fields of Jewish history and literature. For example, the Association des étudiants israélites russes in Paris organized lectures to educate its members on various topics of Jewish history—from the ancient kingdom and its demise at the hands of the Babylonians to the modern success and allure of Zionism.[111] In 1898 the same organization hosted a lecture by the Zionist leader and medical doctor Max Nordau at the Hotel des sociétés savantes—tickets, as the press informed readers, were available at all major Jewish restaurants.[112] Similarly, various organizations in Berlin held lecture evenings in hotels halls, such as the Cassels Hotel, with the purpose of using Jewish history and religion to relate political, frequently Zionist, narratives.[113] These organizations' clear political goals and Zionist inclinations should not cloud the fact that young Jewish students used new consumer sites, including hotels and restaurants, to teach new lessons that would create novel forms of Jewish belonging.[114] And political-Zionist lessons did not monopolize the field.

In late 1909 and early 1910 the Jews of St. Petersburg gathered on a number of different occasions to celebrate the twenty-fifth jubilee of the literary works of S. Ansky (now famous for his later play *The Dybbuk*). On December 27, 1909, the Jewish literary society held a jubilee celebration at the Jewish school. Attended by a large public, the event took place in the school's auditorium and included lectures by the historical and literary scholars S. M. Ginzburg and S. L. Tsinberg.[115] On January 9, 1910, a banquet was organized in S. Ansky's honor and took place at the Central Jewish restaurant R. O. Mikhelevich on Nevskii Prospekt.[116] The journal *Novyi Voskhod* reported that more than 100 people attended the event and that S. Ansky himself was present at the banquet. The esteemed author responded to the outpouring of praise and admiration in a speech he delivered to those assembled.[117]

Likewise, in the spring of 1914 the intellectual and financial elites of the St. Petersburg community were again abuzz, thanks to a visit from the German Jewish philosopher Hermann Cohen. Cohen gave a lecture at the great hall of the Pirogov Museum on Friday, April 25. The following day, a banquet attended by 120 people was held in his honor at the M. A. Gintsburg Jewish almshouse, a building that also housed the Jewish Historical-Ethnographic Society.[118]

Thus by the early twentieth century Jewish intellectual, literary, and political figures came to serve as cultural heroes for a community that was in the process of evaluating the foundations of its identity (what did it mean to be Jewish and on what basis would this Jewishness be formed?) and reassessing its history. Using historical narratives, contemporary culture (mainly modern literature), and traditional folk culture, significant members of the Jewish community of all three cities invested meaning in secular activities and historical artifacts. Yet the 1920s and 1930s would see a greater differentiation between the three cities and the local Jewish communities' ability and propensity to use social and leisure space as a stage on which to play out Jewish belonging. Larger political forces would determine much of the fate of public Jewish solidarity.

Closing the Doors

World War I and the resulting food shortages, as well as the Russian Revolution and civil war, had a significant impact on the population of Petrograd (as St. Petersburg was called after August 31, 1914), Jewish and non-Jewish alike.[119] The liberal Russian Revolution of February 1917 occasioned two major legal-political changes for Jews: civic emancipation and the abolition of the Pale of Settlement. These positive measures along with the beginning of a new wave of anti-Jewish pogroms in the former Pale between late 1917 and 1921 provoked a massive wave of migration into European Russia, demographically changing the nature of Petrograd's Jewish community.[120]

The Jewish population of Petrograd thus exploded as Jews left the former Pale in the wake of civil war, famines, and violent pogroms.[121] Between 1920 and 1939 the Jewish population of Petrograd/Leningrad (the name changed once again in 1924) rose in absolute numbers from 25,543 to 201,542, representing an increase from 0.9% of the general population to 6.31%.[122]

Much of our impression of Jewish life in Soviet Petrograd/Leningrad, however, has been tainted by the fate of Jewish culture under Stalin and during the cold war. As a result, some scholars and many members of the public have assumed that Soviet officialdom immediately set about repressing and destroying all expressions of Jewish political, social, and cultural life within its grasp. Yet a growing number of scholars of Russian and Soviet Jewry[123] have proven that this was not the case and have pointed to a brief Jewish renaissance that took place in the early years of the Soviet Union, beginning in the heady days of the 1917 revolutions and taking different directions after the civil war. On the whole, we must note that Soviet Russian policy toward the Jews, especially in cities such as Petrograd/Leningrad, was never coherent or consistent over long periods of time. It vacillated between the tolerance of those expressions of Jewish culture that were or could be made compatible with the political and ideological goals of the state, and, later, especially under Stalin, clear antisemitic persecution.[124]

In the early days of the revolution, there was an explosion of Jewish cultural and political activity in Petrograd, from Zionist groups (who organized a Palestine Week in 1918)[125] to the creation of a radical, symbiotic, and largely short-lived Soviet Jewish culture. In the chaos of the first couple of years, the Soviet authorities were either less interested in or, in other instances, simply lacked the resources for monitoring all activities and ensuring that they were politically correct. It was during this time that fascinating developments were made on the Jewish stage.

Petrograd in the early 1920s was home to a number of independent Jewish organizations. Members of the Jewish community who had settled in the city during the Imperial era formed religious, charitable, social, and cultural organizations. In addition to feeding poor university students and funding a Jewish old-age home and polyclinic, the OPE ran a library and the Jewish Historical-Ethnographic Society operated a museum.[126] Jewish social spaces became central staging grounds for Jewish culture; these included libraries and reading rooms, such as that of the Society Ivrio; Jewish theaters; vocational schools and other sites of higher education; sports groups such as Maccabi; Zionist clubs such as He-haluts and "Gatikvo" (Ha-tikvah), founded in 1918 to teach the history of Zionism; and the Jewish press.[127] The city, for about six years, also was home to a Jewish university.[128]

Further, Jewish organizations were created under the auspices of the new party apparatus, including the Evsektsiia (the Jewish section of the Communist Party established in 1918 under Seymon Dimanstein and disbanded in 1929). The Evsektsiia was tasked with spreading revolutionary values to the Jewish worker in what was deemed to be their national language, Yiddish. Aggressively antireligious in nature, the Evsektsiia was an expression of early communist policy toward Judaism and religion more broadly but also a reflection of the wider Soviet nationalities policy.

Berta Ioffe, daughter of the St. Petersburg/Leningrad rabbi David Tebele Katzenellenbogen, wrote years later that "Petersburg was rich with Jewish cultural institutions, museums, it was the center of many societies for enlightenment. Over the course of the first years of the Revolution, when well-educated—according to the Jewish meaning—youth arrived to Leningrad, this national cultural life even expanded and acquired a more organized character."[129]

Yet, for political-ideological reasons, consumer sites, such as restaurants, significantly declined in importance.[130] The social and cultural world of the Jews of Petrograd/Leningrad during the 1920s and after had to rely mostly on noncapitalist sites. This would be critical for the fate of independent Jewish organizations when, in the mid- to late 1920s, Soviet authorities began closing a number of institutions and organizations, including Hebrew-language schools and noncommunist Jewish groups. The formal nature of Jewish organizations and the concomitant absence of open public spaces for informal gathering meant that the array of available Jewish spaces shrank considerably.[131]

By the 1930s most of the autonomous and communist-run Jewish associations were shut down by the authorities. One of the solitary remnants of Jewish nonreligious life was the Jewish House of Public Education, which had "a library, a choir, a theatre studio, and held literary evenings."[132] Throughout the Stalinist era, avenues for public or semipublic Jewish sociability remained curtailed.

Opportunities for Jews to meet socially came through other spaces, including the city's only functioning synagogue, private apartments, and institutes of higher education.[133] Yet the postsecondary schools, including the university, were not replacements for sites of sociability and never served as the basis for new communal cohesion. And over time, precisely because of their high visibility, Jewish university students became an easy target for exclusion.[134] The city's one remaining synagogue, though open throughout the Soviet period, was essentially a politically incorrect space, and many Jews avoided it for that very reason. This left the Jewish home, which, though important, poorly satisfied the needs of public sociability and togetherness. Further, it was more restricted in size and in audience. Meeting in the family home, usually a small apartment, posed the additional problem of eavesdropping neighbors. The closings of consumer spaces and of Jewish organizations and associations would have critical repercussions for Jewish life in Leningrad (or the general absence thereof); the demise of public Jewish spaces influenced other features of Jewish life in the city. However, the consequences were rarely as dire as what Jews in Berlin faced with the Nazi rise to power.

Space and Exclusion

Nazi racial policies would infamously lead to the mass murder of millions of Jews,[135] but they also first led to the forcible exclusion of Jews from political, civic, economic, cultural, and social life.[136] The social death experienced by Jews before World War II included their prohibition from swimming pools,[137] theaters, cinemas,[138] parks, and some, though not all, restaurants and cafés.[139] By the end of the 1930s the regime quickened the destruction of Jewish life across the country, closing and destroying countless Jewish establishments, from synagogues to libraries and archives. By the beginning of the war, Jewish social space had been nearly ruined.

Thus few spaces existed where Jews could safely, even surreptitiously, meet. In a fascinating account of survival, Inge Borck recalled years later in a published interview how she would meet a friend at Café Melodie (earlier, Café Kurfürstendamm) on the Kurfürstendamm to buy ration cards on the black market, because she had no legal access to them. "Although it was very dangerous living illegally, there were many underground contacts between those who had gone under and also ways to meet," she stated in the interview. She explained that she and a close friend "would go together to the Café Melodie and arranged ration cards for other people since we looked entirely harmless."[140]

Information about Café Melodie is scant, though it appears to have been one of several cafés where Berlin Jews met during World War II.[141] Borck mentions in the same context that "above in the café older Jewish people met and drank coffee there, did their business and talked."[142] She adds that some of her friends were still living legally at that time.[143] From Borck's description, Café Melodie, until relatively late in the Nazi era, served as a sanctuary where Jews who still lived legally and those who lived clandestinely could meet. In the end, Café Melodie was a site for Jewish solidarity and survival in a city whose leadership nefariously no longer accorded a place for its Jewish inhabitants.

Conclusions

The development of modern leisure culture and space influenced the ways that Jews rebuilt bonds of solidarity and belonging and even created friendships in a changing landscape. These were important patterns for new Jewish organizations and have since repeatedly served as models for creating Jewish community. Arguably one of the most important innovations in contemporary Judaism has been the expansion of the Chabad-Lubavitch movement under its last rebbe, the late Menachem Mendel Schneerson. Chabad-Lubavitch is known for its Jewish outreach and the establishment of Chabad houses across the world, even in remote locations disconnected from existing Jewish communities. Chabad is also famous for its methods, which merge sociability and leisure with observant Judaism. Chabad houses are modeled along the perceived need for a stable Jewish home (and a site of entertainment and friendly interaction) to serve as the basis for Jewish friendships, relationships, solidarity, and observant Judaism—in effect, these are not unlike the clubs and associations that were created during the late nineteenth and early twentieth centuries. These similarities are not random or accidental. Among the many individuals to make their journey from Eastern Europe to America during the twentieth century, Rebbe Schneerson and his wife, Chaya Moussia, spent their formative years making the long westward journey across the European continent, eventually settling in New York City.

In late 1926 Schneerson moved to Leningrad, where he would spend eleven months auditing mathematics and engineering at the local university. It was also during this time that he courted his future wife, a courtship that was particularly unusual in Hasidic circles both for its length and for the fact that the two often stayed out late unchaperoned.[144] After their wedding the couple lived in Berlin from late 1927 to early 1933, during which time Schneerson continued his studies and Moussia pursued her own. From 1933 until the summer of 1940, the couple lived in Paris, where Schneerson finally completed his diploma in mechanical and electrical engineering.[145] Although hagiographic accounts are typically silent on (or downplay the importance of) these years, a recent biography reminds us that the future Chabad rebbe and his wife enjoyed the social and leisure world of these cities: "They were young newlyweds in Berlin, students tasting the cosmopolitan life of the German capital—a life in which they would go out together, usually on Monday nights to enjoy the city."[146] And even though their life in Paris was dominated by Schneerson's rigorous schedule as a student and by his increased involvement in his father-in-law's (the sixth rebbe) activities, the couple still did not live the insular life of a devout Hasidic family.

Schneerson and Moussia were far more modern than narrow renderings of ultra-Orthodox life suggest (or later retellings of their biographies might allow). They were two individuals with modern educations who moved within the social and leisure world of these major cities, even as they adhered to observant Judaism. These experiences were important to them as young Jews, and from them we can extrapolate part of the last Chabad rebbe's vision for a living Judaism that reflects modern understandings of individuality and sociability.[147] In the context of modern Jewish belonging, Chabad has clearly acknowledged the dynamics of the individualization of Jewish belonging. The movement has used methods and patterns that are common to nonreligious and trans-"denominational" organizations, even if it has done so for quite different purposes.

CHAPTER 2

A Place for Love

Autonomy, Choice, and Partnership

By the turn of the twentieth century, commentators in the Jewish press, sociologists, and community leaders seemed to agree on one fact: The Jewish family was changing in unprecedented ways. Just as Jewish belonging had increasingly become a matter of personal choice, so too had individual prerogative become the rationale according to which young Jews sought a life partner. As young individuals took the lead in determining the shape and composition of their own family, they fundamentally altered the parameters along which the community had been reproduced for generations.[1]

There was a real, concrete context for these developments. The transformation of Jewish marital patterns took place not only when a growing number of young Jews began placing greater emphasis on individual satisfaction but also when they had the space to exercise this desire. On a practical level, much of this autonomy resulted from urbanization and migration, a macrospatial transformation that took a generation of young Jews far away from the family home and, not incidentally, also led to the explosion of the Jewish populations of Paris, Berlin, and St. Petersburg. Distance from home and the emergence of a new capitalist market helped promote individual autonomy in ways that directly challenged parental authority. New leisure spaces, including cafés, restaurants, and vacation resorts,[2] provided an important and real physical context for this social change and helped undermine the institution of arranged marriage that had brought so many young Jews together over the previous generations.

In addition, the legal option of civil marriage in France and Germany confirmed the move toward personal volition as state authorities took the matter of marriage out of the hands of religious communities, a legal decision that made intermarriage possible for the first time.[3] Changing socioeconomic and gender relations also led many European universities from the mid-nineteenth century onward to open their doors to female students, though in some cases, including in St. Petersburg, in separate women-only programs. Similarly, an increasing number of women entered the workplace, a development that took off exponentially during and after the Great War. In France and Germany postwar economic instability and inflation destroyed family fortunes and with them the potential to provide dowries for young female family members, a turn that effectively marked the end of arranged marriages on a large scale.[4] In Russia the revolution and civil war had similar repercussions, bringing with them political and personal insecurity; the demise of capitalism and the loss personal fortunes; and social revolution, which sought to overturn all trappings of bourgeois society, including in the early years the institution of marriage. These economic, educational, and legal changes further reinforced the younger generation's quest for individual satisfaction as they moved through the lively metropolises.

To say that the transformation of the Jewish family provoked anxiety would be a great understatement. Many contemporaries from the late nineteenth century onward, certainly those who published on the topic, believed that the new and "modern" choices of young Jews had the potential to threaten nothing less than the very future of Judaism. The metropolis, with its many leisure sites and mixed sociability, was frequently seen as the source of this worrying state of affairs. Arthur Ruppin notes in his study *The Jews in the Modern World* that large cities were always the sites of revolution and dramatic change. For Jews moving to major urban centers, the city "freed [them] from the hold which tradition had on [them]," and "strong communal life is dissolved," giving way to widespread individualism.[5]

In contrast, many commentators romanticized the past, depicting it as a quieter, frequently more rural (or at least far less urbanized) realm of security, stability, and almost unquestionable solidarity. Nostalgic renderings of the Jewish family "attributed the long survival of Jews as a people to the special qualities of the Jewish family,"[6] especially its supposedly clear and uncontested order of relations. Parents and children, husband and wife, were bound together by defined and accepted relational hierarchies, and when all members respected these hierarchies, they together formed a harmonious unit. Although such an image is clearly romanticized, highlighting perhaps more the nineteenth-century preoccupation with the nuclear family as an ideal institution rather than reflecting the early modern Jewish family as a historical artifact, historians have identified a relatively stable pattern of customs and practices that for centuries determined the formation of Ashkenazi Jewish marriages. It was the upending of this same set of customs that concerned so many commentators at the time. Understanding these patterns helps us appreciate the revolution of Jewish marital patterns at the turn of the twentieth century and the role that leisure spaces would play in this transformation.

The Long History of Arranged Marriages

Until the late nineteenth century, family members, with or without the help of professional matchmakers (*shadkhanim*), arranged marriages for eligible young Jews. Marriage was primarily a socioeconomic relationship; personal desire played little role in its formation. Yet over the course of a short and dramatic thirty years—from the late nineteenth century until the 1920s—the dominant marital paradigm was overturned. Companionate marriages became the prevailing marital pattern among most European Jews, even if most still "manage[d] to fall in love with someone in their socioeconomic bracket."[7] To be sure, arranged marriages continued throughout the twentieth century and into the twenty-first, but they were increasingly reserved for the (ultra-)Orthodox milieu.[8]

As a basic and constitutive institution of the Jewish community, marriage played such a central role in Jewish life that the choice of a partner was not left to the whims of the young couple; it was a decision that concerned both families and was made according to well-defined social rules.[9] Importantly, social, religious, and economic considerations and not individual feelings of affection were of the highest importance. Marriage served both religious and socioeconomic functions, and these factors influenced the choice of a partner.

The institution of marriage satisfied several religious demands. It guaranteed the fulfillment of particular mitzvot (i.e., commandments), including procreation, and thus ensured the continuation of the community. It also contained the sexual desires of young men and women, because sexual purity was considered a virtue equally applicable to young women and men.[10] As socioeconomic units, marital unions were made generally among members of the same class. The family of the bride would provide a dowry or other economic advantages, such as employment or a share in a family business commensurate with its status and class. And in the interests of maintaining the family fortune and esteem, it was relatively common that cousins, including first cousins, would marry, a trend that continued into the twentieth century.[11] Indeed, Baron David Günzburg married his cousin, Mathilda, having decided at the age of 12, or so their daughter maintained, that his cousin was the perfect match.[12] In addition to the dowry, young couples could often count on further material support from parents or older family members. Couples often spent the first few years of their marriage living with one set of parents, a practice known as kest. This time also offered young men the opportunity to continue their religious studies.[13]

Given the socioeconomic nature of marriage, professionals and businessmen often used their professional contacts to arrange marriages for their children. Helen Veitel, for instance, married the Berlin merchant Joseph Eyck in 1876. Eyck and Veitel's father had been business associates, and these work-related connections between future in-laws served as the starting point for the closer relationship between the two men.[14] Similarly in France, Alfred Dreyfus's sister, Henriette, met her future husband, Joseph Valabrèque, through the family's industrial textile network. In the same way, his brother Jacques became engaged to and married the daughter of an industrialist from Philadelphia. Finally, Mathieu, another brother, married Suzanne Marguerite Schwob of Héricourt; Suzanne was the daughter of a textile manufacturer in the same town.[15]

In Imperial Russia the new financial elite used marriage alliances to help further their status and business connections. Yaakov, Shmuel, and Eliezer Poliakov, leading bankers and financiers of railway projects, arranged marriages for their daughters to "different dynasties of European bankers," who, in addition to enjoying massive fortunes, also often held aristocratic titles.[16] Each of these unions reflected the business interests of the extended families and could certainly be called good marriages by the standards of the time.

Moreover, the economic incentives that employment or dowries provided helped preserve the continued practice of arranged marriages, offering obvious material incentives.

Another contributing factor in arranging a match between two Jews included *yihus*[17]—"pedigree" or the background and heritage of the potential partners. Coming from a family of illustrious rabbis, for instance, ranked among the most valuable forms of social capital and one that could be potentially exchanged for a relative lack of economic capital. In her unpublished autobiographical sketch, Ester Calvary relates how her father, a rabbi, had broached the subject of marriage.

> Listen, Child, you are twenty now and we want you to get married. We have picked a good man from Posen, the offspring of Jewish scholars, a devout man with a good heart and simple being. Tomorrow he will come to meet you and we hope that you will give your consent to marry him.[18]

Naturally, the daughter of a rabbi would be married to a family with good *yihus*, in this case, "the offspring of Jewish scholars." His religious devotion, good heart, and simple being (i.e., modesty) were important personal and moral traits.

Once all these considerations had been taken into account and an appropriate match had been found, the engagement was arranged. As was increasingly common over the course of the nineteenth century, the young couple was frequently allowed to meet. By this time Jewish men and women did, at least ideally and sometimes in practice, have the right to agree to or decline a union upon meeting one another (as in the case of Esther Calvary).[19] Yet most often the engagement was concluded after an initial visit. As one memoirist noted, in recounting the story of her own parents' engagement:

> If the external criteria such as family, profession, fortune, and health were suitable then the parents of the girl would give their permission so that the young man could come for "inspection." Rarely would the young man leave unengaged. That was a very great insult, since one actually married "into the family" and not the individual girl.[20]

To be sure, Jewish marital patterns were not entirely static. Historians have noted a number of important changes in courtship customs, including the increasingly common practice of effusive and affected letter writing between young couples before marrying.[21] Some scholars have even suggested that the introduction of romantic rhetoric and a discourse on love mark the beginning of the transformation from arranged to companionate marriage.[22] Yet, looking closely, most changes in courtship patterns were relatively minor modifications of the well-established institution of arranged marriage—they were changes in custom but not in content or form. Whether a young couple wrote "love" letters before marrying or whether they had the opportunity to meet and "fall in love" before the engagement cannot and did not take away from the critical fact that these marriages were still arranged.

Historians have also pointed to the growing criticism of the institution of arranged marriage, especially among *maskilim* (followers of the Jewish Enlightenment, or Haskalah), as a determining factor in the institution's ultimate decline. These scholars cite intellectual ideas as the prime factor that precipitated a top-down assault on arranged marriage. One of the most famous and influential of these texts is the autobiography of the *maskil* Moshe Leib Lilienblum, *Hatot neurim* (Sins of Youth).[23] In it Lilienblum decries the common practice of early marriage among Eastern European Jews by recounting his own tragic story. Stressing his and his bride's age (he, 15 years and 10 months old; and she, 13 years and 4 months), Lilienblum remarks bitterly how the *mazel tovs* (congratulations) at his wedding were to signal not a joyful future but a tragic biography, filled with intense misery.[24]

Despite the various rhetorical and intellectual challenges that arose during the nineteenth century, arranged marriage as a practice did not disappear. Instead, the relatively swift and definitive transition from arranged to companionate marriage took place in the late nineteenth and early twentieth centuries just as a growing number of young Jews finally had the *social environment* where they could meet members of the opposite sex. Without the practical, concrete spaces in which to interact, the "social need" reflected in the love rhetoric had no room to grow.

It is also important on an emotional register to note that the significance placed on love before and during marriage was an outgrowth of a broader and *new* desire for self-fulfillment. The pursuit of self-actualization and individual growth led young Jews to seek out like-minded friends and life partners, just as it had led them to pursue activities that appealed to their personal tastes and interests. The increased use of social and leisure space and the growing desire to express personal autonomy were interrelated. Changing emotional registers and forms of expression also needed social outlets and contexts for their production and manifestation. In the end, the catalyst to social change of Jewish marriage practices was neither the ideology of elites nor a clash with abstract ideas but the development of spaces where one could make autonomous decisions.[25]

Space for Endogamous Choice

By the end of the nineteenth century, a growing number of young Jews were on the move. Many migrated from small towns to the big city; some even left their home country behind. Others adopted social and leisure practices that allowed them to spend their leisure time beyond their parents' constant gaze (even if many young women still went out in pairs or with chaperones). This space and distance allowed for the formation of companionate partnerships, not infrequently provoking social tensions and contravening social norms.

In 1882 the famous historian Simon Dubnow was reunited with a long-time friend, Ida Freidlin, in St. Petersburg. The two had met in their hometown of Mstislavl' and become close during their youth. Sharing progressive ideas with her future husband, Ida had decided to leave the family home, though without her mother's approval, and was nearly penniless when she arrived in the capital city. Their first task as a new couple was to find a means by which she could acquire a residence permit so that she could legally stay in the city. Ida obtained a permit through a fictitious employment arrangement, and the two initially moved into separate apartments in the same building.[26] Because they were quite poor, Dubnow worried how he would provide for both of them.[27] In early 1883 Dubnow and his not yet wife chose to live together, something that transgressed social norms even in the more cosmopolitan capital. In his memoirs Dubnow notes that "for those times it was a very audacious step, not only with respect to [our] relatives in the provinces, but also for our social circle in Petersburg."[28]

The couple's final decision to marry in St. Petersburg was prompted by their imminent return to Ida's parental home in their hometown of Mstislavl' and the "acute" need to legitimize their marriage.[29] The match did not, however, please her parents, who were, in the words of Simon and Ida's eldest daughter, Sophie, "deeply shocked when their oldest daughter Ida decided to unite herself with a young man who had the reputation in his native town of being a hopeless freethinker and was wretchedly poor."[30] Clearly, the autonomy afforded by both partners' distance from their hometown allowed

not only for a self-made match but also for the couple to transgress many social and cultural boundaries of the time, as well as the desires of Ida's parents.
By the time the Dubnows' children had grown to adulthood in the early
twentieth century, it went without saying that they too, along with many of
their generation, would make their own matches.[31]

The example of the Dubnows might have been quite exceptional for the
1880s, but other Jews in turn-of-the-century St. Petersburg found that
the modern city offered them a space to determine their own life choices,
and it also offered them more spaces to meet potential spouses. In her late
teens Anna Pavlovna Vygodskaia[32] left her home in Vilna for St. Petersburg
to pursue her studies through the Bestuzhevskie Courses. While in St. Petersburg she became reacquainted with Mikhail Markovich Vygodskii, a man
whom she had met at a party a couple of summers before. Although the
two had initially corresponded after this first meeting, their relationship had
cooled, the two lost touch, and Anna set her sights elsewhere. In St. Petersburg she learned that her onetime suitor also lived in the capital, where he
was practicing medicine. After a year without contact, he decided to visit her,
and the two began an extended courtship. In addition to frequent visits to
her apartment, the couple regularly attended the theater, went to the opera,
and attended concerts. Anna even complained in her memoirs that despite
her best efforts to encourage his appreciation of high culture (opera and concert music), he enjoyed the more pedestrian form, the operetta, to which he
convinced her to join him on one occasion. The couple would also walk to a
local café, even though, as she wrote, he would have much preferred to hire
a carriage. Their courtship, she noted, was therefore a time when they not
only fell in love but learned what made each other different and, most important perhaps, learned that "two people need not be alike in every way to
spend a happy life together; they need only to respect and love each other."[33]

Being far from home certainly gave Vygodskaia the opportunity to make
her own match, but the many sites of leisure in late 1880s and early 1890s
St. Petersburg offered her a suitable place to court her future husband. These
same places facilitated heterosocial interaction and sociability and also gave
the young couple time and space to get to know one another.[34] When the
couple made the decision to marry, Anna suggested keeping "our decision a
secret from my parents" and eloping. However, her fiancé could not imagine
insulting her parents so and decided to tell them himself. In the end, her
parents were delighted by the news, happy that their daughter was finally

getting married at the "late" age of 24.[35] Thus, despite the potentially destabilizing nature of heterosocial sociability in new sites of leisure and consumption, parents were often relieved that their daughters were marrying at all, especially when the match was a socially and religiously appropriate one.[36]

The Great War led to a much more abrupt and dramatic mobilization, uprooting and displacing men and sending them far from home. This mobilization had clear repercussions for the marriage market. Eligible young men went off to war, many not to return, leaving the pool of potential spouses conspicuously reduced. In Germany, for instance, the war saw a decline in marriages among Jews and Christians alike.[37] Whereas in 1911 there were 8.0 Jewish marriages per 1,000, by 1915 the number had dropped to 5.0 per 1,000.[38] Yet in several cases the mobilization also brought couples together. Those enlisted in the war effort were the most obviously affected.

Louis Posner's (Lutz Posener) father, Kurt, a German Jewish soldier stationed in Poland for two years during the war, met his wife while "his patrol was resting in a suburb of Lodz on a Friday afternoon." Peering out at the soldiers, a local rabbi noted the young German soldier's tallis (prayer shawl), apparently somewhat prominently wrapped around his backpack. Bidding his daughter, Lea, to invite the Jewish soldier—"German soldier or not"—to join them for the Sabbath evening meal, the rabbi inadvertently introduced his daughter to her future husband. Following this unlikely act of fate, the young couple saw each other frequently, and after a whirlwind five-day courtship, Kurt Posener proposed to Lea. According to their son, she agreed immediately and her father not only gave his blessing but also performed the religious ceremony. Shortly thereafter, Kurt brought Lea back home to Berlin, helped her set up their new home, and then returned to the front.[39]

The war clearly precipitated rather extreme situations for young Jewish couples (and their families) who risked the odds and chose to marry despite the obviously uncertain future soldiers faced. This uncertainty, combined with the general dearth of men in civilian life, naturally also contributed to the fact that marriage rates remained low throughout the war.

The Poseners were not the only couple to meet as a result of military mobilization. Alexander S. Spiegel, a young Jewish man who had come to St. Petersburg to study medicine, served as an assistant physician during World War I. After Russia's withdrawal from the Great War and following the 1917 revolution, Spiegel decided in early 1918 to resign from the Red Cross, where had been working, to finish his medical studies and become a full-fledged doctor. His plan was complicated, however, by the civil war that had erupted, and Spiegel found himself drafted into the Red Army. Arriving for duty in Moscow, Spiegel was told that his presence would be better served if he were in Tula, a decision that would have interesting consequences.

Both in Moscow and in Tula, Spiegel regularly attended religious services, and in Moscow Spiegel formed a close relationship with the chief rabbi of Moscow, Rabbi Jacob Mazeh (also known as Yaakov Maze). Although Spiegel no longer described himself as particularly religious, he did come from a Hasidic family and shared with Rabbi Mazeh a strong interest in and commitment to Zionism.[40] Through a local rabbi in Tula, Spiegel met Isaac Baumstein, whose daughter, Sonia, studied dentistry back in Moscow. Returning to Moscow, Sonia's brother, Issai, engineered a meeting to introduce the pair, enlisting the help of Rabbi Mazeh. On the night they met, the rabbi formally engaged the young couple and the pair would remain married until after World War II.[41]

The revolution had promoted remarkable mobility, but for those with close connections to observant communities, marriage could follow earlier patterns. Yet observant Jews were increasingly a minority in the communities, not just in Soviet Russia. Furthermore, the social instability of the war and postwar years, combined with new leisure patterns, meant that a noticeable number of Jews began not only to marry partners of their own choosing but also to wed non-Jewish partners.

Intermarriage and the "Crisis" of Choice

> Get up, my wife, take off your shoes, and let us sit down and mourn our child as God has commanded. "The Lord hath given and the Lord hath taken away." We are neither the first nor the last. Let us imagine that we never had a daughter named Chava, or that like Hodel she went off to the ends of the earth.
>
> Sholem Aleichem, *Tevye's Daughters*, 103

Not everyone mourned a child's marriage to a non-Jew as did Sholem Aleichem's Tevye the Milkman, telling everyone that "there was no more Chava. Her name had been blotted out."[42] Yet throughout the late nineteenth and twentieth centuries community leaders, rabbis, and journalists in the Jewish press seemed to paint a bleak picture: Both intermarriage and divorce rates appeared to be on the rise; fertility rates were on the decline; and more and more young Jews seemed to be bent on challenging the authority of their parents by, among other things, choosing their own life partner. The new world order of individual prerogative and open sociability appeared to threaten the very foundations of Jewish life, or so read the pages of countless Jewish newspapers in all three cities.

A pervasive sense of nostalgia clearly clouded many writings of the time—from newspapers to historical articles to memoirs—just as it was apparent in articles in the German and French Jewish press. Historical articles, such as those that could be found in the journals *Perezhitoe* and *Univers Israélite*, might have endeavored to provide a seemingly descriptive historical account of marriage patterns and practices over the centuries, but in essence they romanticized the past and strengthened the pervasive belief that something fundamental had changed.[43] These were not just misapprehensions and baseless fears. Jews studied and worked alongside non-Jews and participated in social activities that were not only heterosocial but also religiously mixed. In France and Germany civil marriage was a legal reality, and the law permitted interfaith marriage without the conversion of one of the partners; a similar legal change would come into effect in Russia in 1918. As a result, by the interwar years intermarriage had become a growing reality.

A number of Jewish sociologists at the turn of the twentieth century seemed to confirm the deepest, most worrying suspicions, offering statistical evidence of the "decline" of the Jewish family.[44] Statistical analysis showed that Jews frequently married at lower rates than their Christian neighbors in Germany and Russia.[45] Fewer marriages at an older age meant fewer children, and if the low birth rates were any indication, Jews were relatively quick to take advantage of modern methods of birth control.[46] Statistics on intermarriage appeared to be no less reassuring.[47] In general, in Germany in 1901 for every 100 endogamous marriages among Jews, there were 16.97 mixed marriages. By 1909 this number had risen to 25.36 for every 100 endogamous marriages.[48] The general consensus on the marriage patterns of Berlin Jews was that roughly a quarter of the population was in a religiously mixed marriage before the Nazi takeover in 1933, with more Jewish men marrying out than women.[49]

Similar statistics for Parisian Jews are lacking, making an equivalent analysis of intermarriage rates impossible. Some observers have argued that intermarriage in France was frequent, especially among the higher classes,[50] whereas others, such as Arthur Ruppin, suggest that the influx of Eastern European Jewish immigrants beginning in the 1880s influenced the overall numbers (according to Ruppin, these immigrants were far less likely to intermarry).[51] Paula Hyman argues that the rates remained negligible for the French Jewish community during the Second Empire and suggests that even for the Parisian Jewish bourgeoisie during this era the rate of intermarriage remained below 14%.[52] Yet in both France and Germany what seemed to concern commentators was not so much the absolute number or the relatively high rates of intermarriage in a given year but the overall trend, which seemed to point to an unstoppable and exponential growth in mixed marriages.[53]

Intermarriage, like conversion, was interpreted as an abandonment of Jewishness and Judaism.[54] The fear was not only that individuals were leaving Judaism and taking with them any future offspring but also that "this intermarriage has assumed such proportions as to threaten the *integrity of Judaism*."[55] From a demographic standpoint, some argued that intermarriage, combined with low birth rates, would result over time in the gradual disappearance of Jews as a people.[56] Although the situation in Imperial Russia differed, importantly because any marriage between a Jew and a non-Jew had to be preceded by conversion (from Judaism to Christianity),[57] commentators voiced their concern for demonstrable and seemingly irreversible changes in the Jewish family.[58]

Critics in the Jewish press offered various diagnoses for the "illness"[59] of intermarriage and related changes in the structure of the Jewish family, including secularization, transforming gender roles, new political beliefs (especially radical political movements and the women's movement), or a combination thereof. The decline in religious observance or religious sensitivities was cited as the underlying cause behind mixed marriage; one writer complained that Jews and Christians alike "no longer recognized any God."[60] Secular tendencies were seen as having lessened the differences between Christians and Jews who, in any event, were "neither [really] Christians or Jews, but simply 'modern.'"[61] For this reason, a "strong religious self-awareness" was seen as a "sturdy dam" against the very thought of marriage with someone from a different faith.[62]

Across Europe observers cited the decline in traditional values (religious and social) as a clear reason for the transformation of the Jewish family.

One article from 1911 published in the *Univers Israélite* argued that the "well developed individualism" of the age was at fault for the rising tide of divorce among Jews.[63] In an article published in 1918 in the Hebrew-language journal *He-avar* out of Petrograd, E. Tsherikover echoed the general pan-European mourning over a bygone era. Tsherikover suggested that a loss of traditional and religious values, paired with a subsequent decline in patriarchy, was leading contemporary Jews down a dangerous path.[64] The loss of a "religious-moral idea that focuses the spiritual strengths," Tsherikover suggested, would have disastrous repercussions.[65]

Hippolyte Prague, the longtime editor of the *Archives Israélites*, wrote in August 1925 against the "independent spirit of the century" that manifested itself in the "religious decadence" and the "abandonment of [religious] practices." At the heart of these worrisome transitions stood the loss of respect for one's parents, which had formed the basis for the Jewish family for centuries. "One no longer speaks to one's father with the traditional deference," he opined. "One no longer obeys his commands with the respect of yesteryear, and the mother that one still, of course, quite loves, is no longer listened to as before like an oracle." Instead, the young generation's "thirst for pleasure" prevents them from performing the critical fifth commandment (to honor one's parents) and leads to the decline in religious practice and morals. Intermarriage and "prohibited relationships" were further evidence of these disconcerting modifications in French Jewish society, or so the article's author maintained.[66]

Changing gender relations were frequently cited as causes for shifting marital practices. The conservative *Univers Israélite*, voice of the Consistoire and platform for French rabbinic opinions, reminded its readers through various articles and reprinted sermons that mothers were responsible for the moral education of their children, just as they were the keepers of tradition.[67] The Jewish woman of valor lauded in these pages was not a modern woman who sought political and legal equality but a woman modeled on the legendary matriarchs. Her primary, and exclusive, tasks were therefore to be in charge of domestic religiosity and the education of children, as well as to practice charity.[68] Jewish women, endowed with greater spirituality, were created not only "to pursue their own happiness but to ensure the happiness of others." Thanks to their supposedly less egotistical nature, Jewish women were given the task of gently influencing men and encouraging in them "the most noble feelings" and helping them to shed their "purely mundane preoccupations."[69] These idealized portraits of the perfect Jewish wife and mother—educator and priestess in the home— placed much responsibility (and potentially blame) for the future of the Jewish family.

Hippolyte Prague, for instance, quite unequivocally blamed women for intermarriage in an article written in 1909.[70]

> The ideas of women's emancipation that currently enjoy great popularity permit, with the tacit agreement of parents too cowardly to resist this dispossession of their natural rights, young girls to follow their hearts as they wish; and for too many of them, a difference in confession would not hinder their choice.[71]

Although Prague conceded to the various challenges faced by young Jewish women to find a Jewish husband, he nevertheless focused his criticism on women, the women's movement, and the decay in patriarchal authority.[72] His depiction of women as weak-willed and easily swayed by (non-Jewish) male influences was repeated in another article that recounted the story of a devoted and religious father who was forced painfully to watch as one of his two daughters was wooed by a young Catholic officer. The suitor, according to the account, not only desired the young woman as his wife but also tried to convert her and "bring a recruit to the Church."[73] This example further highlights the belief that intermarriage was seen as yet another facet of conversion.[74]

Prague's opinions aside, others in the French Jewish press maintained that fathers should also play their part in the raising of good Jewish children.[75] An article from 1911 stressed the need for love and respect between children and parents for the "reconstruction" of the family, suggesting both the supposedly abysmal state of the modern family and the burden placed on both parents to rectify it.[76]

In the German Jewish press Jewish *men* were noticeably and frequently blamed for intermarriage. Statistically more likely to enter into a mixed marriage, "selfish" Jewish men were faulted for leaving their female coreligionists with fewer options in the Jewish marriage market, thus forcing them to look beyond the confines of the Jewish community to find a partner.[77] Others blamed Jewish men for expecting unreasonably high dowries, thereby forcing less fortunate Jewish women to seek a non-Jewish spouse.[78] Finally, the looser morals of Jewish men were highlighted as a cause of their choice to pursue romantic relationships with non-Jewish women, who also were not infrequently characterized as being less morally (read: sexually) restrained.[79]

Memoir literature tells a similar, gendered story of change. Pauline Wengeroff complains at length in her well-known and often studied memoirs about the decline of the traditional Jewish family as a result of *male*-led and *male*-driven modernization.[80] Nostalgia, a sentiment present throughout Wengeroff's memoir, was a common reaction and was shared by both men and women, who at times felt a sentimental longing for a traditional Jewish home run by a capable matriarch.[81] The sense of decline would only grow after World War I. Indeed, the loss of fathers, sons, and potential mates, in addition to the growing financial independence of women, only further exacerbated an already seemingly acute problem.[82]

Leisure practices were also identified as contributing factors in the rising number of intermarriages, just as the ethos of individualism had been branded a new and disruptive value.[83] In an article from 1917, Rabbi Max Eschelbacher broadened his criticism of the social habits of contemporary German Jews to include the growing instance of women's paid work, longer periods of bachelorhood among men, and, no less important, the nefarious influence of cafés, cinemas, and other sites of leisure. New modes of leisure and sociability opened various avenues of social interchange. For Rabbi Eschelbacher, spaces of leisure and sociability were directly responsible for the rising rates of intermarriage among Christians and Jews. "We need only step into a big-city café and immediately we see the root of this evil," he intoned.[84]

Rabbi Eschelbacher was far from being alone in his criticisms of the modern city, the coffeehouse, and the supposedly pernicious influence of the city's leisure spaces. In a speech at the Bnai Brith Lodge in Berlin in 1919, Gustav Loeffler argued that the survival of Judaism depended on defeating the threats of declining marriage and fertility rates, changing sexual mores, and the growing number of intermarriages; he declared that Jews needed to defend themselves against the "sensuous stimulants of over-refined urban culture."[85]

Across Europe, sociability in the modern city posed a fundamental danger to the morality of good Jewish men and women. In this context the café (and, in particular, its nightlife) served as a potent metonymy for the modern city, recalling its particular allure and the sexualized threat it posed to the many men and women who entered it.[86] Even memoir literature from before and after the Great War tells similar moralizing tales about the sexual dangers of modern sociability. Sophie Dubnova-Erlich, for instance, unexpectedly found herself in an uncomfortable and sexually charged conversation with the poetry editor of a leading literary journal in St. Petersburg before the Great War. The poetry editor had casually suggested that they continue their conversation at a local restaurant, but instead of sitting in the main dining room, he requested a private table, and at once there was "a change in the tone of the conversation."[87]

For Lotte Strauss, her first unsuccessful marriage to a non-Jew, who courted her by showing her "Berlin, its museums and environment," stood in stark contrast to the morally beneficial, mutually supportive (and also self-chosen) marriage with her second husband, Herbert Strauss. Both Jewish, the couple met after 1938 through their work for the Jewish Emigration Organization in Berlin.[88] Thus, just as intermarriage rates rose, a counter movement grew that argued that both the general future of Judaism and the individual futures of Jewish youths would be better secured and more prosperous if endogamy were actively encouraged.

Fighting Against the Tide:
Jewish Leisure Space and the Unarranged Arranged Marriage

> No matter whom a youngster thought he loved, Yona [the matchmaker] could make him think otherwise, and whomever his parents thought he should love Yona could make him love too, so that in the end, as it were, he fell in love with her all by himself while Yona simply gave his approval. There were some quite educated people in Szybusz who snorted at the notion of an arranged marriage without knowing that they themselves were a match made by Yona.
>
> Agnon, *A Simple Story*, 36–37

Parents, family, and community members did not simply or passively fret over changes to the Jewish family and rising rates of intermarriage. Instead, by the late nineteenth century many families and matchmakers succeeded in perpetuating the institution of arranged marriages by harnessing the very same leisure spaces that some commentators had decried. As Marion Kaplan has argued, across Germany many arranged marriages were covered up so as "to look as though the partners had met by coincidence."[89] German Jews were not alone in their practice of hiding arranged marriages or orchestrating meetings between suitable men and women. In all three cities new spaces and modes of leisure were harnessed for the purpose of ensuring appropriate matches. As we have seen, balls became an important way for the Jewish community and Jewish organizations to celebrate together and raise money for charitable causes. Typically they were held in hotel halls or at Jewish organizations that were large enough and wealthy enough to own or rent their own permanent space (e.g., Bnai Brith lodges).

But more than raising funds and offering entertainment to those assembled, these gatherings used new patterns of leisure to create a chaperoned Jewish marriage market. Yet balls were not infinitely open, not even to all members of the local Jewish community. Economics and politics were important fault lines that separated various subgroups. In Paris young women of the better classes who were of marrying age (about 19) would attend society events in the company of their mothers. These included balls held by the Friends of Jacob that took place every year at the Hotel Moderne.[90] Society balls, like the Friends of Jacob ball, brought together elites of the community, winnowing the potential marriage market to an already appropriate set of suitors.

Holiday, society, and charitable balls thus served as sites of inclusion and exclusion. They brought together a Jewish audience and, in so doing, promoted endogamy, using specifically Jewish social and leisure spaces to curtail the influence of more open leisure spaces. At the same time, specific balls had the power to exclude politically or socioeconomically undesirable individuals from their midst. Ticket prices or political agendas (e.g., Zionist groups held holiday balls in all three cities) helped control the choice of attendees. Despite certain voices that decried the morally questionable practice of mixed-gender dancing and the larger dangers involved in participating in frivolous leisure activities,[91] it is a bit ironic that such balls were ultimately conservative efforts to maintain the social order in the Jewish community and support endogamy. Because personal choice was seen as a threat to order and social stability,[92] especially among the older generations, participation in new leisure activities such as balls could help maintain marriage traditions and the patriarchal order.

In addition to balls, young Jews set up in arranged matches might meet for the first time in a café, at a restaurant, the market, or the home of a friend or associate, or while on vacation.[93] In each instance families could still oversee their children's courtship, engagement, and marriage. In this sense, a quieter and more modest form of matchmaking developed that permitted the creation of a myth, namely, that the relationship developed out of love and not through the intercessions of a *shadkhan* or the extended family.[94]

This tension between arranged and companionate marriages was a relatively common topic in early-twentieth-century Jewish literature. By pitting "modern" children against their practical, tradition-minded parents, such authors as Sholem Aleichem, S. Y. Agnon, and Sholem Asch poked fun at arranged marriages and the recent changes in Jewish society. The "modern" young man did not "let his parents do all his wooing," we learn, even if the parents arranged the match in the first place.[95] And increasingly the young man was supposed to ask his prospective bride for her hand before speaking to her parents.[96]

Sholem Aleichem parodied the new practice of hiding an arranged marriage in his novel *Marienbad*. The author satirizes both the matchmaker and the search for suitable partners, with the action taking place in the cafés and restaurants of the fictionalized spa town. The character Pearl Yamayiker explains to her husband in a letter home how the matchmaker works there. She knows all too well, because she has come to marry off not one but all three of her daughters.

> [The matchmaker] says that he doesn't arrange marriages in the normal fashion; instead [he does so] through acquaintanceship and love. That means, first one meets in Café Egerländer, it's a garden with music and lots of tables. There one makes each other's acquaintance, almost entirely by chance, but through him, the shadkhan. Then one meets by the fountain, where one drinks water, already without the shadkhan. Thereafter one goes to the theater or to the concert and still the shadkhan is nowhere to be seen. And there, in the theater or concert, they then fall in love, and after falling in love, then comes the engagement. And only at the engagement does the shadkhan suddenly pop up again to pocket his fee.[97]

Sholem Aleichem's *shadkhan* arranged marriages "through acquaintanceship and love." Having established the match, the pair would engage in an extended courtship that took them from a café, to the waters of the spa, and to the theater or to a concert. Finally when the couple agreed to marry, the *shadkhan* reappeared to collect his fee. This mode of arranged marriages merged old matchmaking with new spaces of leisure. And in Sholem Aleichem's fictionalized version of Marienbad, sites of leisure became synonymous with the marriage market.

Another character, Chaim Soroker, complains in a misogynist letter to his wife, Esther:

And Marienbad itself is just as it was a couple of years ago. . . . The same fat women with their pearl-necklaced necks, who come here with their past due young daughters in order to find grooms, to nab a son-in-law.[98]

"Very, very rarely," he lies, "does it happen that I go to Café Egerländer to drink a glass of tea and read a newspaper. One cannot sit there very long because of the fat mamas who have brought with them their daughters for 'exhibit.' "[99] It is not entirely clear how the reader is supposed to understand this rather nasty remark. Soroker's suggestion, read directly, seems to imply that only the lazy or unmarriable needed to resort to such measures to find a spouse. Reality, however, suggested a far more widespread use of leisure spaces for these purposes.

After the Great War the leisure cultures of Paris and Berlin continued to grow and the options for sociability expanded noticeably. In no small measure, the post–World War I sense of freedom and liberation, some might even say hedonism, influenced the sociable patterns of young men and women seeking amusement and companionship. At the same time, the Roaring Twenties were also a time of changing conceptions for the Jewish populations of these cities, especially regarding their self-identification and a seemingly renewed intentionality to self-identify with the larger Jewish collective. This had a spatial dimension as well and one with roots in the pre–World War I era.

For example, already by the late nineteenth century Bnai Brith had seen a pressing need to foster youth sociability through youth clubs and to pro-vide "homes away from home" to young commercial workers who had left the parental house and their hometowns.[100] As the popularity of such youth-oriented programming grew and the audience expanded, so too did the possibility of these interactions serving as the basis for endogamous, companionate marriages. By this point, arranged marriages had largely be-come a thing of the past, but concerned community leaders (and parents) were intent on encouraging young Jews to choose a Jewish partner. To this end, in 1920s Berlin the Bnai Brith lodges began to organize dances for a Jewish audience. Their decision to do so reflects the realities of the chang-ing Jewish marriage market and new attitudes toward sociability and lei-sure time, just as it offers evidence of the organization's clear interest in promoting endogamy. Dances at Bnai Brith lodges thus served as sites of exclusion, separating Jews from non-Jews. It was at one such occasion sometime around 1925 that Ruth Gützlaff met her future husband, Walter Lichtenstein.[101] The dance provided the first step in their courtship.

This spatial strategy—the creation of even temporarily insular Jewish spaces to encourage endogamy—had become so commonplace and well known by 1930 that when the editors of the *Univers Israélite* received a letter ostensibly from a Jewish mother calling for the organization of balls to encourage endogamy (apparently ignorant of the phenomenon), the editors questioned the authenticity of the letter. Incredulous, the author of the short response listed a couple of associations in Paris, including the Union Scolaire, that held such dances and noted that these events were even "honored by the presence of representatives of the rabbinate."[102] The short article highlights the extent to which balls and dances had become recognized as popular ways to promote endogamous marriages, a goal considered so vital to the continuity of the community that rabbinic authorities and official community representatives sanctioned them. The revolution of spatial practices in the early twentieth century had provoked remarkable religious accommodations.

Jewish youth movements and associations also entered this expanding social and leisure market. The early twentieth century witnessed the establishment of Jewish youth movements and sport clubs, which served as popular meeting sites for young men and women.[103] And even though many youth organizations emphasized the clean and decent nature of the interaction between young men and women,[104] romantic relationships were almost unavoidable. Robert Gamzon, the founder in 1924 of the first scouting troop in France, the Éclaireurs israélites de France (Israelite Scouts of France),[105] met his later wife, Denise, in the late 1920s through the same organization.[106] Mixed-gender sociability was bound to foster romantic relationships based on autonomous and individual consent.[107]

Yet not everyone found a partner in the social sites of the city or through traditional channels. The desire and the social and familial pressure to marry a fellow Jew prompted some individuals in Berlin and Paris (though to a much lesser extent in St. Petersburg) to turn to a virtual space: the Jewish press and a new addition to its pages, personal ads.[108] Just as balls could help hide arranged marriages, early ads actually confirmed and promoted the practice as well.

Announcements for Jewish women at the turn of the twentieth century were generally placed on their behalf and typically concentrated on advertising what were deemed to be the most salient qualities of the hopeful brides, reproducing the same characteristics outlined at the beginning of the chapter. These included responsibility in business and household affairs; standards of morality or religiosity, often phrased as "from a good home"; beauty;[109] and a dowry befitting the woman's socioeconomic background. One succinct example reads, "A strongly religious match is sought for a beautiful girl, 20s, with 10,000 [dowry]."[110] Likewise, turn-of-the-century ads for Jewish men generally included the employment and/or educational level of the man. Such information was a window into his present but, more important, his future socioeconomic status. Mostly these ads focused on a description of the desired qualities of the prospective bride, which frequently amounted simply to a stated sum of the expected dowry.[111]

This was not always the case, however. The following 1905 ad from the popular, mainstream *Israelitisches Familienblatt* both stresses the economic status of the man, showing not only his present condition but also his future earning potential, and places attention on the qualities desired in the prospective bride—in particular her domesticity and religiosity. What makes the ad amusing, however, is also what makes it atypical.

> Looking for an appropriately aged match with [a dowry of] 25–30,000 for *a relative*, a 30 year old, able businessman who for the last five years has run a well-earning wholesale business in Berlin, however [he] is not tall. Women of average height with a modest, domestic sensibility and a religious upbringing are preferred.

To be clear, most ads of the time did not make any mention of a man's appearance. Regardless of the serious or unintentionally humorous nature of these ads, all reflect centuries-old customs of Jewish marriage brokerage. What was new was the medium, not the message.

Yet increasingly and relatively quickly the same format began to serve the needs of individuals looking for a Jewish spouse. The growing individualization of the marriage market thus came to be reflected in the personal ads themselves. Personal ads placed in the *Israelitisches Familienblatt* before the Great War reflected some changes that were slowly under way. In particular, the growing autonomy of women can be seen in the small but rising number of women who began placing ads on their own behalf, as in the following ad from 1910:

> Marriage! I would happily marry a young widower or bachelor in Berlin or surrounding area. I am 28 years old, with a beautiful and interesting appearance, personable [*goldenes Gemütlichkeit*], able in business and running a household.[112]

Another ad from the same year ignores monetary concerns completely in favor of relocating to a rural area: "I long for a happy home, preferably in a beautifully situated small town, for a man whom I can give love, joy and cheerfulness. Who will try it?"[113] The ad is quite exceptional for both its tone and its content, just as it raises the question of whether all personal ads placed in the press were seriously intended.

Although it is impossible to know whether these ads were written by young women, as they appear to have been, taken as a whole the ads reveal important characteristics of companionate marriages. Worded in the first person, they suggest personal volition and an individualized search for a spouse who will satisfy the wants and tastes of the person writing the ad (earlier ads for women were written in the third person and placed by family members on their behalf). Certain concerns typical to arranged marriages, including economic status, remain relevant in a number of such announcements but are not the primary determining factor for the union.

After World War I the Jewish press in Germany and France continued to offer a forum for individuals to find a Jewish spouse. Certainly, one could still find the rare ad in the late 1920s placed by parents seeking a spouse for a child, even on behalf of young women who had their own professional careers, including the following ad from the *Univers Israélite*:

> Parents seek to marry young daughter, 29 years of age, slim waist, educated, intelligent, job in State administration, 10,000 fr annually, with retirement, small amount of assets and savings, to a young man, French by birth, honorable, comparable financial standing.[114]

Nevertheless, more and more ads expressed the desire not only to marry into a good family along older patterns but also to enter into a marriage of choice and affection. In the German Jewish press the terms *Neigungsehe* (marriage of affection) and *Selbstinserent* (ad placed on the author's own behalf) became increasingly common in the 1920s. The wording of the texts themselves also clearly changed to highlight the greater importance of personal choice in finding that perfect match.

The following ad from 1927 provides a concrete example:

On my own behalf [*Selbstinserent*]. Businessman, 34 years old, handsome, German citizen, with his own, debt free cigar store in Berlin, would like to meet a beautiful, thin, business-minded lady for the purpose of marriage.

Although economic (and political) considerations are clearly important to the writer of this ad, so is personal desire and attraction. A "handsome man" seeks a woman who will compliment his professional and personal life.

And because a main factor in placing an ad in the Jewish press was to find a Jewish spouse, we not surprisingly see ads that stress the desire to meet a coreligionist, such as this ad from the *Univers Israélite*: "Gentleman 32 years old, foreigner, Israelite, good family, well-off, wine merchant, would marry a young woman between 22 and 25, Israelite, of a very good family, a good musician, if possible with a knowledge of English."[115] In other cases the degree of religiosity was particularly important, as can be seen in the following ad placed by a rather self-assured businessman in the *Israelitisches Familienblatt*:

Lady's choice! Business manager, Eastern Jew, born in Berlin, 32 years [of age] medium height, desires to exchange letters with a beautiful, blond, traditionally raised lady for the purpose of marriage.[116]

In the final analysis, although intermarriage rates in interwar Paris and Berlin did begin to rise, both cities were equipped with concrete leisure sites and thriving virtual spaces that provided contexts for the creation of self-determined and autonomously chosen endogamous marriages—unions in which personal taste and attraction and shared values and faith cemented the bond between two individuals. The spatial landscape for Jews in postrevolutionary Leningrad, by contrast, shared little in common with interwar Paris or Berlin before the rise of the Nazis.

Political Change and the Jewish Marriage Market

In Petrograd/Leningrad, Jewish marriage patterns and family life were dramatically affected by the Russian Revolution. Certainly in the early years of the revolution, the regime sought to overturn patriarchy and bourgeois institutions, including the family, challenging earlier religious and social taboos and customs.[117] Although these new official policies against the traditional family would be reversed in the late 1920s, the general tone of social and political revolution changed the marital landscape for young Jews. The Code on Marriage, the Family, and Guardianship of 1918 did more than legalize civil marriage (and thus make intermarriage legal); it permitted no-fault divorce and guaranteed parental support to all children, regardless of the marital status of their parents.[118] In the context of the radically modernizing and changing world of Soviet Jews, many Jews placed their faith in the communist regime and sought to integrate fully into both the political and the social order. Intermarriage also became increasingly common.[119]

According to Leo Goldhammer (a Zionist, sociologist, statistician, and lawyer), in 1925 there were 18.8 mixed marriages for every 100 endogamous Jewish marriages in European Russia; 25 per 100 in 1926, and 27 per 100 the year after that.[120] By 1936 the rate of intermarriage in Leningrad was 42.3% for men and 36.8% for women, and this pattern would only increase over time.[121] The historian Mordechai Altshuler offers slightly different statistics for the same year, but the overall picture remains the same, with Jewish men in Leningrad intermarrying at a rate close to 42% and Jewish women intermarrying at a rate just under 30%.[122] Thus in interwar Leningrad the Jews of the city had caught up with and even surpassed German Jewish intermarriage rates.

The precarious place of the Jewish family in Leningrad seemed only to be further destabilized by the overall decline in consumer spaces and the closure of specifically Jewish spaces in Leningrad. Indeed, the Bolshevik Revolution and the eventual closure of specifically Jewish institutions had a dramatic effect on the Jewish marriage market in that city and substantially increased the number of intermarriages. Whereas the Jewish communities of both Berlin and Paris faced the same thorny issue of mixed marriage, the young generations there could still rely on thriving Jewish social scenes, which promoted the creation of endogamous unions. In Soviet Leningrad the gradual closure of Jewish spaces in general, not just leisure and consumer sites, effectively closed many spatial options for young Jews to meet one another. This meant that the workplace, universities, and other general, not specifically Jewish sites of interaction and sociability took their place. Many Jews continued to practice endogamy, but intermarriage rates rose and remained the highest of the three cities under investigation.

Political realities clearly had the power to affect intermarriage rates and practices in 1920s and 1930s Leningrad. With the rise of the NSDAP (Nationalsozialistische Deutsche Arbeiterpartei, i.e., the Nazi Party) to power in Germany in 1933, state policy influenced Jewish marriage practices in a radically different and much more sinister direction. The social ostracism and state-sponsored discrimination experienced by German Jews in the first year of the new regime led to a quick decrease in the number of intermarriages between Jews and non-Jews: 44% of German Jews married a non-Jewish spouse just before the rise of Nazism, but by 1934 the number had fallen to 15%.[123] For "full" Jews and those of partial Jewish background, social exclusion influenced sociability and encouraged endogamy. Such was the case with three of the four Chotzen brothers, who, in the eyes of the Nazi state, were half-Jews (their father being "racially" Jewish and their mother being "racially" Aryan, who had converted to Judaism). Hugo-Kurt, Erich, and Ullrich would all marry Jewish women, whom they met through various Jewish circles and sociable activities. Hugo-Kurt met Lisa Scheurenberg through the Jewish sports association; Erich met Ilse Schwarz through a mutual friend he studied with at the Jewish trade school; and Ullrich met Ruth Cohn at the house of friends, all of whom were young Jews.[124] With fewer and fewer options but to socialize and marry another Jew, endogamy rates rose.[125] As well, pressure placed on non-Jewish Germans not to marry Jews, already in the summer of 1933, discouraged intermarriage.[126]

In 1935 the state took an active role in preventing mixed marriages by outlawing them through the statutes of the Nuremberg Laws, though, importantly, existing marriages were not dissolved. In 1938 legislation was passed that aimed to facilitate divorces between Jews and non-Jews.[127] Nevertheless, despite these policies, the great majority of these couples remained married.[128] Of the existing intermarriages in Germany at the time, somewhere between two-thirds and three-fourths were between non-Jewish women and Jewish men, and in addition, nearly half of all intermarried couples lived in Berlin.[129] The twisted logic of Nazi policy toward mixed marriages is reflected in the variety of legislation on the topic. Again, in 1938, existing mixed marriages were divided into two categories—privileged or nonprivileged[130]—"in order to placate the 'German-blooded' relatives as the measures taken against the Jewish population were becoming more and more radical."[131] In fact, many non-Jewish spouses continued to protect and advocate for their Jewish spouses, leading in numerous cases to the partner's survival.[132]

Conclusions

Memoir literature in the late nineteenth century and early twentieth century time and again attests to the growing importance that the various writers placed on personal choice and the opportunities available to follow one's heart. The intimate sphere of love and marriage is but only one part of a larger picture of changing conditions across Europe, especially from the perspective of Jewish women.

Puah Rakovsky's memoir reminds us that this push for female autonomy extended well beyond the three cities. Her own story weaves together a tale of personal emancipation from an early arranged marriage and her two subsequent marriages of choice. The narrative highlights her professional leadership and independence as a teacher and principal of a Jewish girls school in Warsaw. Determined to live her life as an autonomous and independent person, Rakovsky played the role of feminist activist on an immediate and personal level: "My independence upset my parents' house. My sisters and brothers considered my example and they too became boundary breakers."[133] And in the larger world of Jewish politics, Rakovsky also fought against conventional attitudes toward women and their subservient role.[134] This independence of spirit and mind determined her life choices and partnerships. Not without its subtle ironies, she fell in love with her third and last husband, a man several years her junior, while reading Karl Marx.[135] Love was a symbolic emotion that underscored personal desire and choice.

The shift from arranged to companionate marriages occurred concurrently with the modernization of the Jewish community and the society around it, a modernization that had led to the birth and self-awareness of the Jewish individual. The modern city—magnet for migration, site of institutions of higher education, and home to an expanding capitalist network of leisure spaces—served as an important backdrop to these developments. On an emotional level the search for a partner became based on personal prerogative. For all the various differences among the communities in the late nineteenth and early twentieth centuries—including the popularity of personal ads and the possibility of civil marriage—Jews living in the three cities at the turn of the twentieth century faced many of the same choices and dilemmas: how to meet, whom to marry, and how others in the community would react to these individual choices.

Yet with World War I and its aftermath, the nature of the marriage markets in Paris, Berlin, and St. Petersburg diverged significantly. Communism changed the social scene in Petrograd/Leningrad. Jewish spaces were closed along with Jewish newspapers. The agenda of the Soviet state only further weakened the bonds of the Jewish community and led to rising rates of exogamy. The rise of Nazism in Berlin (and in Germany) led to a decline in intermarriage rates, but this in fact placed increased numbers of Berlin Jews in grave danger; they lacked the protection a non-Jewish spouse could offer. The repercussions of personal choice and self-made unions were thus numerous and often unexpected.

Room to Grow

Children, Youth, and Informal Education

The Century of the Jewish Child

"Our task is to create an oasis in the middle of the non-Jewish desert of *Galuth* [exile], and we believe that we can create these Jewish oases in the tight communities [*Gemeinschaften*] of our youth organizations."[1] Written in 1919 Dr. Salli Hirsch's call to action reflects two key aspects: a growing awareness of the spatial realities of European Jews, seemingly wandering in a vast desert of non-Jewish culture yet still keen to build spaces that could facilitate personally meaningful connections with other Jews; and the belief that the key to solving the new Jewish question would be found in the Jewish youth and children of the day. Although Hirsch was a dedicated Zionist and his political mission did not reflect the ideologies of all Jewish Europeans, his insistence on youth-focused and spatially grounded Jewish belonging reflected larger trends in Jewish society that emerged in the late nineteenth century and continued for decades to come.

The spatial revolution that brought increasing numbers of Jewish adults into new venues of leisure and mass consumption was quickly extended to include Jewish children and youth. Just as parents had used social spaces to affiliate with a Jewish community of their own choosing and to find a spouse, the hope was that their children would also continue to express solidarity as Jews through social and leisure sites. A growing number of associations and movements reacted to the expanding market of Jewish families who desired to send their children to specifically Jewish leisure sites and places of informal educational. In addition, teenagers and young adults were instrumental in the proliferation of other youth-oriented spaces through youth movements and popular sports groups, helping to create and design new Jewish spaces following their own social and cultural needs and political agendas.[2]

The creation of spaces for Jewish children and youth coincided with the larger changes in Jewish society. By the end of the nineteenth century, in the face of the radical alteration of Jewish self-definition and affiliation, anxious calls to preserve, protect, regenerate, rebuild, and save Judaism, Jewishness, or the Jewish family, depending on one's cause, could be heard from any number of directions. What ultimately united these various voices was not a shared agenda but a common and repeated concern for the future of Jewish life and a desire to have a say in its vision. The young were evident targets of these efforts,[3] and children's and youth spaces were seen as ideal venues for formal and informal education, which the organizers hoped would help achieve their goals.[4]

The concern for the young, however, was not merely an outgrowth of the confrontation of European Jews with the effects of emancipation and the growing market of sociability; it was also part of a broader, general reassessment of childhood essentially related to the late-nineteenth-century "discovery of the child."[5] The twentieth century was to be the "Century of the Child," as some European intellectuals proclaimed it.[6] From an explosion in children's literature and periodicals to new ideas about education, children became the focus of much intellectual activity.[7] By the late nineteenth century, new pedagogic schools of thought, novel approaches to child psychology, and advances in medicine combined to reshape the way the adult world saw, understood, and treated children. One of the more important sea changes was that contemporary scholars no longer viewed children as adults in miniature. At the same time, "youth" was also "discovered"; youth movements, clubs, and associations were founded and proliferated.[8]

Jewish academics and intellectuals joined their non-Jewish colleagues and participated in these developing schools of thought and in their concern for the family and future generations. They also engaged these debates for particularly Jewish causes. By the end of the nineteenth century, Jewish doctors, psychiatrists, pedagogues, philanthropists, religious figures, lay community leaders, parents, and even youths themselves came to be involved in a variety of discourses and movements that sought to save or regenerate young Jews and, through them, contemporary Jewry. Medical figures worried about the physical and psychological health of Jews of all ages, because the health of the individual purportedly reflected the health of the people.[9] Doctors and nationalists responded to (and thus accepted as truth) the widespread claims that Jews were prone to certain illnesses or were less physically fit than non-Jews.[10] The rhetoric concerning good health could have class-based implications as well; being of sound mind and body was synonymous with the adoption and active demonstration of the bourgeois virtues of "discipline, success, good morals, and social integration."[11] Thus those who aimed to reform the poor, sickly Jewish body were in effect trying to reform the Jewish working class and instill in them the values of the middle class, just as much as they were responding to negative physical stereotypes.

To confront the real and imagined deleterious state of European Jewry, Jewish philanthropists and activists set about finding practical solutions. Invariably these took a concrete spatial form through and in summer camps, kindergartens, children's homes, recreation centers, clinics, and clubs. Physical exercise and sport purportedly strengthened the body; kosher food and religious activities and programs nourished the Jewish soul.[12] The lawyer and Zionist Salli Hirsch imagined these spaces as oases in the desert, whereas others would understand their mission as creating homes away from home. Jewish spaces designed for children and youth invoked notions of intimacy, security, and respite; they were to serve as insular environments that encouraged deeper relationships between participants.

Because time and space do not allow me to examine all places designed for children and youth, I focus predominantly on summer camps and several types of youth clubs. The creation of these new spaces marked an enormous transformation; if before the twentieth century the main spaces of Jewish childhood were the home and the heder (Jewish elementary school, more important for Jewish boys than girls), after the turn of the twentieth century there was a significant increase in the number of different venues that combined new leisure culture and informal education for a young but individualized audience.

At first, philanthropists targeted poor Jewish children and youth, creating new charitable organizations and spaces to these ends—these were in effect places *for* Jews, places where young Jews could be protected from outside (and frequently Christian or antisemitic) influences.[13] As the twentieth century wore on, the desire to impart Jewish education to all children, regardless of socioeconomic class, increasingly became an important motivation for the continuation and further creation of such sites in Paris and Berlin, and the spaces increasingly took on the characteristics of *Jewish spaces*—sites that not only catered to Jewish audiences but also had significant Jewish cultural, religious, and/or political content. Accepted into the mainstream of Jewish life, Jewish summer camps and youth clubs remained important sites well past the first half of the twentieth century. In contrast, political developments in Petrograd/Leningrad stymied the growth and development of the same spaces. Although St. Petersburg/Petrograd was home to a growing number of venues sponsored by Jewish youth movements during and after the Great War, these organizations would be forced to close their doors by the late 1920s. Jewish communist equivalents to the previous nationalist or religion-based Jewish organizations did not take their place in Leningrad.

Summer Camps

Beginning as philanthropic endeavors, summer camps emerged as a popular solution to the unsanitary conditions in which poor urban children lived. In the late nineteenth century, in response to innovations made by Christian organizations, Jewish associations across Europe began to organize summer holiday camps for the less fortunate members of their local communities. Berlin was home to one of the first Jewish summer camps on the European continent. In 1884 the men's only Berliner Logen UOBB (Bnai Brith Lodges of Berlin) founded the Berliner jüdische Ferien-Kolonie. Its creation fell on the heels of the first organized summer vacations for Christian children in Switzerland in 1876 and the introduction of similar Christian institutions to Berlin in 1880.[14]

The decision to create a Jewish summer camp arose out of the perceived need to provide children of poor and working-class families with kosher food and a Jewish environment where, among other things, they would not be subject to Christian proselytizing.[15] The children's camps in Germany offered a chance for exercise, fresh air, convalescence, and good nutrition,[16] underscoring their primary concern for the health of poor Jewish children.[17] In addition, the organization ensured that the children would receive medical attention.[18] In their first year the Berliner Logen UOBB provided a four-week summer vacation in Neuruppin (about 60 kilometers northwest of Berlin) to twelve children of lower socioeconomic backgrounds, and in the late 1890s, they expanded their offerings to include a winter camp. By 1908, 409 underprivileged children participated in holiday camps at a variety of sites, including a villa in Misdroy (on the Baltic Sea) and a home in Elmen (in the Austrian Tyrol).[19]

In 1891, when asked whether such endeavors merited imitation across Germany, Adolph Mayer, a leading figure in the management and organization of the Bnai Brith holiday camps from 1887 until his death in 1906,[20] emphatically pointed to the health benefits of such camps (after all, healthy children meant a healthy future working class) but also to the educational and moral benefits that the less fortunate children reaped at the camps. Boys and girls returned to school from their summer vacation "better mannered," more interested in learning, and more attentive in class. In addition, the time spent at the holiday camps was believed to stimulate love for one's neighbor.[21] The civilizing mission of this paternalistic endeavor, at least as Mayer phrased it in 1891, is striking for its lack of emphasis on Jewish education—the camps were in many respects camps for Jews but not yet Jewish camps. Improving the physical and moral condition of the Jewish proletariat in Berlin dominated Bnai Brith's early agenda, in keeping with the project's larger goals for social, pedagogic, and hygiene reform.[22] These goals were also consonant with that generation's larger concern, across Germany, of making good citizens out of German Jews, regardless of their age, gender, or class.

Similarly, the Jüdisches Kinderheim, founded around 1896 and inspired by the Pestalozzi-Fröbel-Haus, organized a day camp (*Halbkolonie*) during the summer months in Niederschönhausen (today a northern neighborhood of Berlin).[23] Intended for the children who frequented the organization's daycare and kindergarten, the camp catered largely to a poor clientele.[24] The exclusive focus on social and moral improvement characterized by the Jüdisches Kinderheim and Berliner Logen UOBB would not continue for long. Although helping poorer members of the community remained a central motivation behind many summer camps (just as paternalism was a frequent sentiment underlying much of these efforts), increasingly camps and children's organizations desired to offer greater Jewish content and provide cultural, linguistic, historical, or political bases for Jewish self-identification, thus evolving into Jewish spaces (i.e., spaces not only for Jews but with clear Jewish content).

World War I sparked a mass migration of Jewish immigrants and refugees from Eastern Europe toward Germany. Further enabling actual encounters between German Jews and their eastern cousins, the influx of tens of thousands of *Ostjuden* into German lands provided a concrete basis and means to pursue a particular search for Jewish "authenticity." Nationally minded German Jews, such as Siegfried Lehmann (who also went by the name Salomon Lehnert), created spaces that brought together German and Eastern European Jews. In 1916 Lehmann founded the Jüdisches Volksheim, which was modeled on the English settlement system and was inspired by certain values of the German youth movement. The Jüdisches Volksheim, located in the Scheunenviertel District, was to serve as an educational station and place of social integration for the Jewish working class.[25] Still paternalistic in many aspects, the Jüdisches Volksheim combined a belief in the need for social welfare and education among Eastern European Jews with the no less critical conviction that German Jews would benefit from contact with "authentic" carriers of Jewish tradition. Lehmann insisted that the solution be spatial because nationalists could not live in "this cold airless room" but required "earth under our feet."[26] This statement was not a simple call for return to a national homeland but a plea to build concrete spaces more locally in Europe. Lehmann argued that at least provisionally this "earth under our feet" could be as simple as "a house with a Jewish flag on it, a place where Jewish past and German-Jewish spirit become a living synthesis and where we all can be carried into the people [*Volk*]."[27]

The broad program of the Jüdisches Volksheim, which was to serve as a space for community and the promotion of Jewish nationalism, included a children's summer camp, a kindergarten, children's clubs, and adult education. For children the educational mandate included teaching practical skills, such how to grow vegetables (in keeping with the broader Zionist goals of preparing young Jews to work in agriculture in the Land of Israel).[28] Children were also taught Hebrew, a fact that fascinated Franz Kafka and inspired him to help the organization by providing the children with reading materials.[29] Even though at times he was critical of the institution, Kafka was excited by the children's access to Hebrew education when the author himself was trying to learn the language. Although Jewish nationalism remained popular only among a small cross-section of the larger German Jewish community, even in Berlin, Hebrew was a key instrument in disseminating this old-new culture for those Jews who sought a form of Jewish identity that included nationalist expressions.[30]

The story of these spaces is not only or always a top-down tale of philanthropists and elites encouraging frequently poor and immigrant Jewish children into educational spaces of their own design, molding them according to their will in the process. The financiers' initial motivations might have been paternalistic, provoked by a desire to improve the physical and mental health of Jewish children, who were often of lower socioeconomic means, and over time to instruct them in various aspects of Jewish learning. Yet parents necessarily had to consent to sending their children away for weeks at a time. Regardless of the intentions and nature of their initial creators, each group and organization required the acquiescence of Jewish parents, who had to be convinced that their children benefited from attending the camps. Parents' choice to enroll their children in Jewish educational programs expressed a degree of a priori Jewish self-identification and the desire—articulated or mute—for their children to attend a Jewish space, even if Jewishness was not the only or primary motivation.

In France, too, concerns over class and hygiene were important to the founders of children's vacation camps for Jews. In early French holiday camps we also see a greater role of women in the establishment and running of the organizations. Thus we learn from the *Univers Israélite* that one early Parisian Jewish vacation camp from the late 1890s came about thanks to the efforts of various "fairy godmothers [*bonnes fées*]" who belonged to the organization Cagnotte des enfants (literally, "the children's nest egg"). The camp offered "poor" Jewish children "distractions during summer vacation," "pure air far from Paris," and the opportunity "to walk in the woods, through the fields, and provide[d] them healthy and restorative food from the fields." The author of the short news report on the camp happily noted how all campers had gained weight over the course of their stay.[31] Although the goals of the camp clearly echoed the same concerns of camps in Berlin, it is noteworthy that there was a general absence of women among the founders of Jewish summer camps in Berlin (at least those *publicly* acknowledged).[32] In the case of the Cagnotte des enfants camps, women were the driving forces behind the work, including the group's president, Mrs. Jules Ephrussi, and its secretary, the "tireless" Mrs. Ferdinand Dreyfous.[33] Ferdinand Dreyfous himself was a medical doctor who studied and wrote on illnesses typically associated with poverty: tuberculosis and alcoholism.[34] We can presume that the couple shared an interest in these larger medical questions and possible solutions to them.[35]

The children who attended the first Cagnotte des enfants camp, organized in the summer of 1899, were divided into two groups, with twenty-four girls and then twenty-four boys sent to a farm less than 145 kilometers from Paris. The activities included excursions and walks in good weather or lectures and games on rainy days; girls could entertain themselves with the additional task of sewing. Critically, the boys camp was held during the holidays of Rosh Hashanah (Jewish New Year) and Yom Kippur (the Day of Atonement), and the camp organizers made sure to arrange religious services and special holiday dinners.[36] Clearly, the intentions of the camp organizers were not simply that the boys be given a safe space to camp but that they offer them a religiously Jewish space and encourage them to participate in holidays that would normally have been celebrated at home and in the synagogue. In that sense, it is surprising that the camp would coincide with central Jewish holidays and thus take the boys away from the family home. Yet, seen with a more paternalistic gaze, the schedule actually offered the perfect occasion and venue to ensure that the young men participated in religious services. The timing thus suggests the organization's desire to have greater oversight and control over the boys' religious education.

Like examples from Berlin, this early camp was the result of the efforts of Jewish elites to help the poor. Over time and with the considerable growth of the immigrant Jewish community, however, self-help organizations began to organize summer camps for their own subcommunity. These new spaces also highlight the at times hostile relationships between the two communities. Although the discord between French Jews and Eastern European Jewish immigrants has been at times overstated, in some cases the stereotypical animosity was based in reality.[37] One anonymous article from the *Archives Israélites* tells of the creation of the Colonie Scolaire, a Russian-Polish Jewish summer camp organization, which targeted "feeble" children (*enfants débiles*), who were, the author unkindly stressed, "so numerous among the new immigrants."[38] The creators of the Colonie Scolaire offered more complex reasons, however, for their decision to create these camps.

In 1925 two *landsmanshaftn* (self-help organizations)—one composed of individuals originally from Brest-Litovsk and the other consisting of former residents of Piotrkow—set about creating a summer camp that would help ease the "gulf" that had been created between Yiddish-speaking parents and their assimilated, francophone children. Until that time, most if not all educational activities of the Eastern European Jewish community focused on adults, not children.[39] The Colonie Scolaire sought to "awaken the conscience of the Jewish population in order to make it understand that the concern for the health and the education of the youth was a national problem and responded to an absolute necessity."[40] Their goal was to create a "healthy Jewish generation" and to bring them into nature, giving them "sun, air and sea."[41] They did target the poorer strata of the immigrant community, though they did not use the kind of rhetoric used in the aforementioned article from the "native" French Jewish press.[42] In 1927 the group sent 115 children to Berck-Plage, a popular sea resort more than 200 kilometers north of Paris.[43] In 1928 the Colonie Scolaire sent 200 children and had the eventual goal of sending 500,[44] which they exceeded in 1934 when they sent 570 children.[45]

The children amused themselves with games, gymnastics, competitions, playing in the sea, singing, walking, and going on excursions, but the camps also had educational goals. They were not simply spaces for Jews (or, here, Jewish children). Rather, they were Jewish spaces, imbued with culturally relevant content. Children were encouraged to develop a sense of community and to learn stories from Jewish history and folklore.[46] Seen as "ambassadors of Jewish culture" (most likely to other children who did not participate), the children were taught about holidays, history, and Yiddish songs.[47] To pursue further their educational and cultural aims, the Colonie Scolaire created a children's club in Paris in 1930 that remained open throughout the year. Activities included games and crafts as well as Jewish storytelling, recitations, and singing.[48] Stories about history and folklore were clearly intended to help individuals cultivate a sense of self-identification based on historical, cultural, and religious precepts. By fostering solidarity and providing access to Jewish education, it was hoped that greater meaning would be conveyed through the summer camps.

By the late 1930s the number of Jewish summer camps in France had grown considerably. The OSE, which had a long-standing office in Paris, organized summer camps in Enghein-les-Bains and served as a bridge between the French Jewish population and immigrant Jews.[49] The group Pour nos enfants (For Our Children) organized monthly vacations at the popular resort town of Berck-Plage for needy children from the "most unsanitary streets of

Paris." By 1936 the organization had provided 4,297 children with summer vacations, quite an accomplishment for its short six years of existence. The organization further supplied the children with clothing, shoes, medical care, and much food (including kosher meat), provoking the organizers to note proudly how all children had gained at least 1 kilogram.[50]

Other Jewish organizations created camping and hiking groups as a means to integrate Jewish children and youth and build solidarity between them. The Réunions amicales de la jeunesse israélite, for instance, organized hikes and picnics in the summer.[51] Summer camps and hiking groups brought Jewish children together to improve their health, allowed them to enjoy the fresh country air, and provided opportunities to play with other Jewish children. Song, stories, history, and outdoor activities helped strengthen bonds between children and allowed them to participate in Jewish learning in an increasingly popular Jewish space.

The state of Jewish holiday camps in and around St. Petersburg was, by contrast, markedly less lively. Existing more in theory than in practice, the rare passing references to a local summer camp appear to be the only lasting sign of its existence. Thus we learn from a front-page article published in 1896 in *Nediel'naia Khronika Voskhoda* that Imperial Russia was home to a handful of summer camps, including apparently one in St. Petersburg along with camps in Odessa, Warsaw, and Moscow.[52] Yet the goal of the article was not primarily to laud their present achievements but to encourage further expansion and imitation in Russia, and the article offered no details regarding the vacation camp(s) established in St. Petersburg.[53] Instead, the author focused on the generally underdeveloped and preliminary state of affairs in Russia, which he compared with the established and flourishing situation of Jewish vacation camps in Germany. He also offered the reader an overview of the recently opened summer camp in Odessa but declined to give further information on other summer camps in Russia.[54]

Essentially, then, only a rhetorical reality in the Russian capital, the subject of Jewish summer camps in late Imperial Russia was one that concerned a small number of philanthropists and intellectuals. Like their contemporaries to the west, the main concerns and motivations for the creation of these institutions were hygiene and class. Articles on Jewish education and Jewish schools more generally placed significant attention on the physical health and condition of young Jews. The progressive Jewish press in Russia questioned the hygienic standards of various educational institutions, from heders to independent trade schools.[55] And the necessity of physical educa-tion in various guises was seen as all the more acute among Jewish youth, because they were considered "physically far weaker than non-Jews of the same age."[56]

Yet the target of the summer camps according to one article was not merely the stereotypically physically disadvantaged and underdeveloped Jewish youth but also the urban poor among them. Coming from "worn-out and unseemly domestic situations in the city," the children of the lower classes were depicted as malnourished and in need of restorative vacations.[57] Echoing rhetoric from Western and Central Europe at the end of the nine-teenth century, the author explained how the physical frailty of Jewish youth was a result of urban poverty and ethnostructural conditions that privileged mind over body. Summer camps thus appeared to be the panacea that would allow pupils to recover their strength for the coming academic year, attending to their "physical and spiritual" condition. This regeneration was geared not only toward the Jewish body and mind but also to the Jew-ish occupational structure. At least a couple of summer camps in the Pale of Settlement included agricultural work, sometimes in the form of vegetable gardening, on their agenda.[58]

Yet precisely in their activities and geography we see the greatest dif-ference between Russian Jewish summer camps and their counterparts to the west. The existing summer camps could be found overwhelmingly in the Pale of Settlement, not in the capital. Whereas Berlin and Paris were leading centers in the creation and organization of such institutions, St. Petersburg remained an intellectual and rhetorical outpost and, instead, the Pale, with the majority of the Jewish population of Russia, served as the heart of the actual activities. The pivotal Russian Jewish organization OZE (the Society for the Protection of the Health of the Jewish Population) ex-emplifies this pattern. Established by doctors in St. Petersburg in 1912, the OZE focused its task on providing medical help and food for Jews in the Pale of Settlement, where, from 1914 until roughly 1920,[59] the group or-ganized 160 kindergartens and youth hostels serving 50,000 children; 17 milk "kitchens" providing milk for 5,000 infants; and 66 summer camps for 8,400 children.[60] This situation reflected a fundamental difference between the three cities. Whereas St. Petersburg was the capital of the Russian Em-pire and a vital cultural capital of Russian Jewry, it was not the stronghold of the Jewish population of the country. Yet the overall absence of summer camps in St. Petersburg reflected the idiosyncrasies of that city more than they did any particularly distinct Eastern European or Russian Jewish path (compared to other parts of Europe). After all, Odessa and other parts of European Russia were home to Jewish summer camps, including those organized and run by the OZE.[61]

We must acknowledge, however, that we do not really know how successful the summer camps across Europe were at immediately altering or reinforcing the self-perceptions of the children involved. Most articles in the Jewish press, a critical source of information on these spaces, were written by people close to or positively predisposed to the camps. The articles thus tend to be glowing and self-congratulatory in tone, reflecting both their obvious bias and their clear need for financial support to continue pursuing their mission. Post-Shoah documents suggest that the goals were not always immediately successful, at least in the one or two instances where we have sources written by children themselves. Children were entertained by the leisure activities, but it is hard to determine to what extent nationalist, educational, moral, or religious goals were on their minds, even while still at camp. The case of youth spaces offers another vantage point from which to see the involvement of young adults in the formation and continued operation of various leisure spaces and organizations.

Placing Earth Under Their Feet: Youth Clubs and Youth Movements

The founders and members of youth clubs, movements,[62] and sporting organizations responded to a clear desire for Jewish sociability by creating spaces and practices that aimed to inspire Jewish youths to maintain a connection with some element of tradition, community, or Jewish culture. Repeatedly, the initiators spoke explicitly of the need to create sites where Jewish youth could interact and where bonds of friendship and community could be formed.[63] By the outbreak of World War I Jewish youth organizations in all three cities had created popular second homes for young Jews. Young men *and* women, rejecting the bourgeois morality and highly individualized Judaism of their parents, turned to collective, seemingly "authentic" notions of Jewish self-identification.[64]

From the beginning, then, many if not most organizations sought to establish Jewish spaces, sometimes temporary and transient and at other times in more concrete and permanent clubhouses. As Michael Brenner reminds us,[65] the generation that came of age around the time of World War I sought togetherness, sources of communally based self-identification, and even, at times, spiritual fulfillment.[66] Yet it was the very individualization of the community that propelled young men and women toward the collective, not simply a preexisting sense of community that motivated their search for togetherness. As an anonymous member of the Éclaireurs israélites de France (EIF) stressed in the late 1920s, "Scouting is an educational method that appeals to the imagination and the sensitivity of the child, [and] develops his *individuality* all in making him understand that he should perfect himself in order better to help others."[67] By appealing to the individual, her creativity, and her distinct personality, this scouting group attempted to bind her to the collective and activate her energies for the benefit of the community. Only in the context of an increasingly autonomous and voluntaristic Jewish world were these goals and concerns even conceivable.

At the same time, although youth revolt served as the source of much of the initial motivations behind youth movements and helped promote a fertile period for the flourishing of youth spaces, these same anti-establishment sentiments dissipated in Paris and Berlin as a general consensus was reached between the generations by the end of the 1920s. With the rise of Nazism, the spread of antisemitism, and the outbreak of World War II, the 1930s and 1940s would see a significant change in priorities of all groups and organizations. In early postwar Petrograd/Leningrad, the impetus to recreate society in general and Jewish society in particular took a radical turn. The generational struggle ended quite differently, as the 1920s witnessed the demise of Jewish spaces much more broadly.

Before the turn of the twentieth century, the members of Bnai Brith in Berlin charged themselves not only with the task of promoting the health of poor Jewish children through summer camps but also of playing an important role in the lives of Jewish youth in the metropolis and country more generally. In 1891 members of the Great Lodge of Berlin articulated an interest in organizing Jewish youth to contribute to their education and welfare and to preserve Judaism from the "centrifugal forces" that pulled Jewish youth away from the community.[68] In particular, they hoped to redirect Jewish youth toward the community through the creation of youth clubs and not through religion, distinguishing between alternative bases for Jewish self-identification, essentially a spatial resolution to the problem faced.[69]

These early efforts would result in 1909 in the creation of the Verband der jüdischen Jugendvereine Deutschlands (VJJD), an umbrella organization that brought together twenty-five member clubs. Created for educational and, especially, sociable purposes, the VJJD was modeled along the American YMHA (Young Men's Hebrew Association). It and its member organizations were funded and supported by Bnai Brith, the Centralverein (CV), and the Deutsch-Israelitischer Gemeindebund.[70] Together the various sub-organizations and the VJJD itself sought to create homes away from home for young men[71] who worked as commercial apprentices and employees in the pre–World War I period.[72] By the 1910s this organization included women as well.[73]

Apolitical in its orientation, the VJJD hoped to offer "valuable leisure-time activities" and "Bildung" while also combatting a sense of "dejudaization."[74] To this end, one of its central tasks was to compose and distribute educational materials among the various member associations and to organize lectures on themes of Jewish life and courses on general education and practical training.[75] Self-improvement, liberal values, and respectability—the keys to successful integration in the minds of the post-emancipation generation and representatives of Bnai Brith and the CV who helped fund the VJJD—served as the focus of many of these lectures.[76] At the same time, weekly social events were held on Friday evenings and Jewish holidays were celebrated as a way of connecting young Jews to Judaism.[77]

The VJJD was part of an early attempt to direct youth activities from above. As the years wore on, this organization—and through it the official Jewish community—pursued a continued and intensifying co-optation of the youth movement culture and at the same time appealed to the members of youth-run organizations who desired to be admitted to the VJJD.[78] The VJJD organized athletic and social activities, such as sports and dances, which were intended to promote physical health, foster group discipline, and, perhaps most important, by the interwar years encourage a connection to the wider Jewish community that would satisfy the need for "self-knowledge and identity."[79] At the same time, the VJJD also inspired the creation of the Jungjüdische Wanderbund (JJWB), which despite its early affiliation with the VJJD, quickly became an independent youth movement with its own political predilections.[80] Participants in the JJWB engaged in folk dancing and singing, and there was not an insignificant number of Eastern European immigrant children and youth among its members.[81]

A further early example of youth sociability came with the creation of the Bar Kochba sports club in Berlin, on October 10, 1898. Predating the creation of the VJJD by more than a decade, the Bar Kochba club was the world's first Jewish gymnastics association (*Turnverein*).[82] Formed on the heels of Max Nordau's famous speech calling for the creation of a Jewry of muscles, the gymnastics association pursued the goal of improving the physical health and overall condition of Jewish youth and of encouraging Jewish nationalism among them.[83] Gymnastics in particular was seen as the ideal cure for the supposed degeneration of the urban Jewish man, designated by various "types," including the "coffeehouse Jew"[84] and the caftan Jew.[85] This was the primary motivation for the members of Bar Kochba, who sought to improve (and prove) the health of the male Jewish body.

In 1900 the men's section of Bar Kochba would meet twice a week at two Jewish schools in the Scheunenviertel: on Mondays at Gipsstrasse 23a (at the Jüdische Knabenschule, or Jewish boys school) and Wednesdays at Hamburgerstrasse 27 (today, Grosse Hamburger Strasse, at the Jüdische Oberschule, or the Jewish secondary school). The women's section would meet on Tuesdays and Thursdays at Auguststrasse 67–68, a sports field also located in the Scheunenviertel.[86]

Yet additional forms of sociability were important to the movement and served to reinforce nationalist values that captured the hearts and minds of the seventy original members of Berlin's Bar Kochba section.[87] After exercising, the members would gather at the bar (*Hauskneippe*) of the municipal gym (*Turnhalle*), where they socialized and sang national-Jewish songs.[88] The song of the Bar Kochba association, "Allmächtig durch die Herzen ruft," composed by Israel Auerbach, stressed the basic and essential entitlement of Jews to an equal place in the world alongside other national groups. Neither particularly profound nor poetically inspiring, the song uses romantic national imagery not unlike that found in German nationalist lyrics of the time (including mountains, forests, and eagles). Stressing that only strength could help them achieve their final goal of national equality, the fourth and last stanza concludes with the declarative statement, "The world belongs to us too!" ("Auch uns gehört die Erde!").[89]

Much attention has rightly been placed on the male-oriented nature of the early gymnastics and sports clubs in general.[90] Yet by 1900, two years after the founding of Bar Kochba, the association already had a women's section, with a girls' section to follow. By 1903 there were 129 female members (most, by the looks of it, young and single), accounting for about 34% of the total membership in Bar Kochba.[91] Nonetheless, discontent with the Bar Kochba leadership led a substantial number of women to leave. In 1910 they founded the Jüdische Frauenbund für Turnen und Sport (Jewish Women's Union for Gymnastics and Sports), or Ifftus.[92]

Ifftus was decidedly more Zionist in orientation and by 1914 had 181 members.[93] One early member, Käte Dan-Rosen, recalled how she gladly gave up her membership in a (non-Jewish) German gymnastics association and, after joining Ifftus, took a leading role in the creation of a hiking group. Despite the feelings of alienation she felt as a result of the antisemitic taunting she experienced on the streets of pre–World War I Berlin, Dan-Rosen was far from a convinced Zionist when she joined Ifftus. Instead, she found herself having to familiarize herself with central Zionist writings, including those of Herzl, Pinsker, and Ahad Ha'am, in order to arrange social evenings for the group.[94] Such evenings were key to the group's task of providing informal ideological education.

Yet Ifftus had other purposes as well. As Johanna Tomaschewsky, founder of Ifftus, wrote in 1919, friendships were essential for the success of the Zionist sports groups and their goals of physical and moral improvement: "In addition to one or two athletic evenings [*Turnabende*] a week, hiking trips and afternoons spent playing sports have to be arranged and gatherings must take place in a comfortably set-up clubhouse [*Vereinsheim*]."[95] Tomaschewsky further proposed that this sociability would help create a particularly inviting atmosphere, which would entice participants to return regularly.

The clubhouse in particular became a space where young participants could gain access to nationalist literature and familiarize themselves, much like Dan-Rosen had done, with Zionist periodicals and the writings of leading Zionist thinkers of the time. Such spaces were vital to sporting and youth groups like Ifftus, creating a stable environment for members to gather and learn more about the ideological position and goals of the movement. Within these walls members could participate in "Palestine classes," learn Hebrew, and acquaint themselves with Bible stories and Jewish history.[96] The interwar years witnessed an overall increase in the number of women who participated in a variety of sports activities.[97] The appeal was multifold: Jewish sports and gymnastics associations organized more sporting and gymnastics activities but also celebrated Jewish holidays, held lectures, and organized trips and excursions.[98]

Regardless of the particular activity or even the ideology that under-pinned each organization, there was a fairly stable consensus in the early decades of the twentieth century that spaces for youth leisure and sport-ing were ideal conduits through which to encourage members to learn about Jewish tradition and politics and at times also observe customs and holidays.[99] By combining informal education with young people's growing interest in participating in physical activities, Jewish youth clubs and move-ments provided the physical context for Jewish identity formation.

Another advocate of Jewish youth, Moses Calvary, argued that such groups and the spaces they established offered a nonreligious Jewish envi-ronment for the development and expression of Jewish self-identification.[100] Writing about the goals of Blau Weiss (first founded in 1907 in Breslau and in 1912 in Berlin),[101] Calvary explained how this alternative Jewish sense of belonging was to come about: "In and by hiking one becomes aware of one's Jewishness [*Judentum*]." This awareness, he continued, was to encourage "a deepening of community life [*Gemeinschaftsleben*], which today has already

Figure 3. Members of Bar Kochba Berlin on a field trip, 1926. Courtesy of the Jewish Museum Berlin; gift of Ann Stieglitz. Reprinted with permission.

engendered the desire to take possession of historical Jewishness among the hiking youth." The "desire" to express their Jewishness manifested itself, according to Calvary, in the fact that the youths "learn Hebrew, they want to give new meaning to the holidays, they begin to delve into the history of Jewry [*Judentum*]."[102] The communal act of hiking—not only or exclusively prayer, study, or the observance of Jewish law—with other Jews was meant to arouse within the individual a sense of identification and to prompt each individual to seek the roots of his or her Jewishness in a common history, language, and the shared celebration of holidays. In this sense, Calvary took a step further: sociability itself was a form of Jewish learning and served as a mechanism to construct and cement Jewish belonging.

The insistence on the centrality of hiking in nature made by Calvary and other members of the Blau Weiss mirrored the importance of that activity among non-Jewish German youth groups, such as the Wandervogel, on which Blau Weiss was modeled. We should recall that both Jews and non-Jews experienced a rapid rate of urbanization that made the return to a rural setting all the more appealing. Ideologically, the authenticity that a pastoral setting seemed to offer provided an ideal (or at least idealized) location for the rejuvenation of the (predominantly) *male* body.[103] Politically sympathetic to Zionism, Blau Weiss articulated strong connections to German self-identification; its basic aim was simply to "bring back pride to Judaism"[104] while at the same time stressing German patriotism.

Yet, according to historian Glenn Sharfman, the apparent absence of Jewish content in its early years (and its focus on hiking in nature) was precisely what irritated other German Jews of the time. Gershom Scholem vehemently argued that Blau Weiss had no Jewish content and that its romantic emphasis led it in the direction of fascism in the 1920s. In practical terms, though, by the 1920s imitation of the Wandervogel movement gave way to preparing members for immigration to Palestine and rekindling a personal spirit of Judaism.[105] Blau Weiss did not organize hikes on Saturdays and the group served kosher food on trips. They greeted each other with "Shalom" and were "encouraged to learn Hebrew and celebrate the Jewish holidays": "Hanukkah was especially singled out, and the flames of the menorah were compared to the flames of the campfires which took on mystical qualities."[106] Blau Weiss also played an important role in offering a context for Jewish self-identification in nonreligious spaces.[107]

One of the most important youth groups during the 1920s was the

Jugendverband jüdischer Deutscher Kameraden, founded in 1919, an umbrella organization that brought together a hiking league, a sports and gymnastics association, and a youth league (*Jugendbund*). Having its roots in the CV, the Kameraden was nonetheless officially independent from this organization.[108] Open to members of various different religious streams of Judaism and both genders, the larger movement sought both to fight antisemitism and to challenge those Jews who desired "to organize German Jews" according to national-Jewish principles, encouraging instead stronger ties to the "deutschen Heimat." At the same time, absorbing central goals of the sports and gymnastics movement, the group stressed the need for the "bodily recovery [*körperliche Gesundung*]" of Jewish youth.[109] As outlined in *Im deutschen Reich*, this task involved the "tempering [*Stählung*] of the body through hiking, sport, gymnastics [*Turnen*] and a healthy, simple lifestyle."[110] This physical regeneration, and in particular the suggestion that this could be accomplished through a "healthy, simple lifestyle," was to be accompanied by a spiritual component that rejected "religious and social materialism." The quest for simplicity and authenticity was to be found in "in-depth engagement with the religious, ethical and moral values of Judaism," with the hopes that this would encourage inner and outer freedom.[111] Yet, more than functioning on an individual level, this physical and spiritual revitalization was to have a communal dimension as well. Whether in the gym, on the field, or in nature, these activities, it was hoped, would create convivial confraternity among the organization's members.[112] It would foster the birth and development of a sense of community and communal responsibility free of the various deformities of modern society.[113] In an effort to promote Jewish self-identification and offer a new communal form of Jewish belonging that scorned the apparent lack of spirituality ensconced in the Judaism of their parents, some chapters of the Kameraden began to study Hebrew and organized readings of the Bible.[114]

Despite the antisemitism that had prompted the creation of several of the German Jewish youth movements and what one might be tempted to call a hostile environment, these spaces actually flourished in the relative openness of the late Imperial era and the Weimar Republic, especially during the latter's most prosperous years. Their popularity was immense; Michael Brenner estimates that in the 1920s a full one-third of all German Jewish youths, male and female, belonged to a Jewish youth movement. The VJJD alone had 41,000 members.[115] This success not only speaks to these groups' ability to address communal concerns about the health and education of Jewish children and youths but also highlights the general desire and need felt by the Jewish population of the city (and the rest of the country) for such sites of leisure and sociability. Without this demand, it is hard to imagine the increasing number of vacation camps, youth clubs, and sports groups.

The variety and intensity of youth clubs and movements in interwar Berlin are reminiscent of similar developments in Paris. In 1882 the Union Scolaire was created to help school graduates find employment. The group changed its mandate, however, and in 1897 the organization opened the first Jewish community center in the city at 19, rue Béranger (near the Place de la République). Extending its membership beyond its original constituency, a celebratory article in the *Univers Israélite* proclaimed that the Union Scolaire was now open to "Israelites of all classes and walks of life [*de toute catégorie et de toute condition*]." Open afternoons and evenings and boasting of "spacious rooms, electrically lit," the center had conference and reading rooms, a library (with periodicals in multiple languages), smaller rooms for

Figure 4. A Bar Kochba Berlin gymnastics class with Olga Löbel-Glücklich (second row, first person on the left), Berlin, ca. 1930–1938. Courtesy of the Jewish Museum Berlin; gift of Ann Stieglitz, Olga's daughter. Reprinted with permission.

games, and even a fencing room and one for hydrotherapy. Membership was 6 francs for regular members and 3 francs for those between the ages of 15 and 20.[116] By the summer of 1897, the Union Scolaire had more than 600 members.[117] The following year they held monthly concerts, lectures, and weekly language courses in English and German.[118] Three years later, in 1900, the Union Scolaire created a sporting group. The young (presumably male)[119] members participated in a variety of activities: Meeting on Sundays in the Vincennes woods, they might run or play *ballon* (perhaps rugby, football, or another game involving a similar-sized ball), or they might do weightlifting and gymnastics in a small room in the association's headquarters on rue Béranger.[120]

The Union Scolaire was not the only Jewish association to emerge at the turn of the twentieth century. Nadia Malinovich has chronicled the early development of Jewish youth clubs in France.[121] As she has rightly pointed out, the developments of the early years paled in comparison with their explosion in the 1920s and even well into the 1930s. The new youth groups and clubs reflected the ethnically, religiously, and politically diverse Jewish population and were especially important because, unlike earlier examples, these were most often created by the youths themselves.[122] Popular among immigrant Jews and those with links to the Zionist movement, the Maccabi sports club was founded in 1922 and by the late 1920s had 1,300 members.[123] Bene-Mizrah, or Sons of the East, was founded around 1924 and brought together Sephardi Jews. The Cercle de la jeunesse juive religieuse de Paris (Circle of Religious Jewish Youth), catering to the observant, was founded in 1930. The Union des jeunesses israélites de France (Union of Israelite Youth of France), an immigrant association formed in 1929, organized basketball and soccer games for men, basketball games for women, and rugby games and track and field events.[124] The Jewish press helped inform readers about the various activities that took place in those venues and regularly reported, for instance, on the exploits of the Maccabi sporting club.[125]

Another important group was the EIF, particularly noteworthy because of the centrality of its creator, Robert Gamzon, and because of the organization's later activities during the Shoah. In a personal and immediate way, Gamzon bridged the two halves of the Jewish population in Paris. On his mother's side, he was the grandson of a consistorial rabbi, Alfred Lévy, and thus had strong roots in French Judaism.[126] His father, by contrast, was a Russian Jewish immigrant. At age 16 Gamzon had attended a camp of the

Éclaireurs unionistes, a scouting movement with Protestant origins. The following year, in 1923, he organized a small Jewish scouting troop with the encouragement of the consistorial grand rabbi Maurice Liber.[127]

The EIF would mix scouting culture (e.g., Gamzon adopted the totem *Castor Soucieux*, or Cautious Beaver) with Jewish imagery and religious practice. They used Jewish symbols, including the Star of David (which adorned their uniforms until 1942, when the infamous decrees forced Jews to wear the yellow star in occupied France) and the lions of Judea holding the Ten Commandments.[128] The first troop went on an excursion to Versailles that culminated in an evocative ceremony at a local synagogue, reflecting the group's early ties to the Consistoire. "The grand rabbi Liber, who never

Figure 5. Members of the Éclaireurs israélites de France gathering for an outdoor prayer service, ca. 1930s. Source: United States Holocaust Memorial Museum, courtesy of Janine Storch. Reprinted with permission.

missed an excursion of the Boursiers Lauréats des Écoles,[129] took his place at the *Almemor*,[130] along with Gamzon and [André] Kisler-Rosenwald."[131] Together with the remaining young men of the troop, they made an oath, or *promesse*, to serve "God, Judaism and France. To render service at every opportunity." The ceremony concluded with the recitation of the Shema.[132]

In 1924 the statutes of the David troop became official, and in January 1927 the society became the EIF. That same year the group registered 150 members, and by 1930 it had already grown to a total membership of 1,200 scouts in 27 troops.[133] Also in that year, the EIF held a ceremony at the same synagogue where members of the nascent movement had taken their oath for the first time. Holding the afternoon prayer service (*minhah*), the group recited the Ma Tovu prayer ("How goodly [are your tents]"), Psalms 115 and 118 (part of the Hallel, or the prayer for thanksgiving), after which Rabbi Jacob Kaplan, Robert Gamzon, and the writer and novelist Edmond Fleg gave speeches.[134] Religious services continued to be an integral part of the group's activities.

The relative success of the organization can be attributed to Gamzon's desire to appeal to a broad swath of Jewish youth, including girls and young women. By the late 1920s and early 1930s the group had expanded beyond its strong consistorial basis and sought to be more inclusive and pluralistic. The EIF desired to integrate French Jews from outside Paris, North African Jews, immigrants, Zionists, and the nonreligious.[135] Its stated goals included the "physical, practical, moral and religious development of the Israelite youth through scouting methods; to make scouting accessible to observant Israelite children; to 'Frenchify' the young foreign Jews arriving to France; to arouse interest in works of mutual aide and for the reconstruction of the National Home."[136] The group also hoped to return "certain young and entirely dejudaized French Israelites" to Judaism.[137]

Edmond Fleg reflected that, whereas "40 years ago," when the great tragedy facing Jewish families was the "disintegration of Israel" as fathers "watched with pain and often with anger as their [sons] abandoned" tradition, today "the tragedy of Israel is no longer in its disintegration but in its very renaissance." Fleg explained the problem: "One feels that one is Jewish, one wants to become Jewish again," yet whom was a young person to ask and how was this return to be accomplished? History and literature spoke only to a certain section of these individuals; Zionism was a lofty but distant goal; becoming halachically observant was made complicated by other family members who were religiously indifferent. To rediscover Judaism, one had to "rebuild a Jewish life," Fleg maintained. The great supporter of French Jewish scouting, Fleg lauded the scouting movement's ability to do just this and to do it "victoriously." "The Jewish soul" is cultivated and strengthened; biblical epics come alive and are celebrated in the great outdoors, "our holidays regain their naïveté and their primeval meaning."[138] This was the Jewish renaissance in practical terms, and the leaders of the EIF believed that they were in the position to effect palpable changes in Jewish life through and by the creation of Jewish youth spaces and leisure practices.

By contrast, the renaissance of Jewish youth spaces in St. Petersburg was more restricted and short-lived. Several key factors stymied the growth of these spaces, certainly compared to similar organizations in Western and Central Europe. These included a small number of postsecondary students, hostility from the Slavic gymnastics organization Sokol, and official, state-sponsored restrictions against non-Russian groups that were perceived to be nationalistic and separatist.[139] Add to this the political disruptions of the

Figure 6. Members of the Éclaireurs israélites de France resting on a fence while on a hiking excursion through the French countryside in Saint Gervais les Condamines, August 1938. Source: United States Holocaust Memorial Museum, courtesy of Janine Storch. Reprinted with permission.

age, and we see that late Imperial and early postrevolutionary St. Petersburg was not particularly a fertile field for the growth or development of these organizations. Nevertheless, by World War I there were in fact a growing number of gathering sites for Jewish youth sponsored by variety of organizations, from political groups such as the Tseire Tsiyon (Youth of Zion), to sport clubs and youth movements such as Ahdut (Unity), Maccabi, and He-haluts (Pioneers).[140] The creation of such places reflected the growing interest of youths and young adults in confronting questions of identity, health, and the future of the Jewish people.

As had been the case in Berlin and to a somewhat lesser extent in Paris, concerns about hygiene and health contributed to the developing Jewish sports movements. The involvement of the OZE in the establishment of the first Jewish gymnastics club in Russia just before World War I was a clear reflection of this.[141] On February 10, 1914, a sporting and gymnastics group opened in St. Petersburg under the auspices of the OZE and headed by the "famous Jewish sportsman" Grigorii Abramovich Palepa. By the fall of 1914 the group had fifty-four members, split into two groups—one for men (with thirty members) and one for women (consisting of the remaining twenty-four members). Despite the outbreak of the war, their numbers continued to grow. Following the ideals of the ancient Greeks, members aimed "to be healthy, strong, agile and beautiful." The group also took thirteen "health trips" between 1915 and 1916. On one such excursion, the eighteen participants played a variety of games, sang, and danced. Another trip was planned to coincide with Purim.[142] In 1916 this Petrograd Jewish gymnastics circle became an independent organization (one of the first Jewish sports organizations in the Russian Empire) and in 1917 was named the Evreiskii gimnasticheskii-sportivnii kruzhok Ahdut (Jewish Gymnastics-Sportive Circle Ahdut), putting Petrograd at the forefront of the Russian Jewish— and to an extent even the European Jewish—sports movement.[143] Although primarily focused on youth health and sport, Ahdut encouraged brotherhood and fraternity among Jews, as reflected in its motto, "Strong in spirit, strong in body—for our people."[144]

Petrograd also served as the birthplace of the All-Russian Union of Maccabi Sporting Clubs in April 1917 at the sixth congress of the Zionist student group He-haver (The Friend). The group's task was the "physical rejuvenation of Jewish youth."[145] Although the first Maccabi club had been founded in 1913 in Odessa, this new umbrella organization was key in spreading and organizing the wider Jewish sporting movement. Maccabi Petrograd was founded in August 1917, and in addition to promoting physical rejuvenation, the club offered a space for fraternity among the younger Jews of the capital city.[146] The same year, the organization began publishing a monthly journal that promoted its goals and advertised its events. Serving as the voice of the Union of Maccabi clubs, the journal sought to encourage the "physical regeneration of the Jewish masses." The physical and the spiritual were linked, and sport had the power, the leading article proclaimed, to cultivate "strong spirits."[147] Yet the timing of these developments could not have been more dramatic. Pogroms beginning that year provoked Simon Dubnow to remark on the sad timeliness of this "self-defense" in a letter addressed to the journal. He encouraged the Jewish youth of the day—"healthy of soul and body"—to declare, "We are here, we the guardians of the national honor."[148]

The spectrum of Jewish youth and sports movements in Petrograd further included the youth movement He-haluts,[149] which was responsible for creating the Ha-thiyah (The Revival) Club in 1920.[150] The club catered to Jews with nationalist leanings and was linked to the Zionist movement. The club housed not only the youth group He-haluts but also He-haver (The Friend) and collaborated with other Zionist organizations and activists, including those from Maccabi. By adorning rooms "with blue and white banners, portraits of Zionist leaders, and Hebrew inscriptions" and in singing "Ha-tikvah" (The Hope) "and other Zionist songs," the club used Jewish and Zionist symbolism. In so doing, the organization functioned in many ways as a school for Jewish identity building. Yet it used more than symbolism to educate its members; the club organized lectures on Jewish culture and life in Palestine.[151]

These youth organizations, including Maccabi and Ahdut, not only offered Jewish spaces for youths to meet and gather for leisure time activities and political agitation but were also instrumental in creating other Jewish spaces, a process witnessed in Paris. The youth group He-haluts, for example, organized a workshop designed to train pioneers for future agricultural work, which eventually became a labor cooperative called Amal ("labor," in Hebrew).[152] More than a workplace, Amal served as a gathering site for cultural and educational events, including a memorial evening for Joseph Trumpeldor in March 1925 and an evening dedicated to the Yiddish writer I. L. Perets that took place on the eve of Passover.[153] Jewish youth groups in the city created sites for education and celebration that were similar in form, if not content, to those in Berlin. In addition, the examples of such youth groups further demonstrate how these venues engendered the creation of more Jewish sites—giving life, as it were, to a larger culture of Jewish spaces interwoven with one another through association, education, and self-identification.

Around 1921 the consolidating regime began to alter its policy on national and religious organizations.[154] The change from an official but passive to an actively antireligious position resulted in the official closure of branches; some organizations changed their names, and others went underground. Nevertheless, even in 1924 there were still eighty branches of Maccabi with 15,000 members in Soviet Russia and thirty branches of the socialist Ha-shomer Ha-tsair (The Youth Guard) with 6,000 members. The left wing of these organizations continued to function for several more years.[155]

Yet the number of Jews involved in these youth spaces in Petrograd/ Leningrad was in any event quite small. As youth and sports groups closed, most youth turned toward non-Jewish, non-Zionist communist youth organizations.[156] By the early 1930s Jewish youth and sports clubs in Leningrad no longer existed, and the city's Jews were not in a position to recreate them in later years. Jewish children and youths could and did integrate into the existing leisure structures, joining the pioneers, the communist youth movement, and/or the Komsomol (literally, the Communist Union of Youth) and attending vacation camps for all children.[157] Yet separate leisure spaces for Jewish children—either religiously or ethnically focused—did not exist.

Exclusion, War, and Rescue

By the late 1920s in both Paris and Berlin the Jewish youth movement had become an essential component of the Jewish community. With the rise of Nazism and the outbreak of World War II, children's and youth organizations and spaces were forced to address even more urgent tasks than informal education. No longer places to grow, they became networks for rescue and escape.

In the increasingly hostile atmosphere of Nazi Germany, "Jews badly needed places where they could be amongst their own . . . in which they could feel secure from the humiliation and persecution."[158] For Jewish children and young adults, summer camps and youth clubs played important roles in creating a sense of normalcy, even for short periods of time, preparing them physically and mentally for emigration, and later, during the war years, aiding in their rescue. As the Nazi regime sought to progressively exclude Jews from the public sphere, laws were enacted to bar Jews from using public spaces (such as youth hostels).[159]

In 1935, for instance, the Nazi authorities promulgated regulations concerning Jewish youth movements and camping groups. Accordingly, "Jewish camping grounds [were] forbidden except when they [were] on land owned by Jews and not in the area of dwellings of non-Jews." Hiking excursions involving groups with more than twenty Jewish youth were also forbidden.[160] Regulations excluded Jews from "Aryan" sports groups and associations. Further laws prevented Jewish organizations from using public spaces and institutions for their own activities.[161] German Jews therefore had to make arrangements on their own, at least until the Nazis dissolved all political Jewish organizations, including the Zionist associations, in 1939.[162]

Repeatedly, memoirs from the 1930s stress the restricted social and educational options for Jewish children and youths as the primary impetus to join Jewish youth programs. The self-proclaimed atheist Peter Gay joined the Ringbund, a "Jewish boy scout troop," in 1934 because his parents wanted him to get more exercise. By this time, a Jewish youth movement was his only option.[163] Ilana Michaeli became a member of the Werkleute (the Workers, a splinter organization of the Kameraden)[164] after 1935. The group appealed to her, at least in part, because it offered educational activities, trips to museums, and excursions.[165] Another contemporary, Louis Posner, a fairly rowdy child and teenager, found comfort and meaning in physical education through a Jewish sports club. In the spring of 1937 Posner was chosen to represent the "Maccabee-Hakoah" Athletic Club at an athletic meet. He joined the boxing team, training three days a week with "wrestling, a little jujitsu, punching bags, rope skipping, and shadow boxing." The training not incidentally furthered his reputation as a "roughneck."[166]

Yet physical education and athletics were only part of what these youth activities could offer. As Herbert Strauss notes, the youth movement helped him sever contacts with German society. The psychic trauma felt by so many German Jews, especially by the older generation who had believed that being German and Jewish were entirely consonant, was lessened and smoothed over by participation in youth movements that explicitly sought to separate Jews from German culture and from Germany. The Zionist youth movements in particular, even for members who were not convinced

Zionists, helped young German Jews come to terms with the move that many hoped to make: to leave Germany and find a new home. Norbert Wollheim's role first in organizing summer camps for Jewish children in Denmark and Sweden and then later in the *Kindertransport* that saved roughly 10,000 Jewish children[167] mirrored a similar trajectory from disengagement to rescue, a pattern that would be repeated in France.

Jewish children's and youth organizations in France became the foundations for the significant efforts to rescue Jewish children during the Shoah. Broadly, the various youth clubs and associations created to help the young continued to pursue their educational agendas when and where possible, but they also participated and organized rescue and engaged in resistance.[168] They provided individuals with forged documents, helped with travel, provided childcare, and smuggled children to Switzerland and Spain. The youth movements "assumed complete responsibility for the care of 10,000 children whose parents had been expelled."[169] And members of the Jewish scouts also joined armed partisan groups.[170]

Shortly after the Nazi invasion of France, on June 15, 1940, a group of Jewish activists, including Léo Glaeser and David Rapoport, gathered to reestablish a free medical clinic and cafeterias. The group would come to be known as the Comité de la rue Amelot, named after the road on which the clinic La mère et l'enfant (mother and child) was located.[171] Including members of the Colonie Scolaire, ORT,[172] the OSE, and other groups, over the course of the war the committee provided free food, ration cards, money, medical care, and false identification cards; they helped numerous families emigrate or flee to Vichy France and also helped those held in internment camps such as Drancy; finally, they ran an orphanage and helped rescue children.[173] The member institutions of the Comité de la rue Amelot also worked on parallel projects. The OSE, along with ORT and the EIF, organized the evacuation of thousands of Jewish children, placing them in houses established to take care of them, and helped them to emigrate.[174] For example, by 1941 the OSE had more than 1,000 children living in their homes in the Free Zone. Once the raffles began in the second half of 1942, these homes no longer provided safety from deportation.[175] Those who worked for the various Jewish organizations, such as Vivette Samuel, continued to struggle on behalf of Jewish children and helped them to go underground or emigrate.[176] The efforts resulted in a remarkable number of rescues, with thousands surviving thanks to the work of youth advocates, their networks, and homes.[177]

Conclusions

The growing interest and concern for the future of Jewish children and youth was an outgrowth of the increased anxiety over the future of Jews, the Jewish community, and Judaism. Jewish organizations for young Jews sought to merge sociability with informal learning, encouraging Jewish solidarity through play and learning. By the turn of the twentieth century, Jewish leisure became a central conduit for the instruction of Jewish values for young members of the community, a fact that was recognized across Europe and would remain important after the Shoah in Western and Central Europe.

Yet in Imperial St. Petersburg summer camps were essentially theoretical in nature. They served as the subject of discussion and interest; but for a passing example, however, they remained a reality only in the Pale of Settlement and further to the west. In addition, the consolidation of the Soviet system led to the progressive closure of youth spaces for and by Jews. The mid-1920s again serves as a decisive moment in the notable and considerable divergence in the experiences of the Jews of Leningrad from those of the Jews of Paris and Berlin. Whereas the three communities had shared common concerns, by the 1920s the political changes in the Soviet Union meant that the future of youth spaces in Leningrad would be vastly different from those in Berlin and Paris.

Politics were essential elsewhere as well. The rise of the Nazis had a devastating effect on the lives of Jewish children and youths across Europe, but in the 1930s especially, German Jewish youth movements found themselves engaging in new tasks and playing quite different roles in the lives of young Jews. Instead of creating new Jewish spaces, they became instrumental in helping young Jews prepare for new lives abroad. By the outbreak of World War II, in both Germany and France youth movements and organizations served as essential networks in the rescue of young Jews and in the larger resistance to Nazism.

CHAPTER 4

A Space for Judaism

Rites of Passage and Old-New Jewish Holy Days

One critical aspect of the transformation of European Jewry during the nineteenth century was the gradual disintegration of Judaism as a way of life into splintered, multiple, and frequently privatized expressions of Jewishness. The processes of secularization by definition did not result simply or straightforwardly in an abandonment of "tradition" by the growing number of European Jews but in the alteration of religious beliefs and practices (from liberal to Orthodox guises). These in turn led to noticeable changes in the type, nature, and emphasis of Jewish spaces for ritual and holy day participation.

In the wide historiography on the subject, much of the story of Jewish secularization has focused on the clear decline and/or privatization of religious observance. Michael Brenner and Leora Batnizky have noted how the religious world of German Jews was spatially reduced "to the narrow sphere of the synagogue."[1] Judaism in post-emancipation Germany came to be for many Jews "purely a religious denomination," and the synagogue was transformed from a communal space into a highly sacralized one.[2] By using a confessional definition, Jews compartmentalized their religious identities into specific and private spheres. As Franz Kafka's bitter letter to his father suggests, if the family was not engaged in that narrow sphere to any considerable degree, then one had no access to Jewish religious knowledge.[3] The German state, for its part, also approached and understood its newly emancipated Jewish citizens in denominational terms.

Similarly, "nineteenth-century French Jews operated from the assumption that they could only legitimately assert their place in the French nation as members of a religious minority," as opposed to a distinct ethnic or cultural group.[4] In this capacity French Jews maintained public identities that were politically republican and secular, and at home and in the synagogue they saw themselves as *confessionally* Jewish. This divide only widened in 1905 with the law that formally separated church and state and removed public funding from the Consistoire, a move that officially sanctioned the inner Jewish perception of privatized religious identities.

In Russia the process of secularization was noticeably different. Officially, Jews continued to be seen both by insiders and outsiders as an *ethno*religious community, not just as a faith. This definition itself, though, was a reflection of changing understandings of group identity, as previous notions of Jewish peoplehood evolved in response to modern nationalist conceptions. In addition, growing groups of Jews, especially those in the capital, began to challenge these ethnic definitions, seeking to adopt the maskilic and individualized definition of Jewish belonging: being Jews at home and Russians on the street.[5] Thus in St. Petersburg some chose to abandon halachic Judaism in favor of forms of ethnic, and often political, self-identification (e.g., Bundism, Zionism, autonomism), whereas others adopted patterns of acculturation that we typically associate in almost clichéd fashion with German Jews (especially the latter's purported love affair with the Christmas tree).[6] Yet Eastern European immigrants to Central and Western Europe also destabilized the confessional definitions of Judaism in Paris and Berlin—and France and Germany more broadly—a point that could lead to tensions between members of the various groups.

The story of secularization as merely one of decline and privatization misses another important component of the process underway: Jews in the late nineteenth and early twentieth centuries frequently undertook to *remake* religious practice. As a result of the transformation in social and cultural patterns among European Jews over the course of the nineteenth century and in reaction to changing political conditions, Ashkenazi Jews began to alter the ways they celebrated bar mitzvahs, weddings, and certain holy days. They also in several instances created new rituals, including initiation rites for young teens. This too was a form of secularization, though not one we always associate with the term. In this context, Jewish customs were changed as their celebration was moved in and out of traditional Jewish spaces and sites of consumption and leisure.[7]

Rites of Passage

Among the various celebrations to change during this era were rites of passage. For instance, the bar mitzvah ceremony increasingly became a family affair in which religious meaning held secondary or little importance at all, depending on the views and values of the parents. This meant that for many families, the critical space of the bar mitzvah ritual was less the synagogue and more the site of family interaction: the home.[8] This transformation, along with apparent declining numbers of children participating in religious services and education, provoked concern among religious leaders, both clerical and lay. Fearing for the spiritual condition of the coming generations, they regularly bemoaned what they interpreted as the decline in Jewish religious observance and practice. Opinion editorials about the decay of Judaism pervaded the Jewish press.[9] Not willing to concede defeat, however, the writers sought to address the supposed decline in observance and religiosity by redoubling their efforts to promote the salutary benefits of Jewish education, in the process giving further importance to the role children and youth were to play in safeguarding the future of Judaism. The belief in the power of religious education to secure the future of Judaism continued well into the twentieth century.[10]

Writers in the Jewish press expressed a strong desire for improved Jewish education. In Paris journalists for the *Archives Israélites* and the *Univers Israélite* turned to religious education as the panacea that would rescue Paris's (and France's) children.[11] The lack of participation in religious services was seen as the first of many problems plaguing the community. Many pieces written by Hippolyte Prague, editor of the *Archives Israélites*, pointed to the declining religious observance and synagogue attendance of Parisian Jews, which he characterized with the evocative term *dejudaization*. Prague also criticized the meager Jewish knowledge possessed by a large segment of the community's children who were "abandoned . . . to the assault of pleasure-seeking materialism."[12]

поютъ и пляшутъ. Радость, подлинная, искренняя, захва-
тывающая радость такъ и брызжетъ изъ глубины души
еврея, сквозитъ въ каждой чертѣ лица, проявляется во
всѣхъ его движеніяхъ, которыя становятся какъ-то живѣе
и свободнѣе.

И неудивительно: его полные глубокаго смысла осенніе
праздники заканчиваются блестящимъ торжествомъ въ
честь его Торы, его святыни, его гордости и утѣшенія...

Figure 7. Children waving flags on Simchat Torah. Source: M. Daikhes (ed.), *Eveiskie osennie prazdniki* (St. Petersburg: Gutzats, 1913), 19. Courtesy of the National Library of Israel.

In addition, an anonymous writer in the *Univers Israélite* bemoaned that religious instruction no longer took place at home and complained that young boys came to the synagogue only during major holidays, and girls came even less.[13] In the face of these complaints, not surprisingly other articles reproached parents and urged them to take a more active role in the religious education of their children. Some writers reminded readers of the familial nature of Judaism and of parents' role in the instruction of their children. It was not merely the task of parents to bring their children to synagogue and religious school (both of which were repeatedly urged); they were also supposed to model Jewish values in the home.[14]

The Russian Jewish press before World War I echoed some of these concerns, but typically with a lesser degree of hysteria. Articles concerning children's religious education pointed to developments further to the west. The writers argued for the introduction of children's services, citing the creation of new initiation rites and the general attempts to make Judaism a living religion.[15] The Biblioteka Evreiskoi Sem'i i Shkoly (Library of the Jewish Family and School) published small didactic booklets explaining major Jewish holidays and life cycle events in a semiprescriptive fashion for youths and parents alike, clearly with the desire to increase Jewish celebration and observance among Russian-speaking Jews.

Similarly, journalists and commentators in the German Jewish press wrote at length about the nature and goal of Jewish religious education. Though not always as dire or pessimistic as Prague's writings in the *Archives Israélites*, these texts shared an assumption regarding the necessity and salutary benefits of religious education.[16] In all three cities Jewish education was seen as key to the future of Judaism and Jewishness.

Rites of passage thus stood at the heart of an attempt to encourage participation in Jewish educational programming. The ceremonies themselves further marked the entry of the individual into the community and allowed the child to celebrate and affirm "collective identity even as it welcomed the individual into its ranks."[17] Bar mitzvah ceremonies and the later introduction of alternative coming-of-age rituals in Paris and Berlin—the *initiation religieuse* and the *Konfirmation*, respectively—allowed Jewish children to join the community and become active members in it through a public celebration in the synagogue. It confirmed their Jewish religious learning and marked their path into adulthood. It also allowed them to participate as members of their community and engage in the public staging of religious Jewish self-identification in the synagogue.

To be sure, the bar mitzvah ceremony remained an important rite of passage across the period of study and beyond, though the level of participation and the young boy's level of engagement did vary from family to family and were subject to change over time. The bar mitzvah was and remains a ceremony that took place publicly in the synagogue, and it is characterized by the public performance of mitzvot. At the same time, this ceremony is not ageless, nor has it had a monopoly on Jewish childhood rites of passage.[18] Only by the late Middle Ages did the bar mitzvah become a public coming-of-age ceremony that cemented the age of majority among the Jews of Ashkenaz at 13, establishing the age at which a Jewish boy was obligated to perform the mitzvot.[19]

The format of the bar mitzvah ceremony was similar in all three cities at the end of the nineteenth and beginning of the twentieth century. Typically, a young Jewish boy in late-nineteenth- and early-twentieth-century Paris, Berlin, or St. Petersburg read a section of the Torah and Haftarah (section from the Prophets) and gave a *dvar torah* (speech on matters of Torah) at home or in the synagogue,[20] after having prepared for the ceremony by learning Hebrew and attending a religious school or studying privately for the ceremony.[21] Such was the case for Fritz Seliger, who celebrated his bar mitzvah in Berlin in 1917. He recited the blessing before the reading of the Torah in German and then read the *maftir* portion of the weekly *parashah*.[22] The formal bar mitzvah ceremony was then followed by a celebration, frequently in the family home. The *Univers Israélite* noted the celebration of Nathan Klein's bar mitzvah in 1894 in the Orthodox *oratoire* (prayer room) on Cadet Street, which was followed by a reception hosted by Nathan's mother.[23]

For many in the Jewish community of Paris and Berlin, the religious significance of the ritual was eclipsed by the familial importance ascribed to the occasion, a shift that placed greater emphasis on celebrations in the family home over and above those in the synagogue. It remained a Jewish experience, but one bound to family and friends. Recalling her eldest son's bar mitzvah, Helene Eyck, a Jewish mother living in Berlin, wrote in her diary in 1891, "It [Hans's bar mitzvah] was—regardless of what I think about the religious side of the celebration—a true family celebration [*Familienfest*] and we were surrounded by all of our friends and family that day and had

45 people over for dinner that evening." The religious value of the ceremony took a distant second place in her telling of the event. More important for Eyck was the familial aspect of her son's bar mitzvah. The rest of her entry reflects her pride as a mother: "Hans recited a sort of profession of faith and in such excellent fashion I could not have imagined possible." She concentrated her comments on the people who came together both to celebrate and to hear Hans give his speech, characterizing the event as a special familial gathering, a fact further exemplified by her notation of the "long list of presents" that he received.[24]

The lengths to which this coming-of-age ceremony could be emptied of all religious meaning can be seen in the following rather exceptional anecdote. When Peter Gay, under the influence of the troop leader of his Jewish scouting group, suggested to his parents in 1935 that he wanted to have a bar mitzvah ceremony, the antireligious couple simply responded that they would support such a project if he really wanted to do so, but if he was simply interested in extra presents, "they would see to it that my thirteenth birthday produced an exceptionally rich haul." The young Peter Gay was easily persuaded to forgo the ritual requirements of the event and simply enjoyed the extra gifts.[25]

Because the religious value of the bar mitzvah ritual seemed to take a distant second place to familial celebration in certain circles and because it gradually became a ceremony that was celebrated primarily in the family home with relatives and friends, religious leaders from various sectors voiced their apprehension. With religious values deemphasized, Orthodox rabbis, such as M. Grünfeld, wrote about their concern over the children's ability to maintain their faith. The rabbi poignantly ended his essay on the bar mitzvah, published in the mainstream *Israelitisches Familienblatt*, with a quote from Proverbs 29:18, which he evocatively and somewhat erroneously translated into German as "Ohne Religion entartet ein Volk; Heil ihm, wenn es an seiner Lehre festhält." ("Without religion a people degenerates [!]; heal he who holds fast to his teachings").[26]

One solution to the perceived decline in religious instruction was the creation of new rituals: confirmation ceremonies, which sometimes substituted for and at other times accompanied the bar mitzvah ceremony.[27] In Berlin and Paris some congregations promoted new rites of passage, desiring that through them children and families would return to the synagogue. They hoped that through the Jewish education that preceded the new initiation rites, Jewish children would be inculcated with sufficient Jewish values that they would feel a stronger attachment to the synagogue. Importantly, these ceremonies aimed to educate Jewish children of *both* sexes about Judaism and its main religious tenets and to make the religion relevant to them.[28]

In this attempt to bring children and youth back to the synagogue, religious leaders somewhat ironically found themselves compelled to invent new traditions in old spaces. We must be clear, however, that not all synagogues held such rites of passage in Paris and Berlin. At least initially, reformist groups instigated the new rituals (i.e., Reform congregations in Berlin and liberal French Jewish circles within the Consistoire in France).[29] This would change in Berlin over time, but it is worth noting that new rites of passage could at times highlight the fault lines between liberal and Orthodox and between native and immigrant Jews in the two cities.

Already by the early nineteenth century, reformist religious leaders in France and Germany had created confirmation ceremonies (the *Konfirmation* in Berlin and the *initiation religieuse* in Paris), celebrated around Shavuot (the Festival of Weeks),[30] that replaced or supplemented the bar mitzvah ceremony. The terminology itself both reflects and suggests the integrationist policies of the early-nineteenth-century rabbis and leaders who encouraged the adoption of the new rites. It is clear that these new initiation rituals developed in dialogue with initiation ceremonies from the dominant culture, and it is not surprising that these ceremonies demonstrate a playful reformulation of Christian rituals. Even though the name "religious initiation" has no obvious Christian religious influence, religious educational literature—in the form of "catechisms"—reveals this influence.[31]

This is not to say, however, that the confirmation or religious initiation ceremonies were copies of Christian rites of passage. These newer ceremonies had links to earlier Jewish rites of passage[32] even as they had clear inspiration from the surrounding Christian society. In addition, religious leaders did not believe that they were Christianizing Judaism; they were hoping to renew and rediscover an authentic expression of Judaism.[33] Religious leaders designed these ceremonies out of a desire to encourage Jewish identification, in order, at least in part, to make Judaism relevant to the new generations. French Jewish leaders hoped that the religious initiation ceremony would "provoke a deeper emotion in the soul of the assembled children" and bring them closer to "tradition."[34] Furthermore, French Jewish consistorial authorities created other rituals in addition to the *initiation religieuse*, including a public presentation of newborns of both sexes in the synagogue.[35] Both rituals made the synagogue the focal point for Jewish celebration.

In early-nineteenth-century Germany, liberal communities introduced the *Konfirmation*, which, like its French counterpart, was a ceremony intended to strengthen the religious sensibility of youths of both genders.[36] In fact, the desire to include girls was cited as a central impetus behind the creation of such rites.[37] These services, their creators hoped, would strengthen the bonds between children and the Jewish religion through the synagogue at a time when many felt that religious observance was declining and the integrity of the religious community was at risk.

Religious instruction preceded the event. Upon passing an examination, the youths were able to participate in the collective ceremony in the synagogue. The age prescribed for these rites of passage was slightly different: Confirmands in Berlin came of age when they were roughly 15 years old; girls in Paris came of age at 12 and boys at 13.[38] In each case children would recite various prayers and listen to a sermon.[39] Because of the mixed-gender nature of the program, the German variant was not integrated into regular religious services where the presence of girls might conceivably offend more observant members, but it was celebrated as a *Feier* (celebration) that was "conducted entirely in German without Torah reading or prayer book."[40]

The first confirmation ceremony appears to have taken place in Dessau in 1803.[41] Early German Jewish confirmation ceremonies followed the Protestant pattern and were originally held in Jewish schools or private homes and not, as would later be the case, in the synagogue. The young confirmands took an exam on religious fundamentals, recited a public oath, and listened to a sermon in German. The precise timing of the annual event changed from place to place and school to school.[42] By midcentury the practice of holding group confirmations as a way of concluding religious learning became popular and widespread.[43]

Yet the format of these rituals itself varied from community to community. The Consistoire de Paris decided in 1852 that the religious initiation service would take place once a year, always around Shavuot, and only in 1864 did religious leaders in Paris codify the format of the religious initiation ceremony.[44] The *Univers Israelite* published a description of the initiation ceremony at the main Temple de la Victoire in 1897. According to the report, after the temple choir sang several songs, the young "neophytes recited the Shema, the decalogue, [and] the thirteen articles of faith." This was followed by a speech by M. Dreyfuss, the chief rabbi of Paris. That particular year, the speech was about the love between parents and children as well as that between God and his people. Following Rabbi Dreyfuss's speech, the chief rabbi of France, Zadoc Kahn, urged the youths to remain true to their religion and to be courageous as Jews in the face of insult—a clear allusion to the social and political challenges facing the Jewish population during the unfolding Dreyfus affair.[45]

Three years later, on June 7, 1900, just a few days after Shavuot, nearly 400 children gathered for the annual religious initiation ceremony at the synagogue on the rue de la Victoire. The service began with a short address by Chief Rabbi Dreyfuss. Then the confirmands recited the prayer Ma Tovu ("How goodly [are your tents . . .]") and Psalm 118, and this was followed by a longer, sentimental speech by Rabbi Dreyfuss on the virtues of children and childhood. After his speech, the youths recited the Decalogue and the Shema and Chief Rabbi Zadoc Kahn gave a lengthy speech about the young people's need to remain committed to Judaism despite external challenges.[46]

It is clear that religious leaders expressed anxiety about the engagement of Jewish children with the synagogue and with Judaism. Yet, was this fear based in a measurable decrease in participation rates? Records show that in Paris and Berlin, at least in the early twentieth century, parents did send their children to religious education and did encourage the children's participation in rites of passage. However, they also appear to have insisted on actively contributing to the creation of specific noninstitutional meanings by bringing the bar mitzvah celebrations into the family home. In the late nineteenth and early twentieth centuries, in Berlin (and Germany more generally) most bourgeois Jewish boys participated in a bar mitzvah or *Einsegnung* ceremony.[47] Moreover, Jewish Berliners continued to celebrate *Konfirmation* ceremonies throughout the twentieth century.[48] Only after the Shoah did the religious community face more significant challenges in enticing Jewish children to attend religious schools and participate in such ceremonies.[49]

Although the number of initiates in Paris was rather low in the 1890s, with only about 170 children (mostly girls) participating in the religious initiation service in 1890 and 335 children (190 girls and 145 boys) participating in 1895,[50] the number of participants in the French capital continued to rise along with the number of children attending religious instruction. By the turn of the twentieth century, religious education, which was to precede both the religious initiation and the bar mitzvah ceremony,[51] was becoming fairly popular. In a meeting held on April 5, 1906, by the Commission de Propagande of the Consistoire, a member reported that there were 2,000 children taking religious instruction out of an approximate total Jewish population of 60,000 individuals (their own estimates).[52] At first glance, this might seem like a small number (representing only 3% of the total Jewish population). Yet, if we consider the probable number of children in the overall community[53] and account for the children who were either too old or too young to partake in this instruction, the total reflects a sizable number of children who participated in the Consistoire's educational program.

The numbers nonetheless raise a related question: Who opted out? According to historian Béatrice Philippe, only children from modest families attended the consistorial schools; bourgeois children did not.[54] Thus class differences accounted for the fact that some youth did not attend the consistorial religious classes. These same youths might have nevertheless celebrated their bar mitzvah but were possibly prepared by a private tutor, something that the economic means of their family would have made possible.

Family background might have also played a determining role. In Paris there were many nonconsistorial synagogues and *oratoires*, notably those organized by Eastern European immigrants. These would have provided religious education for the children of their members as well. In fact, after 1905 it is almost certain that, by necessity, these organizations would have offered programs for their own children. That year the "Consistory, in its new nongovernmental form, had recently voted to admit to its membership only those Jews who had lived in France for ten years, with foreign-born Jews not to exceed a quarter of the membership."[55] This meant in no uncertain terms that Jewish families (and their children) from Eastern Europe were systemically excluded from consistorial life, including religious education. This planned exclusion continued for some time. Immigrants also responded with their own desire to maintain this separation, a fact reflected in the establishment of a synagogue on rue Pavée in the Marais in 1914 through the efforts of the Orthodox Agudat Hakehilot (Union of Communities).[56]

Despite complaints in the Jewish press suggesting the contrary, significant numbers of Jewish parents in Paris and Berlin insisted that their children participate in these rites of passage and in the religious education that preceded them. We also know that at least in some cases these rituals had the effect of confirming a sense of Jewish self-identification among the children.[57] For example, William Stern, an important psychologist and pedagogue, recalled the preparation for his own confirmation (or *Einsegnung*), which took place at a Reform congregation in Berlin in the late nineteenth century when he was 15 years old. His religious studies the year before the ceremony, attendance at weekly religious services, and the ceremony itself were all important for him and strongly reinforced his commitment to Jewish self-identification.[58] Even years later, this religious education and the significant amount of time spent in the synagogue remained an essential experience in his biography.

In addition to absolute numbers of participants, religious authorities singled out a specific target audience—girls—in an effort to encourage their participation. This desire could transcend the Reform/Orthodox divide in Germany. The Orthodox Schul- und Talmud-Torah-Vorstand (School and Talmud-Torah [religious school] Board) explained in a letter from 1907 to the board of the Jewish community to which it belonged[59] that "it seems advisable to further develop the confirmation courses," because they would help to strengthen and revive the "religious feelings in the female youth of our community." By 1908 the board had established confirmation classes for girls and had specifically made arrangements for four classes, mandating that a maximum of forty girls be in each class.[60] Gender equality was not the purpose of this education, nor was the decision based on a desire to be more inclusive of girls. Rather, "the goal of this instruction is to give the girl a conclusion to her religious education, especially to make her familiar with the duties of the Jewish woman in the synagogue and in the house."[61] Girls were to have a place in the synagogue and a place in the ritual participation, but in certain Orthodox circles in Berlin this education was intended to prepare them to be good Jewish homemakers and mothers, competent in their gendered roles in the synagogue and home.[62]

The gendered expectations behind Jewish education were visible in the French Jewish case as well. In the 1892 program for the *initiation religieuse* service, we can clearly see that girls played different roles in the service. Consistently, the boys were expected to recite in Hebrew, whereas the girls spoke in French, reflecting a different level of knowledge and familiarity with Hebrew that was expected of the children. Thus, whereas boys recited the Ten Commandments in Hebrew, the girls did so in translation.[63] Highlighting a further set of gendered considerations, in his speech at the *initiation religieuse* ceremony of 1900, Rabbi Kahn voiced his hope that the youths' professional careers would serve as "schools in obligation, honesty and conscience"—a message intended for the boys alone. To the girls assembled, he entreated them to "cultivate gentleness, simplicity, goodness, because these are the true finery of women." After extolling these "natural" traits, he encouraged them to use them to immediate effect and "begin now your apprenticeship in charity!"[64] The message was clear: All were to be devout and devoted Jews, but in different ways. The boys were to become upstanding and productive citizens; the girls were to rely on their "natural" gifts of gentleness and goodness and turn to philanthropy. Far from representing gender equality, the Jewish education and role given to girls in these new rites of passage reflected the desire to prepare them for their "rightful" place in the Jewish home as mothers and wives. Yet the inclusion of girls in these relatively new ceremonies nevertheless highlights their novelty and importance in the reformulation of Jewish ritual in Paris and Berlin. One article in the French Jewish press from 1911 even suggested that it represented a "small revolution."[65]

The situation in St. Petersburg differed in several key ways from that in Paris and Berlin, even as the bar mitzvah became and remained a family event just as it had further to the west. As in the other capital cities, Jewish commentators in St. Petersburg expressed their concern for Jewish children and the future of Judaism and Jewishness in the Jewish press. However, this concern did not translate into the restructuring of Jewish religious spaces, nor did it induce religious leaders to create new rites of passage, despite the clear awareness of similar programs across Europe, including other parts of the Russian Empire.[66]

Indeed, new rites of passage caught the attention of observers in St. Petersburg, who reported them, praised them, and extolled their benefits. Citing youth services in synagogues and the confirmation ceremony, an article written for the *Nediel'naia Khronika Voskhoda* asserted that Jewish feeling, more than simple Jewish learning, was an essential component to a successful Jewish education and was to be its primary goal.[67] The synagogue and Jewish educational institutions—with new rituals and new services directed toward children—were to be the central Jewish spaces for young Jews on the verge of becoming adults. Jewish education, new rituals, and children's religious services were potential means to reassert the bonds between individual Jewish children and the religious community, bringing them back to the

Баръ-Мицво.

Литературно-художественный сборникъ для еврейской семьи и школы.

Подъ редакціей М. ДАЙХЕСА.

Выпускъ X.

С.-ПЕТЕРБУРГЪ.
Паровая Скоропечатня М. М. Гутзана. Шпалерная, 26.
1914

Figure 8. Cover of M. Daikhes (ed.), *Bar-Mitsvo: Literaturno-khudozhestvennyi sbornik dlia evreiskoi sem'i i shkoly* (St. Petersburg: Gutzats, 1914). Courtesy of the National Library of Israel.

synagogue. Nevertheless, this concern did not propel the adoption of a new ritual in St. Petersburg. It did resonate, however, in publications intended for Jewish children and youth, including those designed to teach young Jews about holidays and rites of passage.

The small book *Bar-Mitsvo*, published as part of a series by Biblioteka Evreiskoi Sem'i i Shkoly, began with an outline of the main aspects of the typical bar mitzvah as it was (or ought to be) celebrated in Russia and Poland generally.[68] According to the sketch, the bar mitzvah ceremony in the synagogue included an *aliyah*[69] to the Torah and the reading of the *maftir* portion and the Haftarah, all standard practices for bar mitzvah boys across Europe.[70] Beyond offering a depiction of the "typical" bar mitzvah ceremony, the semidescriptive, semiprescriptive nature of the book speaks to a belief in the decline of Jewish ritual and religious participation, similar to the rhetoric expressed in the French and German Jewish press.

Other Russian Jewish commentators lamented the decline in ritual participation and active religious learning. Already before the turn of the twentieth century, an anonymous author of an article on Jewish religious youth education in the Russian-language Jewish newspaper *Nediel'naia Khronika Voskhoda* bemoaned that, because of the general lack of Jewish knowledge, "the custom of the bar mitzvah seems like a lifeless act, devoid of all meaning."[71] Other nostalgic and historical articles about the bar mitzvah only reinforced such feelings.[72]

Yet, rather than simply reflecting the lifelessness of the occasion, the articles nonetheless point to an important change in the rite's celebration in the Russian capital. By the end of the nineteenth century the bar mitzvah in St. Petersburg had become a family event, like farther to the west, and the festivities centered on the family home. There, the young boy would give his *dvar torah* and the boy's family would invite guests over for a large feast.[73] Rabbi Ben-Doiv, in his sentimental bar mitzvah reminiscences, described his own bar mitzvah ceremony. Even for this (at least later in life) religious figure, the celebrations at home with guests and the large meal take a central place in his narrative, as he recalled the "guests, a feast, songs and merriment!"[74]

As the bar mitzvah became a family affair, significant aspects of its celebration moved out of the synagogue and into the family home or even a restaurant.[75] This process was facilitated by the fact that parents, not religious leaders, typically determined the level of participation and the form of celebration of the ritual. The increased individualization of the Jewish community placed the control over ritual observance and religious participation in the hands of parents. Although this transition had less impact on the overall decision to participate in such ceremonies in Paris and Berlin and instead informed the spaces and emphasis of their celebration, the same was not the case in Petrograd/Leningrad. The political changes concomitant with the consolidation of Bolshevik power and the acceptance of predominantly negative attitudes toward religion on the part of many Soviet Jews combined to decrease the overall popularity of Jewish rites of passage, not just change the venue or meaning of the celebrations themselves.

Going to the Chapel? The Place of Religious Weddings

If new social and leisure spaces had helped young Jewish adults to find partners of their own choosing, the consequences of these individual desires and the related spatial developments affected the choice of venue in which weddings were held. Far from being a straightforward or uncomplicated process, the Jewish wedding ceremony revealed a long-standing debate over the legitimate and acceptable location in which to hold a religious wedding. Before the sixteenth century, Ashkenazi Jews typically married inside the synagogue under a cloth or tallis (prayer shawl), possibly in imitation of local Christian customs. The first mention of a wedding held outside under a portable chuppah (wedding canopy) comes to us from Rabbi Moshe Isserles in the sixteenth century.[76] Rather than both traditions existing simultaneously, over three short centuries the spatial innovation of holding the wedding ceremony outdoors, frequently in the courtyard of the synagogue, became an almost sacrosanct custom.

By the nineteenth century, as European Jews, especially those of the middle classes, strove to acculturate and fashion Judaism along bourgeois lines of respectability, increasingly calls were made to bring wedding services back into the synagogue.[77] However, this move to return the wedding service to the synagogue, a suggestion made by both liberal and Orthodox Jews, itself caused an uproar. Indeed, the placement of the chuppah and the "proper" location of a Jewish marriage ceremony even became subjects of dispute between Orthodox and "ultra-Orthodox" Jews by the mid-nineteenth century. The *psak din* (religious ruling) of Michalovce of 1865 explicitly rejected the "innovation" of holding a wedding inside the synagogue, arguing that one should not erect a chuppah in the synagogue. The debate over the appropriate place for Jewish weddings was, in this context, a debate over rabbinic authority and the acceptability of making changes to religious customs (or in this case, ironically, reverting to older practices) as well as a debate about the place of Jewish practice in European society. The 1865 *psak din* was but the beginning, or perhaps middle, of a larger theological and practical debate about the acceptable location of Jewish marriages.

The nineteenth century witnessed not only the sometimes contested move of the wedding ceremony back into the synagogue building[78] but also the opening up of a number of other venues, from the family home to hotel halls and restaurants. Frequently, the choice of a space reflected more than prosaic concerns about how to accommodate a specific number of guests and could have social-political and, at times, as already suggested, religious implications.

That being said, from a comparative perspective the questions of wedding venue and whether to celebrate a religious wedding were *on the surface* the least fraught in Berlin in the late nineteenth and early twentieth centuries. Berlin Jews in the early twentieth century were generally committed to holding religious weddings in addition to the civil services that legally had to precede them. Roughly, 85% of the Jewish couples who married in 1905 held a religious wedding.[79] It is quite possible that a lack of sufficient funds prevented some segment of the remaining 15% from celebrating their nuptials twice. Given the overwhelmingly bourgeois nature of the Jewish community of Berlin, class clearly could explain these statistics. The location of the wedding ceremony was equally uncontested.[80] Whether held at home, in the synagogue, or at a local hotel or restaurant, the choice frequently appeared to have been based more on tastes and budget and less on ideology or politics. Although there was significant discussion and debate over the proper place of religious weddings in Paris and France, such a discourse was far less palpable in Berlin.

This is not to say, however, that religious politics were not at play in Berlin. The decision to bring the wedding service back into the synagogue reflected concerns of propriety by a community that sought inclusion into German Christian civil society.[81] This desire for inclusion could and did have an architectonic dimension. Across Europe the place of Jewish communities in larger society was reflected in the building of grandiose central synagogues, which were erected over the course of the second half of the nineteenth century. Ostentatious edifices, these synagogues also featured wedding chapels or rooms.[82] The impressive Neue Synagoge on Oranienburgerstrasse, a Reform synagogue that seated 3,000 people, was no exception and included a wedding room (*Trausaal*), as did the lavish Choral Synagogue in St. Petersburg. Bourgeois manners and propriety were values that Jews went to great lengths to demonstrate in ritual and architecture.

In addition, hotels and restaurants became welcome and acceptable fixtures in the nuptial plans of Jewish couples in Berlin by the late nineteenth century. Hotels and restaurants frequently placed advertisements in the German Jewish press to promote their large halls for weddings celebrations.[83] For example, the Hotel Münchener Hof advertised their elegant celebratory halls (*Festsäle*) in the pages of the *Berliner Vereinsbote* and assured prospective clients that "weddings and the direction of festivities on and off premises" could be done at "affordable prices."[84] Furthermore, the hotel boasted a kosher kitchen, literally catering to observant members of the community. The popularity and general consensus on hotels as legitimate staging grounds for religious weddings extended across the religious spectrum of the Berlin Jewish community.

Indeed, the 1907 wedding and postwedding celebration of Henriette Hirsch, the granddaughter of the Orthodox rabbi Esriel Hildesheimer, took place in a hotel. She described the day in her memoirs, noting how her "father waited—proud and happy—by the door of the hotel in which our wedding party was celebrated and where also the nuptials took place." She continued, "And with me on his arm, [we] went up the stairs into the ballroom. . . . My father beamed with happiness as he brought me past the many, many guests."[85] The size of the wedding reminds us why such spaces became popular for the reception in the first place. And there must have been added convenience to holding both the wedding ceremony and the reception in the same location. The availability of funds most likely influenced the choice of venue more than religious belief. Yet, holding a wedding in this space reflected a new use of the hotel and became an acceptable practice in Germany by the early twentieth century, continuing until the early 1930s.[86] The political changes with the rise of the Nazis and their extension of antisemitic policies across Germany would change this, however. The willingness of Jews to make public expressions of Judaism and Jewish belonging quickly disappeared.

With Hitler's takeover at the end of January 1933, a growing number of Jewish couples understandably preferred holding marriage ceremonies in Jewish institutions or private homes. This turning inward was frequently motivated both by the closure of certain sites, including restaurants, to Jewish consumers and also by a desire to seek protection behind the closed doors of Jewish organizations and institutions, places that non-Jews in the Nazi era would have had no reason or desire to enter. Fear and uncertainty were powerful motivators in Ilse Rewald and her husband's decision to hasten their marriage plans after Kristallnacht in 1938. Concerned that the Nazis might prohibit Jewish marriage, the couple chose to marry at home in December of the same year. The wedding, as she recalled years later, was not a joyful celebration, as it was clouded by recent events.[87]

The constricting spatial and social world of Berlin Jews under the Nazis can be further seen in the example of Walter Besser and his wife, Eva. Walter had proposed in a Jewish café, but the couple chose to hold the marriage ceremony in the prayer room of a Jewish community building on Joachimstalerstrasse in March 1942.[88] Their hands were ceremoniously bound with a tallis as they stood under the chuppah. Then they exchanged rings (a novel practice at the time; traditionally, only the groom placed a ring on the bride's finger), were blessed in both Hebrew and German, and drank from a ceremonial wine cup. The couple then celebrated the wedding with family and friends at the bride's parents' house, the women of the family cooking the festive meal. In his memoirs Walter wondered whether theirs was not perhaps the last Jewish wedding in Berlin before the end of the war.[89]

However, other memoir literature from the Nazi era suggests an alternative narrative, one that stresses the *religiosity* of a parent or spouse as the reason to hold the wedding service in the seemingly more appropriate space of the synagogue. In September 1933 Kurt Posener and his second wife were married in an unnamed Berlin synagogue. The wedding was a modest affair with a small reception in the vestibule following the ceremony. The new couple then joined friends and family at a relative's home, where they held a party at which Louis's aunt played piano and his uncle sang. Kurt's son, Louis, explained in his autobiography that his stepmother's greater ties to Judaism and stricter observance were motivations behind this choice.[90] Similarly, in the group biography of the Chotzen family, the choice of Erich Chotzen and Ilse Schwarz to marry in one of Berlin's synagogues on November 7, 1941, was justified by the fact that Ilse's mother was apparently "religious" and wanted her daughter to marry in the synagogue.[91]

Whether or not the religiosity of the partners or their families was in fact the real reason for the choice of venue is impossible to tell, and we should

PARIS. — *Temple Israélite (Rue de la Victoire)*.

Figure 9. Temple de la Victoire, Paris. Courtesy of the National Library of Israel.

not deny the importance of religious belief for some members of the Jewish community of Berlin. Yet we can surmise that after the Nazi takeover, the synagogue might have additionally offered a safer and closed environment. Also, by the late 1930s and early 1940s, the synagogue might have been one of the few spaces available to hold a Jewish wedding, especially with so many other spaces closed to Jews.

The choice of venue worked according to a slightly different set of parameters in imperial St. Petersburg, because, most important, religious weddings were the only legal option there. This fact, however, had no real bearing on the location of the wedding, just the person officiating it. As in Berlin, class, personal tastes, and even politics influenced the choice of venue. For instance, the elites of the community repeatedly made a point of marrying publicly and ostentatiously at the Choral Synagogue. This should come as no surprise; the grand Choral Synagogue was essentially an institution created by and for the St. Petersburg elites. For example, Evgenia Isidorovna Gintsburg, the niece of the important financier and railway man Avram Zak, married in the Choral Synagogue.[92]

Other leading St. Petersburg families chose to have "destination" weddings.[93] The wedding of David Günzburg, heir to arguably the most important and influential family in Imperial St. Petersburg, to his cousin Matilda on December 18, 1883, took place in the distinguished central synagogue of Paris, the Temple de la Victoire.[94] The same synagogue was the site for the wedding of another Russian Jewish couple: Jacques Poliakoff, son of the important Moscow financier Lazare Poliakoff, and Claire Brodsky, daughter of Leon Brodsky from Kiev. Various Russian aristocrats and leading members of the Jewish community of Paris attended the wedding service.[95] Display, grandeur, and prominence were all essential aspects of both the weddings themselves and the attention they garnered in the Jewish press.

France was a popular wedding destination for Russian Jews for other reasons. Simon Dubnow and his soon-to-be wife also hoped to travel to France to marry. Their motivations were political-religious, and the couple had hoped to forgo a religious wedding, which was their only option in Russia. In the end, the conclusion of their time in St. Petersburg and their impending return to their hometown precipitated speedier nuptials, and the couple married quietly at the home of cousins, the Emanuils.[96] Despite their desire for a modest affair—Dubnow had even requested that the St. Petersburg rabbi Dr. Drabkin "send some less known person from the synagogue"—the well-known and respected Rabbi Landau, the Orthodox leader of the Jewish community of St. Petersburg, was sent instead. The wedding remained a quiet event, with most friends learning of the wedding only after the fact.[97]

Nearly thirty years later, when their daughter Sophie married, she and her husband held a modest wedding in St. Petersburg in "a synagogue chapel." She recalled the event in her memoirs: "Under a worn little old canopy I stood in a gray cloth overcoat, with a bag over my shoulder. The witnesses were three old parishioners. H. [Henryk, her husband] got the words of the wedding service mixed up, and I had to prompt him in a whisper." Afterward, the couple left the city and went to Linka to be with her parents; it was her father's birthday, and they celebrated both their wedding and Simon's birthday together. Then the newlyweds traveled to Poland and visited Henryk's parents in Lublin, where "they fed me, showered me with gifts, smothered me in embraces; the number of aunts and cousins grew ominously by the day."[98]

Given that so many Jews in St. Petersburg had recently migrated to the city, not all of them married in the capital or held their postnuptial celebrations there. Anna Vygodskaia and her fiancé, Mikhail Markovich Vygodskii, both legal residents of St. Petersburg during much of their courtship, celebrated their wedding in Vilna, where Vygodskaia's parents lived and where she was living at the time, having completed her studies in St. Petersburg. Although she had actually wanted to run away with her fiancé and marry in St. Petersburg, her fiancé did not want to begin their married life by "[inflicting] any grief on my parents."[99] Instead, their self-made match was celebrated in a combination of traditional and innovative ways, including an impressive trousseau and a dowry of 10,000 rubles (made possible by her father's rising fortunes as a merchant of the first guild and a factory owner).[100]

The search for an appropriate space for the wedding ceremony itself reflected the changing spatial options. Noting the absence of alternative venues, Vygodskaia remarked that "we finally found an unlet apartment that consisted of several spacious rooms"; "in those days," she explained, "we had no social clubs or restaurants in town." This is a telling remark, suggesting that the customary changes made to the marriage ceremony were noticeable across Russia during the years between Vygodskaia's wedding and the late 1930s, when she wrote her memoir. The choice of space meant that her family would have to decorate the apartment in addition to preparing the wedding feast, which included, along with the "traditional fish and poultry," a number of unnamed "curious and exotic dishes."

On the day of the wedding, March 11, Vygodskaia found herself surrounded by seamstresses and a hairdresser, helping her into an extravagant outfit that included a dress of "expensive damask silk" and a veil that required an elaborate hairdo, which she likened to "a real Eiffel Tower . . . atop my head." Brought to the apartment by carriage and then surrounded by her family, Vygodskaia's father "took me by the arm and walked me past a long row of guests, who stood on either side of the carpet that ran through all three rooms of the apartment, leading all the way to the dais. Children ran in front of me, throwing flowers at my feet." After being allowed to take a seat, the chuppah was placed in the middle of the apartment, and the bride and groom were each led by two other young couples to the canopy. The ceremony was followed by a lengthy meal that Vygodskaia, according to her memoirs, could not have been more impatient to see come to an end.

Vygodskaia's detailed account of her wedding is interesting for one significant omission: There is no mention of a rabbi or any religious aspect of the service, with the exception of the wedding canopy itself. Yet the wedding, by virtue of its time and place, must have been a religious ceremony. The material opulence of the event and the bride's feeling of being out of her element are the main aspects of her telling of the wedding.[101]

With the Bolshevik Revolution, the previous constellation that had banned civil marriage and upheld only religious marriage was officially reversed in early 1918 with the decree "On the Freedom of Worship, the Church and Religious Societies."[102] According to the decree, civil marriage became the only legal means to marry and all weddings were to be held in the offices of the personal status registry; religious weddings were private matters. In some cases authorities attempted to stop religious services and ceremonies, but in large part, at least initially, this decree in effect privatized religious weddings but did not call for their immediate abolishment.[103] So long as they remained private affairs, held in religious buildings or private homes, religious marriages were not illegal, and, in fact, according to circulars from the mid-1920s, "Servants of the cult who perform rites of baptizing, weddings, etc., before the registration of births weddings, etc., by organs of ZAGS [the civil registry] are not transgressing law."[104] Thus, despite the official legal changes, in the early years after the Bolshevik Revolution, many Jews, especially those living in rural areas, continued to celebrate religious weddings.[105]

Such was the case of Alexander Spiegel, who had been studying medicine in St. Petersburg since 1913. During World War I Spiegel had worked for the Red Cross while continuing his medical studies. With the Bolshevik Revolution, Spiegel decided to resign from the Red Cross and dedicate his time to finishing his studies and passing his exams. His intention was to move to Moscow for that period of time, but he was drafted into the Red Army and joined the Tula garrison as company doctor instead. During these tumultuous months, Spiegel was frequently in touch with the chief rabbi of Moscow, Rabbi Jacob Mazeh, for advice, and the rabbi also proved instrumental in arranging Spiegel's engagement to Sonia Baumstein of Tula.

Spiegel and Baumstein's engagement and wedding were highly traditional and religious affairs. The engagement was celebrated with a rich "banquet for more than two hundred Jewish guests." On the following Saturday at the synagogue, Spiegel was called to read the Haftarah and "again deliver a sermon." Sonia's father provided a sizable dowry of 400,000 gold rubles. The wedding ceremony was celebrated in the garden at the home of Sonia's parents on the afternoon of Friday, May 13, 1918, with more than 300 guests, and it was officiated by not one but *four* rabbis. The following day, Spiegel was again called up to read the Haftarah, and after Shabbat morning services, the couple celebrated a "'Seven blessings' feast."[106] Despite the changing political circumstances and legal decrees, Spiegel and his wife had an elaborate religious wedding ceremony. Moreover, his memoirs make no mention of a civil ceremony or how they informed the new authorities.

Yet, Spiegel's experiences notwithstanding, increasingly, political ideologies influenced the perception of religious weddings in the larger Soviet context, and religious ceremonies came to be seen in a pejorative light. The first Jews to abandon religious weddings were, not surprisingly, those who were the most ideologically committed to the new path. Thus Komsomol[107] members typically registered their weddings according to the civil practice. By the 1930s, as a result of both growing antireligious propaganda and the rise of intermarriage, the number of religious weddings precipitously declined.[108]

In contrast, politics of another sort played out in France. If the French Jewish press is to be trusted on the matter, the location of the religious wedding was hotly contested in Paris. In the face of the declining power of the central religious authorities as a result of changes in the civil law, the

Consistoire repeatedly attempted to assert its control over the Jewish wedding ritual. By the turn of the twentieth century the synagogue became the focal point for this debate. The Consistoire made few compromises: Jews who desired to have a religious wedding ceremony were compelled to do so in one of the consistorial synagogues. Only under specific conditions could one chose to have the religious wedding (referred to as the nuptial blessings) performed at a private home.[109] The Consistoire did not hide its motivations for this policy and made clear that these ceremonies provided it with important funds, a factor that only increased in significance when the state withdrew public funding for religious institutions through a law passed in 1905.[110]

To accommodate couples' varying budgets, each consistorial synagogue established a multitiered system that, it was hoped, would encourage even those on a modest budget to hold a religious wedding.[111] One article in the *Archives Israélites* chided its readers and reminded them that it was possible to marry as cheaply as 15 francs in a synagogue; an ostentatious wedding followed by banquet, a ball, and then "crowned with a meal" was not the only option.[112] In reality, little care was paid to where or whether the couple held a celebratory meal *after* the religious service so long as the religious service itself was held in its proper place.[113] The tension over the space of religious weddings in Paris, however, was not just a matter of money. By divorcing rites of passage from religious spaces and Halachah, consistorial rabbis were potentially limited in the power they held over Jewish rituals.

Many French Jews appear to have been ambivalent about the Consistoire's insistence on holding a religious wedding in one of the consistorial synagogues. The repeated pleas made on behalf of the religious community to hold religious marital ceremonies in the synagogues attest to the tensions between the Consistoire and a number of Jewish residents of Paris. It would seem from the historical record that at least some Jews were married religiously but simply not in the synagogue. For example, one father, in a 1911 letter to the Consistoire de Paris, matter-of-factly requested that a rabbi bless his daughter's wedding at an unnamed hall (a *salon*), suggesting the growing popularity of this practice in Paris.[114] It is clear that regulations could not stop Jews from celebrating religious marriages outside synagogues.

Consistorial authorities had to face challenges not only from lay members of the community but also from rabbis themselves. In one case, though not

from Paris, we learn in the pages of the *Univers Israélite* that the marriage of
a French rabbi took place in a hotel. The small piece from 1920 reads:

> Last Tuesday the marriage of Rabbi Robert Brunschwig, Israelite military
> chaplain with the Sarre troops, to Miss Lucie Meyer, daughter of Dr. and
> Mrs. Ernst Meyer of Mulhouse, took place in Strasbourg in the halls of the
> Hotel Continental. The nuptial blessings were performed by Rabbi Arthur
> Weill, of Bischheim, the brother-in-law of the groom.[115]

Even in the face of regulations and repeated pleas from the Consistoire regarding the location of religious marriages, not even all rabbis could always
be convinced to have a religious wedding in the synagogue.

At least one group, however, required no convincing to hold their weddings at consistorial synagogues: the elites. Both wealthy and influential
Parisian Jews and even important Jewish families from Russia, as we saw
earlier, held their weddings in the main synagogue of the city, the Temple
de la Victoire—with considerable pomp. The religious marriage of Alfred
Dreyfus, for example, took place at the grand synagogue. After the ceremony the family celebrated at the home of Dreyfus's wife, Lucie.[116]

The French Jewish press participated in such spectacles by routinely recording the details of "grands mariages." In 1895 the young baron Henri
Rothschild married Mathilde de Weisweiller, a wedding that made the
pages not only in the Jewish press but of the *Figaro* as well.[117] The weddings
of other members of the Rothschild family were similarly recounted in the
Jewish press, all taking place, it goes without saying, in the synagogue on
rue de la Victoire.[118]

Even well into the interwar period, such marriages continued. The
Archives Israélites reported in 1930 that "with great pomp" Jacqueline de
Rothschild, the daughter of Baron Edouard, married Robert Calman-Lévy,
heir to the major publishing house of the same name, at the central consistorial synagogue (i.e., the Victoire). The chief rabbi of France, Israël Lévi,
conducted the service. The article continues with a lengthy description of
the music performed and of the bridal dress (including the number of children who helped carry the train). Following the wedding ceremony, the
parents of the bride held a reception in the "magnificent hotel de la rue
Saint-Florentin," whose halls were overwhelmed by the "inordinate quan-
tity of bouquets presented to the young couple."[119]

Financial elites were not the only ones to celebrate their weddings in the central consistorial synagogues; families with a significant stake in the institutions of the Jewish community (including the Consistoire and the Jewish press) shared in this custom. With relative frequency the children and grandchildren of leading consistorial rabbis married in the consistorial synagogues, and the journalists of the *Univers Israélite* (the voice of the Consistoire) reported on these weddings in customary hyperbole. In late June 1889 Jules Franck, harp soloist with the Paris Opera, married the granddaughter of the chief rabbi S. Ullman, Miss Clémence Braun. The short notice in the newspaper noted the "splendors of the Temple de la Victoire," the "charm" of the musical service, the eloquence of the chief rabbi's speech, and the many, many guests.[120]

When the only son of the editor of the *Archives Israélites* married in 1902, the same newspaper was sure to fill an entire page detailing the wedding ceremony of the young René Cahen and Marguerite Hayem. "All the notables of the Community of Paris, the medical world and the world of finance" gathered together in the Temple de la Victoire. The "imposing ceremony," "embellished by the joyous harmonies" of an orchestra and the "melodious voices of artists of the first rank," included tributes to prominent family members. The musical accompaniment featured psalms and blessings but also Bach's *Andante du Concerto*. The article ends with a list of prominent guests who attended the wedding.[121]

Elites also used weddings in the consistorial synagogues to display their philanthropic largesse in special ways. Several women who lived at the Toît Familial—a charitable home for young girls and widowed or abandoned women between the ages of 16 and 25—were married in the consistorial synagogues. The home sought to protect these women from falling into disrepute and to provide them with a moral and religious framework. It was funded and organized by the CBIP (Comité de bienfaisance israélite de Paris; Israelite Charitable Committee of Paris). Although the sources are silent about who exactly paid for the wedding ceremonies themselves, at least one reference makes clear that one young bride received many gifts from friends and was "above all spoiled by her benefactress."[122] By helping these women celebrate their own weddings in consistorial synagogues, the elites encouraged and rewarded "proper" behavior on the part of a particular segment of the Jewish population.

In the end, the practical options for Parisian Jews up until the outbreak of World War II included holding a religious wedding at a consistorial synagogue or in a private home, convincing a rabbi (perhaps one unaffiliated with the Consistoire) to perform the wedding at a location of one's choosing, or forgoing a religious wedding entirely, though the latter alternative remained less significant than the Jewish press in France might have wanted its readers to believe.[123]

Religious weddings in the three cities were far more than occasions for couples "to build a house in Israel" in front of their family, friends, and community. The staging grounds of these ceremonies could reflect individual tastes, the intentions of religious leaders to exert influence, and the attitudes of non-Jewish political authorities. Individual choice, communal authority, supervision, and ideology were thus all components of a larger practical project of maintaining and changing the Jewish ritual celebration of weddings.

Holy Days to Holidays

Each Jewish holy day or festival comes with its own story, rationale, and set of celebratory customs—some determined by local and regional practice and others codified in Jewish law.[124] Hanukkah (the Festival of Lights), for instance, commemorates the rededication of the Second Temple in Jerusalem following the Maccabean revolt in the second century BCE. Celebrated for eight nights, Jews light an additional candle on the *hanukkiah* (a special menorah) for each passing night (one candle for the first night, two for the second, and so forth), and place the *hanukkiah* in a prominent window of the family home. Purim is a joyous celebration commemorating the rescue of the Jews of ancient Persia from a cruel and murderous plot, thanks to the efforts of Queen Esther and her cousin Mordechai. According to Jewish law, Jews are expected to listen to a public reading of the scroll of Esther ideally in a large gathering place, such as the synagogue. Jews are also expected to give charity to the poor and send gifts of food (*mishloah manot*) to friends. Yom Kippur (the Jewish Day of Atonement) is a solemn fast day, the holiest Shabbat of all *shabatot*. Spent in the synagogue, Jews focus their prayers on penitence and seek divine forgiveness for sins and misdeeds.

Yet, for all these generalizations and despite the many halachic rulings concerning each holy day, over time and on a sociological level these occasions changed their degree of importance just as Jews changed the form and mode of celebration for each occasion.[125] Importantly, many holy days have undergone important changes in the last two centuries, as Jews interacted with other cultures, beyond what might have occurred before. In other words, over the last two centuries customs were not simply adapted or adopted into the framework of halachic Judaism. Instead, the process of secularization had a decisive effect on Jewish holy days as newer practices marked conscious breaks with previous customs and sometimes even with Jewish law. Cultural appropriation, new spatial practices, and politics influenced the ways that Jews understood themselves as Jews and how they chose to celebrate.

As Jews increasingly saw themselves as individuals who could select the manner of their own personal affiliation and cultural practice, they sought out new methods of celebration. Part of this transformation included moving the location of old holy days into new spaces. Outside the confines of traditional Jewish spaces, Jewish holidays could be celebrated in a variety of ways and be imbued with different meanings determined by the users, not just by religious authorities.

One of the most vivid examples of this process came as growing numbers of Jews in the late nineteenth century started celebrating Hanukkah, Purim, and other Jewish holidays with balls, gala dinners, concerts, and quite frequently some combination thereof, adopting a fashionable and popular activity across Europe. The use of balls—an unconventional and, even to some extent, radical mode of sociability for observant society—reflected the individualization of the community and the rifts between past customs and present norms. This transformation in the celebration of Jewish holy days was made possible by the existence, use, and popularity of modern sites of sociability and reflected the individual desires and tastes of the participants.

A minor holiday, Hanukkah has become a widely celebrated and quite important family holiday in Christian countries—exceeding its religious significance on the Jewish calendar—thanks to Hanukkah's proximity to Christmas.[126] This transition was a dialectical process that began in the nineteenth century, when growing numbers of Jews in Europe (and North America) abandoned halachic observance of Judaism and Jewish holy days. To be sure, the observant continued to celebrate the occasion, but participation rates and the popularity of the holiday were ebbing. In this context a number of factors and voices came together to repopularize Hanukkah, but not necessarily along older patterns of celebration.

At least two distinct and quite divergent movements were important in this process: religious leaders and nationalists. First, religious leaders, including liberals and reformers, sought by the end of the nineteenth century to re-energize the holiday in the face of the growing interest in Christmas among coreligionists. Already in 1871, in Germany the progressively minded rabbis who convened at the Augsburg synod unanimously agreed that observance of Hanukkah must be strengthened and fostered, though beyond such grand intentions little information can be gleaned regarding just how exactly they hoped to effect this.[127] Similar rhetorical concern was voiced in the French Jewish press. For example, Rabbi Mathieu Wolff wrote about Hanukkah and Christmas, complaining about the "frightening decline in the Israelite faith." In a didactic fashion, the rabbi explains the holiday, hoping that with greater awareness about their own traditions, Jews "would stop needing encourage-ment to celebrate the 'festival of lights' at Christmas time."[128]

The second group to help reenergize the holiday of Hanukkah was the nationalists.[129] Arguably, the nationalists were the more successful of the two because they offered much more than mere words; their celebrations were, in fact, quickly imitated by other Jewish organizations. The nationalists' task was nevertheless particularly challenging. Before they could create a new nation-state, they first had to make Jews into a modern nation. This im-plied the creation of the new expression of Jewish belonging, one that was decisively secular and replaced a religious notion of a people chosen by God with the idea of a natural-historical nation, a process that required a new set of Jewish heroes and a new interpretation of old messages. Religious stories were replaced by new national myths and historical lessons.[130] In a struggle for national self-determination, the Maccabees were ideal role models in the nationalists' quest for political and national power. Practically, from Moscow westward, the celebration of Hanukkah became linked to the aspirations of the Jewish national movement.[131] Other holidays were similarly embraced. Purim, with its carnival atmosphere and tale of collective rescue, was quickly adopted and given a "strong nationalist coloration," as was Tu b-Shvat (arbor day, or new year's for trees, a holiday Zionists used to promote the settle-ment and development of the Land of Israel).[132]

Across the Russian Empire, nationalist Jewish organizations sought to combine Jewish activism with holiday participation and fundraising, in-cluding balls, with the goal of preparing for the eventual return to Eretz Yisrael. These celebrations were particularly popular among young Jews, es-pecially students, who sought ways to combine conviviality with a political-ideological message. One of the earliest balls held in Europe to mark the

festival of Hanukkah took place in St. Petersburg. In 1879 a group of students organized a ball on the eighth day of Hanukkah. The event was a clear
demonstration of the student organizers' advocacy for a return to Zion as a
solution to the Jewish question.[133]

Few details are available about this early ball, but holiday parties of this
nature continued in the Russian capital for quite some time. In 1907, for instance, Zionist circles held a "Palestinian Evening." The event consisted of a
full musical concert and dance held in the hall of the Blagorodnoe Sobranie
(a popular location for balls and Jewish gatherings) on February 15, the day
of Purim.[134] Three years later the Purim "Palestinian Concert-Ball" was held
in the Pavlovoi Hall, and the dancing was scheduled to continue until the
early hours of the morning.[135] In addition to fundraising, this event brought
together a Jewish holiday with ideological mobilization and entertainment.

Events such as these had become established patterns of celebration in
the community such that by 1914 a short ad in *Novyi Voskhod* could casually
note that Jewish students at the Petersburg University were organizing their
"*traditional* Jewish students' party [emphasis added]" on the day of Purim.
That year's event was held in the halls of the aforementioned Blagorodnoe
Sobranie.[136] The political inclinations of the student organization were left
unmentioned; yet we can see through this event and others like it that Jewish youth were important actors in changing the structure and meaning of
the holidays.

The Zionists of the city also quickly took up the task of encouraging even
younger members of the community to celebrate in a similar fashion and, of
course, in the process become dedicated nationalists. In 1900 the Jewish Palestinian Society of St. Petersburg held their inaugural children's celebration
in the Zal Pavlovoi (Pavlovoi Hall) for Tu b-Shvat. According to an article in
the journal *Budushchnost'*, the event "attracted a large public, consisting of
mainly women and children." The celebration began with hymns sung by a
children's choir composed of boys and girls from the Jewish orphanage. The
children also recited poetry, including a poem by the Jewish author Shimen
Frug. The political message of the event was manifest in the children's various
costumes. Decked out according to the theme of agricultural colonization of
the land, the mini-pioneers held rakes, hay forks, and carried Stars of David
in their hands.[137]

Holiday parties were quickly imitated across Europe. Entertaining and
fun experiences, the celebrations found eager audiences. In 1896 the Zionist

organization Ichoub Eretz Israel: Société d'assistance aux colons israélites en Palestine (Yishuv Eretz Israel: The Society for the Assistance of Jewish Colonists in Palestine) held an artistic and musical party to celebrate Hanukkah on Saturday, December 5, with an attendance of more than 400 people, including the editor of the *Archives Israélites*, Hippolyte Prague. The event took place at the Grand-Orient de France (the local Masonic temple) and was reported in the French Jewish and Russian Jewish press. The gathering featured speeches by prominent members of the Jewish community, including Rabbi Weiskopf, the president of the society, who thanked everyone assembled and reminded them of the political-ideological goals of the organization. Another featured speaker was somewhat surprisingly the chief rabbi of France, Zadoc Kahn, who, despite personally being on good terms with Herzl, was nonetheless apprehensive about the Zionist movement as a whole.[138]

Rabbi Kahn's speech began with a brief overview of the Maccabees' place in Jewish history, but the heart of his emotional talk focused on a different patriotic lesson from what one might expect for a Zionist event. Kahn emphatically stressed that "we have the good fortune of being French and being citizens of this France that, first, emancipated our fathers and made them free men, of this France that, rightly, is regarded by our brothers abroad as a center of Judaism." He stressed, "Let us be French and good Frenchmen and let us proclaim loudly our love for the motherland [*patrie*]."[139] The message was intended for both those present and the detractors outside less than two years after Alfred Dreyfus's initial conviction for treason.

The speeches at the Ichoub Eretz Israel society's ball were followed by music and artistic performances that either had a Jewish theme or were the works of Jewish artists.[140] The event thus also makes clear that non-Zionists were more than willing to use the new holiday parties for their own purposes.

In 1897 the Association des étudiants israélites russes (Association of Russian Jewish Students) held its annual ball during the holiday of Purim. The short article in the *Univers Israélite* reminded readers in passing that having fun and dancing were commanded activities for the holiday, insisting that the ball's activities were in keeping with good Jewish practice.[141] The next year, the same association held its annual ball on Purim at the "grands salons de la Marquise," close to Monceau park and not far from the Sorbonne university; the ball evidently catered to a student audience.[142] We do not know, however, if the Russian students brought this practice with them from home or whether they adopted the practice in France. The group's apolitical leaning,[143] however, suggests that already by the turn of the twentieth century a broader segment of the Jewish population, albeit clearly a young one, had begun to accept the holiday ball as an appropriate means to celebrate certain Jewish holidays.[144]

Berlin Zionists were similarly happy to celebrate Hanukkah and Purim with concerts, balls, and parties. The Berliner Zionistische Vereinigung (BZV) regularly held Hanukkah balls, including one in December 1900 at the Hotel zu den vier Jahreszeiten and another on December 1906 in the Hohenzollern Sälen. For Hanukkah 1904, out of respect for the passing of Theodor Herzl, the association held a musical evening without a ball at the Ausstellungspark near the Lehrter Bahnhof.[145]

The BZV did not work alone in organizing these Hanukkah festivities. On December 25, 1902, for example, the BZV and the Jüdisch-nationale Frauenvereinigung (Jewish National Women's Association) co-sponsored a Maccabee festival and ball at the Hotel Imperial. The event included a speech, musical and dramatic performances, including a satire against assimilationists, and the ball itself.[146] The January 2, 1903, issue of *Jüdische Rundschau* reported with much delight that more than 500 people attended the celebration, some staying into the wee hours of the morning. The same article noted that among those assembled were individuals who were not (or not yet) Zionists and that a speech given during an intermission sought to explain the main tenets of the movement for the politically mixed audience.[147]

Also in 1902 the Jewish sports movement Bar Kochba held its own "Maccabee party," which was attended by more than 400 people. Again, speeches explained the program of the movement and the meaning of the holiday and were followed by songs, theatrical performances, and dancing.[148] Five years later, the BZV held another "Makkabäer-Feier nebst Ball" at the Brauerei Königstadt in December 1907. Tickets were sold for individuals as well as for families, suggesting the broader audience to which the event catered.[149]

For Purim the Bar Kochba sports association held a costume party at the Dresdner Casino on the evening of Saturday, March 14, 1903.[150] The BZV and the Jüdisch-nationale Frauenvereinigung held an annual Purim costume festival.[151] A short article in the *Jüdische Rundschau* from 1903 informed readers that the committee responsible for the ball was working hard to prepare Jewish emblems and decorations for the halls of the Hotel Prinz Albrecht. The committee also requested that guests put in extra effort that year to dress as Jewish heroes (including those associated with the holiday, such as Esther and Mordechai), historical figures, or in "colonial costume in colorful orientalist fashion"; "naturally" the ball would be incomplete, the committee suggested, without a "Polish-Russian Jew."[152] One wonders what, if any, reaction this politically incorrect suggestion garnered among the Eastern European Jewish community living in Berlin. In addition to these events primarily targeting adults, the Jüdisch-nationale Frauenvereinigung held children's balls, expanding the audience for such events and introducing children to the novel celebration of the holiday from an early age.[153]

Figure 10. Advertisements for various communal events in Berlin, including several Purim balls. Source: *Berliner Vereinsbote* (March 12, 1897): 2. Courtesy of the Universitätsbibliothek Frankfurt am Main/Digitale Sammlungen Judaica. Reprinted with permission.

Although many of the first Hanukkah and Purim parties were held by Zionist organizations, the popularity of such festivities grew over time. In Berlin Bnai Brith began holding similar holiday dances in the 1920s, at the latest. For instance, on Monday, December 6, 1926, Bnai Brith held a Hanukkah party at the Berthold Auerbach Lodge. The evening included a musical concert (featuring singers and a performance by a member of the Volksbühne) and a dance. In addition, the Spinoza and Akiba Eger Bnai Brith lodges organized a costume ball held in the Kleist Logenhaus for Purim on March 17, 1927. The short ad announcing the event promised two jazz bands and "surprises."[154]

By 1927 the nationalist Israel Auerbach could triumphantly write in the pages of the *Monatsschrift der Berliner Logen* about the renaissance of the holiday of Hanukkah, the "rejuvenating Jewish development," and the part Bnai Brith played in both. His article focused on how the menorah reflected the values of "irresistible progress and victory of intellectual prowess [*geistigen Mächte*] over the powers of violence and darkness," arguing that the holiday could be read as a lesson in what he saw as the values of Bnai Brith.[155] Out of the grasp of religious authorities, Jewish holidays could be remade according to other agendas.

To be sure, additional holidays were similarly refashioned, and the popularity of holiday balls and parties spread across both time and place. The organization Parizer Bundisher Ferayn "Kempfer" (Parisian Bundist Association "Fighter") held a ball for Sukkot on the evening of Saturday, October 18, 1913, at the Grand Orient de France. In addition to the ball, the organization advertised an "excellent, rich concert and various amusements."[156] Years later, in 1929, the Maccabi sports club of Paris organized a ball for Simchat Torah (Rejoicing of the Torah) in the salons of the Palais des Congrès; the activities included the crowning of ten Maccabi "queens," the distribution of toys to children, and jazz music by two bands. Here again, organizers took care to offer entertainment not only for men and women but also for their children.[157] Targeting children was also a clear way to achieve goals of political, cultural, and religious education. Sociability served as a gateway to different forms of Jewish practice and expressions of belonging.

The celebration of Jewish holidays with fashionable balls marked an important shift in values, in addition to a change in venue. The changes did not go unnoticed. Even Purim balls, celebrating a holy day known for its carnival-like practices, were met with certain unease. Dr. Simon Bernfeld,

writing in the mainstream *Generalanzeiger*, pointed to the Purim masquer-
ade ball as an innovation of "modern Jews" in which personal entertainment and enjoyment, "according to [individual] inclinations and tastes,"
took precedence over the meaning of the holiday. The individualized experience of holiday celebration, with its focus on personal meaning and
entertainment, provoked a clear sense of discomfort. Yet in the end Purim
and Hanukkah balls did not disrupt the social order significantly enough
to cause a serious backlash among most members of the community, and
the balls continued to be central ways to celebrate the holidays after World
War II in Paris and Berlin. The same cannot be said, however, for a short-
lived and highly controversial holiday ball.

The new custom of celebrating Jewish holy days with balls took an extreme turn at the end of the nineteenth and beginning of the twentieth
centuries when in several cities, including Paris, Jewish anarchists celebrated
lavish balls on Yom Kippur. Two such balls were held in Paris, first in 1900
and then in 1901, and, according to reports, 400 individuals took part in the
first.[158] Following on the heels of similar events in London and New York,
the two Yom Kippur balls in Paris continued a trend of anarchist provoca-
tion.[159] For obvious reasons, in each city where they took place, these balls
raised significant furor among the Jewish communities, exactly what the
event organizers wanted.[160] Intentionally arranged and publicized to garner
the greatest reaction, the anarchists sought to advance their own political
agenda through these balls. And the French Jewish press gladly obliged.

Quick to decry the ball of 1900, an article in the *Univers Israélite* tried
to deflate the anti-establishment sentiments and intents of the event by
noting that, although the anarchists ostensibly rejected religion, the staging of such an event on Yom Kippur reflected a connection to Judaism,
however upturned. As the writer remarked, a house is still a house even if
"the roof is below and the basement is on top." These "banqueteurs," the
author continued, "continued to celebrate Kippur." Trying to be provoca-
tive, "the organizers of the banquet" were nonetheless "much more Jewish
than they thought," following in a long line of Jews who did not always
remain faithful to the mitzvot. Trying to seem unimpressed with the anarchist Jewish spectacle, the author pointed to other Jews who "didn't want
to fast for Yom Kippur" and so "would simply go to a restaurant," sometimes furtively, sometimes openly.[161] Nevertheless, by holding a Yom Kippur ball, the participants transgressed the fundamental component of what

was largely recognized and accepted as normative Judaism. During these events the dance halls became at once a profoundly Jewish and also a radically anti-Jewish space.

Even though the Yom Kippur balls amounted to a passing fad, the overall tension that emerged out of the at times radical use of spaces of consumption provoked apprehension. One joke, published in the *Univers Israélite* only a few years later, in 1908, exemplifies the concern over the decline in strict religious observance and returns to the restaurant as the scene of this religious upheaval.

> In a restaurant on Yom Kippur, Hayim Leib and his son complete their lunch. After coffee, the young man stands up to go. But his father says, "Hey, hey!?" "What do you want from me?" the son asks. Outraged, the father cries, "*Posché Isroel* [Sinners of Israel]! On a day like this, at least you could *bench* [say the blessings after a meal]!"[162]

The humor of the joke stems from the father's ironic demand that his son say grace after meals on a day when the very act of eating and drinking is a serious sin. The decline in Jewish observance—and the lack of proper Jewish education—gives the joke its bitter humor.

Similar anxieties were voiced elsewhere, and an analogous joke made its way around Berlin, told separately by Sammy Gronemann and Gershom Scholem. Scholem suggested that "malicious souls used to say in the years before World War I that a headwaiter stood at the entrance to the well-known restaurant next to the Grosse Synagogue on Oranienburger Strasse (corner of Artilleriestrasse) and addressed the guests in their holiday finery as follows: 'The gentlemen who are fasting [for Yom Kippur] will be served in the back room.'"[163] In Gronemann's version the venue is identified as Café Loy and it was a sign that supposedly greeted the furtive and not so observant guests.[164] Whether any truth lies behind these jokes is unclear and not particularly relevant. Participation in a leisure world that enabled Jews to celebrate Jewish holidays on their own terms provoked anxiety among those who longed for an earlier time when Jewish conduct was seemingly more controllable and uniform.

Nowhere, however, were the challenges to religion and Judaism more extreme than in revolutionary and Soviet Russia. The political changes that occurred as a result of the Bolshevik Revolution meant that radical, politically charged, and antireligious versions of Jewish holidays were not merely the work of a select group of dissidents; rather, in the 1920s they became state-sponsored activities. As Anna Shternshis has effectively shown in the early years of the Soviet Union, Jewish communists attempted to reformulate and refashion Jewish holidays. While the authorities undertook the process of closing synagogues across the country, they also sought to teach their new political message by both attacking certain religious practices and infusing specific holidays with alternative meanings. Between 1921 and 1928 this included anti–Yom Kippur campaigns waged in the press by the Yiddish communist journal *Der Apikoyres* (The Atheist) and in deeds by Jewish Komsomol members who demonstratively entered synagogues and ate before the fasting congregants. In trying to dissuade Jews from celebrating the religious holiday, these efforts were aimed at denigrating organized religion and challenging the authority of "bourgeois" religious leaders.[165] At the same time, in practice, not all Jews heeded this ideological message. Antireligious ethnic Jewish activists met with "staunch resistance" in the 1920s, including fistfights.[166]

Other holidays, such as Passover, were harnessed as occasions for propaganda. Not long after the revolution, in 1921, "the Central Bureau of the Bolshevik Party's *Evsektsii* sent instructions to all local branches to organize 'Red Passovers.' Popular brochures that came to be known as 'Red Haggadahs' were published, specifying how to conduct the alternative celebrations."[167] These Haggadot, published into the 1930s, reinterpreted the traditional story of liberation from bondage as, not surprisingly, the struggle from bourgeois capitalism.[168] Yet these Jewish communist celebrations were short-lived, especially for the Jews of Leningrad. Indeed, religious holy day celebrations declined significantly after the 1920s as the pace of antireligious propaganda and political censure increased.

Conclusions

The secularization of Judaism and of Jewish communities in Paris, Berlin, and St. Petersburg did not result simply in the decline of Jewish observance or in the confessionalization of Judaism. Instead, the process included a significant restructuring of Jewish practice, just as it reflected a diversification of Jewish communities along secular, cultural, religious, and national lines. Everyday Jews took the celebration of Jewish rites of passage and holy days into their own hands and imbued them with their own meanings, sometimes in ways that contradicted the goals and desires of religious elites. Responding to these perceived challenges and acts of "dejudaization" and fearing for the very future of Judaism, many religious authorities and some lay leaders attempted to reassert their control over proper conduct and observance by stressing the role of religious education and of the synagogue in rites of passage.

Yet the story told here is not just a narrative of struggle, certainly not in the cases of Paris, Berlin, and imperial St. Petersburg. The early reformulation of the celebration of Jewish holy days, such as Hanukkah and Purim, were co-opted by wider constituents of the Jewish communities. In Paris and Berlin many of these same rituals and celebrations continued well past the Holocaust. By contrast, the stark antireligious nature of the Soviet regime led to a radical reorientation of Jewish holy days into celebrations of communism. Yet these communist Jewish celebrations did not last, and Jewish holidays and rites of passage declined significantly in their importance for the Jews of Leningrad. This was not simply a result of the attack against capitalism (and sites of leisure) but a consequence of the significant restriction in the number of spaces that stood outside the grasp of the central authorities. Jewish religious celebration quickly became politically incorrect under the Soviets, and there were few safe sites in which to hold them.

CHAPTER 5

Rebuilding After the Shoah

The Challenges of Remembering and Reconstruction

The devastation wrought by the Shoah cannot be overestimated. The Jewish population of Europe in 1939 stood at 9.5 million. During the Holocaust, the Nazis and their collaborators murdered a full two-thirds, leaving 3.8 million Jews alive in Europe in 1945, including 2 million in the Soviet Union. The Shoah had particularly tragic consequences for Jewish children, who died in higher proportion than Jewish adults,[1] and many of those who did survive were orphaned. The OSE estimated that 40,000–45,000 Jewish children and adolescents were orphaned or abandoned in Europe at the war's end.[2] By 1960 the Jewish population of Europe had declined further to 3.2 million as a result of emigration,[3] despite an influx of Jews coming to France from North Africa.

Given these statistics, it is little wonder that the overwhelming majority of historical narratives choose to present the Shoah as an end point in the history of European Jewry, a zero hour of another sort. The biblical term that Jews after the war used to describe those who survived, *sh'erit ha-pletah* (the surviving remnant), suggests unprecedented and insurmountable destruction, confirming the sense of obliteration and loss. It would be irresponsible if not morally objectionable to suggest that World War II was not a tragic watershed in the European Jewish experience. The Jews who survived the war—be it in camps, in hiding, through mixed marriages, in exile, or in parts of Europe beyond the Nazis' genocidal reach—faced a series of existential questions, including the fundamental question of whether or not to stay on the Dark Continent (or in some cases, whether to return to the blood-soaked lands).

At times this decision was not really a choice. Some simply *could not leave* on account of their own or a loved one's poor health, family ties, or political circumstance. In other instances, some Jews felt they *could not stay*, as the post-Holocaust pogroms in Poland and the anticosmopolitan campaigns of the early 1950s across Eastern Europe made painfully clear. For those who did consider leaving, the promise of a new life abroad in Palestine (as of 1948, Israel), Canada, Australia, and the United States was a powerful pull factor.

If historical monographs on the subject are any indication, the topic of continuity between the pre- and post-Shoah period remains largely understudied. Yet, as Maud Mandel has carefully reminded us in the case of the Jews of France, "The Holocaust was part of their history, not its end."[4] In this final chapter I return to several of the main themes explored in this book and point to the social and structural changes resulting from persecution, the war, and genocide; but I also note certain instances of continuity in cultural patterns between the pre- and post-Shoah eras. For those who stayed or returned, many expressed a desire to rebuild some semblance of Jewish life, to find spaces and ways to create togetherness and raise a new generation. Yet they also frequently experienced deep insecurity, fear, and distrust of the surrounding non-Jewish world. As they searched for a way to rebuild their lives, they often turned, when and where possible, to patterns created in the pre-Shoah era. In Leningrad, Berlin, and Paris, external political conditions and the strength of the Jewish communities are the two main factors that conditioned the success or failure of these ventures, but they also account for the significant differences that can be seen between the three communities.

Space for Togetherness

TWO BERLINS

At the war's end Berlin's Jewish life was all but decimated. The city's once thriving Jewish community of 170,000 people was nearly entirely annihilated. In 1947 there were 7,000 Jews registered in Berlin, of which a little more than 1,400 survived by going underground.[5] Most of the remaining Jews had survived the Shoah thanks to their non-Jewish spouses (whom, we recall, they had married before such unions became illegal in 1935); approximately half of the surviving Jewish population was in a so-called privileged marriage, and another quarter were in nonprivileged marriages.[6] There were also few children in postwar Berlin. In 1946 roughly half of the population was age 50 or older, and 6.8% were under 18.[7] These figures meant that the community was not going to grow through natural means anytime soon.

Although many Jewish refugees from Eastern Europe temporarily lived in displaced persons camps in Berlin immediately after the war, the overwhelming majority left.[8] These temporary residents were joined in their decision to leave by numerous German Jews who felt that Germany was no longer their home. For many Jews around the world, the idea that any Jewish individual would want to rebuild a life in Germany was anathema, and the topic of the small but persistent Jewish community in Germany provoked heated debate.[9]

Life in early postwar Berlin reflected the general problems faced by the city's residents, including shortages of food and shelter caused by the heavy bombing of the capital city during the war. Most Jews were also dependent on public welfare and social assistance, some of which came in the form of CARE packages, whereas other assistance came from Jewish organizations and from the German governments.[10] Even as basic material conditions gradually began to improve, the remaining Jews, a tiny fraction of their original population, found it impossible to reestablish the once-flourishing Jewish cultural and social life in Berlin, especially after the official split of the religious community of Berlin in 1953 into the Jüdische Gemeinde zu Berlin (in West Berlin) and the Jüdische Gemeinde von Berlin (Ost). These divisions were defined further and more profoundly with the establishment of the Berlin Wall in 1961.

By 1954, the year after the momentous split of the Gemeinde, West Berlin's Jewish community had three functioning synagogues, a Jewish hospital, and an old-age home as well as three religious schools.[11] In the east, the district of Prenzlauerberg was home to the sector's only synagogue, the Friedenstempel (or Freedom Temple, as it was renamed in 1953) on Rykestrasse, which served as a focal point of the community's activities. From 1953 until the end of the regime the only kosher butcher was located in the same district (on Eberswalderstrasse).[12] In addition, many East Berlin Jews lived in the borough of Pankow, immediately to the north.[13]

The West Berlin community faced certain challenges stemming from political infighting and its small size (5,000 to 6,000 members in the 1950s) but was spared the larger external political persecution that the East Berlin community experienced in the early 1950s (see later discussion). Its members were overwhelmingly German Jewish, many having lived in the city since before World War II. Thanks to the relatively tolerant social and political atmosphere, the Jewish community was able to function and develop its institutional and social base. With government help and funding, the Jewish community renovated several synagogues, organized children's programs and a kindergarten, and secured rabbis to serve both the community's liberal and Orthodox members. In 1957 the Jewish community of West Berlin requested the property at 79–80 Fasanenstrasse for a community center (the Gemeindehaus), and the foundation stone was laid that same year.[14]

One obvious and striking characteristic of the post-Shoah Jewish community in Berlin was its greater reliance on the official community (the Jüdische Gemeinde zu Berlin) and its spaces for cultural life and gatherings. Given the tiny Jewish population of Berlin, the Jewish population was not in the position to maintain the wide variety of associations, organizations, and institutions that had existed in the city before the war. On top of this, membership in the existing associations was frequently quite small.

This situation led to an important change in the official institutional framework. Namely, the official community took over a number of non-religious tasks that had previously been in private hands. The Jewish Community Center of West Berlin (the Gemeindehaus) was in some respects the most obvious example of this. Built on the ruins of the old Fasanenstrasse synagogue, it was to be the hub of Jewish life in the western sector of the city, housing a kosher restaurant, a library, and, a couple years after its establishment, a *Volkshochschule* (an adult education program).[15] It catered to Jews of different levels of religious observance and self-identification, including those who felt drawn more by cultural and social programs than by religious rituals.

The creation of the Gemeindehaus reflected multiple purposes and intentions and can serve as an entry point to a host of larger issues that faced the Jewish community, including a new consensus on Jewish nationalism, changing understandings of what it meant to be a German Jew, the memory of the

Holocaust, and the myriad compromises that came with living on German soil. On a spatial-symbolic level, the choice to renovate an old synagogue for (more) secular ends was telling, an architectonic sign of the processes of secularization that had affected the Jews of Berlin since the nineteenth century. In a sense reinforcing the architectural repurposing, the activities in the Gemeindehaus clearly followed the needs of a community that expected more than narrow confessional expressions of Jewish belonging. This was not simply the result of local factors. After World War II, communities across the West sought to imitate the American Jewish community center and YMHA (Young Men's Hebrew Association) models to "[reinforce] the notion of Judaism as a communal way of life rather than merely a belief system."[16]

On another level the new community center clearly emerged as a symbolic response to persecution and genocide. To be sure, numerous attempts by the Jewish community and by non-Jewish Germans to counteract antisemitism and alter the perception about Jews in Germany preceded the establishment of the Gemeindehaus. Serving the community from 1950 to 1953, the Berlin-born rabbi Nathan Peter Levinson[17] noted that by the early 1950s Berlin had become a vibrant city where "exciting political and cultural things happened." It was in this not yet fully divided city that "in the East sector, [the communist Jewish actor] Helene Wiegel played *Mother Courage* in the Theater on Schiffbauerdamm . . . and in the West [the Austrian Jewish actor] Ernst Deutsch played *Nathan the Wise*."[18] These were the (literally) dramatic signs of but two artistic and directorial attempts to reverse the antisemitic propaganda of the Nazi years. Both the place of Jewish actors on the German stage and the staging of a stark antiwar and antifascist play by Berthold Brecht and Lessing's classic Enlightenment play (and plea) for tolerance demonstrated a determined overturning of recent attitudes within the city's cultural sphere. Naturally, other public acts of denazification, including those done officially by the West German government, emerged from a certain self-interest in international recognition and normalization on the world stage.[19] Yet some individuals as well as governmental and informal groups in Germany were determined to overturn the past, and the Jewish Gemeinde participated in these activities.

Working with the Society for Christian-Jewish Cooperation (Gesellschaft für Christlich-Jüdische Zusammenarbeit),[20] in 1954, for example, the Gemeinde co-sponsored the exhibition "Alt-Neuland Israel," held in the Maison de France on the Kurfürstendamm. The exhibition showcased the new Jewish state and offered an overview of its historical origins; it also made claims to Israel's current status as a democratic republic that respected the equality of minorities and freedom of speech and religion (perhaps also implicitly suggesting a model for emulation for the new West German republic). The exhibit included lectures, a recital in Hebrew and German, and a film.[21] Organizers clearly designed the program not just for Jewish residents of the city but especially for non-Jews as a means to promote positive images of Jews and of the newly founded State of Israel. A vocal segment of non-Jewish Germans faced their past and the role of their prejudices and deeds in the fate of their neighbors and attempted to change these destructive stereotypes.

We thus need to see the creation of the Gemeindehaus as a continuation of this larger process of *Vergangenheitsbewältigung* (the struggle to come to terms with the past). Financed by the city government, the community center demonstrated the goodwill and obligation of the non-Jewish city authorities and an institutional desire to see the renewed visibility and presence of the Jewish community and thus of Jewish life in the city. Mayor Willy Brandt, for instance, attended the laying of the cornerstone in 1957. The renovated building thus stood as a site of outward reconciliation and the inward rebuilding of (a mostly) secular Jewish belonging.

Yet this belied another important aspect of the story—the Gemeindehaus was also a guarded space. The Gemeindehaus, on the grounds of a once large and imposing synagogue, was nonetheless located on a side street and was built at an obvious distance from the road, in a sense sheltering members from the outside non-Jewish world. Even though Jews had previously come together in specifically Jewish spaces, they had also felt comfortable moving in and out of non-Jewish spaces, thereby publicly displaying Jewish belonging. After the war, despite public attempts to renew Jewish presence and confront the Nazi legacy, Berlin's Jews were not necessarily eager to be always in the limelight.

In this regard, the legacy of the Shoah expressed itself in unexpected ways. After the Shoah, Jews of Berlin on both sides of the city noticeably preferred to gather in sheltered spaces, be they explicitly Jewish spaces (such as the Gemeindehaus or a kosher restaurant) or semiprivate venues. A few examples of this phenomenon should suffice to highlight this fact and to point to the complicated realities of Jewish belonging after the war.

The small Berlin chapter of WIZO (Women's International Zionist Organization) held its founding meeting in 1952 at the Konditorei Neumann, a kosher establishment on Mommsenstrasse in Charlottenburg.[22] As another example, an informal group of German Jews who had made aliyah (i.e., immigrated to Israel) but then chose to return to Germany regularly met in the backroom of the nonkosher Café Moehring on the Kurfürstendamm every Friday.[23] And the Vereins Brith Rischonim/Bund der Alt-Zionisten (Association Brith Rischonim [Covenant of Pioneers]/Union of Old Zionists) founded in 1960 held their first meeting at the Hotel Bristol-Kempinski on the Kurfürstendamm, a Jewish-owned hotel that was opened in 1952 by Frederick Unger (heir to a notable Jewish family of local restaurateurs and hotel owners whose legacy included the Haus Vaterland and the Weinrestaurant Kempinski on the Kurfürstendamm).[24] In the context of a lively city, with "artists and literati [sitting] in the cafés on the Kurfürstendamm," as Rabbi Levinson noted, it is significant that Jews chose to meet in sheltered spaces, be they specifically Jewish spaces (e.g., a kosher restaurant or a Jewish-owned establishment) or the backrooms of popular non-Jewish cafés that had been around since the turn of the twentieth century.

Naturally, other factors played a role as well, but these are no less telling. Clearly, Jews who observed Jewish ritual dietary restrictions would not eat in a nonkosher restaurant, and it therefore seems reasonable to assume that ritual needs played at least a partial role in the WIZO chapter's choice for a kosher establishment. In this regard, their choice was the most straightforward. The decision of German Jews who had immigrated to Israel and then returned to Germany to meet in a backroom, however, suggests multiple interpretations: from the mundane (the desire to sit in a quieter space in the back of a popular and therefore possibly loud café), to possible anxiety at gathering publicly as Jews, to concern over being noticeable as a group of returnees. Returning to Germany from Israel was a decision fraught with conflict in the Jewish world, and thus the more isolated location could have additionally reflected apprehension about publicizing a particular element about the group's life choices. After all, their choices—intentionally or not—challenged a wider Jewish consensus.

After the Holocaust and certainly after 1948, Zionism increasingly became a component of Jewish identification in various communities across the globe.[25] On top of this, Germany was viewed by many members of the Jewish community (including German Jews who left for America or Israel) as a land in which Jews should no longer dwell. Prominent intellectuals and

Israeli politicians publicly called for Jews to abandon Germany, and then Jews abroad urged those who chose nonetheless to live there to leave.[26] Especially in the early 1950s, there was a desire to isolate those Jews who remained in Germany as a way of encouraging their departure.[27] The group of German Jews who had returned from Israel and met in a café's backroom might have had many reasons to meet and share their common stories and experiences, but they also might have wanted to minimize their visibility.

The decision of the Union of Old Zionists to meet at the Hotel Bristol-Kempinski was similarly overdetermined. The group brought together men over the age of 50 who had, according to its charter, spent at least twenty-five years involved in Zionist activities. These were men who had lived through the war but for unspoken reasons, perhaps simply because of age, had stayed in Berlin.[28] Just as they had deep roots in the city, the hotel in which they met was also linked to the longer outline of Berlin Jewish history (one that included "Aryanization" under the Nazis and escape). The newly established hotel, building on the legacy of two previous generations of Jewish hotel and restaurant owners, conformed to the story of German Jewish returnees and their desire to rebuild a Jewish presence in Berlin. Here, obliquely, we can see the legacy of the Holocaust at play: the desire to recreate aspects of that which had been painfully destroyed but also the desire to cling tightly to those who remained. This was a community in mourning that sought out others with a similar set of experiences and beliefs (including nonreligious ones).

Even on an individual level, the choice of leisure site could reflect these same feelings. In a passing but powerful anecdote, Rabbi Levinson recounted how in the early 1950s whenever he entered the Café Wien in Berlin, the orchestra would play "Kol Nidre."[29] The orchestra's selection—picked most likely because the Ashkenazi melody is well known and particularly beautiful—serves as an unintentional metaphor for the community's mourning. Kol Nidre (all vows) is the emotional declaration that begins Yom Kippur. The Kol Nidre declaration begs God to annul all vows made in vain before God, and prayers throughout the entire day focus on seeking forgiveness and reconciliation with the divine. Yom Kippur is also traditionally the day on which God determines the fate of all in the coming year (who lives and who dies and by what means). The choice of music, again probably unintentionally, thus evoked a series of strong emotional associations, connections that reverberated even with the history of the café itself.

Opened after World War I by the successful restaurateur and Hungarian Jew Karl Kutschera, Café Wien had been a popular institution on the Kurfürstendamm. Under the Nazis the café and Kutschera's other restaurant, the Zigeunerkeller, were "Aryanized." Kutschera, his wife, Josefine, and their two children, Clara and Gerhard, remained in Berlin, however, and appear to have been some of the last Jews of the city to be deported in 1943. First sent to Theresienstadt, the children were ultimately sent to Auschwitz, where they perished. Yet Karl and his wife survived, returned to Berlin after the war, and reopened Café Wien. When Karl died in 1950, Josefine continued to run the café. Just as the Union of Old Zionists met in the newly opened Jewish-owned Hotel Bristol-Kempinski, it was probably not by chance that Rabbi Levinson frequented Café Wien. His short story serves as yet another example of the tendency among Jews of Berlin to meet in specifically Jewish spaces, an act that held particular meaning for a community that was seeking to hold onto its past and reclaim its presence in the city.

There are many ways we can interpret the behavior of certain Jews in Berlin: again, out of anxiety or uncertainty toward the non-Jewish world; in the cases of Hotel Bristol-Kempinski and Café Wien, as a desire to support the reestablishment of Jewish-owned businesses and assert resilience despite the past; or for these two eateries, possibly as a sign of nostalgia and longing for a bygone era. Coming together as Jews in West Berlin was thus emotionally complicated. It involved new consensuses regarding the importance and place of Jewish nationalism (through the victory of Zionism), challenges to German Jewish self-definition, memory of persecution and genocide, and the complications of a life of compromises. Creating the basis for Jewish self-identification among the city's few children was no less fraught.

In the immediate post-Shoah period, the basic needs of Berlin's Jewish children were acute. In the early 1950s Rabbi Nathan Levinson wrote to a congregation in the United States requesting aid. In his letter he explained the Berlin community's desire both to bring the children closer to Judaism and to help satisfy their basic needs: "We are trying to draw many children who have become lost to us, partly through mixed marriages, partly through communism, back to Judaism." However, the problem was not merely spiritual. Rabbi Levinson explained that the community had formerly aided those without sufficient food with care packages from the American Jewish Joint Distribution Committee (JDC). Presently, he continued, "Some of our teachers lend a helping hand to the children by buying for them clothing, shoes and other needed articles." The poverty of the students preoccupied Rabbi Levinson. He wrote in the same letter, "The children here are so poor, that as a rule we have to supply them with fare and some with food."[30] Religious spaces were to be both a physical and a spiritual lifeline, a means of helping ensure the physical and religious survival of those few young Jewish Berliners who had survived the Shoah and whose parents had decided to remain in the city.[31]

To these ends, Rabbi Levinson organized an annual summer camp in Berlin-Wannsee in the early 1950s; the camp played an important part in the lives of Berlin's Jewish children. Bringing together children from all over the city, Rabbi Levinson ran the camp with his wife, Helga. "We had children from all sectors of the city, in particular from the East. They could experience wonderful holidays in a Jewish atmosphere that they otherwise would not have been offered."[32] This Jewish atmosphere included "religious instructions by the rabbi and teacher" and "a service each Friday and Saturday." In addition, they held "a discussion concerning synagogical [sic] life."[33]

In 1952 the children wrote letters to the American Jewish congregation that had donated some of the necessary funding for the summer camp's functioning. The children wrote to their "American friends," giving a sense of their activities at the camp. Several older children reported that twenty-five children between the ages of 6 and 15 participated in the three-week-long summer holiday. Most letters referenced the good food they ate, the sports activities they engaged in, and the other leisure time activities. The only reference to religious learning comes from K. (age 12), who simply mentioned that she knew several of the other children from the religious school. M., an articulate 11-year-old, wrote that she had been in Wannsee the previous year. She added that there had been some issue of whether she would be able to come this time, because she lived in the east (outside Berlin).[34] She noted in her letter that the camp allowed her to meet children she knew from the year before.[35] The social aspect of the summer camp appears to have been more important—at least immediately—to the children and youth than any particular formal lesson they learned.

Around 1954, after Rabbi Levinson had left the city, the community succeeded in "placing the children in groups of 40 for 3 weeks in a holiday-camp in the Walter-Rathenau-house."[36] By 1960 the activities of the official Jewish community of Berlin had expanded to include a kindergarten and a center for children and youth. Approximately 180 school-age children would come each week to the center; there they would engage in discussions, play music, sing, play, do crafts, and participate in classes, including sports lessons. In the same year, 140 children participated in the summer camp and 24 in the winter camp also organized by the community.[37] Because "religious forma- tion [and] the education, instruction and engagement of our young people, is quite dear to our hearts,"[38] the community also established a kindergarten on Joachimstalerstrasse that took care of forty-five "little citizens." For these children, too, the need to promote Jewish education and belonging was considered self-evident. The Gemeinde's monthly periodical stated clearly, "That they are to be raised as conscious Jews is obvious, that occurs with good contact to religion, history and the land of the Jews."[39]

In Berlin the Gemeinde was charged with far more than attending to the religious needs of the Jews living in the city. Jewish Berliners came to expect the Gemeinde to offer a variety of Jewish social programs, such as those that had existed in the pre-Shoah era. The Gemeinde's participation in the support and further creation of Jewish spaces points to an evolutionary process of Jewish space and Jewish community in which self-identification was based on interaction in new spaces. In a sense, the Gemeinde needed to fulfill West Berliners' expectation for a market of leisure and social programs that would also incorporate the children of the community through various social activities and offer them spaces of inclusion. Its task was to recreate a haven for Jewish life that would answer parents' expectations of Jewish socia- bility for their children but that would also offer safe spaces in a controlled, Jewish environment.

Until 1953 the Jewish community of both West and East Berlin was one unified religious organization, and, as the example of the early summer camps showed, it served members on both sides of the city.[40] In early 1953, however, this would change. The division of the community emerged as a result of antisemitic persecution, which began in the Soviet Union in the late 1940s and spread outward with anticosmopolitan show trials staged in Prague (the Slansky trials) and Moscow in 1952–1953.[41] Although a number of German Jews had returned to East Germany with the hopes of building a new socialist society, their Jewishness, euphemistically revealed through terms such as *Westemigranten*,[42] made them suspect during this time.[43] The Jewish Gemeinden across East Germany were targeted, and in January 1953 many East Berlin (and East German) Jews fled to the West, drastically re- ducing the Jewish population of the eastern half of the city and precipitating a further political crisis.[44] A number of the Jews who chose to stay in East Germany opted to renounce their membership in the Jewish community in favor of membership in the ruling Socialist Unity Party (Sozialistische Einheitspartei Deutschlands; SED), feeling that membership in both was no longer possible or desirable.[45]

Even though most of the tensions of the early 1950s receded by the second half of the decade, the official religious community never recovered. By 1955 the Jewish communities of East Germany registered only 1,715 members, and in 1959 this had dropped to 987 individuals, of which more than 75% were older than 50.[46] By the early 1960s, religious services both on Shabbat and during the High Holidays were poorly attended, with only twenty individuals coming for regular services and between eighty and a hundred attending for the High Holidays.[47] Nonetheless, a striking number of socialists and communists were of Jewish descent, including such prominent politicians as Albert Norden and such literary figures as Arnold Zweig, Anna Sehgers, Jurek Becker, and Stefan Heym.[48] Yet the extent to which such individuals engaged in Jewish activities, were moved by Jewish themes, or even considered themselves Jewish varied greatly.

Thus in East Berlin the political setting conditioned different parameters. Individual expressions of Jewish self-identification played out under the context of specific social and political restrictions. Unlike in the Soviet Union, in East Germany Jews were considered a religious group and not a nationality,[49] and Jewish religious activity was tolerated in East Germany to a far greater degree than in Soviet Russia. In fact, the East German government subsidized the Jewish community and its institutions (this is perhaps ironic, given Marxist attitudes toward religion and certainly a policy that contradicted that of Soviet Russia).[50] Yet the city's one synagogue came to enjoy a significant monopoly over organized Jewish life. Those who felt little affinity to Judaism as a religion or to the official religious community had few other social outlets. In short, in East Berlin after 1953 there were basically two legitimate Jewish identities: as members of a community of fate (*Schicksalsgemeinschaft*), or, more officially, victims of fascism (*Opfer des Faschismus*); or as members of the religious community. The situation resulted in a more distinct split between the religious on one hand and socialists and communists on the other.

Unlike the West Berlin Jewish community, which possessed more than one synagogue and was able to cater to Jews of differing religious inclinations, the East Berlin Jewish community was, strictly speaking, defined by membership in the religious Gemeinde (i.e., the Jüdische Gemeinde von Berlin (Ost) established in 1953), which had but one synagogue and leaned in the direction of Orthodoxy. The sector also had a kosher butcher, but there was no institution similar to the Jewish Gemeindehaus of West Berlin. A further challenge for those seeking to lead a religious life was that both the Gemeinde and the synagogue were subject to surveillance by members of the Ministry for State Security (Ministerium für Staatssicherheit, or Stasi) and its informants, the latter including the leadership of the Gemeinde itself.[51]

Nonetheless, the Rykestrasse Synagogue in East Berlin did function as more than a religious space and served as a site for gathering. For instance, academics would give talks at the synagogue, and concerts were held there throughout the year as well.[52] These included an annual concert every February that was open to the Jewish and non-Jewish public. In 1961 the event showcased performances by the cantor from West Berlin and several opera singers.[53] Nonetheless, the highpoint in the Gemeinde's calendar was arguably its annual commemoration of Kristallnacht (Night of Broken Glass, also known as Pogrom Night).[54]

Cultural programs for Jewish and non-Jewish audiences could aid in relegitimizing the Jewish presence in the city, but they could also serve as official acts of anti-Nazism. In the wake of the Shoah, we cannot underestimate the importance that these public concerts held for these communities and, through them, the recognition from the public and civil authorities. If the Nazi goal had been to delegitimize the Jewish presence in the public, the authorities and communities of West and East Berlin recognized the importance of allowing the staging of Jewish self-identification and commemoration for a wide audience. Yet this was only a small part of the story.

During the cold war the East German government pursued a policy of publicly delegitimizing the West German state by, among other tactics, publicizing the names of former Nazis who continued to live and work in West Germany. The goal was to discredit the West German state and its various agents, highlighting its own supposed lack of racism and emphasizing the degree of denazification that East Germany had undertaken (and West Germany had not). Public demonstrations of solidarity with Jews and events commemorating Jewish persecution were rhetorical tools in the cold war between the two Germanies. The rhetoric spoke far more to the non-Jewish aspirations than to Jewish memory, especially because over time

Holocaust survivors—seen as "passive" victims of the Holocaust—were accorded fewer privileges than the "active" and ideologically motivated "fighters against Fascism."[55]

On top of this, as the Jewish population of East Berlin (and East Germany more generally) declined and membership in the official Gemeinde decreased, the synagogue came to have even greater importance as a space for the visible confrontation of *non-Jewish* Germans with the Nazi past. For those who hoped to live an observant Jewish life, the lack of a religious Jewish community thus became problematic. A year after leaving East Germany in 1984, Peter Honigmann summarized the situation of the remaining Jews in East Germany succinctly in *Tribüne* magazine: "When there are more Christians present in the synagogue for religious services than Jews, and when this becomes a permanent condition, soon the Jew feels like a living museum piece. And in fact he will be enlisted exactly in this capacity."[56]

As the East Berlin synagogue gradually evolved into a non-Jewish space harnessed to cold war ends and the number of practicing Jews declined, other Jews derived their self-identification from a shared past and sought each other out in different spaces. For them, informal modes of meeting were the only platforms for the expression of any type of Jewish belonging. Barbara Honigmann recalled the social world of her parents, who had spent the war in England and came to live in East Berlin after the war for ideological reasons. Not being religious, her parents were among those East Berlin Jews who felt solidarity with other Jews and émigrés as a result of their similar heritage and fate. They would gather with friends who had emigrated during the war at Die Möwe, an artists' club opened in 1946, which provided comfort in the face of their alterity; it was a club "in which no one, at least, had to suspect the other of being a Nazi."[57] Like Jews in West Berlin, they too sought out a sheltered space that brought together others from the same *Schicksalsgemeinschaft*. The war and its experiences, in this case persecution and exile, conditioned a new and particular form of belonging.

PARIS

By the end of the war the Nazis and French collaborationist authorities had sent one-fourth of the Jews living in France to their death.[58] Through deportations and murder, the Jewish population of Paris had lost 70,000 members by the time the city was liberated in August 1944.[59] The death toll amounted to nearly half the number of Jews living in the city right after the Nazi occupation began in 1940. In addition to the massive loss of life and trauma of the occupation, the overall disorder and shortages at the war's end further added to the challenges faced by the Jewish community. Looking forward, the Jewish community of Paris faced an unprecedented and enormous task of rebuilding.

As had been the case in Berlin, the immediate postwar situation was characterized by harsh conditions, food shortages, and a lack of proper housing; there were nevertheless a series of striking differences. The Jews of Paris (and France more broadly) faced several unique challenges in the postwar era. First, in France there was a different national narrative at play, one that included a thoroughgoing denial of the participation and complicity of non-Jews in the carrying out of the Final Solution on French soil. Many Jews who came back to Paris to recover their property faced hostility upon their return, and the heart-wrenching stories of parents and relatives who tried to find and reunite with children who had been placed in hiding during the war made international headlines well into the early 1950s.[60]

One of the most pressing issues faced by the Parisian Jewish community was how to help the large number of orphaned Jewish children who had survived the Shoah.[61] Historian Katy Hazan estimates that there were 8,000–10,000 abandoned or orphaned Jewish children in France alone, including children whose parents were simply unable to care for them;[62] David Weinberg suggests that the number hovered between 5,000 and 15,000.[63] Jewish groups such as the OSE had the task of finding the children who had been sent into hiding and establishing homes for Jewish children who had nowhere else to go (including those returning from concentration camps). The significant number of displaced persons coming through the country as well as the large number of Jews who needed help in France in general placed huge amounts of strain on communal resources. The postwar task of rebuilding the Parisian (and French) Jewish community was thus immense and relied largely on a variety of local[64] and foreign Jewish organizations, especially the JDC.[65] Yet, even in the face of these enormous challenges, by 1946 "Paris housed nearly two hundred different Jewish organizations representing every religious, ideological, and political strand that had been present before the war."[66]

The task of rebuilding became even more complex as the Parisian Jewish community began to grow after the war, with Jews from Central and Eastern Europe immigrating to France.[67] By the time of the Suez Canal crisis in 1956, a second influx of migrants from Egypt had come to France. They accounted for roughly 7,000 individuals. With Moroccan and Tunisian independence (1956), the Franco-Algerian war, and the Évian Accords (1962), which ended the conflict, the Jewish population of France had swelled, gaining 235,000 Jews between 1956 and 1967.[68]

The growth of the Sephardi population dramatically altered the demographic composition of Paris and its Jewish cultural-religious content. The neighborhood of Belleville,[69] which by the interwar years had become "the largest immigrant Jewish community in Paris"[70] and a center of Yiddish life with ateliers, shops, cafés, and unions,[71] was transformed through this North African migration into a Jewish immigrant neighborhood of another kind.[72] Despite this important demographic change by the end of the period under examination, the case of Paris demonstrates a significant degree of continuity in institutional and practical forms. Yet changes in politics, the longer process of secularization, and the numerous repercussions of the Shoah shaped the changing content of Jewish belonging during the 1950s. Thus forms of sociability and the spaces in which it took place remained noticeably consistent across the century, even as the political messages evolved.

Continuing a widespread practice already popular by the turn of the twentieth century, various organizations held balls and parties to raise funds for various causes. In numerous cases groups that had been created long before the Shoah continued to function in Paris. For example, the Union Scolaire, founded in 1882, held their annual "Grand Bal" on Saturday, February 9, 1952, at the Salle des Ingénieurs des Arts et Métiers; the event included live musical performances, a buffet, and a fundraising raffle.[73] As before, the Union Scolaire was also engaged in a variety of additional activities; for example, the organization held educational talks and organized theater performances and dances.

Aided by the Consistoire, the Union Scolaire also promoted a combination of secular and religious Jewish education for the young. On the one hand, the group continued to appeal to universalist interests. Various lectures included presentations such as "A Look at Modern Jazz" and "French Opera in the 17th Century—Lully." The group also continued to encourage Jewish learning, pride, and self-identification. Other lectures featured discussions of leading secular Jewish figures, such as Einstein (subject of the ambitiously titled lecture "The Life and Works of Einstein"), presenting a new set of heroes for Jewish audiences, just as topics like *Pirke Avot* (Ethics of the Fathers) sought to add a strong foundation in Judaism to the array of educational resources.[74] On the other hand, the group also began to encourage the learning of Hebrew, suggesting more recent and broader acceptance of Zionism and the newly created State of Israel (a distinct break in political attitudes from those widely held before the Holocaust), and further organized lectures on Israel, including one in April 1957 titled "Israel and Its Accomplishments." The Union Scolaire clearly tried to appeal to a wide Jewish audience by using older methods and themes but also by adopting newer political messages.[75]

The importance of Zionism and the State of Israel were clear features of postwar French Jewish attitudes. Another grand fundraising gala held at the Hotel Continental on October 19, 1953, aimed to pay for Jewish children to travel to Israel. The previous trip had sent 300 children.[76] A brochure published by the Comité national des colonies de vacances en Israël (National Committee on Holiday Camps in Israel, part of the broader Fédération sioniste de France) announced in 1954 with much enthusiasm that the organization aimed to send 500 children during the summer vacation of that year. In the preceding three years, the group had "only sent 600 children." More work was needed, the brochure suggested, to protect the children from the "vast ocean of assimilation that surrounds us."[77] Numerous French Jewish organizations were convinced that the state of French Judaism was abysmally poor and in dire need of "rejudaization."

The process of secularization had certainly played a role in the social world of Jews in the city. As much as various associations and religious organizations in Paris had long attempted to determine the contours and content of Jewish identity and give it both a spiritual and institutional basis, memoirs suggest that other Jews found solidarity beyond their walls. In addition to the kosher restaurants in the city, a number of cafés emerged in the 1950s as sites where Jews could publicly socialize with one another, as annual guides for Jewish travelers noted.[78]

Henri Raczymow recounted in his memoirs how he and his younger brother would accompany their grandfather to a café on the corner of boulevard de Belleville and the rue Ramponneau, where their grandfather treated them to a drink of their choice.[79] Still a center for Yiddish and Eastern European Jewish life into the 1950s, cafés in Belleville catered largely to the men of the neighborhood, notably on Shabbat, when they would have the day free from work. Raczymow likened the social world of the boulevard of his grandfather during the 1950s to a synagogue, making explicit the process by which consumer and leisure spaces became central sites for secular Jewish belonging: "It was their very own *shul* [synagogue], the boulevard, and they had fresh air too."[80]

For Raczymow and many others, the boulevard and the café had created a de facto Jewish space that was more relevant, it would appear, for them as Jews than the synagogue. The tension between religious authorities and secular senses of belonging that had already emerged in the early twentieth century (if not earlier) became considerable sources of tension between the Jews of the city and the religious and communal leaders of the city. Much of the latter's efforts, especially those directed at children, were focused on combatting the apparent widespread dejudaization, a phenomenon believed to be all the more threatening to the future of Judaism in the wake of the Shoah.

Many sectors of the postwar Jewish community believed that the future of Jewish children—orphaned or not—was a critical issue and posed a central challenge to their efforts to keep French Jewry alive. By the post-Shoah years, parents, Jewish educators, and communal leaders had arrived at a clear conclusion: Jewish leisure spaces for children were essential for the future of Judaism. The Consistoire therefore played a much more significant role than it had before World War II by funding and founding Jewish spaces for youths and children. Informal education became an important part of the communal agenda, and vacation camps and youth clubs sought increased attention and funds.[81]

At the same time, the motivations behind the renewed interest in Jewish summer camps, for example, stemmed not merely from the desire to foster positive Jewish identities; they also explicitly emerged in reaction to the assumed dangers posed by Christian camps.[82] The fear of Christian proselytizing, rather than abating over the century, had grown in the wake of the Holocaust. The experiences of numerous Jewish children during and after the Shoah conditioned this anxiety. In many instances, Jewish children survived the Holocaust because Christians had helped rescue and hide them. Yet, in some instances, these children had been baptized (with or without the consent of their parents). At the war's end, as family members returned to claim these hidden children, not all were welcomed with open arms. Instead, a number of Christians refused to return the children and were at times even supported by members of the church in their refusal to reunite children with surviving family members. The famous Finaly affair (named after the two young Jewish boys at the heart of the story) would take nearly eight years to resolve, and only at its conclusion were the two boys reunited with their aunt, but not before being baptized *after* the war and hidden by church officials.[83]

It is perhaps not surprising, then, that after the war many organizations created programs specifically for Jewish children. In 1950, for example, a variety of French Jewish organizations—including the Colonie Scolaire, the OPEJ (Oeuvre de protection des enfants juifs; Organization for the Protection of Jewish Children),[84] the OSE, and the EIF—went to great lengths to organize summer vacations for several thousand Jewish children between the ages of 10 and 18. During these vacations, the children played, spent time in nature, and participated in Jewish studies.[85] In 1955 about 5,000 children attended 35 summer camps, in addition to a number of children who went abroad.

Reflecting the diversity of the Jewish community in Paris, different camps offered distinct programs for the children. The Foyer ouvrier juif (Arbeter Heim, or the Workers' Home) sought to foster Yiddish and Hebrew and culture. The CRJTF (Conseil représentatif du Judaïsme traditionaliste de France; Representative Council of Traditional Judaism in France) largely attended to the condition of North African Jews living in France. The Cercle amical (Arbeter-Ring, or Workers' Circle) promoted Yiddish language and culture, and Yechouron offered a summer camp for religiously observant children.[86]

What all camps had in common was their mutual concern for the physical health of the children and their ability to cater to the needs of Paris's diverse Jewish population. The sponsoring organizations frequently provided summer vacations free of charge for children in financial need or subsidized the costs of attending. Many of these organizations relied on other philanthropic associations, including the JDC, the CBIP,[87] and, after its founding in 1950, the FSJU (Fonds social juif unifié; United Jewish Social Fund), to garner the needed funding to provide subsidized vacations. A central task was to make Jewish belonging and Judaism relevant and meaningful. Although each group expressed a distinct form or angle of Jewish self-identification, they all shared a common devotion to transmitting Jewish self-identification to the children and promoting solidarity among them.

The consensus on the usefulness and necessity of holiday camps was expressed in an article in the *Journal des Communautés*, which began, "No one any longer doubts the importance of vacation camps for the rejudaization of our children." The author continued, "For the vacation camp [*colonie de vacances*] is an excellent means of bringing to us a large number of young Jews who risk being lost to Judaism." The camps, with their "Jewish ambiance" and their "Jewish instruction," were ideal spaces to teach Jewish history and values.[88]

The recognition of the potential of leisure spaces as popular venues and as sites through which particular visions of the Jewish future could be molded prompted the Consistoire to participate more proactively in subsidizing and creating summer camps. They, too, shared in the desire to "bring Jews back to Judaism" and renovate the spirit.[89] To these ends, the Consistoire increasingly promoted Jewish leisure spaces, working with various youth organizations and helping to create additional Jewish youth clubs and "homes,"[90] including the Centre des Jeunes. Opening in 1955, the Centre des Jeunes organized various activities, including sports activities, a movie club, a choir, a drama group, and music classes; the center itself also housed a library along with photography, ceramic, and painting studios. In addition, it offered kosher food, observed Jewish holidays and Shabbat, and held Friday evening services.[91] By 1958 the Centre des Jeunes also offered Hebrew classes, had a television and a ping-pong room, and boasted 800 young members. Not to be outdone, the organization also ran annual summer camps and a winter ski camp.[92] The center's organizers might have hoped that the wide variety of leisure activities would encourage Jewish children and youths to participate, but their goal was to use the space and the activities held there as a means to offer access to Jewish education and a Jewish framework. Put otherwise, the children and youth might have come for the ping-pong, but it was hoped they would stay for the Jewish values, or at least come away learning more than how to paint.[93]

Even those over the age of 18 were targeted by such educational-spatial solutions. Under the auspices of the CBIP, the Toît Familial was created to house young adults enrolled in postsecondary educational institutions.[94] The goal was to help students both materially, in the face of widespread housing shortages in the city, and spiritually, to provide postsecondary students with a Jewish milieu.[95] An undated introduction and list of rules for the house states that the Toît Familial had the goal of bringing together "Israelite students registered in courses at the faculties or schools of higher education, to establish bonds of fraternity between them and to contribute to the harmonious development of their personality. In a familial atmosphere, they can complete their knowledge of traditional values of Judaism and its history."[96] The organizers designed the home for the accommodation of 100 male students and included a music studio, workout room, bicycle storage room, common room, a library, and a garden.[97] From its opening in 1955, the young men began to organize activities, including a cinema club and their own journal.[98]

Youth and children's spaces continued to be created for the express purpose of building and fostering their emotional, physical, and personal well-being as individuals but especially as Jews. Creating and strengthening solidarity among them was deemed vital for the future of the community. The widespread popularity of such spaces suggests their perceived need among parents, educators, and organizers and perhaps also points to a degree of their success. By the 1950s the Parisian Jewish community already had a long history of Jewish spaces designed for Jewish youth and children. The creation of Jewish spaces in the post-Shoah era, often helped by the Consistoire, the JDC (in the immediate postwar era), and other Jewish philanthropic agencies, reflected the belief that Jewish education, solidarity, and self-identification could and ought to be fostered in a variety of spaces. After the war the number of Jewish children from Paris participating in Jewish summer camps, youth movements, and clubs would only grow.

The combination of numbers and openness distinguished the success and variety of Jewish spaces for children, youth, and adults in Paris from those in Berlin and Leningrad. Unlike postwar Berlin, postwar Paris continued to have a sizable Jewish population, one that had the necessary manpower and means to offer a larger variety of Jewish sites (even if much of the money came initially from the United States). In contrast to Leningrad after the late 1920s, the Jews of Paris for most, though of course not all, of the period under study were fortunate to enjoy an open and welcoming social environment that permitted the growth and development of different Jewish movements and organizations, and the narrative of inclusion was one that French Jews and French authorities were eager to tell and retell.

The memory of the Holocaust was harnessed in immediate ways to strengthen the Jewish community and to reassert republican values and make claims for Jews' full civic inclusion in the Fourth Republic. Despite certain assumptions to the contrary,[99] Jewish organizations and especially the Consistoire set about publicly and officially commemorating the Holocaust soon after the war, even if in some cases these early efforts at commemoration involved heated debate.[100] Local political contexts influenced and colored Holocaust commemoration in Paris, just as it had in Berlin and would in Leningrad. Whereas in East Berlin the Holocaust was read into a story of the cold war and the general struggle between capitalism and socialism, in Paris early Holocaust commemoration on the part of Jews was largely subsumed into a republican and assimilationist narrative.[101]

Commemorative events included annual public ceremonies, first at the Drancy internment camp and then from 1948 onward at the main consistorial synagogue on the rue de la Victoire; two memorials were also erected (one at the Temple de la Victoire and the second on the rue Geoffroy l'Asnier). The memorial at the Temple de la Victoire was dedicated tellingly to "the memory of our brothers who fought in the war and in the liberation, martyrs of the resistance and of the deportation, and to all victims of German barbarity."[102] Universalist in its attention to all victims of the war, the wording also clearly ignores the French collaborators by insisting that the real enemy had been Germany. The unveiling of the monument took place in early 1949 and was attended by the French president, Vincent Auriel, a remarkable and almost unprecedented aspect of the ceremony.[103]

In addition to the monuments, annual ceremonies held at the Temple de la Victoire reiterated republican narratives and infused them with a religious Jewish message. In 1958 the "Memory of the Victims and Heroes of the Deportation" ceremony, held at the Temple de la Victoire, for example, began with the afternoon *minhah* prayer service and was then followed by the "entrance of the flags." The ceremony alternated religious motifs with secular republican ones. Thus, after the recitation of the memorial prayer Av Ha-rahamim (Father of Mercy), Rabbi Bauer's speech, and the recital of the funeral prayer El Male Rahamim (God Full of Mercy) and the mourner's Kaddish, the ceremony continued with a commemorative bugle call used by the French army (the *sonnerie aux morts*), a minute of silence, and the *sonnerie aux champs*, another bugle call used to greet high military officials. The ceremony ended with the Prayer for the Republic, yet another traditional Jewish prayer, Yimlokh (And God Shall Reign), and the evening prayer service (*maariv*).[104]

The back and forth between Jewish religious texts and French republican (and military) features and between liturgical and musical recitations in the annual ceremonies confirmed year after year a republican model of official French Jewish identity. Over the years French governmental personnel attended various ceremonies. In addition to the presence of the French president at the 1949 unveiling ceremony, at the 1954 service the Jewish press noted that a significant number of local and national French officials attended. The repeated presence of government representatives gave further support to the new political policy of "reconciliation."[105]

LENINGRAD

The process of closing and dismantling openly Jewish religious and cultural spaces, institutions, associations, and clubs in Leningrad had already been largely completed before World War II. Yet Soviet Russian policy toward Jews, especially in cities such as Leningrad, was never coherent. It oscillated between tolerance of expressions of Jewish culture that were or could be made compatible with the political and ideological goals of the state and clear antisemitic persecution.[106] On the one hand, the Soviet authorities sponsored and developed a number of Jewish national institutions, including Jewish sections of the Communist Party; during World War II the Jewish Anti-Fascist Committee was foremost among them.[107] On the other hand, the postwar period under Stalin witnessed unprecedented antisemitism.

Yet the experience of the war and the ways in which it was later integrated into collective memory further highlights the profound differences between the Jewish experience in Leningrad and that in Paris or Berlin. On a simple, factual level, the inhabitants of Leningrad experienced World War II quite differently from the inhabitants of Paris or Berlin (Jewish and non-Jewish alike). Whereas Leningrad's Jewish population was saved from Nazi occupation and the death camps by virtue of being physically outside the killing zone, the siege of Leningrad brought devastation to nearly all residents of the city. For 872 days, from late 1941 to early 1944, the city was blockaded by Nazi forces and continually bombed. Rations during the winter of 1941–1942 were at starvation levels, and a massive famine was the result; the death toll was staggering.[108]

The immediate postwar era did not bode well for Soviet Jews. In Leningrad and in Soviet Russia more generally many Jews preferred to maintain relatively weak connections to Judaism and understood their Jewish self-identification in personal terms, if at all.[109] This distance to Judaism only grew in the late Stalinist years in the face of deepening and widespread antisemitic persecution. Seen as internal threats to the nation, Soviet Jews became the targets of officially sanctioned and organized antisemitism, which was expressed in the anticosmopolitan campaigns beginning in the late 1940s and culminated in the doctor's plot in 1952–1953. The death of Stalin in March 1953 put a stop to the persecution, and the following years saw amelioration in the condition of the Jews and their place in the Soviet public. During the "thaw" under Khrushchev, there was even a sense of cautious optimism, though this too was short-lived.

As a result of both this antisemitic persecution and the fact that religious ceremonies and practices were ideologically out of step, only a devout minority of Soviet Jews participated in Jewish rituals, and the only public Jewish space was the highly monitored Choral Synagogue. The devout minority of the city's Jewish community who desired to participate in religious ceremonies and maintain Jewish religious observance felt that their activities required a level of secrecy, and this had immediate repercussions for the place in which Jewish education and various religious ceremonies took place. For Jews who wanted their children to prepare for and become bnai mitzvah in Leningrad, the project involved a great deal of secrecy, particularly in the first years after World War II, when antisemitic persecution still raged under Stalin.

Berta Ioffe, the daughter of the former rabbi of St. Petersburg and Leningrad, Rabbi David Katzenellenbogen, briefly recalled how her sons prepared for their bar mitzvah ceremonies in the early years after World War II. Their preparation—learning Hebrew, grammar, literature, and Bible—was done in secret, as was the celebration of the event: "We celebrated their bar mitzvah, of course, entirely secretly, we were utterly *conversos* [the author uses the Hebrew term *anosim*], like *marranos* in medieval Spain."[110] This comparison to the earlier dangers faced by converso Jews living under the threat of the Inquisition reflects not only Ioffe's sense of secrecy in her family's Jewish practice but also how she interpreted the dangers of openly practicing Judaism in Soviet Leningrad. Like conversos, her family had to outwardly appear to have converted to the general system of belief; in Leningrad this was, of course, communism. Only at home and secretly could they celebrate their real faith. The remaining Jewish population, by her analogy, either lived a double life or internalized the public conversion.

Other accounts of secret bar mitzvah preparations and ceremonies from the post-Shoah period further demonstrate the peculiar quality of the Soviet bar mitzvah in postwar Leningrad. In 1950 Avraham Belov's eldest son, Eliyahu, celebrated his bar mitzvah in the family home. The family was observant and nationalist; Avraham had taught his son Hebrew from an early age. He also prepared his son for the bar mitzvah ceremony, studying various biblical passages, including the binding of Isaac, the stories of Joseph and his brothers, and the first chapter of the book of Isaiah, and selections from rabbinic literature (including *Pirke Avot*), the prayer Nishmat Kol Hai,[111] a poem by Hayim Nahman Bialik, "Mete midbar ha-ahronim" (The Last Dead of the Desert), and another poem by Shaul Tchernichovsky, "Ani ma'amin" (I Believe).[112] To conceal the fact that they were holding a religious celebration in the building and to explain the large number of guests, the family told their neighbors that they were having a double party on the occasion of the son's birthday and the father's completion of a book. To buy their neighbor's good will, the family visited them before the event and gave them various snacks and treats. In reality, of course, they had invited a sizable group of friends and family to celebrate Eliyahu's bar mitzvah.

The young boy read the "Binding of Isaac" in Hebrew and Russian and recited the poems by Bialik and Tchernichovsky from memory. In addition, Abraham gave a speech on the meaning of the two poems, though he made no mention of the nature of his remarks in his memoirs. After the ceremony, all present enjoyed a "festive mid-day meal of traditional Jewish foods." Following the meal, a family friend who played the piano accompanied the family and guests as they sang "old and beloved Jewish songs" and even "contemporary Israeli" songs.[113]

As one of the few remaining Jewish sites in the city, the family home was an essential space for the practice and transmission of Jewish self-identification. In this space Jews could sing Hebrew songs, eat Jewish food, and celebrate Jewish rituals together. The home allowed for the expression and continuation of Jewish self-expression and ritual and was one of the only spaces that afforded the requisite privacy. The Belov family might have thought that the political climate of the time warranted their caution in keeping Eliyahu's bar mitzvah a strictly private affair, limited to close family and friends. Later examples, however, suggest that the same perceived need for privacy continued, despite the political thaw.[114] Later examples also highlight the religious inclinations of the families who chose to hold such celebrations.

For example, Rabbi K., born to a religious family after the war, celebrated his bar mitzvah around 1959. His Jewish education began at an early age, and various members of the Jewish religious community, including the shohet (ritual slaughterer) and the mohel (man who performs ritual circumcisions) of Leningrad, taught him Yiddish and Hebrew in a private location. He celebrated his bar mitzvah not in the city of Leningrad but in a "summer camp," again purposefully beyond the gaze of others.[115] Far from being a regular summer camp, this camp was organized by elders of the community, and the bar mitzvah was held in a private home with a full minyan (quorum of ten men) and directed by a rabbi. Rabbi K. stayed two days but no longer. The entire experience was veiled in secrecy, much like his overall observance of Jewish ritual at the time.[116]

Thus, despite the political thaw and decline in official expressions of antisemitism, space for Jewish life and religion was highly restricted in Leningrad. The late 1950s witnessed only passing attempts to revive Jewish culture and life in the capital city. The experience of the Holocaust, the memory of the war, antisemitic persecution under Stalin, and then expectations for cultural renewal during the thaw were all reflected in one rare instance of Jewish public gathering in Leningrad. In 1957 the Department of Culture connected to Leningrad's trade unions together with a number of interested Jewish actors organized a Yiddish-language musical and theatrical group.[117] Performing in the culture club of the Svetoch paper factory in April 1958, the group presented excerpts from a rendition of Sholem Aleichem's Dos groyse gevins[118] and a patriotic, pro-Soviet monologue by an old Jewish woman who had lost her sons and husband at the front during World War II.[119] The unusual event caught the attention of the Soviet Yiddish press. The Folks-Shtime (Warsaw) reported that "the concert made a deep, unforgettable impression on all audience members. The artists received much applause. and baskets of fresh flowers from the appreciative hall, for the great pleasure that they created."[120]

Beyond any sense of enjoyment the performance might have elicited, the event was remarkable for its engagement with war memory. Commemoration in Berlin (East and West) was predicated on an awareness of a particularly Jewish angle to the story, even if in East Germany this aspect was frequently downplayed in favor of the experiences of the more "active" socialist and communist fighters. In Soviet Russia, by contrast, the great patriotic war was understood and commemorated as a universal struggle for the nation that in the end privileged the memory of Russians and communists over Jews and other ethnic victims.[121]

The monologue by an old Jewish woman whose sons and husband had died at the front conformed in many ways to the universal narrative of valor on the battlefield and common suffering through military struggle with the Nazi-Fascist enemy. In this way it probably also helped the performance to pass the censor's audit. However, the universalist message was disrupted profoundly by the subsequent singing of a song that ended with lyrics from the well-known "Song of the Partisans (We Are Here)," so named because the song ends with the words "Mir zenen do / Mir zenen vider do" ("We are here / We are here again").[122] The allusion to the partisan's song broke with the Soviet narrative. Considered an anthem for Holocaust survivors, it was written in 1943 by Hirsh Glik, a member of the socialist-Zionist Ha-shomer Ha-tsair (The Young Guard). His song was perhaps "the most emblematic and well known of the ghetto songs." Ostensibly a partisan song, it "was less a battle cry than a defiant affirmation of Jewish endurance."[123]

In a rare moment, a specifically *Jewish* memory of World War II was staged for a crowded audience. It is unlikely that this message was lost on those present, and the reprinting of those particular lines in the Yiddish press out of Warsaw suggests that the song was especially significant. This brief case of public Jewishness, produced for and consumed by a Jewish audience, is indicative of the poor state of Jewish life in Leningrad. Although those in the audience might have hoped that the refrain "We are here, we are here again" could be taken as a sign that Jewish life in Leningrad had again become legitimate, with the benefit of hindsight we know that this dramatic production was episodic. The Yiddish theater production in Leningrad offered a momentary possibility for Jewish selfhood—or at least a state-sponsored and partially sanitized version of it—to be expressed openly and on stage, but it could not satisfy any need for spaces of Russian-language Jewish culture. The performance had little actual meaning or importance for the future of Jewish public space and belonging in Leningrad. And herein lies the biggest challenge that Jews of Leningrad faced.

Attending a performance in Yiddish might have been emotionally or personally moving—evoking nostalgia for a bygone era, the familial language and culture now largely erased—but it amounted in effect to a performative museum exhibit. Meaningful Jewish culture in Leningrad after World War II almost necessarily would have had to have been in the Russian language for it to have resonated and offered a deeper connection to the majority of Jews living in the former capital. It was the absence of Russian Jewish culture that was devastating for the city's Jews. Instead, Jews found that the private apartment was one of the few spaces to hold necessarily private gatherings (as it was for all Soviet citizens), and this made the reproduction and dissemination of Jewish culture difficult.[124]

Yet it was in fact in an apartment that years later, in the mid-1970s, another group of Jewish artists—this time visual—gathered together to hold an exhibit of their works. The Aleph Group,[125] as they called themselves, displayed Jewish folk art and self-portraits in the Leningrad apartment of Evgeny Abezhaus. The practice of holding politically "nonconformist" art exhibitions in private homes had become popular in the mid-1970s, and this Jewish expression was a reflection of this larger pattern. Visited by several thousand people in less than a week, the art show became another rallying point for the display and celebration of Jewish self-identification in the city.[126] By this time, the Jewish protest movement had solidified. No longer did numerous Jews of the city hope for officially sanctioned Jewish culture; they rebelled against its suppression. For a significant section, though not the majority, of the Jewish population of Leningrad, the search for Jewish expressions merged with Jewish nationalist aspirations and political dissatisfaction.[127]

Conclusion

In this chapter I have returned to several of the major themes explored throughout this book—how modern spaces of leisure and consumption served in the creation of Jewish solidarity and the education of children and youth—and have explored how patterns that began in the early twentieth century at times manifested themselves in the post-Shoah era. The story of contingent continuities is in itself noteworthy. Jewish individuals in Paris and Berlin (especially West Berlin) continued to seek out meaningful connections to other Jews through leisure spaces and consumer sites; summer camps continued to serve as important sites of children's education, even gaining in importance and popularity in Paris. In both Paris and Berlin the official Jewish communities increasingly played instrumental roles in the creation of Jewish social spaces.

Yet Jewish life in the early years of the cold war differed considerably as well, both from city to city and in relation to the prewar years. The devastating effects of the Shoah and the political-ideological distinctions between various regimes contributed in momentous ways to the lives of the Jews living in each city. The legacies of persecution and genocide in Berlin and Paris could be felt on a number of levels. The Jews of West Berlin appeared to favor communal insularity just as they sought to continue or rebuild their lives on this unsettling ground. Jews in East and West Berlin again hoped to encourage their children's formal and informal education through summer camps, but only to note with distress their small numbers. In Paris the concern for the youngest members of the community revealed religious struggles over hidden children and only increased the anxiety felt over the future of Jews and Judaism in France. The Jews of Paris, though stronger in numbers, also faced challenges of both asserting their desire again to be part of the republican ethos and confronting the forgetfulness that stood behind the national narratives of resistance and bravery.

Cold war ideologies made their way into self-understanding and influenced institutions. Soviet attempts to suppress distinctly Jewish forms of self-identification, which began before the war, continued to determine the general absence of Jewish culture, religion, and life in Leningrad. Yet the desire to give voice to some sense of particular Jewish belonging occasionally broke through the surface, even if it reflected the positions of a minority of the largely disinterested Jewish population. Cities that had, at the turn of the twentieth century, shared much in common, by 1945, at the latest, came to follow different trajectories and expressed quite distinct answers to questions of Jewish belonging and practice.

Epilogue

European Jews over the first half of the twentieth century sought spatial solutions to the existential questions raised as Jewish communities became more individualized and voluntary. European Jews, under these new circumstances, attempted to define, create, and express their commitment to Judaism and Jewishness using tools at their disposal. To these ends, they employed existing consumer and leisure spaces and created new sites in order to build homes in Europe. These places allowed Jews to expand the array of Jewish expressions, gathering *as* Jews in a remarkably different set of spaces from those frequented by previous generations. By carrying out these activities in semipublic spaces, Jews were able to perform new modes of self-identification, which became part of the Jewish cultural vocabulary. This spatial transformation radically changed the face of the Jewish community, because individuals were able, more than ever before, to establish and maintain Jewish affiliations that were neither dependent on nor limited to the demands and expectations of the official religious community. This process allowed them to create bonds of friendship and solidarity in new ways and places, revolutionize the nature of the Jewish family, change the ways in which Jewish values were transmitted to future generations (in addition to the nature of these same values), and alter the face of Jewish celebration. By the post-Shoah era, the spatial revolution that had begun in the late nineteenth century had been consolidated. This spatial revolution transformed Jewish life from the intimate sphere of the family to the wider level of the community. It allowed many individuals to form—through a change in social practice and not just through a shift in rhetoric—their own distinct Jewish belonging based on personal prerogative and individual choice.

Yet what also emerges from this discussion is that the lachrymose narrative of Jewish history, which reduces the long tale of Jewish life in the Diaspora to the story of repression, oppression, and survival despite all odds, does injustice to a longer and much richer history. It is also simply incorrect. All too often it has been assumed that the persecution of the Jews created solidarity among them and, conversely, that tolerance toward them led to the weakening of communal bonds and ultimately to their complete assimilation into the wider society. My work shows the opposite. In the modern era, the more open a society has been, the greater the number of ways Jews could affiliate with and express their sense of solidarity with the Jewish community and Judaism. Jewish belonging thrives in places of choice, and Jews find more reasons and ways to remain connected to their culture and to each other in cities and countries with multiple viable options.

Jews in Paris enjoyed the greatest and the most consistently supportive environment for the creation and display of Jewish belonging of the three cities under study. The demographic strength of the community, coupled with a generally and comparatively more tolerant social environment across most of the nineteenth and twentieth centuries, helped foster a fertile space for the development of multiple expressions of Jewish self-identification and for the flourishing of Jewish life—socially, culturally, and religiously—despite the anxiety that was frequently voiced over the future of Jews and Judaism in that city (and country). Indeed, modern Judaism in France and elsewhere has changed, and the process of secularization has led to an experience geared to and based on the desires of the individual. Although some might bristle at these changes, transformation is not the same as the demise of the culture or religion.

On the other hand, the closure of almost all Jewish social, leisure, and religious spaces in Leningrad significantly limited the forms and scope of

Jewish expressions. With the Bolshevik consolidation of power, the shutting of consumer-based sites of sociability,[1] and the progressive closure of formal Jewish spaces, Leningrad's Jews were left with few actual outlets in which to build, express, and promote Jewishness and Judaism. Despite the size of the community, which was similar to that of Paris in the post-Shoah era, expressions of Jewish culture and solidarity were scarce. The lack of Jewish sites of sociability had a significant effect on the marriage market and resulted in high levels of mixed marriage. The question of exogamy touched Jews of Paris and Berlin as well,[2] but spaces of Jewish sociability and leisure in the post-Shoah era offered greater options for the Jewish marriage market for those who desired an endogamous union.

The Jews of Leningrad had limited access to Jewish education, little opportunity for religious practice (whether Orthodox or liberal), few cultural activities and social programs, and no organized programs for Jewish children. In addition, Jewish holy days and rituals were largely ignored by most of the Jews of the city, frequently out of fear that public or even semipublic celebration could have negative repercussions in other realms of life. Simply put, by the postwar period most Jews in Leningrad did not live actively Jewish lives, however defined. The lesson of Leningrad is quite simple. Persecution does not create community and belonging but has the power to extinguish the flame of faith and community.

This general insight—that the variety of places for the expression of Jewish belonging proportionally affected the scope of Jewishness—was at the forefront of the minds of post-Shoah Jews in Paris and Berlin. After the war, as these communities sought to rebuild, they looked to their past and yearned to recreate at least part of that former life. By midcentury the Jewish public had come to expect a wider social and cultural program that would cater to different guises of Jewish belonging beyond strict religious definitions. This expectation is above all evident in the variety of social spaces created for Jewish children and youth. Originating in the prewar era, these sites served as templates for how Jewish values could be transmitted to future generations. In the post-Shoah era, parents and community leaders continued to turn to these sites precisely for this reason.

In this book I have explored the new patterns of Jewish belonging that emerged in the early twentieth century and that, for all practical purposes, remained the model along which Jews in Western Europe and North America continued to affiliate for the better part of the twentieth century.[3] Yet the realities of early-twenty-first-century Jewish life in the Diaspora seem to raise an essential question regarding the viability of such forms and spaces of commitment in the long run. That these changes have happened is irrefutable. We can note how Orthodox and even Haredi communities, most noticeably the Chabad-Lubavitch movement, have followed some of the trends we have surveyed, albeit to promote their own exclusive form of Judaism.

Chabad in particular has also capitalized on communal anxieties and emotional longings that are in themselves not unlike what we have observed since the late nineteenth century—namely, Chabad has succeeded in many ways by, first, pointing to a clear decline in Jewish observance and a perceived weakening of Jewish belonging, and, second, positioning themselves as the representatives of "authentic" Judaism ready and willing to step into the perceived void. The popular Jewish concerns over authenticity and the appeals to a romanticized (and necessarily homogenized) past have allowed Chabad to echo concerns voiced for now well over 100 years in the Jewish press.

These debates over authentic and viable Judaism and Jewish belonging have made their way into academic discourse as well. Zvi Gitelman has recently offered a litmus test for the viability of a culture, arguing that "[Jewish culture] should be more than symbolic and be able to constrain and direct behavior"; it should also "be transmissible across at least three generations."[4] In his reading, no expression of modern Jewishness has really emerged and remained a lasting anchor to a nonreligious expression of Jewish identity.[5] Certainly, if we follow his definition, we must concede that the modes of Jewish belonging that were fashioned in consumer and leisure spaces, by their very nature, resisted the ability to "constrain and direct behavior" and were particularly attractive, at least initially, because of their nondogmatic, relaxed nature. According to Gitelman, this would be a sign of their weakness: "The vast majority of Jews in the Diaspora give only occasional expression to their Jewishness. It is a pastime, not a vocation; a luxury, not a necessity; occasional rather than constant and all embracing. How much stamina does thin culture have?"[6] Gitelman's questions and answers demonstrate grave concern if not downright pessimism for the future of Jewish culture, a sentiment familiar to so many writers in the Jewish press across the twentieth century.

Are pessimism and anxiety therefore permanent states for Jews in the Diaspora? Must we assume that if most Jews are not continually aware of or focused on their Jewishness, there is an existential threat to the community? To be sure, Judaism for most Jews is no longer a way of life as the vast majority had practiced it before the modern age. At the same time, the transformation of Judaism and Jewishness in the modern era is not a problem or challenge particular to Jews but a result of fractured and multiple senses of self that are expressed and experienced by all members of modern society. We might instead focus on the continued need for a conscious dedication to pluralism, choice, and the maintenance of multiple forums for interaction—not in order to create one unified form of solidarity but to enable multiple and overlapping expressions of it, to create homes away from home.

Notes

NOTES TO INTRODUCTION

1. Staatsarchiv Hamburg, Polizeibehörde-Kriminalwesen C Jahrgang 1819, Nr. 199, pp. 1–4.

2. In many ways this book is an investigation of the multifold secularization processes among European Jews. I have taken preliminary inspiration on the nature of secularization from the work of Karel Dobbelaere, who notes several overlapping definitions that are relevant to my study. I see secularization as linked to the decline of community and the rise of the individual—a process that is related to autonomy and freedom, according to which the "'autonomous' individual is free to follow his own subjective preference." Of equal importance is the fact that this same process has generally taken place in the capitalist West, where "the private sphere is consumer-oriented" and "the 'autonomous' consumer selects certain religious themes from the available assortment" (Dobbelaere, *Secularization*, 33, 34). For more on secularization and Jewish history, see Joskowicz and Katz, "Introduction."

3. On the diverse paths to emancipation, see Birnbaum and Katznelson, *Paths of Emancipation*.

4. Again, Dobbelaere notes the personal search for meaning. See Dobbelaere, *Secularization*, 143.

5. Volkov, "German-Jews," 5.

6. Valensi, "Multicultural Visions," 198.

7. In his introduction to *Hannah Arendt in Jerusalem*, Steven Aschheim cites Dan Diner's distinction between the Western and Eastern Jewish narratives: Western Jews' identity is fragmented, whereas Eastern Jews' sense of self is based on collective, national experience. This strikes me as a false dichotomy that romanticizes the Eastern European experience and overlooks the radical changes to that society and the sense of dislocation expressed. Aschheim, "Introduction," 2–3.

8. Feiner, "Pseudo-Enlightenment," 67.

9. S. R. Hirsch, "Religion," 224. These transformations began slowly in the eighteenth century and have been noted by such historians as Azriel Schochat (Shohat), Jacob Katz, Jay Berkovitz, and Shmuel Feiner. See Schochat, *Der Ursprung*; Katz, *Tradition and Crisis*; Berkovitz, *Rites and Passages*; and Feiner, *Origins of Jewish Secularization*, 7–10. Feiner provides in the cited pages a historiographic survey of this debate.

10. M. A. Meyer, "How Awesome," 59.

11. On the history of consumerism, see Williams, *Dream Worlds*; Auslander, *Taste and Power*; Grazia, *The Sex of Things*; Roberts, "Gender"; V. Schwartz, *Spectacular Realities*; Strasser et al., *Getting and Spending*; Tiersten, *Marianne in the Market*; Confino and Koshar, "Regimes of Consumer Culture"; and Reuveni, *Reading Germany*. On consumption and consumerism and Jewish history, see Heinze, *Adapting to Abundance*; Wobick-Segev, "Buying"; Wobick-Segev, "German-Jewish Spatial Cultures"; Lerner, *Consuming Temple*; Stein, *Plumes*; Kobrin and Teller, *Purchasing Power*, esp. the introduction; and Sutcliffe, "Anxieties of Distinctiveness."

12. It is particularly interesting to note the historiographic interest in leisure culture in Imperial Russia. See Stites, *Russian Popular Culture*; and McReynolds, *Russia at Play*. Jeffrey Veidlinger notes that "the commercialization of leisure through theaters, nightclubs, restaurants, tourist groups, and movie houses transformed the ways that middle-class Russians spent their time" (Veidlinger, "Jewish Cultural Associations," 199).

13. This statement might come as a surprise when we include the Soviet Union in the investigation. Yet, as David Shneer has correctly noted, we cannot or should not back-project the purges and antisemitism of the late 1930s or the post-Shoah period onto the 1920s. Jeffrey Veidlinger, David Shneer, Kenneth Moss, and Anna Shternshis, among others, have shown how "Soviet Jewish cultural activists were actively, not passively, fostering Jewish identity" (Shneer, *Yiddish*, 3). See Moss, *Jewish Renaissance*; Shternshis, *Soviet and Kosher*; and Veidlinger, *Moscow State Yiddish Theater*.

14. For example, Endelman, "Introduction"; Caron et al., *Jewish Emancipation Reconsidered*; Green, "Modern Jewish Diaspora"; Sorkin, "Enlightenment"; V. B. Mann, *Tale of Two Cities*; Stein, *Making Jews Modern*; Knörzer, *Expériences croisées*; Kleinmann, *Neue Orte*; and Hyman, "Two Models." Finally, the awareness of internationalism and connections among Jewish communities and organizations across national borders is another important turn in the research. See Leff, *Sacred Bonds*.

15. Based on secondary literature, it would appear that Warsaw, for example (along with other cities), could offer an equally illuminating and comparable case study. For example, Scott Ury's recent work on the revolution in 1905 explores the importance of the Jewish public sphere, including cafés and theaters. See Ury, *Barricades and Banners*, esp. ch. 4. Yet, including Poland in this monograph would exceed my linguistic competencies.

16. By 1872 the Jewish population of Paris amounted to 25,172 individuals, according to the census. See Hyman, *Jews of Modern France*, 1, 58; and Philippe, *Les juifs à Paris*, 20.

17. The migration wave had significant repercussions on the Berlin Jewish community more broadly, as the number of native-born Jews became proportionally much less than the number of Jews born in other provinces. See Lowenstein, *Berlin Jewish Community*, 3, 11; and Königseder, *Flucht nach Berlin*, 19, 21.

18. Höppner, "Ostjude ist jeder." Höppner ascribes the phrase to a "bon mot" of Jacob Toury.

19. Horowitz, *Empire Jews*. For a discussion of the overlap between liberalism and nationalism among Jews in Russia, see Horowitz, *Jewish Philanthropy*.

20. Acculturation and liberal politics were also options that motivated and inspired European Jews, even in Russia. See Horowitz, *Empire Jews*. Also, on the influence of antisemitism on the increased sense of Jewish solidarity, see Wiese, "Modern Antisemitism," 145.

21. To be sure, Brian Horowitz's book on the OPE also refutes a simplistic view of the OPE as a "liberal" organization. It was politically far more complex: "The activity that took place in the society cannot simply be categorized as bourgeois, nationalist, radical, liberal, or conservative. Some individual members fit in several categories at once, and as people changed, so their classifications also changed" (Horowitz, *Jewish Philanthropy*, 11).

22. Charnow, "French-Jewish Identity," 66–67. By the 1920s we can find any number of examples of greater interest in Jewish topics and an overall process of closing of ranks. On changes made in Germany to the CV in interwar years, see, for instance, Barkai, "Deutschtum and Judentum," 78. The Bnai Brith in Germany also turned inward in certain ways. Consider the small but revealing example of a concert of Jewish folk songs hosted in the large hall of the Kleist Lodge by the cantor Leo Gollanin. See *Monatsschrift der Berliner Logen* (June 1927): 43.

23. For example, consider Zweig, *Face of East European Jewry*; and Ansky, *Enemy at His Pleasure*. Russian and German Jews especially found themselves writing about the war and a renewed sense of collective Jewish belonging. Jews in France joined in this desire for explicit togetherness in the interwar years, and this influenced the interactions between "natives" and new Jews. See Malinovich, *French and Jewish*, 108–15.

24. For a full discussion of this process, see Nathans, *Beyond the Pale*, 45–79; and Altshuler, *Soviet Jewry*, 219. Problems concomitant with census data are well known and are nowhere more acute than in Russia, where these data often reflect censuses asking about religion and mother tongue. For a critical discussion of these censuses, see Kleinmann, *Neue Orte*, 136; and Nathans, "Mythologies," 108. On top of these more local challenges, population statistics are always troublesome and certainly are no less problematic in the field of Jewish history. Questions of identification, self-identification, religious or ethnic origin, and language all come into play in Jewish census data. Issues of official communities and illegal ones in St. Petersburg make the data even more complicated and only partly reliable. The situation in France is particularly complicated because official censuses ceased inquiring about religion in 1872.

25. See Stanislawksi, *For Whom Do I Toil*, 109; and Nathans, "Mythologies," 122.

26. Weinberg, *Les juifs à Paris*, 8. Scholars estimate that the Jewish population in Paris rose to the low 40,000s between 1880 and 1890. Philippe, *Les juifs à Paris*, 20; Nord, *Republican Movement*, 64. The bulk of the Russian Jews who settled in France did so after 1905 and left as a result of worsening economic conditions. Scholars mark 1905 as another year of pogroms and, of equal significance, as the year that

Great Britain closed its borders to refugees. Patrick Weil, "De l'affaire Dreyfus," 107. From 1906 to 1939, between 150,000 and 200,000 Jews came to France and predominantly settled in Paris. Hyman, *Dreyfus to Vichy*, 31.

27. Maurer, *Ostjuden in Deutschland*, 76.

28. For a history of the OSE near the end of and after World War II, see Hazan, *Les orphelins*.

29. This was the third newspaper to bear this title. Beizer, *Jews of St. Petersburg*, 25. On the detailed history of the various names changes—and there were several—of this journal, see Slutsky, *Ha-itonut*, 203n3.

30. Foucault, "Of Other Spaces."

31. Accordingly, the earlier model of religiously based and sociopolitically autonomous *kehillot* was replaced by a model of voluntary associations, which could include religious institutions but was not centered on them. Philippe, *Les juifs à Paris*, 81–82, 119–23. In a similar vein, since the 1990s, historians have made extensive inroads into the associational history of the Jews in Germany and France, and somewhat more recently historians of Russian Jewry have taken up a similar task. For several examples, see Pickus, *Constructing Modern Identities*; Hofmeister, *Selbstorganisation*; Lässig, *Jüdische Wege ins Bürgertum*; Baader, "Rabbinic Study"; Sorkin, *Transformation of German Jewry*; and Mosse, *German Jews*. For further examples of how sociability, leisure, and associationalism have made their way into the recent historiography, see Brenner, *Renaissance of Jewish Culture*; Malinovich, *French and Jewish*; Veidlinger, *Jewish Public Culture*; Veidlinger, *Moscow State Yiddish Theater*; Moss, *Jewish Renaissance*; Shneer, *Yiddish*; Shternshis, *Soviet and Kosher*; and Nathans, *Beyond the Pale*. And no work of this kind could be conceivable without the groundbreaking contributions of Marion A. Kaplan; see M. Kaplan, *Jewish Middle Class*.

32. The early interest in specific spaces was sparked in no small part because of the publication and later translation of Jürgen Habermas's *Strukturwandel der Öffentlichkeit*, published in English as *The Structural Transformation of the Public Sphere: An Inquiry into a Category of Bourgeois Society*. In this work Habermas paints a narrative of a bourgeoning, politically active public sphere, the foundation of democracy. The politics of associations and certain spaces of gathering, such as coffeehouses, thus caught the attention of historians. Since then, the popularity of Habermas's thesis has waned, but historians have continued to be interested in connections between behavior and social spaces. Other theoreticians, such as Pierre Bourdieu, have been invoked, and scholarly discussions have been reoriented to focus on practices in which all forms of consumption are conspicuous and create distinction. Bourdieu, *Distinction*, 31, 55.

33. Lipphardt et al., "Exploring Jewish Space," 2; Kümper et al., *Makom*; Schlör, *Das Ich der Stadt*; B. Mann, *Place in History*; Gilman, "Introduction"; Baker, *Rebuilding*; Benain, "Bâtissez des maisons"; Fonrobert and Shemtov, "Introduction"; Herz, "Institutionalized Experiment"; Roemer, "City of Worms"; Gregor et al., *German History*; Pinsker, "House of Study"; Pinsker, "Urban Literary Café"; Miron, "Lately."

34. Space, a seemingly "neutral, pre-given medium," a companion to time, is frequently presented as the field on which "the particularities of culture and history come to be inscribed, with place as the presumed result." Accordingly, human experience and culture emerge in the context of a "blank 'space' to which placial modifiers . . . are added" (Casey, "How to Get from Space to Place," 14, 15).

35. Edward Casey reminds us that knowledge emerges from experience and that experience is by its nature localized and specific. Places themselves are not merely locations but are linked to our interactions in them; places "happen" just as much as they exist. Casey, "How to Get from Space to Place," 16, 27.

36. In addition to a growing interest in space, there has been a clear increase in the number of studies on the cities themselves. For several notable examples, see Clark, *Petersburg*; Buckler, *Mapping St. Petersburg*; Steinberg, *Petersburg*; Kelly, *St. Petersburg*; Webber, *Berlin*; Föllmer, *Individuality*; Harvey, *Paris*; and Rearick, *Paris Dreams*.

37. Heidegger, "Building, Dwelling, Thinking."

38. Gluck, "Budapest Flâneur," 8.

39. Cohen, "Nostalgia," 131.

40. Hödl, "Turning to History."

41. Cohen, "Nostalgia," 131–32. David Harvey notes that authenticity as a concept is modern. See Harvey, "From Space to Place," 12.

42. Mark Steinberg's recent and excellent study, which explores modernity in Russia through the case of St. Petersburg, offers an extended analysis of modern urbanity, its spaces, and the emotional experiences and rhetorical utterances made about them. See Steinberg, *Petersburg*.

43. Harvey, "From Space to Place," 17, 21.

44. Harvey, "From Space to Place," 23. On everyday life and its connection to emotions, see Matt and Stearns, "Introduction," 3.

45. Harvey, "From Space to Place," 22. Much of this thinking has its origins in the works of Henri Lefebvre, more recently interpreted by David Harvey and Edward Soja. See Soja, *Thirdspace*. Lefebvre suggests a three-way dialectic between the materiality, representation, and imagination of a given place. Lefebvre, *Production of Space*.

46. Frevert, *Emotions in History*, 213.

47. Matt and Stearns, "Introduction," 2.

48. Foucault, "Of Other Spaces," 24.

49. Foucault, "Of Other Spaces," 25.

50. Kesten, *Dichter im Café*, 12–13; translation mine.

51. Foucault, "Of Other Spaces," 27.

NOTES TO CHAPTER I

1. Agnon, *Twenty-One Stories*, 72–78.

2. For a few examples, see Simmel, "Metropolis"; Ruppin, *Jews in the Modern World*; and Benjamin, *Das Passagen-Werk*.

3. In modern Jewish literature, consider the following writings: Bergelson, *Shadows of Berlin*; Döblin, *Berlin*; and Vogel, *Married Life*. On David Vogel, see Abramson, "Vogel and the City." Abramson notes that, "whether or not the poets had been affected by the First World War, they expressed an awareness of an evil embodied in some kind of massive force against which they could not prevail. The city becomes 'the emblem of an insoluble historical crisis'" (Abramson, "Vogel and the City," 46). This image was not simply a literary trope. Béatrice Philippe notes that "in the warmth of the backrooms of Parisian cafes or in very modest homes, the up-rooted comforted their identity [*confortent leur identité*]: in other places, other immigrants, Poles, Italians or even Corsicans and Bretons tried, too, 'to not lose their soul in the big city'" (Philippe, *Les juifs à Paris*, 123; translation mine).

4. Hyman, *Jews of Modern France*, 91–92.

5. Paula Hyman notes that "the social mobility of French Jewry and their integration into state institutions was more far-reaching than in any other European country" (Hyman, *Jews of Modern France*, 95).

6. By 1897 a growing number of intellectuals began to support Dreyfus. Yet a key moment in the affair came with Emile Zola's publication of "J'accuse . . . !" in the newspaper *L'Aurore* on January 13, 1898. See Hyman, *Jews of Modern France*, 104.

7. Hyman, *Jews of Modern France*, 96–97.

8. Also consider the example of Edmond Fleg, as cited in Malinovich, *French and Jewish*, 54–56.

9. Hyman, *Jews of Modern France*, 125; Green, *Pletzl of Paris*, 165–71.

10. Pulzer, *Jews and the German State*, 88.

11. Pulzer, *Jews and the German State*, 114–17.

12. Pulzer, *Jews and the German State*, 152–53.

13. In addition to the clear anti-Jewish policies of Tsars Alexander III and Nicholas II, we can also point to the attitudes and influences of antisemitic individuals in the government, including Konstantin P. Pobedonostsev, who served as the chief procurator of the Holy Synod and was instrumental in drafting anti-Jewish legislation in 1882.

14. Frankel, *Crisis*, 59.

15. In 1904 the Russian intelligentsia began what was called the banquet campaign and in 1905 founded the Union of Unions. The growth of a public sphere allowed for Jewish liberals to join and give voice to specifically Jewish issues, and they proceeded to create the Soiuz dlia dostizheniia polnopraviia evreiskogo naroda v Rossii (Union for the Attainment of Full Rights for the Jewish People in Russia), which was open to all Jewish political groups and gave voice to Jewish concerns (e.g., demands for equality). Gassenschmidt, *Jewish Liberal Politics*, 19–22. For more on the banquet campaign, see Emmons, "Russia's Banquet Campaign."

16. Horowitz, *Jewish Philanthropy*; Horowitz, *Empire Jews*.

17. Horowitz, *Jewish Philanthropy*, 178.

18. Veidlinger, *Jewish Public Culture*, 8, 16–18.

19. Brian Horowitz notes that, "although Jewish nationalism took various forms

in the two decades before October 1917 . . . the central point for all these groups was that the Jews were entitled to political self-determination as individuals and to collective cultural rights as a nation" (Horowitz, *Jewish Philanthropy*, 169).

20. Benbassa, *Histoire des juifs*, 208, 231.

21. Vogt, *Subalterne Positionierungen*.

22. Stites, *Women's Liberation*; Anderson, *Utopian Feminism*; Edmondson, *Feminism in Russia*; Engelstein, *Keys to Happiness*; Reagin, *German Women's Movement*.

23. Béatrice Philippe suggests that Jews transformed the basis of their identity around the concept of associationalism. Quoting Annie Kriegel's *Les juifs et le monde moderne*, she argues that "the Jewish group did not find itself dissolved, but transformed partly by the changes that affected its internal mechanisms, and partly by its exposure to a global society undergoing urbanization and industrialization, in which aggressively secular themes centered on the nation, democracy and science" (Phillippe, *Les juifs à Paris*, 126; translation mine). Other scholars who have explored the emergence of distinct (and modern) Jewish identities through social and cultural change include Sorkin, *Transformation of German Jewry*; Lässig, *Jüdische Wege ins Bürgertum*; Brenner, *Renaissance of Jewish Culture*, 20, 32–33, 35, 46; Malinovich, *French and Jewish*, 3, 25; Moss; *Jewish Renaissance*; Veidlinger, *Jewish Public Culture*; and Nathans, *Beyond the Pale*.

24. As Michael Brenner has noted, "The Jewish renaissance in literature, art, music, and scholarship was no return to traditional Judaism but an attempt to integrate selected aspects of this tradition into the framework of a modern secular culture. And it was the task of the modern organizations to promote such a renaissance" (Brenner, *Renaissance of Jewish Culture*, 21). Also consider the writings of Richard I. Cohen and Klaus Hödl in regards to the role of history and nostalgia: Cohen, "Nostalgia," 130–155; and Hödl, "Turning to History," 17–32.

25. In this sense Jews were much like other Europeans; they adopted new leisure patterns on the basis of their means, interests, free time, and the larger market availability of particular activities. Memoirs make clear that across Europe middle-class Jews were often avid theatergoers and frequently attended the opera and various concerts. For instance, see Leibovitch, *La moitié de beaucoup*, 26–28. Leibovitch grew up in St. Petersburg. Evgeniia Isidorovna Gintsburg went to charitable concerts and was active in the local music scene; see Gintsburg, *Vospominaniia ionosti*, 31. Balls were also popular, especially before World War I. Some brought together Jews and non-Jews. See Dr. Adolf Asch, *Memoiren*, Leo Baeck Institute/Jüdisches Museum Berlin, MM3, pp. 2–3. Asch worked in Berlin as a lawyer from 1908 to 1914. Alexander S. Spiegel writes of mixed sociability and of attending concerts and balls in Petrograd; see Spiegel, *Through Fire and Water*, 47, 56–57, 62.

26. The Bestuzhevskie Courses were named after the first director of the program, Konstantin Nikolaevich Bestuzhev-Riumin. They were also known as the Higher Courses for Women at St. Petersburg University. Ironically, it was the fear that women who went abroad to pursue higher education (e.g., to Switzerland for medical training) would bring back radicalism, which motivated the Russian government

to permit the establishment of the Higher Courses for Women in May 1872. Stites, *Women's Liberation*, 77, 81. See also Vygodskaia, *Story of a Life*, 76–78.

27. Vygodskaia, *Story of a Life*, 99 (on dancing), 102–6, 124–25.

28. Of the handful of cafés mentioned in the Baedeker guidebook for Russia, for instance, all but one was located on Nevskii Prospekt. Baedeker, *Russia*, 90.

29. Cheaper public spaces for dining, or *traktiri* (a Russian tavern-like establishment), had a much longer history in Russia, but they were far from modern, fashionable restaurants. On the history of Russian dining before the mid-nineteenth century, see Smith, "Eating Out." See also Goldstein, "Gastronomic Reforms"; and Khmel'nitskaia, "Restorannaia zhizn'." For a discussion on the legal and bureaucratic challenges faced in the Imperial era by owners of *traktiri* and restaurants, see Khmel'nitskaia, "Eda davno minuvshikh dnei." Khmel'nitskaia has written extensively on the subject of restaurants, public dining, and leisure culture in late Imperial Russia, and this was the subject of her dissertation, "Stolichnyi dosug v nachala XX veka: Peterburg i Moskva." The Baedeker guidebook for Russia from 1914 tells the curious traveler that restaurants open at 11 a.m. and remain open until 2 or 3 a.m., serving lunch from noon to 2 p.m. and dinner from 5 to 8 p.m. The guide further explains that "beer-saloons, tea-rooms (*Traktir*), and eating-houses or cook-shops (*Kukhmisterskaia*) are frequented by the lower classes only. *Cafés* exist in a few towns only" (Baedeker, *Russia*, xxvii).

30. Jews were free to choose their place of dwelling in St. Petersburg—affordability was the determining factor. Nathans, "Mythologies," 113–14, 122, 128–30. Yet wealthier Jews tended to live in the Kazanskaya area (between the Griboyedov Canal and the Moika River in the district of Plekhanov Street) and in the Spasskaya area (along Sadovaya Street between the Griboyedov Canal and Fontanka). Jewish craftsmen and intellectuals settled in the Moskovskaya area (around Zagorodny Prospekt). Beizer, *Jews of St. Petersburg*, 7; Kleinmann, *Neue Orte*, 136–39.

31. Karl Schlögel, *Petersburg*, 238–39. As much as individual Jews might have gone to the relatively few cafés in the Russian capital, Jewish belonging was staged elsewhere in the city. One simple though partial reason for this difference is that there were comparatively far fewer cafés in St. Petersburg than in Paris and Berlin, and those that did exist in the city were recent additions to the city landscape. Jews in St. Petersburg went to cafés as individuals (and to be sure they did use other consumer spaces to meet and associate), but the city's few cafés did not attract Jewish literary or artistic circles in the same way that those in Berlin or Paris would. Instead, the literary cafés in Imperial St. Petersburg served the interests of individuals and literary movements, but not Jewish groups. A further impediment to the popularity of cafés for collective Jewish organization, certainly among literary figures, was the age of those who might have gathered there. As Shachar Pinsker has noted, the "café scene was uncomfortable to the premodernist generation of Hebrew and Yiddish writers and intellectuals," including Simon Dubnow, Hayim Nachman Bialik, Mendele Moycher Sforim, and Ahad Ha'am (Pinsker, "Urban Literary Café", 441). This also potentially limited the number of Jewish

literary coffeehouse guests in the Russian capital. Perhaps most critically in the long run, however, was the fact that the Russian Revolution cut short any possible evolution of literary cafés in Petrograd and helped propel growing waves of Jewish refugees westward. Instead of finding a literary home in the cafés of the Imperial Russian capital, many Russian and East European Jewish authors found themselves working and socializing in the coffeehouses of 1920s and 1930s Berlin and Paris. Regardless of the cause, the fact that cafés did not function as sites for the creation or reproduction of Jewish culture is itself one of the key differences between the three cities.

32. For example, Rössner, *Literarische Kaffeehäuser*; Ellis, *Coffee House*, 220–24; Bollerey, "Setting the Stage," 47; Im Hof, *Das Gesellige Jahrhundert*; Grévy, "Les cafés républicains"; and Haine, *World of the Paris Café*.

33. "An hour may be pleasantly spent at one of the small tables in front of the cafés on the Boulevards in watching the life of the streets. Most of the Parisian men spend their evenings at the cafés, where they take coffee, liqueurs, or beer, meet their friends, read the newspapers, or play billiards or cards. Letters also may be written at a café, the waiter bringing writing-materials on application. . . . Good bands play in the evenings at many of the cafés and brasseries, especially on the boulevards" (Baedeker, *Paris*, 24–25). Similarly, the numerous cafés in Berlin provided newspapers, billiard tables, and stationery to write letters, in addition to a long menu of drinks that included alcoholic beverages. See Baedeker, *Berlin*, 11–12.

34. Baedeker guides for the cities of Paris and Berlin and the guide for Russia all took care to note accommodations and eateries where women could comfortably stay or eat alone, and they also highlighted those locales with less than salubrious reputations. The Polish Café in St. Petersburg was "frequented by ladies for luncheon," whereas the Old Donon restaurant was "frequented by the demi-monde at night after the theatre" (Baedeker, *Russia*, 89–90). The Paris and Berlin guides listed hotels where women traveling alone could stay and restaurants that could "without hesitation be visited by ladies," at least so long as they wore the "customary . . . evening dress" (Baedeker, *Paris*, 18; Baedeker, *Berlin*, 5, 8). The Paris guide, however, also advised that Maxim's Bar-Restaurant was "frequented mainly at night (for gentleman only)." Other restaurants were noted as being "similar to Maxim's," including three near the place Pigalle, leaving little doubt that temporary female companionship was also available for a price (Baedeker, *Paris*, 18, 23).

35. Philippe, *Les juifs à Paris*, 31; Green, *Pletzl of Paris*, 71.

36. "Most Jews who opted [to keep French citizenship] in Alsace-Lorraine emigrated to Paris and its suburbs. Between 1866 and 1872 the Jewish population of Paris increased from 20,615 to 23,434, a jump of 16 percent" (Caron, *Between France and Germany*, 72).

37. Philippe, *Les juifs à Paris*, 33–34. Between 1872 and 1905–1907, the proportion of immigrant Jews rose from 16% to 61%.

38. Green, *Pletzl of Paris*, 87–90.

39. Central Archives for the History of the Jewish People, Jerusalem, F Pa 26,

unnumbered documents. Café Trésor had been a haunt for Russian Jewish militants years earlier (e.g., it was a favorite with anarchists near the end of the 1880s). Their activities also included concerts and balls. Green, *Pletzl of Paris*, 97–98.

40. The Chambre syndicale des casquettiers was founded in 1896 and was dominated by poor, Yiddish-speaking Jews from Russia. Michlin, *Aucun intérêt au point*, 32; Green, *Pletzl of Paris*, 134. Cafés were not the only spaces to function in this way. Nancy Green notes that "Razenshtroych's restaurant was a known recruiting center for capmakers, furworkers, and jewelry workers; the furworkers' union section established a more formal placement office at Lander's restaurant" (Green, *Pletzl of Paris*, 89).

41. Philippe, *Les juifs à Paris*, 34, 37.

42. Philippe, *Les juifs à Paris*, 39–41.

43. Philippe, *Les juifs à Paris*, 34–35.

44. Haine, *World of the Paris Café*. Scott Ury notes the intersection of cafés and Jewish politics in the case of Warsaw. See Ury, *Barricades and Banners*, 151–53.

45. Michlin, *Aucun intérêt au point*, 33.

46. The café presently has a website on which one can find a small amount of historical background. See www.lecaféducommerce.com (accessed February 2, 2017).

47. Michlin's father, for his part, belonged to a burial society of Polish Jews (*hevra kadisha*): "Once a year, we went to the cemetery of Bagneaux, where my father and the other members of the association gathered before the headstones in the Jewish section and then left to find a café where everyone would drink schnapps and eat cake" (Michlin, *Aucun intérêt au point*, 29–30; translation mine).

48. Valensi and Wachtel, *Jewish Memories*, 199; Bunim, "Sur les traces," 48–49.

49. Valensi and Wachtel, *Jewish Memories*, 199.

50. Lowenstein, *Berlin Jewish Community*, 16–18.

51. In addition to Café Bauer, which was not Jewish owned or kosher, one could find restaurants that did serve kosher food, including Baumanns Restaurant on Friedrichstrasse 58 (circa 1903). See the advertisement for this establishment in *Schlemiel: Illustriertes jüdisches Witzblatt* (November 1, 1903): 7.

52. Ostwald, "Berlin Coffeehouses," 184, 186. Café Monopol was also known to the authorities because of its diverse clientele. The Königlichen Polizei-Präsidii zum Berlin kept a list of establishments (*Lokale*) that "primarily foreigners frequented." A list from 1909 includes five establishments where "Russians" met, including the well-known "Caffee Monopol" on Friedrichstrasse and an establishment named Simon at Gipsstrasse 12a. The second address is telling because it makes clear that Russians as a group could be synonymous with Russian Jews. Until 1904, Gipsstrasse 12a had been the home of the synagogue for the separate Orthodox community, Adass Jisroel, which in that year moved to its new location on Artilleriestrasse. In early 1905 (perhaps even in late 1904), the Restaurant Simon opened its doors, serving kosher food under the supervision of Adass Jisroel. See Landesarchiv Berlin, A Pr. Br. Rep. 030, Nr. 13503, Bl. 158 recto, 159 recto/verso, 160 recto. On the location of the synagogue of Adass Jisroel, see Hilker-Siebenhaar, *Wegweiser durch das jüdische*

Berlin, 153–60. On Restaurant Simon, see their ad in the *Israelitisches Familienblatt* (Hamburg) (January 5, 1905): 18.

53. Itamar Ben-Avi, translated and quoted in Nash, *In Search of Hebraism*, 173.

54. Nash, "Tmunot," 5–6. Aschheim, *Brothers and Strangers*, 94.

55. Ostwald, "Berlin Coffeehouses," 185.

56. Unsurprisingly, the bourgeois Café Bauer became a popular spot among certain literary circles. Pinsker, "Urban Literary Café," 451.

57. The newspaper directory from 1889 lists 348 titles from Africa, America, Asia, Australia, and many from Europe. At any given moment, Café Bauer had up to 600 publications and a staff responsible specifically for providing guests with the desired reading materials. Petras, *Das Café Bauer*, 52; Grafe, "Café Bauer," 119.

58. Henriette Hirsch, "Erinnerungen an meine Jugend," Leo Baeck Institute / Jüdisches Museum Berlin, MM38, p. 32.

59. Pinsker, "House of Study," 92–94; Pinsker, "Urban Literary Café", 449–53.

60. Pinsker, "Urban Literary Café," 451; Estraikh, "Vilna on the Spree," 112.

61. Goldmann, *Jewish Paradox*, 21.

62. The Romanisches Café frequently served both as a topic of their writings and as a motif therein. See, for example, Ehrenburg, "Briefe aus dem Café"; and Ehrenburg, *Viza vremeni*, 10–20. See also Lasker-Schüler, *Else Lasker-Schüler*, 2: 276. Leah Goldberg also mentions the café in her own *Letters from an Imaginary Journey*; see Pinsker, "House of Study," 90.

63. Paris, Berlin, and St. Petersburg (before the Bolsheviks came to power) all boasted notable cafés where artists and writers met. St. Petersburg was home to the aptly named Literaturnoe Kafe (The Literary Café) on Nevskii Prospekt, a "favourite haunt of Pushkin," and the Brodiachaia Sobaka (The Stray Dog) on Isskustv Square 5, an avant-garde and short-lived literary salon known to be the haunt of Anna Akhmatova, Osip Mandelstam, Arthur Lourie, and Boris Pasternak, the first three all Jewish converts to Christianity. Fitch and Midgley, *Grand Literary Cafés*, 84–88.

64. Estraikh, "Vilna on the Spree," 113.

65. Bergelson was in Berlin from 1921 to 1933. See Murav, *Music*, 52.

66. Estraikh, "Vilna on the Spree," 114.

67. Bergelson, *Leben ohne Frühling*, 284.

68. Estraikh, "Vilna on the Spree," 114.

69. Spiegel, *Through Fire and Water*, 200.

70. Spiegel, *Through Fire and Water*, 225, 224–28.

71. Spiegel writes in typically effusive fashion that he had been instrumental in getting exit visas out of Soviet Russia for Hayim Nahman Bialik and sixteen other Hebrew writers. See Spiegel, *Through Fire and Water*, 140–49.

72. Kesten, *Dichter im Café*, 13.

73. Kesten, *Dichter im Café*, 52, 76.

74. Kesten, *Dichter im Café*, 13.

75. Abramson, "Vogel and the City," 43.

76. Bergelson, *Shadows of Berlin*, 9.

77. Kassow, *Who Will Write Our History*, 7.

78. For example, see Vygodskaia, *Story of a Life*, 89, 93. Vygodskaia noted the growing popularity of balls; even her neighbors held them for entertainment. She also pointed out that the students of the Higher Courses organized grand balls and concerts to raise funds for the program; sometimes "the best Opera singers of the Mariinskii Theater would perform at these galas" (89).

79. *Tzedakah* (variously translated as social justice or charity) was by no means a new ethical value in Judaism, but the methods used at the end of the nineteenth century definitely were.

80. Interestingly, during the Middle Ages and into the early modern era dancing was an acceptable practice among European Jews, from Sephardi and Italian communities to Ashkenazi ones. In German lands there were even dance halls built for weddings and other celebrations. By the seventeenth century, however, an increasing number of rabbis sought to put an end to this practice and to forbid dancing. See Weinstein, *Marriage Rituals*, 383; and N. Roth, *Daily Life*, 46, 88. On the prohibition against dancing, see Brayer, *Jewish Woman*, 145.

81. The question of under what circumstances it would be admissible to hear a woman sing has become increasingly relevant for ultra-Orthodox and Orthodox communities. In a discussion on a woman's public recitation of the Shema, the Talmud rules that a woman's voice (*kol isha*) is nakedness and therefore prohibited; this depiction of the female voice as nakedness is repeated in the *Shulkhan Arukh*. The debate over a woman's public recitation of the Shema was extended, however, over time to other instances of public speaking and singing. In the nineteenth century the Hatam Sofer (Rabbi Moshe Sofer) took a broad approach and prohibited the listening to a woman's singing voice in general (*Hoshen Mishpat* 190). Nineteenth-century modern Orthodox rabbis Samson Raphael Hirsch and Esriel Hildesheimer allowed women to sing with men so long as they were not individually distinguishable. Rabbi Yechiel Yaakov Weinberg's *Teshuvot Seridei Eish*, Part 2, *Siman* 8, echoed this.

82. In fact, in Berlin and Paris the popularity of balls grew during the interwar years, and such events continued to be held well after the Shoah. For examples from Berlin, see ads for a concert and ball on February 13, 1927, at the halls of the Zoologischer Garten and another ad for a ball with Jazzkapelle and cabaret on January 13, 1927, at the Spinoza Lodge in *Monatsschrift der Berliner Logen* (January 1927): cover, 193. In addition, fundraising for the Logenheim in Lichterfelde was done through a society evening and ball; see *Monatsschrift der Berliner Logen* (February 1927): 212. The *Univers Israélite* reported well into the 1930s the regular concerts and balls held by various Jewish organizations. For example, see announcements for a "grand bal de nuit" held by the Keren Kayemeth Leisrael in the "sumptuous" halls of the Washington-Palace and the "grand bal de nuit" organized by the Société de secours mutuel "Les enfants de Cracovie" at the Claridge Hotel (*Univers Israélite*

[October 28, 1927]: 186). In 1932 the Keren Kayemeth Leisrael's grand ball was held at the Salle Hoche and included a raffle. See *Univers Israélite* (October 14, 1932): 90.

83. The Hotel Continental was located at 3, rue de Castiglione. The building faces the Tuileries Garden; today it is the Westin Hotel.

84. *Univers Israélite* (February 16, 1889): 343.

85. *Univers Israélite* (March 16, 1889): 407–8.

86. The group boasted that its membership had more than doubled from 250 to 520 members in just several weeks (*Berliner Vereinsbote* [February 7, 1896]: 4). For information about Rabbi Lipschütz and the Lippmann-Tausz Synagoge, see Singermann, *Die "Lippmann-Tausz" Synagoge*.

87. H. Hirsch, "Erinnerungen an meine Jugend," 9–10.

88. For yet another example of the widespread use of balls, see *Jüdische Rundschau* (January 9, 1903): 15, where there is an announcement that the Jüdisch-Musikalische Vereinigung will have a *Stiftungsfest* with concert and ball on Saturday, January 17, 1903, in the Prachtsälen of the City-Hotel, Dresdnerstrasse 52.

89. Jeffrey Veidlinger notes that balls and gala evenings became popular across Russia in the Imperial era. See Veidlinger, *Jewish Public Culture*, 224–27.

90. "Lektsii i doklady," *Novyi Voskhod* 5.8 (February 27, 1914): 25.

91. Not to be confused with the aforementioned Blagorodnoe Sobranie. I would like to thank Professor Michael Beizer for helping me clarify the locations and difference between the two institutions.

92. *Razsviet* (January 24, 1910): 27.

93. "Breslau," *Der Israelit* (March 10, 1892): 393.

94. See Wasserman, *Shaye*, 165–68.

95. For example, the Verein Ehemaliger Schüler der Knabenschule der jüdischen Gemeinde had a meeting on Tuesday, February 24, 1903, at 9 p.m. in the Hotel zum König von Portugal on Burgstrasse 12 (*Jüdische Rundschau* [February 20, 1903]: 63).

96. As a result of the *numerus clausus* at Russian universities instituted in 1887, many Jewish students began studying in Western and Central European universities. In 1894 there were 500 university students in Paris from Russia and Romania, a number that continued to grow in the early twentieth century. By 1912–1913, more than 2,500 Russian and Romanian students attended the Université de Paris, accounting for 13.4% of the student body. See Green, *Pletzl of Paris*, 76. The numbers in Berlin were equally noteworthy. An article in *Novyi Voskhod* suggests that in the 1912–1913 school year, 10.4% of the university students in Berlin were foreigners, and of those a sizable number (41.9%) were Russian. Among these Russians, a full 97.9% were Jews (i.e., there were 499 Russian Jewish students out of a total of 9,806 university students in Berlin). In other words, 1 out of every 20 university students in Berlin was a Russian Jew. Izrael, "Russko-evreiskaia uchashchaiasia molodezh'." Interest in Russian Jewish students was a recurrent subject in the Russian Jewish press. *Novyi Voskhod* published several articles about Russian students in Germany: for example, Izrael', "Russko-evreiskaia uchashchaiasia molodezh'"; and

Novyi Voskhod (January 30, 1914): 16–18. See also M. I——ch, "K sud'bie nashego zagranichnago studenchestva," *Novyi Voskhod* (September 18, 1914): 9–12.

97. *Univers Israélite* (February 16, 1895): 340–41.

98. *Univers Israélite* (November 29, 1895): 322.

99. Not entirely unlike the CV, which was founded shortly before in 1893 and which also responded to antisemitism but over time became an "association of conviction" that brought together those who shared both a common fate and a common descent, the Vereinigung Monbijou sought to remind potential members of a shared past and future. Barkai, "Deutschtum and Judentum," 76–78.

100. See *Berliner Vereinsbote* (March 13, 1896): 1, 5.

101. "Vereinigung Monbijou," *Berliner Vereinsbote* (March 13, 1896): 5.

102. The emphasis on youth came from all directions. I explore this topic more fully in Chapter 3, but it is interesting to note here how balls were associated with youth and the younger members of the community. A commercial for "youth cream" in the pages of the *Israelitisches Familienblatt* spoke to those who attended "balls and societies," offering them the requisite "smooth, youthfully fresh" hair for a mere 3.2 pfennig. Not only was youth for sale, so was, it would appear, an assimilated physique. The emphasis on smooth hair—that is, not curly (read: not stereotypically Jewish)—resonates with ethnic self-perceptions. *Israelitisches Familienblatt* (February 19, 1903): 15.

103. "Enseignement: Union Scolaire," *Archives Israélites* (February 14, 1884): 51–52.

104. See, for example, the announcement for a ball in June 1889 held at the Salon des Familles: *Univers Israélite* (June 16, 1889): 610–11. The Union Scolaire held another ball, their first "grand bal," in 1900 to fund free memberships at the *halles* of the civil engineers (*Univers Israélite* [March 9, 1900]: 792). See also, "L'Union Scolaire," *Univers Israélite* (June 15, 1900): 401–3.

105. Lévy, "L'Union Scolaire," 758. In other words, Lévy argued that young Jews should be encouraged to participate in the "right" kinds of sociability.

106. "L'Union Scolaire," *Univers Israélite* (June 15, 1900): 401–3.

107. For example, M. F. G., "Kontsert' obshchestva evreiskoi narodnoi muzyki," *Novyi Voskhod* 1.3 (January 14, 1910): 30–32; and Nagen, "Vecher evreiskoi muzyki," 25–26.

108. Nagen, "Vecher evreiskoi muzyki."

109. Beizer, *Jews of St. Petersburg*, 160.

110. "Lektsii i doklady," *Novyi Voskhod* 5.8 (February 27, 1914): 25.

111. *Univers Israélite* (January 8, 1897): 512–13.

112. "Une conférence," *Univers Israélite* (May 20, 1898): 281.

113. See, for instance, the ad for a lecture evening sponsored by the Jüdisch-National Frauenvereinigung at Cassels Hotel (Burgstrasse 16), which featured a discussion of the book of Ruth: *Jüdishe Rundschau* (November 21, 1902): 61. And see an ad explaining that the Allgemeine Sitzung der Akademischen Gruppe was to meet on Saturday, January 24, at the Cassels Hotel for a lecture evening including a discussion about the Jews of Galicia: *Jüdische Rundschau* (January 23, 1903): 28.

114. Such activities continued well into the interwar years. In 1927 the Association général des étudiants juifs de Paris held a literary soirée at the grande salle du Petit Journal that featured Yiddish literature. *Univers Israélite* (October 21, 1927): 153.

115. "Iubilei S. A. An-skago," *Novyi Voskhod* (January 6, 1910): 20.

116. *Razsviet* (January 10, 1910): 34. Ansky participated in a variety of Jewish associational activities in the city, including the Jewish Literary Society (founded in 1908). The Jewish Literary Society had more than 800 members by 1909, a clear sign of its popularity in the city. Veidlinger, *Jewish Public Culture*, 123, 125.

117. G., "Banket v chest' S. A. An-skago," *Novyi Voskhod* (January 14, 1910): 23–24. Similarly, the life and works of Peretz Smolenskin were celebrated on his *yahrzeit* (anniversary of the day of his death) by the Society "Khoveve sfat' eiver" on March 16, 1910. Ben-Aaron, "Chestvovanie pamiati Peretsa Smolenskina v S-. Peterburgie," *Razsviet* (March 28, 1910): 30–31. In 1914 the jubilee of Ahad Ha'am was the focus of similar attention on the part of the Jewish Literary Society. *Novyi Voskhod* (March 19, 1914): 39–40.

118. "Prebyvanie prof. Germana Kogena v Peterburgie," *Novyi Voskhod* (May 1, 1914): 11–13.

119. The social-political campaign against capitalism resulted initially in the official closure of private restaurants, and public cafeterias took over in their stead. Clandestine or semitolerated private restaurants did continue to operate in the intervening years. Collective dining in the form of cafeterias remained open. It would be only under the New Economic Policy (or NEP) that private restaurants were again legalized. Borrero, "Communal Dining," 162, 163, 171–73. Despite their reemergence on the official dining scene, restaurants and public dining spaces took on cultural meanings that were in some ways incongruent with consumer patterns in the West. The role of restaurants in Soviet Russian society ebbed and flowed as their use fluctuated. Sheila Fitzpatrick notes that from about 1930 to 1934 restaurants were frequented almost exclusively by foreigners and the rare but perhaps more audacious Soviet citizen. In 1934 restaurants and leisure spaces, at least in Moscow and Leningrad, were again open to those who could afford to enjoy them. Fitzpatrick, *Everyday Stalinism*, 93. The functioning of restaurants in Soviet Russia until after World War II was severely hampered by repeated food crises and ambivalent state policies. On bread rationing, which began under Stalin in the winter of 1928–1929 and ended officially in early 1935, see Osokina, *Our Daily Bread*, 35–37, 138–44. On rationing in general, see Osokina, *Our Daily Bread*, 39, 41, 47–48, 144–48. On the food crisis, see also Fitzpatrick, *Everyday Stalinism*, 4, 41–45.

120. Altshuler, *Soviet Jewry*, 70; Beizer, "Jews of a Soviet Metropolis," 113–15.

121. Julie Hessler reminds us that there were three *major* famines in the Soviet Union between its creation and the death of Stalin: 1921–1922, 1932–1933, and 1946–1947. See Hessler, *Social History*, 5. Elena Osokina also notes the rural famines of 1929–1930 and 1936–1937; see Osokina, *Our Daily Bread*, 34–35, 158–63. Valery Gessen, the son of the famous Russian Jewish historian, offers the example of the dire situation of Jewish scholars: "Conditions for scholars were so bad that a special

commission was established, headed by the well known writer Maksim Gorky to improve their lot. The commission compiled lists of scholars who died in 1918–19 and, next to almost every name, the cause of death was shown as exhaustion and related illnesses" (Gessen, "Jewish University," 76).

122. Beizer, *Evrei Leningrada*, 360–61; Beizer, "Jews of a Soviet Metropolis," 113. With the introduction of the internal passport on December 27, 1932, migration slowed. At this time, there was a growing concern for fostering a population of "useful" workers by excluding those whose occupation was not "politically correct." Thus passports were given to those who had "useful" work, and those without passports were not permitted to stay in "closed" cities such as Leningrad. The growth rate of the Jewish population of Leningrad dropped from 17% a year before passports were introduced to 1.2% thereafter. Nevertheless, taken in sum, this demographic shift significantly altered the city's Jewish population; the population of Jews who had come to Leningrad in prerevolutionary times made up only a small segment of the overall Jewish community. Altshuler, *Soviet Jewry*, 11–12; Beizer, "Jews of a Soviet Metropolis," 115. Beizer notes that by the end of 1926, less than one-fourth of the city's Jewish population had been born in the city.

123. See Veidlinger, *Moscow State Yiddish Theater*; Shneer, *Yiddish*; Shternshis, *Soviet and Kosher*; and Moss, *Jewish Renaissance*.

124. Throughout the Soviet era, Jews were recognized as a national minority and many found work within the party, especially in the early years. Jews were Russian Soviet citizens, individuals before the state, and were not necessarily or always viewed negatively. One important example of this policy, insofar as the space or institution was compatible with Soviet policy and ideological goals, was the Moscow State Yiddish Theater (GOSET), which existed from 1919 until it was closed in 1948. See Veidlinger, *Moscow State Yiddish Theater*. More generally, in the Soviet Union, various individuals shared an ideologically based suspicion of religious belief as it was expressed by Jews and members of other religious groups. Officially, Judaism was, in a way similar to other religions, "attacked in statewide propaganda, which aimed, among other things, to separate Jews from Judaism" (Shternshis, *Soviet and Kosher*, 2). Yet this was not only a top-down process of forced secularization. Jewish communists also participated in the early campaigns against obscurantism. The goal of these early participants was to create good communist citizens, who were, if anything, Jewish by nationality but not by religion. Shternshis, *Soviet and Kosher*, 9, 14–43.

125. "Palestinskaia nedielia v Petrogradie," *Razsviet* (April 21, 1918): 28–29.

126. Beizer, "Jews of a Soviet Metropolis," 116.

127. E., "Vospominaniia starogo evreia," Central Archives for the History of the Jewish People, Jerusalem, P200, pp. 1–2, 4; Beizer, *Evrei Leningrada*, 335–50. The club of Gatikvo was located at Torgovaia Street 11. See "V Petrogradie," *Razsviet* (July 21, 1918): 43.

128. The Jewish university was established circa 1919. Berta Ioffe recalled the importance of this institution in her life. Upon completing her university studies

(presumably at the Petrograd State University) and leaving the student milieu, she wrote that she found herself in a vacuum. By chance, a former teacher "dragged [her] to some lecture at the still extant Jewish University." It proved to be a turning point; from then on, she began attending the Jewish University, living on "questions of Jewish culture." Her account raises more questions than it answers, though. She states that she attended the Jewish University between 1924 and 1930. Yet the Jewish University faced serious problems in 1924 and was closed in 1925 (along with many other Jewish institutions). To be sure, Jewish educational organizations continued to exist, including the *rabfak* (workers' faculty) of the St. Petersburg University. Despite these inconsistencies, Ioffe's account does intimate a connection between institutions of higher education, specifically those organs that were dedicated to Jewish learning, and Jewish self-consciousness during the 1920s. Ioffe, *Semeinye zapiski*, 38, 39. Scholars have noted that the Jewish university survived only until 1924 or 1925, after a short six-year existence. For the time that it was active, it served as an important site of Jewish sociability and learning, a place where Jewish self-identification and belonging were at the core of its raison d'être. Gessen, "Jewish University," 73–79; Greenbaum, *Jewish Scholarship*, 9–10.

129. Ioffe, *Semeinye zapiski*, 31.

130. Petrograd/Leningrad also was home to several eating houses and Jewish dining rooms. Several of the specifically Jewish-owned dining establishments in the 1920s included the Jewish students' dining room (near the "Sitny Market") and two private kosher dining rooms (the first on Rubinstein Street and the second, named Lahmaniya, or "dinner roll" in Hebrew, on Sadovaia Street). From roughly 1930 to 1948 a Jewish-style, though not kosher, dining room existed on Nevskii Prospekt. Beizer, *Jews of St. Petersburg*, 307–9. More generally, public eating and drinking were not abolished in the Soviet Union, but increasingly public eating took place at cafeterias and workers' canteens. See the section on elite dining in Osokina, *Our Daily Bread*, 97. See also Fitzpatrick, *Everyday Stalinism*, 93. Fitzpatrick notes that in Moscow restaurants had been open only to foreigners between 1930 and 1934.

131. Pinkus, *Soviet Government*, 2.

132. Beizer, "Jews of a Soviet Metropolis," 116.

133. In fact, by 1939 the percentage of Jewish university students had risen to approximately 20%. Beizer, "Jews of a Soviet Metropolis," 114, 120. Already before the Russian Revolution, Jews represented a significant and disproportional percentage of the student body. In 1911, 661 Jews were enrolled at the St. Petersburg University, accounting for 7.8% of all students. See Beizer, *Yehude Leningrad*, 25; and Beizer, *Evrei Leningrada*, 14. Private apartments were a site for dissident meetings, including Jewish dissidents. See Rubenstein, *Soviet Dissidents*, 159.

134. After World War II the number of Jewish students admitted to universities and colleges was significantly restricted. One outside observer and activist on behalf of Soviet Jewry noted that in 1963 Jews accounted for, across the Soviet Union, 3.1% of the student body at institutes of postsecondary education, including universities, teaching colleges, conservatories of music, and schools for journalism.

Decter, "Status of the Jews," 11. According to Mordechai Altshuler, in the 1960–1961 academic year Jews accounted for 3.2% of the overall enrollment in institutions of higher education. See Altshuler, *Soviet Jewry*, 118. Although Soviet official policy played an important role in the restriction of Jewish students from universities, thus producing these relatively low figures, we must also consider that during this time, enrollment among other nationalities consistently rose. In other words, the proportion of Jewish students was bound to decline as the number of other students increased. Altshuler, *Soviet Jewry*, 116–18. Yet "affirmative action" in favor of other nationalities was not the only cause for these restrictions in the number of Jewish students. Problems for Jewish students arose because in the late 1950s, and more significantly in the 1960s and 1970s, the number of available spaces for students in these institutions did not rise to meet the needs of this expanding student body. Altshuler, *Soviet Jewry*, 117. See also the memoirs of Professor Solomon Mogilevskii, *Prozhitoe i Perezhitoe*, 74–75; Dmitrj, "Ich faste zweimal im Jahr," in Bredereck, *Menschen jüdischer Herkunft*, 53; and Rene Mojsevic, "Es gibt nichts, wofür man kämpfen könnte," Bredereck, *Menschen jüdischer Herkunft*, 57, 59.

135. The history of the Nazi persecution of the Jews has been told in great detail elsewhere and will not be subject to an extensive investigation in these pages. I concentrate my brief remarks simply on how the Nazi persecution affected Jewish life in sites of sociability.

136. For example, see M. Kaplan, *Between Dignity and Despair*.

137. "Badeverbot" (August 22, 1933), in Walk, *Das Sonderrecht*, 48, 262.

138. "Juden ist der Besuch von Theatern, Kinos, Konzerten, Ausstellungen usw. verboten" (November 12, 1938), in Walk, *Das Sonderrecht*, 255.

139. Although Jews were banned from entering particular cafés and restaurants, they were permitted to visit others, including those owned by Jews and cafés in train stations. M. Kaplan, *Between Dignity and Despair*, 45, 59, 136; Grunberger, *12-Year Reich*, 184; Borut, "Struggles for Spaces."

140. Borck, "Ich war nie weg," 60–61. Whether or not "entirely harmless" meant not looking Jewish according Nazi stereotypes is not explicitly stated in this context, but earlier in the interview Borck does note that around 1940 she looked like "the prototype of a German child" (Borck, "Ich war nie weg," 43). The forced deportations of Berlin's Jews began in 1941. Those who would survive the Shoah were able to do so thanks to a non-Jewish spouse (whom they had married before 1935) or because they had gone underground to escape forced labor and deportations to almost certain death.

141. Various memoirs and interviews note the existence of Jewish cafés throughout the Nazi period and even during the war years. See Ilse Stillmann interview, in Herzberg, *Überleben heist Erinnern*, 160. Walter Besser gives the example of Café Dobrien at the Hackescher Markt as a Jewish café he and others frequented during the Nazi era. He even proposed to his future wife in a Jewish café sometime in early 1941 (the couple were married in March 1941). See Walter Besser interview, in Herzberg, *Überleben heist Erinnern*, 226, 235. Lili Nachama notes that Kondi-

torei Teschendorf was a clandestine meeting point of a "clique" of illegals. The owner would provide coffee and refuge to those who came in and even gave bread to those without ration cards. See L. Nachama, "In der Arche Noah," 181.

142. Borck, "Ich war nie weg," 61.

143. Between 1941 and 1943 the Nazi authorities deported the overwhelming majority of the Jews of Berlin to their deaths in the East. The process therefore gradually created a situation whereby some of the community still legally lived in the city while another smaller portion avoided deportation by going underground. M. Kaplan, *Between Dignity and Despair*, 184, 188.

144. Heilman and Friedman, *The Rebbe*, 79.

145. Heilman and Friedman, *The Rebbe*, 114, 121.

146. Heilman and Friedman, *The Rebbe*, 104.

147. Secularization is not just the leaving of religion but its change and fragmentation according to the needs of the individual.

NOTES TO CHAPTER 2

1. The changes wrought to the family as a result of the individuation of Jewish belonging were not incidental or peripheral to the structure of the Jewish community. The family and the family home have often served as the center of much of Jewish ritual and have provided the basis for the continuance of Jewish culture and civilization. Hyman, "Modern Jewish Family," 179–80. See also Hyman, "Introduction" (1986), 3, 4.

2. For more on the Jewish spa experience, see Triendl-Zadoff, *Nächstes Jahr in Marienbad*; and Bajohr, *Unser Hotel ist judenfrei*, esp. 24–25. Bajohr notes that spas functioned as a marriage market for those Jews who desired to avoid mixed marriages. See also Borut, "Antisemitism"; and Lempa, "The Spa."

3. In Germany intermarriage was made possible on February 6, 1875, when civil marriage became obligatory; in France civil marriage was introduced in 1792.

4. Hyman, "Modern Jewish Family," 184.

5. Ruppin, *Jews in the Modern World*, 40–41.

6. Hyman, "Introduction" (1986), 3.

7. Stearns, "Modern Patterns," 25–26.

8. Such was the case of Berta Ioffe, whose father was the rabbi of St. Petersburg and later Leningrad, Rabbi David Tebele Katzenellenbogen. It is not entirely unsurprising, though nevertheless not representative of the Leningrad Jewish community as a whole, that her marriage in 1931, a year after her father's death, was arranged. See Ioffe, *Semeinye zapiski*, 2, 40.

9. See Freeze, *Jewish Marriage*, 11–44, esp. 25; Katz, *Tradition and Crisis*, 114–22; and Katz, "Nisuim v-haye."

10. Katz, *Tradition and Crisis*, 115.

11. For instance, the parents of Henriette Hirsch were first cousins; see Henriette Hirsch, "Erinnerungen an meine Jugend," Leo Baeck Institute/Jüdisches Museum Berlin, MM38, p. 1. Henri Raczymov of Paris notes that his Polish Jewish grand-

parents were first cousins; see Raczymow, *Avant le déluge*, 27. Jacob Teitel married the daughter of a cousin; see Teitel, *Aus meiner Lebensarbeit*, 10–11, 16. Even after World War II, relatives might marry, as was the case with Ignatz Bubis, who married a distant cousin (their mothers were first cousins) in 1953; see Bubis, *Damit*, 80–81. Marion Kaplan discusses this phenomenon in Imperial Germany at greater length; see M. Kaplan, *Jewish Middle Class*, 114–16.

12. Günzburg, "My Father," 250.

13. Freeze, *Jewish Marriage*, 30–31.

14. U. F. J. Eyck, "Einige Bemerkungen zu dem Tagebuch von Helene Eyck," Leo Baeck Institute/Jüdisches Museum Berlin, MM2 41, p. 1.

15. Burns, *Dreyfus*, 59, 65, 81.

16. Poliakov, "Serebrianyi samovar," 34.

17. Katz, *Tradition and Crisis*, 117–18.

18. Moses Calvary, "Erinnerungen," Central Zionist Archives, Jerusalem, A225/15 (personal papers of Hans Klee), p. 7.

19. For the case of Lithuanian Jews, see Etkes, "Marriage and Torah Study," 155.

20. R. Strauss, *Wir lebten in Deutschland*, 19.

21. For instance, consider the comparison that Pauline Wengeroff makes regarding her own courtship and that of her older sister. Her sister, Eva, who married sometime in the late 1840s, was not permitted to meet her fiancé in person before the wedding. In fact, she "saw her groom for the first time in her life right before the wedding ceremony." The young couple nonetheless engaged in a seemingly affectionate correspondence before the marriage, itself an innovation in courting patterns. "The correspondence," as Wengeroff writes, "was already not without a certain sympathy, devotedness and love, but [was] definitely not rapturous. Nevertheless, one had the impression that they pined for one another, and waited and received letters with all their heart" (Wengeroff, *Memoiren einer Grossmutter*, 1: 181; translation mine). Naomi Seidman has also recently written on the two engagements; see Seidman, *Marriage Plot*, 1–6.

22. Most historians have explained the transition through a rhetorical and intellectual change that favored love marriages. To be sure, many of these scholars use the term *love marriages* as shorthand for a wider process in which individuals sought greater personal autonomy and self-expression, including in their married lives. M. Kaplan, "Based on Love," 90–91. Marsha Rozenblit has also suggested that the quest for personal autonomy, and not love, was important but that World War I was the true catalyst for changes in Jewish marriage patterns. See Rozenblit, "Jewish Courtship." Nonetheless, relying largely on the writings of nineteenth-century *maskilim* and of selected memoirists from the time, many scholars have argued that over the course of the nineteenth century "progressive" and "enlightened" individuals began urging for marriages to be based on love and personal choice. The expanding reading culture more generally introduced the avid reader to new values and customs fashionable in "progressive" circles. See Schochat, *Der Ursprung*, 287–308; Katz, "Nisu'im v-haye"; Katz, *Tradition and Crisis*, 113–31; Biale,

"Love"; M. Kaplan, "For Love or Money"; M. Kaplan, "For Love or Marriage"; Maurer, "Partnersuche und Lebensplanung"; Budde, *Auf dem Weg ins Bürgerleben*; Gebhardt, *Das Familiengedächtnis*; Freeze, *Jewish Marriage*, 22–24, 33; Parush, "Women Readers"; Parush, *Reading Jewish Women*, esp. 97–132; Hyman, "Introduction" (1986); Biale, *Eros and the Jews*, esp. 148–75; Dubin, "Jewish Women"; Z. J. Kaplan, "Thorny Area"; and Seidman, *Marriage Plot*, 71–82. Interest in the creation of the Jewish family can be found in earlier writings as well. For instance, consider the example from the Russian Jewish journal *Perezhitoe* (Experiences) by the famous belletrist Lev Osipovich Levanda: "Starinnye evreiskie svadebnye obychai," *Perezhitoe* 3 (1911): 103–35. David Biale speaks of a revolution in values whereby love became a part of a normative system surrounding marriage in the late eighteenth and nineteenth centuries. It is important to note that he is not interested in whether people *actually* felt love. Biale, "Love." The historiographic interest in love, regardless how exactly it was defined or felt, comes largely as a reaction to the works of two historians of England (the "sentiments school"): Lawrence Stone and Edward Shorter. Stone controversially argued that in early modern England, up to and including the sixteenth century, affection and love were significantly lacking in the nuclear family, not only between husband and wife but also between parents and children. Stone, *Family*, 4–5. Edward Shorter's thesis was quite similar. Shorter, *Making of the Modern Family*.

23. Raised in an observant household, Lilienblum became a *maskil* and joined Hibat Tsiyon, serving as its secretary. S. Ansky's short story "The Sins of Youth" uses Lilienblum's autobiography to discuss how maskilic literature infiltrated the world of observant youths and turned them away from religious life.

24. Lilienblum, *Katavim otobiografiim*, 1: 106. Shulamit Magnus, writing extensively on the memoirs of Pauline Wengeroff, argues against this male-dominated, maskilic narrative of "tradition" as an agent of obscurant oppression. Instead, she offers a more nuanced, gendered reading of the modernization of the Jews of Europe that points to the problems caused by modernization and highlights certain advantages of tradition, all the while making room for female agency and voice. See Magnus, "Sins of Youth"; and Magnus, "Kol Isha."

25. Certainly I am not the only historian to look to the actions (rather than the rhetoric) of Jews to determine shifts in behavioral patterns. Jay Berkovitz studies *takanot* and how they reflected concerns over changing behaviors of the Jewish community of Metz. This communal action included regulations against clandestine marriage. See Berkovitz, *Rites and Passages*, 50–52; and Schochat, *Der Ursprung*, 287–308. Also, Immanuel Etkes notes the time delay between the rise in maskilic rhetoric against traditional Jewish marriage and the actual transformation of Jewish marriage practices in Eastern Europe; see Etkes, "Marriage and Torah Study," 153–54.

26. Dubnow, *Kniga zhizni*, 1: 140.

27. Dubnow, *Kniga zhizni*, 1: 140–41.

28. Dubnow, *Kniga zhizni*, 1: 152. Dubnow's was not the only example of how

migration permitted the transgression of social norms. Maxime Rodinson's mother came to Paris from Suwalki, Poland, in 1902 and became pregnant by another Polish Jewish worker, Samuel Rubinstein, who did not want to take responsibility for their daughter. Rodinson's mother would then move in with another man she would only later marry. See Rodinson, *Souvenirs*, 49–51, 76.

29. Dubnow, *Kniga zhizni*, 1: 166–67.

30. Dubnova-Erlich, *Bread and Matzoh*, 10.

31. When Sophie Dubnova married Henryk Erlich in 1911, from the standpoint of the Erlich family, Sophie's lack of dowry was forgiven in part because she was both Jewish (and the family had feared that Henryk's involvement in the socialist movement would lead him to marry a non-Jewish woman) and "an *ikhes*, the daughter of a man of some renown." Clearly, self-chosen matches did not mean that the rest of the parameters of the Jewish marriage market necessarily changed. Ehrlich-Dubnova, *Bread and Matzoh*, 19, 30, 158, 165.

32. Vygodskaia was born in the late 1860s in Bobruisk (now in Belarus). The family later moved to Vilna. Her published memoirs cover the period from her childhood to her studies in St. Petersburg and end with her marriage to M. M. Vygodskii.

33. Vygodskaia, *Story of a Life*, 125.

34. We should remember that women might have begun studying at the local university, but they did so in women-only programs.

35. Vygodskaia, *Story of a Life*, 134.

36. Anna Pavlovna's self-arranged relationship stands in marked distinction to the arranged marriage of her older sister. Her older sister was married off according to earlier customs, a deed made all the easier by her continued proximity to the family. And the choice reflected the interests of the family more than her personal volition. When Vygodskaia's sister reached the age of 18, their father and stepmother decided that the time had come for Anna's older sister to marry. The young bridegroom was a financially independent bank employee who also happened to be the family's boarder and a cousin of Anna's stepmother. For his part, as Anna succinctly notes in her memoirs, the bridegroom required a wife from a good family who was young and healthy and possessed a dowry. The match was made. On the day of the official engagement, Anna's uncle came into her room to inform her of the engagement. Upon hearing the news, Anna burst into tears, crying for her beloved sister, who would have to spend the rest of her life with "this unattractive, uninteresting and, as it seemed, overly respectable fellow." Fortunately for all, the marriage ended up being a happy one. But Anna clearly would have no part in such an arrangement. Vygodskaia, *Story of a Life*, 65.

37. Over all, the number of marriages in Germany in 1914 had already dropped by more than 10%, with Jews being affected the most. See *Zeitschrift für Demographie und Statistik der Juden* 12.7–9 (1916): 110–11. During World War I, the rate for Christians and Jews dropped by nearly half. Only in 1919–1920 did the marriage rate rise to prewar levels. See, Daniel, *Arbeiterfrauen*, 129.

38. *Zeitschrift für Demographie und Statistik der Juden* 15.5 (1919): 112.

39. Posner, *Through a Boy's Eyes*, 5–7.

40. Rabbi Mazeh was the chief rabbi of Moscow from 1893 until he passed away in 1924. An early supporter of Zionism, he was a member of the Hibat Tsiyon movement and a founding member of the Bnai Tsiyon society in Moscow.

41. Spiegel, *A Life in Storm*, 94–106; Spiegel, *Through Fire and Water*, 10.

42. Sholem Aleichem, *Tevye's Daughters*, 104.

43. Levanda, "Starinnie evreiskie svadebnie obichai." Consider also the nostalgic historical article on Jewish marriages in Alsace by Schorestène, "Les mariages israélites."

44. For instance, see Goldhammer, "Die Mischehe," 280.

45. In Germany in 1903 the marriage rate for Jews was 7.10 per 1,000 total population (residents), whereas among Christians during the same year the rate was 8.27. By 1925 the rate was 6.6 per 1,000 for Jews versus 8.8 for non-Jews. Ruppin, *Soziologie der Juden*, 192. In European Russia in 1897, Jews married at a rate of 7.37 per 1,000, whereas Christians married at a rate of 9.48. Furthermore, the age of marriage among Jews, even in European Russia, was by the turn of the twentieth century higher than that among Christians, a telling shift in marriage patterns if we consider the earlier campaign that the *maskilim* waged against early marriages. Statistics from Fishberg, "The Jews."

46. M. Kaplan, *Jewish Middle Class*, 42–43.

47. It is important to note, however, that the way intermarriage rates were calculated differed by methodology. Lowenstein, "Jewish Intermarriage," 54. Lowenstein notes that he calculates his figures according to the American method.

48. *Zeitschrift für Demographie und Statistik der Juden* 8.11 (1912): 166. The same article notes that Jews were not the only ones to intermarry; increasingly common were marriages between Protestants and Catholics (and intermarriage rates for Catholics were higher than those for Jews).

49. By 1933 the rate of intermarriage hovered at 27%. Schmelz, "Demographische," 39. See also Lowenstein, "Jewish Intermarriage," 28–29. Lowenstein also notes the particular volatile nature of the Jewish marriage market from World War I until 1933. This too is an important consideration. I would also like to thank Jonathan Sarna for pointing out that one of the major differences in calculating statistics on intermarriage is to calculate the rate by the number of marriages (which leads to higher rates) versus by the number of individuals.

50. Fishberg, "The Jews," 448.

51. We must also bear in mind the stereotyped characterization that Ruppin made of Eastern European Jews as being more authentically Jewish. Ruppin, "Die Mischehe," 19.

52. Hyman, *Jews of Modern France*, 58.

53. If the rate was 25% in the 1920s, the fear, it would appear, was that eventually the rate would approach 100%. Leo Goldhammer, focusing on the ever increasing rate of intermarriage, makes this explicit in his "Die Mischehe." On the difficulty

in determining French Jewish intermarriage rates and for a wider discussion of the discourse thereon, see Bovy, "It Is Not the Number."

54. Van Rahden, "Intermarriages," 126.

55. Fishberg, "The Jews", 445; emphasis added.

56. Goldhammer, "Die Mischehe," 280. Similar rhetoric can be found elsewhere. See Tänzer, *Die Mischehe*, and reviews on it: "Literatur," *Zeitschrift für Demographie und Statistik der Juden* 9.12 (1913): 181; and *Im Deutschen Reich* 20.3 (1914): 140–41.

57. Until 1905 conversion from Russian Orthodoxy to any other religion was forbidden by law. See Avrutin, "Returning to Judaism," 92.

58. The discussion on Jewish marriage in the Imperial Russian Jewish press and within the state rabbinate focused on "illegal marriage," also known as hidden or unknown marriages. These were marriages that conformed to Jewish laws but contravened state law, for instance, by not being performed by a state rabbi or by not being registered in the metrical books. These illegal marriages were all the more complicated because they were halachically legitimate and therefore required a halachic divorce to dissolve them. For more, see Freeze, *Jewish Marriage*, 122, 124–28. The other pressing concern was divorce. On divorce in Imperial Russia, see Freeze, *Jewish Marriage*, 4; and Goldman, *Women*, 50, 106–8. Even though the national divorce rate for Jews was higher than the average for non-Jews in 1920s Germany, the divorce rate among Jews in Berlin and Hamburg was actually lower than that of non-Jews. See Schmelz, "Demographische," 28. The general divorce rate in France in 1926 was 0.46 per 1,000 people, less than in Soviet Russia and Germany at about the same time, though precise statistics about Jewish divorce rates in France are hard to find. See Goldman, *Women*, 107. The possibility of holding both religious and civil marriage ceremonies caused an unforeseen problem when the marriage failed. For couples who were married both civilly and religiously in France, the issue came to a head in 1907. The question at hand was whether Jews who divorced civilly would have to also divorce religiously by obtaining a *get*, as is generally required by Halacha. A rabbinic council was formed to address several issues, including how to deal with a husband who refused to grant his wife/ex-wife a religious divorce. According to the proposals made by this council, a clause was to be added to the *ketuba* (marriage contract) that would release a Jewish woman from her marriage contract when she obtained a civil divorce. See Prague, "Une dangereuse innovation," 194; M. Lévy, "Juda Lubetski," 129. Another example where the laws dividing state and religious authorities posed problems for inhabitants of France came about because of migrant Jews who lived in France but had foreign citizenship. Such was the case with Jews of Russian citizenship who lived in France. In the end, it was decided in the early twentieth century that foreign Jews whose home country recognized religious unions had to have both a civil and a religious union in France. See "Le divorce israélite et la loi russe," *Archives Israélites* (March 14, 1912): 84; "Le divorce en France des israélites russes," *Archives Israélites* (January 2, 1913): 4–5; "Le divorce en France des israélites russes," *Archives Israélites* (February 27, 1913): 69; and Urbah, "Le mariage des juifs," 58. Finally, the topic of intermarriage, strictly speak-

ing, emerged in rabbinic discussions in Russia but referred, at least in the case of the rabbinic commission of 1910, to the halachic validity of marriage between Jews and Karaites (ruled invalid). See *Razsviet* (March 28, 1910): 29; and Freeze, *Jewish Marriage*, 370n93.

59. The rabbi Dr. Max Eschelbacher, who succeeded Leo Baeck in Düsseldorf, labeled intermarriage an illness, or *Krankheit*, in his article on the topic. See Eschelbacher, "Mischehen," 74.

60. Salzberger, "Die jüdisch-christliche Mischehe," 26.

61. Eschelbacher, "Mischehen," 74.

62. Eschelbacher, "Mischehen," 74. Similarly, see "Unsere Zeit: Die Mischehe," *Menorah* 8.9–10 (1930): 502. Georg Salzberger argued that connecting the youth of the time with their religion was the best way to prevent them from entering a mixed marriage. See Salzberger, "Die jüdisch-christliche Mischehe," 29.

63. R. M., "Le divorce," *Univers Israélite* (January 20, 1911): 581–85. Other articles blamed men and women equally. See, for example, Isaac, "La libre-pensée." On gender and change, note how Joseph Roth, an Austrian Jew and outsider, rather positively noted how young Jewish women, their children in tow, would attend the Yiddish Theater in Paris, "speaking only French" and looking as "elegant as Parisiennes." For Roth, there was no doubt: "The assimilation of a people always begins with the women." In Roth's estimation this assimilation into French culture on the part of these once Eastern European Jews was not a fact to be mourned but something to be admired. J. Roth, *Wandering Jews*, 84–85.

64. Tsherikover, "M-yerushat mishpaha patriarkalit." Certainly at first blush, Tsherikover's article, an extended study of the ethical will of a Warsaw rabbi, appears to argue that one of the many virtuous acts of previous generations was to provide for one's wife and children during and after one's lifetime. Given the general Russian discourse on *agunot* (chained women; those who cannot obtain a Jewish divorce because of an obstinate or absent husband or who cannot prove the death of their husband), it might be easy to assume that this was the context for his more general comments.

65. Tsherikover, "M-yerushat mishpaha patriarkalit," 130.

66. Prague, "Religion et famille."

67. See, for example, I. Schwartz, "Education morale"; and Bauer, "La femme et nos traditions religieuses."

68. Wolff, "Propos sabbatique"; anonymous letter to the editor, "Féminisme juif?" *Univers Israélite* (November 23, 1900): 310–11.

69. L. Lévy, "Les femmes d'Israël." With his article title, Lévy is quoting the recently translated book by Grace Aguilar, *Les femmes d'Israël*.

70. For an example from the postwar era, see Prague, "La marée monte," 93–94. For more information on Hippolyte Prague, see Knörzer, "Hippolyte Prague."

71. Prague, "Toujours les mariages mixtes," 74.

72. Prague, "Toujours les mariages mixtes," 74. A year later, Prague wrote a similar article and cited Grand-Rabbi Haguenauer, who similarly blamed the passivity

of women and charged them with the task of defending the faith. See Prague, "Le rôle," 73–75.

73. Prague, "Contre les mariages mixtes," 365.

74. When the conversion went in the opposite direction, to Judaism, it was reported with triumph. In the context of the Dreyfus affair, the conversion of Gustave Kahn's wife, Elizabeth (the couple had married earlier in a civil service), and their subsequent religious wedding were reported with delight in the pages of the *Univers Israélite*. See "Paris: Une Conversion," *Univers Israélite* (November 18, 1898): 282.

75. "Instruction religieuse de la jeunesse israélite," *Univers Israélite* (April 1, 1910): 77–80.

76. Interestingly, the excerpt quoted in the article comes from a non-Jewish source and reflects larger societal concerns. See Faguet, "Les pères."

77. "Die Mischehen bei den deutschen Juden," *Der Jude* 1.12 (1917): 855; Goldhammer, "Die Mischehe," 283.

78. Eschelbacher, "Mischehen," 79. Till van Rahden's statistical analysis of intermarriage among Jews in Breslau during the Imperial era in some ways confirms this thesis. He points to the larger number of lower-class Jews, men and women, who entered interfaith marriages, as opposed to the middle and upper classes. He maintains that because of working-class Jewish women's entry into the workforce, they had more social contacts with non-Jews. In addition, their parents, being poorer and unable to offer a substantial dowry, were less likely to be able to exert any influence over them. See Van Rahden, "Intermarriages," 141.

79. Eschelbacher, "Mischehen," 79, 85–86. Concerns about bourgeois morality could also be found in discussions on divorce rates. Repeatedly it was noted that Jews in mixed marriages (and especially Jewish men in mixed marriages) were more likely to get divorced than non-Jews in mixed and endogamous marriages. See *Zeitschrift für Demographie und Statistik der Juden* 6.4 (1910): 64. Not all commentators in the German Jewish press blamed men for the decline of the Jewish family. Women were also charged with being responsible for the perceived religious decline. German Jewish women were frequently blamed for not creating a suitable Jewish home or for not sufficiently educating their children in Judaism and Jewish ritual. Frequently, it was seen as the woman's role to educate and raise her children to be good Jews. See, for example, Hirschfeld, "Ordensgedanke," 166; and M. Kaplan, *Jewish Middle Class*, 64. Yet Albert Bloch clearly charges fathers with the task of being good examples for their children, especially their sons, even as he suggests that both parents should work to look after their children's futures. See A. Bloch, "Jugendvereinigungen," 11. As Paula Hyman has correctly noted, the accusation that Jewish women were responsible for intermarriage, repeated even in the earlier historiography on the subject, emerged as a result of reading the experiences of an earlier generation of prominent German Jewish women into later eras (including Henriette Herz and Dorothea von Schlegel, née Mendelssohn, daughter of the famous Jewish Enlightenment philosopher Moses Mendelssohn). The examples of this tiny group were taken to be representative of German Jewish women's prac-

tices more broadly and over a longer period of time. See Hyman, "Two Models," 40–41. Also, as Deborah S. Hertz has noted, Jewish women in Berlin were generally less likely to convert to Christianity than Jewish men and only in one decade between 1800 and 1876 did more Jewish women convert than men. See Hertz, *How Jews Became Germans*, 223–24.

80. Wengeroff, *Memoiren einer Grossmutter*, 1: 123–53. By now the reader will have noted that not infrequently and in each city women, men, or both, in equal measure have been held accountable for the nefarious changes in the Jewish marriage market. Historians have also engaged in these debates. Scholars of the Jewish family in Western and Central Europe have increasingly stressed the conservative role women played in the modernization of the Jewish family. In so doing, they have sought to reject the previous accusations that women were behind assimilation. Yet, at the same time, some scholars of Eastern European Jews have in fact argued for the role that women played as active modernizers, attempting thereby to redress a gender imbalance that they see as having marginalized Jewish women in traditional society and ignored their contributions to Jewish society's self-emancipation. See Baskin, "Piety"; Magnus, "Sins of Youth"; Parush, "Women Readers"; and Hyman, "Introduction" (2002).

81. One short article in *Menorah* reported on a women's Bnai Brith chapter from Cologne that organized an exhibit of different *heimische* scenes from days long gone. Freimark, "Die jüdische Frau."

82. From the French Jewish perspective, this point was made explicit in one short article in *Univers Israélite* that called for a return to traditional Jewish matchmaking. See M. S., "L'école du chadchen," *Univers Israélite* (January 31, 1930): 553. It is also worth noting that Jews were not alone in having these fears. Non-Jewish Germans also commented on the crisis of the family. Sharon Gillerman, "Crisis of the Jewish Family," 176–79.

83. One article from 1930 attacked the Jewish communities themselves for allowing men in mixed marriages to hold positions of esteem in the community and other Jewish organizations. The anonymous writer charged that by accepting these men into leadership positions, the communities were wittingly or unwittingly recognizing and accepting the practice of intermarriage. The article's author concluded that, "if each man who lives in a mixed marriage were excluded from all Jewish posts, then at least the corrosive influence of intermarriage on the lives of the Jewish community would be neutralized" ("Unsere Zeit: Die Mischehe," *Menorah* 8.9–10 [1930]: 503).

84. Eschelbacher, "Mischehen," 78, 87–88.

85. Translated and cited in H. Strauss, "The *Jugendverband*," 220.

86. See Gluck, "Budapest Coffee House," 297–298; and Dickinson, "Men's Christian Morality Movement," 60, 77, 102. Sharon Gillerman cites one letter from a widow requesting help for her delinquent son; the woman knowingly explains, "I don't have to tell you how boys at this age waste heaps of money on smoking, drinking, cafes, and even worse" (Gillerman, "Crisis of the Jewish Family," 181).

87. Dubnova-Erlich, *Bread and Matzoh*, 160–61.

88. L. Strauss, *Over the Green Hill*, 38–39, 43–46.

89. Kaplan continues, "When this was not possible, participants attempted to solve the contradictions between 'love' and 'marriage' by 'falling in love' during the engagement or shortly after the wedding" (M. Kaplan. "For Love or Money," 265). Also see Budde, *Auf dem Weg ins Bürgerleben*, 29–30.

90. Philippe, *Les juifs à Paris*, 82.

91. See Chapter 1.

92. Consider the strong rhetoric against arranged marriage by leading members of the Bund. Bernstein, *Ershte Shprotsungen*, 25–27.

93. M. Kaplan, "For Love or Money," 293–94.

94. M. Kaplan, "For Love or Money," 264–65.

95. Agnon, *Simple Story*, 42.

96. Such is the story of the courtship of the fictional Zachary Mirkin and Nina Ossipovitsch. Nina becomes upset when she learns that Zachary approached her mother first and suggests sarcastically that if her mother could be consulted regarding the engagement, then it should be her mother who decides whether Nina accept the proposal. Asch, *Peterburg*. Interestingly, Gunilla-Friederike Budde cites the case of a real non-Jewish woman whose own story echoes the case of Nina in one regard: Enid Bagnold apparently, around the turn of the century, reacted with great uproar when she learned that a suitor had come to ask her father for her hand in marriage without first speaking to her. Budde, *Aug dem Weg ins Bürgerleben*, 30. By contrast, Sholem Aleichem's Tevye is incensed that Motel had asked for his daughter's hand in marriage before speaking to Tevye. Sholem Aleichem, *Tevye's Daughters*, 32–33.

97. Sholem Aleichem, *Marienbad*, 43.

98. Sholem Aleichem, *Marienbad*, 38.

99. Sholem Aleichem, *Marienbad*, 40.

100. Just before the outbreak of World War I, these German Jewish youth groups, which were predominantly male institutions, began allowing women to join, and over the course of the war years, the number of female members rose. H. Strauss, "The *Jugendverband*," 206.

101. Ruth Gützlaff interview, in Herzberg, *Überleben heist Erinnern*, 90, 93.

102. M. S., "Mariages mixtes et 'demi-juifs,'" *Univers Israélite* (January 31, 1930): 553.

103. Gunilla-Friederike Budde notes that sport became fashionable and acceptable among the bourgeoisie in Germany and England at the turn of the twentieth century. Budde, *Auf dem Weg ins Bürgerleben*, 33–34.

104. This extended beyond leisure groups. Jewish socialists also made much of their members' good values and fair treatment of women as well as their rejection of traditional, patriarchal family values. See Bernstein, *Ershte Shprotsungen*, 25–27; and M. Kaplan, "Apprenticeships," 234.

105. Robert Gamzon was the grandson of Grand Rabbi Alfred Lévy.

106. Gamzon, *Mémoires*, 31–32.

107. The fear of a destabilized Jewish marriage market, rocked by the caprices of individualistic young people, prompted at least two organizations to update older forms of *shadkhanut* (matchmaking). In the fall of 1908 the first edition of the appropriately titled Yiddish journal *Der Shadkhon* (The Matchmaker) was published out of Vilna. In the leading article of the first edition, the author explains the goals of the "one and only . . . illustrated weekly family newspaper for Jews." Appealing to nostalgic visions of the perfect—content, religious, tightly knit, and patriarchal—Jewish family now seemingly long gone, the author contends that the motivation for the creation of the journal came from those dramatic changes in Jewish family life that threatened to undermine it. The author continues with a lengthy depiction of the decline of the Jewish family, stressing the new ideals and ways of today's children and the increasing disconnect between parent and child. By the second half of the article, the tone reaches near hysterical levels as the author characterizes the discord between the older and the younger generations, between wives and husbands, as a "battlefield," a "horrible war" that has led to high divorce rates, family scandals, and the tragic case of wives abandoned by their husbands and thus unable to remarry (*agunot*). Then, using a different but no less dramatic metaphor, the author speaks of the challenges facing contemporary Jewish family life as a "horrible plague," an "epidemic" that spread from Jewish family to Jewish family. The illness at the heart of this misery was none other than bad matches ("unpasende parteyen"). *Der Shadkhon*—a voice for the family that "strengthens our awareness and helps us to understand the issues and questions of daily life"—was the remedy. "Undzer Tsiel," *Der Shadkhon* 1.1 (September 15, 1909): 1. Another organization even suggested the creation of a school for matchmakers. A short article in the *Univers Israélite* from 1930 began with a call for, "and don't laugh, it's very serious," the return of "that venerable institution of the ghetto." The writer was clearly aware of the dramatic changes in the marriage market, so much so that in 1930 the idea of resurrecting the institution of the matchmaker seemed to be both outdated and out of place. Yet, the author maintained, the number of young Jewish women who lacked good marriage prospects was cause enough to consider such, perhaps, drastic measures. M. S., "L'ecole du Chadchen," *Univers Israélite* (January 31, 1930): 553.

108. Examples of personal ads in the German Jewish press can be found beginning in the 1890s. The number of ads placed in the French Jewish press was small until after World War I. Personal ads were significantly more rare in the Russian press, at least in newspapers published in St. Petersburg. One of the reasons for this seems to have been a simple, structural issue regarding the type of newspapers popular in each locality. In Germany "family newspapers" (*Familienzeitungen*) were a popular and common genre already before the turn of the twentieth century, and they frequently published personal ads. By contrast, the major French Jewish newspapers, the *Univers Israélite* and *Archives Israélites*, adopted this format or elements thereof only after World War I, possibly to increase their readership. Another factor for the growing number personal ads in the French Jewish press after World War I might be the significant dearth of eligible young men as a result of war casualties

and thus the perceived need to turn to alternative media to find partners. In St. Petersburg family newspapers were all but nonexistent. Ads placed by individuals seeking employment or by families seeking governesses were frequent enough, but personal ads were not. Family newspapers existed in the Pale of Settlement, however; there we can find examples of personal ads, including one placed by a student living in St. Petersburg (*Der Shadkhon* 1.2 [1909]: 4).

109. If her hair color was mentioned at all, then the young woman in question was almost always blond. For example, consider the following announcement from the *Israelitisches Familienblatt* (March 16, 1905): 16: "Marriage. For a 20 year old, beautiful blond, elegant appearance, good sense for business and from a good family, tentative dowry of 15–20 thousand, looking for a dentist, veterinarian or businessman with a secure position."

110. *Israelitisches Familienblatt* (March 16, 1905): 16.

111. In addition to cash dowries, the economic security of the young couple could also be achieved with the groom marrying into a preexisting business. A number of businessmen, shop owners, skilled workers with their own shops, and even doctors offered their daughter's hand in marriage along with business opportunities, and conversely, parents of the groom looked for similar opportunities for their young sons. The term *Einheiraten*, or "marrying into," appeared regularly in the ads; for instance, "I'm looking [for a match] for my brother, 30 years of age, traveling at present. Prefers marrying into a Berlin business that specializes in fashion accessories, notions or toys [*Galanterie-, Kurz- u. Spielwar.-Branche*]." In this example, the interests of the extended family clearly supersede the tastes and desires of the young individuals to be married, and the desired characteristics of the young bride are not mentioned at all. *Israelitisches Familienblatt* (August 11, 1910): 15.

112. *Israelitisches Familienblatt* (July 7, 1910): 14.

113. *Israelitisches Familienblatt* (August 11, 1910): 15.

114. *Univers Israélite* (February 10, 1928): 657. We can find a similar announcement from the *Israelitisches Familienblatt* placed on November 8, 1933 (p. 8): "We are looking for a capable and cultivated life partner, with good character, for our only daughter, a 23 year old only pharmacist, tall, attractive, 1.75 m tall, businessminded, with varied interests. 20 000 RM and trousseau."

115. *Univers Israélite* (April 23, 1920): 111.

116. *Israelitisches Familienblatt* (March 10, 1927): 7.

117. Goldman, *Women*, 1–4.

118. Goldman, *Women*, 49–51.

119. Shternshis, "Choosing a Spouse," 12. Anna Shternshis notes that her own study contradicts larger statistics about Jewish rates of intermarriage patterns, as most of her early respondents were in fact married to other Jews. Yet she makes clear that her interviewees' decision, at least in hindsight, was not made out of a calculated desire to find a Jewish partner and continue a Jewish life but as a "matter of instinct" or to please one's parents. She also cites historian Mordechai Altshuler, who argues that intermarriage by this point was not a rejection of the past or one's identity.

120. Goldhammer, "Die Mischehe," 280. Similar statistics can be found in Ruppin, *Soziologie der Juden*, 218.

121. Altshuler, *Soviet Jewry*, 74.

122. In 1936, 3,034 Jewish men married in Leningrad: 1,779 married a Jewish woman, 1,143 married a Russian, and the remaining 112 married a woman of another nationality. Of the 2,527 Jewish women who married in Leningrad that same year, 1,779 married a Jewish man, 610 married a Russian, and 138 married a man of another nationality. Altshuler, *Soviet Jewry*, 270.

123. B. Meyer, "Mixed Marriage," 54; Stoltzfus, "Limits of Policy," 122–23.

124. Schieb, *Nachricht von Chotzen*, 74–75, 78, 82. All three men would perish in the Holocaust.

125. It is interesting to note that when Kurt Posener remarried in September 1933, he entered an arranged marriage with a Polish Jewish woman who at the time was living in Breslau. It is unclear whether the marriage was contracted before or after Hitler's rise to power and therefore whether the rise of Nazism influenced his choice of bride and the means by which he met her. Posner, *Through a Boy's Eyes*, 20.

126. Maurer, "Everyday Life," 287.

127. Stoltzfus, "Limits of Policy," 123.

128. Stoltzfus, "Limits of Policy," 118, 123.

129. Stoltzfus, "Limits of Policy," 125, 133.

130. B. Meyer, "Mixed Marriage," 60.

131. B. Meyer, "Mixed Marriage," 61.

132. Nathan Stoltzfus goes to considerable length to suggest that protest was vital in preventing the regime's annihilationist plans, suggesting that "the regime's ideology might never have developed into genocide had the German people not achieved for the regime the social and economic isolation of the Jews, a prerequisite for their deportation and murder" (Stoltzfus, "Limits of Policy," 117). The now quite famous attempt in 1943 to deport a large number of intermarried Jews from Berlin failed as a direct result of the actions of their non-Jewish family members. Rounded up and detained in the Jewish Community House on Rosenstrasse, the non-Jewish family members (mainly wives) staged protests outside the building, growing in size daily until a week later Jews in mixed marriages and their children were released. Stoltzfus, "Limits of Policy," 134; B. Meyer, "Mixed Marriage," 63.

133. Rakovsky, *My Life*, 59.

134. Rakovsky, *My Life*, 82.

135. Rakovsky, *My Life*, 77–78.

NOTES TO CHAPTER 3

1. Salli Hirsch, "Jüdische Erziehung," 6.

2. Children's and youth programs spanned a wide spectrum of activities and involved a host of different actors, including pedagogues, religious leaders, parents, and the youths themselves. Yet, because of the diversity of participants and programs, the programs are usually studied separately. As a result of the nature of my

sources (an extension of a much wider problem concerning sources and perspectives on the history of children), I am quite aware that much of this chapter and discussions in the next focus on the history of Jewish children and youth through the perspective of adults. Stearns, "Challenges"; Gleason, "Avoiding the Agency Trap."

3. Prestel, "Die Jüdische Familie."

4. On the education of Jewish children, especially as it pertains to bourgeois goals of *Bildung*, see Budde, *Auf dem Weg ins Bürgerleben*; Rieker, *Kindheiten*; and Eliav, *Jüdische Erziehung*.

5. Examining the historiography, one cannot help but feel that childhood has always been in a process of discovery. One of the most important contemporary works on the supposed discovery of childhood in the modern (read: post-medieval) world is Philippe Ariès's *Centuries of Childhood*. See also Heywood, *History of Childhood*. In the mid- to late nineteenth century, childhood was given renewed interest as an academic subject of inquiry. Budde, *Auf dem Weg ins Bürgerleben*, 193–94. Yvonne Rieker suggests that in the 1920s, youth (here meant as the period between the ages of 14 and 20) was identified as a separate stage in human development. See Rieker, *Kindheiten*, 87.

6. The term comes from Ellen Key's book *The Century of the Child*, first published in 1900. It was clearly a popular work, and one article, written in 1906 by Charlotte Perkins and translated into German for a publication of the *Jüdisches Kinderheim* in Berlin, picked up on the book's title and referred to the century as the "Century of the Child." See Charlotte Perkins, "Kinder-Kultur," *Jüdisches Kinderheim: Kindergarten und Kinderhort* (1906), pp. 12–14, Archiv des Centrum Judaicum, Berlin, 1, 75 A Be 2, Nr. 312, #542, Bl. 22v–23v.

7. On children's literature and the bourgeois family, see Budde, *Auf dem Weg ins Bürgerleben*, 127–32.

8. Herrmann, "Pädagogisches Denken," 167–69. Germany was on the forefront of pedagogical developments that sought to reform previous approaches to teaching children, especially the previously dominant trend of authoritarian pedagogy. Education was, according to this new paradigm, supposed to both emerge from within the child and reflect an organic, holistic approach to the child. Whether this model was ever fully applied or realized is secondary to the general zeitgeist that extended beyond Germany and focused attention on children's education and well-being. Herrmann, "Familie," 119–20; Herrmann, "Pädagogisches Denken," 148, 159–170.

9. Efron, "Kaftanjude"; Zimmermann, "Muscle Jews," 14–15. This intersection between nationalism and medicine influenced the ideologies and methods of the Zionist movement. Brenner, "Introduction," 4.

10. The Jewish sports movement emerged in part to regenerate the body and invert claims about Jewish degeneracy made both by people within the Jewish community and from without by antisemites. At the same time, the Jewish sports movement can be seen as an example of a larger European-wide sports culture and the belief that individual health reflected national health. The concern for fashioning a muscle Jewry, then, was the outgrowth of this larger trend that linked bodily

ideals to nationalism. See Caplan, "Germanising the Jewish Male," 164; Giller-
mann, "Samson in Vienna"; Berkowitz, *Jewish Self-Image*, 74–77; Zimmermann,
"Zwischen Selbstbehauptung"; Zimmermann, "Muscle Jews"; Eisen, "Zionism";
Hödl, "Der Zionismus als 'Therapie'"; and Mosse, "Nationalism."

11. Gillermann, "Crisis of the Jewish Family," 191.

12. The sociologist Arthur Ruppin, in his two-volume work *Soziologie der Juden*,
devoted Chapter 30 to the issue of the Jewish body and began the chapter with
the question of degeneration among the Jews. Although Ruppin argued that Jews
showed no more signs of degeneration than the peoples (*Völker*) around them, the
question of degeneration was of enough significance to warrant an entire chapter on the topic. He concluded the chapter with two examples of how Jews had
nevertheless striven toward regeneration: sport and hygiene. Ruppin, *Soziologie der
Juden*, esp. 85–95.

13. In 1926 the OSE began to publish a monthly journal: *Revue OSÉ: Organe
Mensuel de l'Union des Sociétés pour la Protection de la Santé des Populations Juives*.

14. The summer camp movement was born independently in the United States
and Switzerland. The first American summer camp was organized in the latter half
of the nineteenth century with the purpose of providing city children with time
outdoors. This first camp—a two-week-long camp in 1861—was part of the curricu-
lum of the Gunnery School in Washington. American Jewish camping began at the
beginning of the twentieth century. This recreational camping was largely aimed at
poor, predominantly Eastern European immigrant children. The goal of this philanthropic activity was to foster the physical health of the children and to "promote
their Americanization." Farago, "Influence," 50–51, 78. At the same time, similar
developments took place in Switzerland, and they appear to have had a significant
influence on the summer camp movement in Europe. The summer camps of Pas-
tor Bion from Switzerland are even mentioned in the *Bericht über das 25 jährige
Bestehen der jüdischen Ferien-Kolonieen, 1884–1908 und Jahresbericht für 1908* (Archiv
des Centrum Judaicum, Berlin, 1, 75 A Be2, Nr. 316, Bl. 37). France's earliest summer camps (*colonies de vacances*) were organized by Protestant evangelicals. Their
introduction into the French leisure landscape coincided with the introduction of
compulsory education of children (the Ferry Laws of the early 1880s). By the late
1890s Catholic colonies were organized. See Downs, *Childhood*, 15, 21, 66, 68.

15. *Bericht über das 25 jährige*, Bl. 36v.

16. "Ferienkolonie für jüdische Kinder," 2. *Beiblatt zum General-Anzeiger für die
gesamten Interessen des Judentums* (April 20, 1903).

17. The physical health of poor Jewish children was the central concern of these
philanthropists, as it was of similar Jewish institutions, including Jewish convales-
cent homes for children. *Bericht über das Jüdische Kinder-Genesungsheim im Soolbad
Elmen, 1907–1908*, Archiv des Centrum Judaicum, Berlin, 1, 75 A Be 2 Nr. 309,
#539, Bl. 13–16. The issue of physical health and body weight emerged repeatedly.
See Wassermann, "Beobachtungen," 79. Other philanthropic institutions in Berlin were created with similar tasks—for example, the Association for Children's

Outings (Verein für Kinderausflüge). This group served as the incentive among young people to create a youth club. "Forderung für das körperliche und sittliche Gedeihen der Jugend unseres Volkes," *Neunter Jahresbericht des Vereins für Kinderausflüge*, Archiv des Centrum Judaicum, Berlin, 1, 75 A Be 2, Nr. 317, #547, Bl. 1–6.

18. *Bericht über das 25 jährige*, Bl. 37–38.

19. *Bericht über das 25 jährige*, Bl. 37–38r, 38v.

20. *Bericht über das 25 jährige*, Bl. 37r.

21. A. Mayer, "Referat," 3.

22. *Bericht über das 25 jährige*, Bl. 36v.

23. Niederschönhausen is a northern suburb of Berlin that was incorporated into the city in 1920. Today it is part of the borough of Pankow.

24. Archiv des Centrum Judaicum, Berlin, 1, 75 A Be 2, Nr. 312, #542, Bl. 18–19.

25. Brenner, *Renaissance of Jewish Culture*, 186–88.

26. Lehnert, "Jüdische Volksarbeit," 110.

27. Lehnert, "Jüdische Volksarbeit," 110–11.

28. Lehnert, "Jüdische Volksarbeit," 104–5.

29. Already from the creation of the Jüdisches Volksheim in 1916, Franz Kafka shared a keen interest in the organization and made a point of visiting the home whenever in Berlin. His contact with the institution inspired his fiancée, Felice, to begin working there. In 1916 and 1917 Kafka took it upon himself to send Felice and the children reading materials, including a Blau Weiss songbook, and helped in that regard to build a library. Bruce, *Kafka*, 119–23. A little bit later, in the early 1920s, Kafka noted how he was particularly struck by the fact that the children at the Kolonie des Jüdischen Volksheims Berlin learned Hebrew. Letters from Franz Kafka to Max Brod and Robert Klopstock, dated July 10, 1923, and July 13, 1923, in Brod, *Franz Kafka*, 435.

30. Brenner, *Renaissance of Jewish Culture*, 186–88.

31. M. Bloch, "Les colonies scolaires," 181, 184.

32. It is not immediately clear what accounts for the difference between the two cities, though in both cities the families responsible for at least part of these efforts came from the elite classes.

33. M. Bloch, "Les colonies scolaires," 181.

34. For example, Dreyfous, *Essai*; and Dreyfous, *De l'hystérie alcoolique*.

35. The group's president, identified through her husband, Jules Ephrussi, was Fanny von Pfeiffer, daughter of a leading noble family from Vienna. Jules Ephrussi was a phenomenally successful banker from Odessa. Recently a popular history of this family has been published. See Waal, *Hare with Amber Eyes*.

36. M. Bloch, "Les colonies scolaires," 182–83.

37. Nadia Malinovich has rightly noted that the two communities were not always at odds with each other, even if conflict did exist at times. Malinovich, *French and Jewish*, 108–15.

38. "Création d'une Colonie Scolaire," *Archives Israélites* (March 7, 1929): 35.

39. *L'association "La Colonie Scolaire,"* 3.

40. Wolski, "L'activité de la Colonie Scolaire," 9.

41. Children were examined medically before the vacations to ensure that they were not infected with a contagious disease (under the direction of Jewish doctors). Similar concern for the children's diet was taken. Wolski, "L'activité," 9.

42. *Dix années de Colonie Scolaire*, 5.

43. Berck-Plage was a common holiday site, popular among Parisian Jews. See, for instance, "Berck-Plage," in *Almanach juif* (Paris: La Nouvelle Génération, 1931), 31.

44. "Création d'une Colonie Scolaire," *Archives Israélites* (March 7, 1929): 35.

45. *L'association "La Colonie Scolaire,"* 3.

46. The Colonie Scolaire's bulletin gives no indication of what type of stories the children learned. Wolski, "L'activité," 14–15, 17.

47. *L'association "La Colonie Scolaire,"* 4.

48. Wolski, "L'activité," 19; *L'association "La Colonie Scolaire,"* 4.

49. "Une fête de Pourim à la Colonie de vacances de l'OSÉ," *Révue OSÉ* (March 1937): 26–27.

50. Biélinky, "En faveur."

51. The girls sent letters confirming that they would participate or expressed their regret that they would not be able to join in the organization's hikes in 1927. See, for instance, Centre de Documentation Juive Contemporaine, Paris, MD 13.2, pp. 5, 6, 70, 89, 94, 98, 99. For letters written in 1928, see Centre de Documentation Juive Contemporaine, Paris, MD 13.3; and for 1929, see Centre de Documentation Juive Contemporaine, Paris, MD 13.4.

52. "O letnikh koloniiakh dlia uchashchikhsia," *Nediel'naia Khronika Voskhoda* (March 24, 1896): 314–16.

53. "O letnikh koloniiakh dlia uchashchikhsia," 314.

54. Unfortunately, other sources have been similarly silent on the subject of summer camps in St. Petersburg. Archival and newspaper sources attest instead to sites in the Pale of Settlement.

55. Untitled lead article (presumably by the editors) in *Nediel'naia Khronika Voskhoda* (May 6, 1890): 449–51.

56. "O letnikh koloniiakh dlia uchashchikhsia," 314.

57. "O letnikh koloniiakh dlia uchashchikhsia," 314.

58. Untitled front-page article about summer camps in *Nediel'naia Khronika Voskhoda* (July 30, 1895): 850.

59. In 1920 or so the Russian government closed the OZE as a result of infighting and conflict with the regime.

60. Davidovitch and Zalashik, "Air, Sun, Water," 133, 133n15; Shtif, "Di tsen-yorike geshikhte fun 'OZE,'" 4–5; Gesellschaft OSE, *Die Entstehung*, 4.

61. For references to summer camps in Russian territories, see the short announcements in *Voskhod* (April 15, 1901): 10; and *Voskhod* (June 14, 1901): 9.

62. Youth movements, clubs, and associations from the tail end of the nineteenth century and during the first thirty years of the twentieth century frequently shared common intellectual and cultural origins. Although in many cases they re-

sponded to growing antisemitism, because a number of hiking and sport movements across Europe had started to exclude Jews from Christian clubs on racist grounds, antisemitism was actually only one of the motivating factors for the creation of uniquely Jewish organizations and was not always the overriding concern. Youth movements had their roots in larger trends common in non-Jewish circles across the continent as well: the influence of the hygiene movement; the popularization of physical activities such as sporting, gymnastics, and hiking; the rise of nationalism as a political ideology; and a general turn toward romanticism that rejected rational, industrial, bourgeois society (a romantic return to nature was less important for Jewish youth groups in Paris and St. Petersburg, though it played a role for those in Berlin). Schatzker, *Jüdische Jugend*, 245; Schatzker, "Special Character," 279–84; Brenner, *Renaissance of Jewish Culture*, 46–47.

63. In the historiography, sports and gymnastics organizations, youth movements, and youth associations have been treated as either separate entities or as though there were no essential differences between them. Youth movements of the early twentieth century were not just for teenagers but appealed to those under age 29, sometimes under 25. Thus all types of organizations often catered to the same demographic, even as they offered sometimes differing activities. Youth associations and clubs typically focused on education and socialization, and events tended to be cultural in nature. Youth movements, by contrast, tended to focus more on physical activity in their general attempts to revitalize Jewish sociability. For definitions regarding youth movements and other youth organizations, see Hetkamp, *Die jüdische Jugendbewegung*, 1: 40–41. In addition, youth movements were created and run in the early twentieth century by the youths themselves and stood in opposition to youth organizations, which were created by established (and older) Jewish groups and individuals. Therefore many of the early youth movements and youth associations emerged out of a generational struggle between the Jewish establishment and anti-establishment youth. At the same time, to separate youth movements founded by youths themselves from youth associations founded by the Jewish establishment creates a false dichotomy, certainly in practical terms. Organizations created by the Jewish establishment quickly co-opted the forms of leisure and sociability that had become popular in the youth movements, including hiking and scouting, whereas youth movements and sporting organizations frequently held and organized cultural and informal educational programs in addition to their athletic activities. Also, youth-run and -directed youth movements were often created in conjunction with organizations of the establishment. On a simple level, the two types of organizations frequently shared activities, approaches, and inspiration. Moreover, they both sought to further their influence and encourage imitation of their means and ideologies through a variety of periodicals. Over the course of the twentieth century, a number of Jewish sports and youth movements even founded their own periodicals, including the *Jüdische Turn- und Sportzeitung* (published in Berlin, 1900–1939), *Makkabi* (originally published in Odessa, 1917–1919), and *EIF: Revue Mensuelle des Éclaireurs Israélites de France* (published in Paris in the 1930s and

again after the Shoah). The connection between sports, sociability, space, reading, and learning repeat throughout this chapter.

64. Brenner, "Turning Inward"; Schatzker, "Special Character," 21, 24, 27. Finally, the three cities under study were not exceptions. Jack Jacobs's recent book seeks to understand the power of the Bund by examining its countercultural activities, not its results in Polish elections. To this end, he explores the Bund's youth and children's movements and the sports movement, Morgnshtern. Jacobs, *Bundist Counterculture*.

65. Brenner, "Turning Inward," 56.

66. Youths who came of age during World War I or shortly thereafter had markedly different expectations of communal belonging than did their parents. Although frequently we hear that the experience of the Great War, especially for German Jews, was pivotal for the renaissance that would flourish in the 1920s, it was a search for authenticity that brought them back to Judaism and Jewishness far more than simply a sense of rejection from the larger, non-Jewish society: "Members of the Jewish youth movement posed a radical challenge to the rational and individualistic ideologies associated with their parents' world," something that was "true for Jewish as well as for non-Jewish youth" (Brenner, "Turning Inward," 60). Nadia Malinovich points out that, in general, antisemitism in 1920s France was on the decline. What propelled Jews at that moment to seek new ways to express a connection to their Jewish identity was the "disillusionment with the 'ideology of assimilation'" (Malinovich, *French and Jewish*, 116). With regard to youth revolt and the young generations' search for an authentic, spiritual Jewish life and community, see also Schatzker, "Special Character," 26–27.

67. "Les Éclaireurs israélites de France," *Archives Israélites* (April 4, 1929): 55; emphasis added.

68. Schatzker, *Jüdische Jugend*, 231.

69. H. Strauss, "The *Jugendverband*," 210; H. Strauss, *Eye of the Storm*, 55; Döpp, *Jüdische Jugendbewegung*.

70. Schatzker, *Jüdische Jugend*, 231; H. Strauss, *Eye of the Storm*, 55–56.

71. Herbert Strauss notes that the core of the VJJD was made up of members between the ages of 18 to 25, sometimes with older members approaching 35 and younger members under 18 joining the ranks. See H. Strauss, "The *Jugendverband*," 208.

72. H. Strauss, "The *Jugendverband*," 206, 208.

73. H. Strauss, "The *Jugendverband*," 206.

74. H. Strauss, *Eye of the Storm*, 56; H. Strauss, "The *Jugendverband*," 216–17.

75. Schatzker, *Jüdische Jugend*, 241. Schatzker provides a long list of lectures given by the CV, including "Die jüdische Weltanschauung," "Antisemitismus," and "Die Juden als deutsche Bürger."

76. H. Strauss, "The *Jugendverband*," 211. Strauss stresses the ideological implications of the VJJD's connections to Bnai Brith.

77. H. Strauss, "The *Jugendverband*," 217.

78. H. Strauss, *Eye of the Storm*, 55–56; H. Strauss, "The *Jugendverband*," 217, 224. By World War I, rabbis and teachers increasingly took over leadership of the VJJD.

79. Schatzker, *Jüdische Jugend*, 242; quote from Elsa Hirschel, cited in H. Strauss, "The *Jugendverband*," 228.

80. Schatzker, *Jüdische Jugend*, 232. Unlike the apolitical nature of the VJJD, the JJWB came to have Zionist tendencies and around 1930 changed its name to "Brith Haolim." See Reinharz, *Dokumente*, 358n; and H. Strauss, "The *Jugendverband*," 224–25.

81. The JJWB, for its part, was a typical youth movement in terms of its "anti-modern, anti-urban, anti-rational educational idea" and in its "protest against a broad range of political, social and intellectual conventions" that members felt characterized mainstream Jewish society (H. Strauss, "The *Jugendverband*," 225).

82. Bar Kochba was one of the first Jewish gymnastics club in Europe. See Eisen, "Zionism," 247–62; and P. Y. Mayer, "Deutsche Juden."

83. Historians have placed much attention on the thoughts and writings of Max Nordau (and those of other, similar-minded Zionists), in particular on his concepts of muscle Jewry and degeneration (seen as a consequence of urban life in the Diaspora) and on his emphasis on the rejuvenation of the male Jewish body through gymnastics. Mosse, "Max Nordau," 566–69.

84. Burin, "Das Kaffeehausjudentum," 74–75.

85. Efron, "Kaftanjude."

86. *Jüdische Turnzeitung* 1 (May 1900): 8.

87. "Correspondenzen: Berlin," *Die Welt* 2.49 (December 9, 1898), 12; "Correspondenzen: Berlin," *Die Welt* 2.50 (December 16, 1898), 12; "Vereinsnachrichten: Berlin," *Die Welt* 2.52 (December 30, 1898): 13.

88. "Vereinsnachrichten: Berlin," *Die Welt* 3.2 (January 13, 1899): 13. In other writings, Israel Auerbach stressed the need for Jewish men to strengthen their bodies and fight back against antisemitism as a means of overcoming the physical and national deformities that were synonymous with life in the Diaspora. Of course, this auto-emancipation was not merely from antisemitism but also from self-imposed stereotypes.

89. See Auerbach, "Sein Junge." The short story is a melodramatic tale of a father, brutalized and lamed by antisemites during his childhood, who lives to see his son, of course a member of a local, nationalist Jewish gymnastics society, defend himself against antisemites and thereby overcome the pernicious influence of life in the Diaspora. For more on the article, see Wildman, *Der veränderbare Körper*, 137.

90. Given the nature of Max Nordau's writings and even of those texts penned by members of Bar Kochba Berlin, such as Israel Auerbach, the historiographic preoccupation with the gendered discussion of the *male* Jewish body comes as no surprise and is certainly justified.

91. This high proportion of female participants and members in Bar Kochba was unusual compared to German gymnastics associations of the time and to other Jewish sports and gymnastics organizations of the same era. Yet, if we consider the intersection between women's expected role as the primary educators of their

children and the ruling scientific conceit of the day that only healthy individuals begat healthy offspring, the existence of a women's section of Bar Kochba is logical in theory, even if it was exceptional in practice. From the creation of the women's chapter in 1900 and as reflected in the charter of the Jewish Sports Association (Jüdische Turnerschaft), women played leading roles in the association and had full voting rights. Pfister, "Die Rolle der jüdischen Frauen," 77, 79.

92. Ultimately, Ifftus would reunite with Bar Kochba in 1924, in the wake of the Great War, during which time the two organizations had begun to work in greater consultation. Pfister, "Die Rolle der jüdischen Frauen," 81.

93. Pfister, "Die Rolle der jüdischen Frauen," 80.

94. Käte Dan-Rosen, "Aus Meiner Erinnerungen," Leo Baeck Institute Archives, ME 104, MM 17.

95. Tomaschewsky, "Mädchenerziehung," 8.

96. Tomaschewsky, "Mädchenerziehung," 9–10.

97. Pfister, "Die Rolle der jüdischen Frauen," 73.

98. Pfister, "Die Rolle der jüdischen Frauen," 83.

99. Salli Hirsch, "Jüdische Erziehung," 6.

100. Calvary, "Blau-Weiss."

101. Schatzker, *Jüdische Jugend*, 267–68.

102. Calvary, "Blau-Weiss," 452.

103. Brenner, "Turning Inward," 62–63.

104. Sharfman, "Between Identities," 200.

105. Sharfman, "Between Identities," 198–200.

106. Sharfman, "Between Identities," 202.

107. For more on the goals of Blau Weiss, see Schatzker, *Jüdische Jugend*, 267–68.

108. "Jugendbewegung 'Die Kamerade,'" *Im Deutschen Reich* (May 1919): 229.

109. Herzfeld, "Kameraden," 317.

110. "Der Reichsbund der Kameraden," *Im Deutschen Reich* 26 (February 1920): 93.

111. "Der Reichsbund der Kameraden," 92–93.

112. Herzfeld, "Kameraden," 317.

113. "Der Reichsbund der Kameraden," 93.

114. Brenner, *Renaissance of Jewish Culture*, 47. On a practical level, the Kameraden shared elements derived from the scouting movement: Participants wore similar uniforms; troop names were inspired by Native American tribes; the group had its own special handshake; members were awarded special decorations; and the group's motto was a direct copy of that of the Boy Scouts ("Be prepared"). They camped, told stories by the campfire, swam, and played games such as soccer and handball. Lippman, *Link in the Chain*, 12, 14–15.

115. Brenner, *Renaissance of Jewish Culture*, 47.

116. L. Lévy, "L'Union Scolaire."

117. "L'assemblée générale de 'l'Union Scolaire,'" *Univers Israélite* (June 4, 1897): 343–45.

118. "Union Scolaire," *Univers Israélite* (December 9, 1898): 379.

119. The Jewish Press makes no explicit reference to women participating in the activities of the Union Scolaire. It is likely that in the early twentieth century they did not participate.

120. "Nouvelles diverses," *Univers Israélite* (July 6, 1900): 503–4.

121. Malinovich, *French and Jewish*, 87–90, 117–36.

122. Malinovich, *French and Jewish*, 119.

123. Malinovich, *French and Jewish*, 122.

124. For their activities, see *Univers Israélite* (January 17, 1930): 503; and Malinovich, *French and Jewish*, 122–23.

125. Relentlessly positive in tone, the *Univers Israélite* seems to have chosen only ever to publicize the group's wins. See, for instance, "Carnet des sociétés," *Univers Israélite* (April 11, 1930): 23.

126. Alfred Lévy served as the grand rabbi of France before World War I. See Gamzon, *Mémoires*, 32.

127. Michel, *Les Éclaireurs israélites*, 17–18.

128. Michel, *Juifs*, 36.

129. Literally, "school scholarship winners," an organizational basis for the later Jewish scouting group, the Éclaireurs israélites de France.

130. The elevated platform in the synagogue from which the Torah is read.

131. André Kisler, quoted in Michel, "Qu'est-ce qu'un scout juif," 78.

132. Kisler, quoted in Michel, "Qu'est-ce qu'un scout juif," 78.

133. Michel, *Les Éclaireurs israélites*, 20.

134. "La fête des Éclaireurs israélites de France," *Univers Israélite* (June 27, 1930): 368.

135. Michel, "Qu'est-ce qu'un scout juif," 79, 81.

136. *Almanach juif* (Paris: La Nouvelle Génération, 1931), 106. See also "Les Éclaireurs israélites de France," undated but ca. 1938, Centre de Documentation Juive Contemporaine, Paris, MD 1.8, pp. 2–3.

137. "Les Éclaireurs israelites de France," *Archives Israélites* (April 4, 1929): 55.

138. Edmond Fleg, "Scoutisme et vie juive," 357–58.

139. Yeykelis, "Odessa Maccabi," 86.

140. Beizer, "Zionist Youth Movements," 11–12.

141. Beizer, "Zionist Youth Movements," 15. "V O-v okhraneniia zdorov'ia evreiskago naseleniia," *Novyi Voskhod* 5.11 (March 19, 1914): 22.

142. Tysler, "Evreiskii gimnasticheskii kruzhok."

143. Yeykelis, "Odessa Maccabi," 86; Beizer, "Zionist Youth Movements," 15.

144. Cited in Beizer, "Zionist Youth Movements," 15.

145. Resolution taken at the sixth congress of He-haver, cited in Yeykelis, "Odessa Maccabi," 87. See also Miller, "Maccabi Russia," 119.

146. "V Petrogradie," *Makkabi* 1.1 (November 1917): 50–51; Miller, "Maccabi Russia," 119.

147. "Nasha Zadacha," *Makkabi* 1.1 (November 1917): 1.

148. "Pis'mo," *Makkabi* 1.1 (November 1917), 5.

149. The organization had a club of its own, on Kazachii Lane, which was closed in late 1919 because of official, legal registration issues.

150. On Ligovskaia Street.

151. The club had about 200 members, and lectures were attended by 20–30 people; cultural events drew 300. Beizer, "Zionist Youth Movements," 16.

152. Beizer, "Zionist Youth Movements," 19.

153. Beizer, "Zionist Youth Movements," 24.

154. On Soviet activities against religious organizations in the 1920s, see Shternshis, *Soviet and Kosher,* 2–4, 7–9; on the decline, see Beizer, "Jews of a Soviet Metropolis"; and Beizer, "Zionist Youth Movements."

155. Miller, "Maccabi Russia," 122–24.

156. Beizer, "Zionist Youth Movements," 31.

157. Transcript of interview with L., Avraham Hartman Institute, Oral History Division, (217) 163, pp. 4–5.

158. Borut, "Struggles for Spaces," 307.

159. Borut, "Struggles for Spaces," 328.

160. "Einheitliche Behandlung jüdischer Jugendverbände," *Sonderrecht für die Juden* (July 10, 1935): 121.

161. "Ausschluß jüdischer Turner und Sportler," *Sonderrecht für die Juden* (April 25, 1933): 18; "Voll-Arisierung der Deutschen Turnerschaft," *Sonderrecht für die Juden* (May 24, 1933): 25; "Jugendpflege," *Sonderrecht für die Juden* (June 2, 1933): 28. In what might appear to be a strange twist of bureaucratic logic, Nazi authorities permitted the Zionist sports groups Schild and Makkabi to continue operation longer than other Jewish groups. Of course, these exceptions existed only because the Zionists' goal of leaving for Palestine conformed to the Nazis' desire to rid the country of its Jewish residents. "Sportbetrieb von Juden und sonstigen Nichtariern," *Sonderrecht für die Juden* (July 18, 1934): 85; "Richtlinien für den Sportbetrieb von Juden und Nichtariern," *Sonderrecht für die Juden* (September 15, 1934): 92; "Erleichterungen für zionistische Jugendorganisationen," *Sonderrecht für die Juden* (January 17, 1935): 102; "Zionistische Gruppen besser behandeln," *Sonderrecht für die Juden* (January 25, 1935): 103; "Jüdische Jugendverbände," *Sonderrecht für die Juden* (February 4, 1935): 104. Certain youth movements, such as "Makkabi-Hazair," helped young Jews prepare for emigration. See Tichauer, "Wer sind wir," 253.

162. "Auflösung jüdischer Organisationen," *Sonderrecht für die Juden* (Anfang 1939): 273.

163. P. Gay, *My German Question,* 54–55, 69.

164. Maoz, "The Werkleute," 154.

165. Hetkamp, *Ausgewählte Interviews,* 75.

166. Posner proudly notes how he would beat up Hitler Youth members. Posner, *Through a Boy's Eyes,* 32–33.

167. Matthäus, *Jewish Responses to Persecution,* 353.

168. Lee, *Pétain's Jewish Children.*

169. Lazare, "Educational, Rescue, and Guerilla Operations," 181.

170. Lazare, "Educational, Rescue, and Guerilla Operations," 182.

171. On the Comité de la rue Amelot, see Hazan, *Les orphelins*, 35.

172. Founded in St. Petersburg in 1880, ORT (Obshchestvo remeslennogo i zemledel'cheskogo truda sredi evreev v Rossii; Society for Trades and Agricultural Labor Among the Jews in Russia) is a worldwide Jewish organization for Jewish education, in particular, trades and technology.

173. Association *"La Colonie Scolaire": Oeuvre juive pour la protection de l'enfance, exercise 1939* (Paris, 1940), 6.

174. In addition to helping Jewish children from Alsace, the EIF evacuated Jewish children from Paris during the war. See Gamzon, *Mémoires*, 8; and Hyman, *Jews of Modern France*, 176–82.

175. Rosengart, "Les maisons de l'OSE," 83–84, 87, 100–101, 106.

176. See the memoirs of Vivette Samuel, who worked for the OSE during this time: Samuel, *Sauver les enfants*, esp. 50, 52–56, 110–11.

177. Lazare, "Educational, Rescue, and Guerilla Operations," 183.

NOTES TO CHAPTER 4

1. Brenner, *Renaissance of Jewish Culture*, 19.

2. Brenner, *Renaissance of Jewish Culture*, 22; Batnitzsky, *How Judaism Became a Religion*; M. A. Meyer, "How Awesome."

3. Kafka, *Letter to His Father*.

4. Malinovich, *French and Jewish*, 4, 15.

5. I am paraphrasing the famous line of Yehuda Leib Gordon's poem "Awake My People" (*Ha-kitsah ami*).

6. On the Christmas tree in German Jewish homes, see M. Kaplan, "Redefining Judaism," 14–17; and Richarz, "Der jüdische Weihnachtsbaum." Yet, to see this as only a German Jewish phenomenon is to miss a larger pattern of acculturation common to Jews across Europe. The issue of the Jewish celebration of Christmas vexed writers in the French Jewish press; see Wolff, "Hanoukka-Noël." Evidence suggests that also in St. Petersburg members of the upper-middle and upper classes at times celebrated Christmas—"the highlight of winter"—even as they might also insist that the holiday "had no religious content" for them. See Leibovitch, *La moitié de beaucoup*, 18–19. Leibovitch also mentions that her family celebrated Mardi Gras (*Maslenitsa*) in addition to Jewish holidays such as Passover; see Leibovitch, *La moitié de beaucoup*, 20, 27. Alexander S. Spiegel notes that "Christmas time in Petrograd was always something special. . . . I had been invited to a number of non-Jewish homes, and also to Jewish homes where Jesus' birthday was celebrated scrupulously, as though it were their very own holy day. The homes were decorated with Christmas trees, which were hung with presents for the children" (Spiegel, *Through Fire and Water*, 49).

7. Studies of rites of passage and rituals have frequently stressed the role of these symbolic acts in creating unity, a fact not lost on those who promoted them. Yet, as scholars of ritual have also more recently noted, these same acts can also highlight

tensions. Just as rites of passage seek to create community (through the inclusion of potential members), they also demarcate all those who were to be excluded from the ritual space and the ritual act. Weitzman, "Feasts"; Lehman, "Gendered Rhetoric."

8. As Gunilla-Friederike Budde notes regarding Wilhelmine Germany, rites of passage became "family festivals," where friends and family gathered to share a festive meal on the occasion of the child's religious coming of age. This development was similar to the experience of non-Jews during the late nineteenth century. Budde, *Auf dem Weg ins Bürgerleben*, 398–99.

9. For an example on the discussion of decadence in the French Jewish press, see Prague, "Contre la décadence," 17–19.

10. In 1946, for instance, M. Cohn wrote a report arguing that the Jewish school, far more than any other institution, was in the position to save French Judaism. See M. Cohn, "L'école juive," August 15, 1946, Archives de l'Alliance Israélite Universelle, Paris, AP 1/43, p. 1.

11. See Bermann, "L'éducation de nos enfants," 269–70; Weill, "De l'enseignement religieux," 19–20; L. S., "Sur l'éducation religieuse," *Archives Israélites* (February 24, 1910): 60; and Lichtenstein, "Notre sabbat et nos enfants," 23–24.

12. Prague, "De l'instruction religieuse," 93. Criticizing the "spectacle of dejudaization," Prague wrote in 1908 that "our youth is lamentable, this youth, which is the future of French Judaism." Blaming the state of education (in particular, "la libre-pensée," or "free thought") and the general, excessively permissive intellectual attitude of society, he stressed, as he did in many other articles, the need for a solid Jewish education. See Hyman, *Jews of Modern France*, 64, 70; and "Défendons notre jeunesse," *Archives Israélites* (June 25, 1908): 201. For further articles of this nature by Hippolyte Prague, see his "Le devoir des parents"; "Ce qui manque au Paris israélite"; "Des actes!"; "Le culte des parents et le respect de la religion"; "Défendons notre jeunesse"; "Après Simchat Tora"; and "Nos jeunes israélites." Prague's comments are by no means exceptional even today. In examining Jewish summer camps for children in the United Kingdom, M. Shabi and W. El Ansari write, "Jews in the Diaspora live in the world of secular culture. Many Jews know very little about Jewish history, literature and Hebrew language. Times have changed and Jewish identity is no longer passed on through the generations by habit, memory and external events. For the young generation, being Jewish is no more than a matter of choice. Who will choose to be Jewish only if they know Jewish history, the richness of Jewish life and become proud to be Jewish" (Shabi and El Ansari, "Youth Perceptions," 51–52).

13. "L'instruction religieuse," *Univers Israélite* (November 26, 1897): 311–12.

14. Prague, "Le caractère familial," 329–30; and Prague, "Le rôle de la femme," 73–75.

15. For example, see "Neudovletvoritel'naia postanovka religioznago vospitaniia evreiskago iunoshestva," *Khronika Voskhoda* (September 27, 1898): 1470–72.

16. For instance, consider Bergel-Gronemann, "Über religiöse Erziehung" (Bergel-Gronemann was the sister of Sammy Gronemann); Bernfeld, "Das europäische

Erziehungsvorbild"; Böhm, "Die neue Erziehung"; Calvary, "Erziehung"; and E. Stern, "Über die Bedeutung religiöser Formen." The Jewish press also served as a means for German rabbis to comment on the issue; see Baeck, "Religion und Erziehung."

17. Marcus, *Rituals of Childhood*, 106.

18. In medieval Ashkenaz, male children around the age of 5 or 6 were introduced to Jewish religious learning during Shavuot. A father would bring his son to his future teacher, and the teacher would introduce the child to the aleph-bet (Hebrew alphabet); then the child was allowed to eat sweets and other treats. The young boy would repeat a formula to help his future learning and would be taken to the river and told that the study of Torah is as ceaseless as the running of the water. Marcus, *Rituals of Childhood*, 1.

19. Marcus, *Rituals of Childhood*, 102–3, 118–26.

20. Grünfeld, "Über Barmitzwah-Vorbereitungen," 9.

21. Letter from Dr. J. Stern, the Schul- und Talmud-Thorah-Vorstand, to the Vorstand der jüdischen Gemeinde, December 15, 1907, Central Archives for the History of the Jewish People, Jerusalem, Folder "Konfirmations-Unterricht für Mädchen und Barmizwa-Unterricht 1907 für Knaben," D/Be4/157. In France and Germany, a growing number of publications were written with the task of teaching young members about Judaism. For instance, see Derenbourg, *Livre de versets*.

22. Archiv des Centrum Judaicum, Berlin, Personal Archive 6.2 (Fritz Selbiger), Nr. 2, Bl. 47. For further examples, see documents pertaining to the bar mitzvah ceremonies of Hans and Herrmann Rathenau, in Stiftung Jüdisches Museum, Berlin, Historische Sammlung, Rathenau Sammlung, 2001/104/952–953 and 2001/105/366; and Arthur Stern, "Mein Leben: Gedanken und Erinnerungen eines Nervenarztes," Leo Baeck Institute/Jüdisches Museum Berlin, MM 73 and MM 74, p. 9. Stern lived in Königshüte at the time and later moved to Berlin.

23. "Nouvelles diverses," *Univers Israélite* (November 1, 1894): 116.

24. Helene Eyck, "Helene Eyck (1876–1898)," January 17, 1891, Leo Baeck Institute/Jüdisches Museum Berlin, MM II 41, p. 47. Unfortunately, there is no record of Eyck's son's response to the event, or her husband's.

25. P. Gay, *My German Question*, 55–56.

26. Grünfeld, "Über Barmitzwah-Vorbereitungen," 10. This translation itself is curious. The original Hebrew reads, "B-en hazon yipara am v-shomer torah ashrehu" ("Without vision the people becomes wild; fortunate is the one who keeps the Torah"; translation mine).

27. In addition to introducing new rites of passage, some communities also created children's religious services to differing degrees of success. On the latter, see M. A. Meyer, "*Gemeinschaft*," 32n29. For more on early confirmation ceremonies, see M. A. Meyer, "Jewish Communities," 122; Wolff, "Première communion," 268; Manuel, "L'initiation," 4; Haus, *Challenges of Equality*, 199n39; and Wormser, "L'initiation religieuse," 8.

28. M. Mayer, *Instructions*; I. Bloch, *Petit catéchisme israélite*.

29. We should also remember that many of the reforms made in consistorial

synagogues in France were aesthetic or cultural in nature. French consistorial Judaism remained wedded to a more observant form of Judaism, and French Judaism did not split along a Reform-Orthodox divide like German Judaism had.

30. In 1852 it was decided in Paris that the religious initiation ceremony would take place before the holiday of Shavuot, but evidence shows that already by the late nineteenth century this was not the case and the ceremony was held as much as a month after the holiday. See Manuel, "L'initiation a cent ans," 4; "Nouvelles diverses," *Univers Israélite* (June 16, 1892): 592–93; and "L'initiation religieuse," *Journal de la Communauté* (June 30, 1950): 6. The writer of the last article notes that the ceremony took place on June 18, and Shavuot that year began on the evening of May 21. Also, a number of children who participated in the Réunions amicales de la jeunesse israélite in 1927–1929 sent letters to the organizers of a hike in June (thus after Shavuot) regretting that they could not participate in the hike because of the religious initiation service, sometimes referred to as confirmation, in which either they or a family member was taking part. See Centre de Documentation Juive Contemporaine, Paris, MD 13.2, MD 13.3, and MD 13.4. In Berlin the ceremony often took place after the holiday. See Letter from Dr. J. Stern, the Schul- und Talmud-Thorah-Vorstand, to the Vorstand der jüdischen Gemeinde, December 15, 1907, Central Archives for the History of the Jewish People, Jerusalem, Folder "Konfirmations-Unterricht für Mädchen und Barmizwa-Unterricht 1907 für Knaben," D/Be4/157.

31. The influence of the Christian surroundings was clear even in the structure of religious lessons. For instance, books printed in France were often based on the Christian instructional model of catechisms. See Débry, *Catéchisme*. We can find similar examples from Central Europe, which made their way to the French Jewish community through translation. See Heinemann, *Profession*.

32. The earlier school initiation ritual also took place around Shavuot. See Marcus, *Rituals of Childhood*, 1.

33. Heschel, *Abraham Geiger*, 14.

34. Wolff, "Première communion," 268.

35. Philippe, *Les juifs à Paris*, 109.

36. As early as 1818, five Jewish girls were confirmed in a public ceremony in Berlin. See Eliav, *Jüdische Erziehung*, 344.

37. "Nouvelles diverses," *Univers Israélite* (June 16, 1889): 609.

38. Haus, *Challenges of Equality*, 143. In the early years of the *Konfirmation* ceremony in Germany, the age varied between 13 and 15. By the late nineteenth century it was common in Berlin to be confirmed at the age of 15. See Eliav, *Jüdische Erziehung*, 338; and W. Stern, *Anfänge der Reifezeit*, 8.

39. On the initiation's early history, see Berkovitz, *Shaping of Jewish Identity*, 216–17.

40. M. A. Meyer, "Gemeinschaft," 21. One exception to this rule was the community that met at the Baruch Auerbach orphanage. There girls were confirmed during a regular holiday service. See M. A. Meyer, "Gemeinschaft," 29.

41. M. A. Meyer, *Response to Modernity*, 39. Mordechai Eliav suggests that the first confirmation was in 1807 in Wolfenbüttel; Eliav, *Jüdische Erziehung*, 339.

42. Eliav, *Jüdische Erziehung*, 330–33, 339–44.

43. Although Germany is often associated with the creation of a defined Reform movement, Jewish rituals and services were "reformed" in other settings as well, including in Paris and St. Petersburg. See M. A. Meyer, *Response to Modernity*, 165–71, 197–200; Nathans, *Beyond the Pale*, 146, 149; Philippe, *Les juifs à Paris*, 109; and Berkovitz, *Rites and Passages*, 139, 142, 193, 200, 206–7, 224–25, 235.

44. M. A. Meyer, "Jewish Communities," 122; Wolff, "Première communion," 268; Manuel, "L'initiation a cent ans," 4; Haus, *Challenges of Equality*, 199n39; Wormser, "L'initiation religieuse," 8. Such ceremonies did make their way to Eastern Europe and were subject to discussion in the Russian Jewish press. See "Neudovletvoritel'naia postanovka," 1470–72. Already by 1813 a book had been written in German and translated into French on preparing children for the confirmation ceremony. See Heinemann, *Profession*.

45. "Initiation religieuse au temple de la rue de la Victoire," *Univers Israélite* (June 18, 1897): 406–7. Béatrice Philippe cites an article from the *Archives Israélites* published in 1875 that summarizes the ceremony. According to the article, the choir sang Psalm 118, and then the children recited a prayer; they stated that they would remain faithful to their religion and asked God to receive them in his covenant. Philippe, *Les juifs à Paris*, 109 (quoted from *Archives Israélites* [1875]: 396).

46. L. L., "Cérémonie de l'initiation religieuse," *Univers Israélite* (June 15, 1900): 398–400.

47. Budde, *Auf dem Weg ins Bürgerleben*, 396.

48. Levinson, *Ein Ort ist*, 136.

49. "Report of Rabby [*sic*] Levinson," ca. late 1940s/early 1950s, Zentralarchiv zur Erforschung der Geschichte der Juden in Deutschland, Heidelberg, B2/19, Nr. 5, p. 3.

50. "Nouvelles diverses," *Univers Israélite* (June 1, 1890), 579–80; "Nouvelles diverses," *Univers Israélite* (June 16, 1895): 590–91.

51. "L'examen de la bar-mitswa," *Univers Israélite* (November 20, 1896): 267–70.

52. Meeting notes from April 5, 1906, Consistoire de Paris, B78, dossier 21, p. 3. In the immediate post–World War II era, this issue was far more acute. See Hazan, "Du heder aux écoles actuelles," 16.

53. Paula Hyman notes that already by 1872 there were little more than two children born per Jewish household. By the early twentieth century, fertility rates would drop even further. See Hyman, "Jewish Fertility," 85.

54. Philippe, *Les juifs à Paris*, 108.

55. Krinsky, *Synagogues of Europe*, 251.

56. Gousseff, "Les juifs russes en France," 9; Hyman, *Jews of Modern France*, 130; Green, *Pletzl of Paris*, 84.

57. At the same time, the anxiety expressed in the press about the lack of Jewish knowledge and participation also suggests that the Jewish press writers might have thought that the religious education that preceded the rites in Germany and France was not sufficient.

58. W. Stern, *Anfänge der Reifezeit*, 8–9, 111–12.

59. This is not incidental. Although the group was Orthodox, they remained part of the larger Jewish community of Berlin and worked with the Reformers of the community. Not all Orthodox Jews of the city agreed with this position and the *Austrittsgemeinde*—or separate community—refused to work with Reform Jews.

60. Letter from Dr. J. Stern, the Schul- und Talmud-Thorah-Vorstand, to the Vorstand der jüdischen Gemeinde, December 15, 1907, Central Archives for the History of the Jewish People, Jerusalem, Folder "Konfirmation und Barmitza Unterreicht," D/Be4/157.

61. Letter from Dr. J. Stern, the Schul- und Talmud-Thorah-Vorstand, to the Vorstand der jüdischen Gemeinde, December 15, 1907, Central Archives for the History of the Jewish People, Jerusalem, Folder "Konfirmations-Unterricht für Mädchen und Barmizwa-Unterricht 1907 für Knaben," D/Be4/157.

62. Despite their interests, however, not all girls participated in this ritual. Interview with Florence Singewald, in Herzberg, *Überleben heißt Erinnern*, 16.

63. *Cérémonie de l'initiation religieuse instituée*. In addition, at times, boys and girls in Paris took the exams separately, further pointing to the different curricula. See the exam schedule, which separated boys and girls, posted in *Univers Israélite* (May 1, 1889): 510; and similarly, *Univers Israélite* (April 29, 1898): 184. Yet two years later, in 1900, boys and girls took their exams at the same time. See "Nouvelles diverses," *Univers Israélite* (May 4, 1900): 214.

64. L. L., "Cérémonie de l'initiation religieuse," *Univers Israélite* (June 15, 1900): 398–400.

65. Wolff, "Première communion," 268.

66. "Neudovletvoritel'naia postanovka," 1470–72; "Prazdnik religioznago sovershennolietiia" (most likely written by M. Daikhes), in Daikhes, *Bar-Mitsvo*, 16–17. Michael Meyer notes the existence of similar rituals across Russia, including in Riga. M. A. Meyer, *Response to Modernity*, 238.

67. "Neudovletvoritel'naia postanovka," 1470–72; other articles also note Jewish youth services, see Vostochnik, "Jugendgottesdienst," *Nediel'naia Khronika Voskhoda* (June 23, 1896): 669–700.

68. The article was written in a semidescriptive, semiproscriptive fashion to a Russian-speaking Jewish audience. "Prazdnik religioznago sovershennolietiia," in Daikhes, *Bar-Mitsvo*, 1–18.

69. The calling of an individual to the *bimah* (the platform from which the Torah is read) to recite the blessing before and after the reading of the Torah portion.

70. "Prazdnik religioznago sovershennolietiia," 10–14.

71. "Neudovletvoritel'naia postanovka," 1472.

72. Pereferkovich, "Bar-Mitsva." Written as a historical-cultural feuilleton, this article explores elements of the rite of passage (including age and key components of the ceremony, such as donning tefillin [i.e., phylacteries]).

73. "Prazdnik religioznago sovershennolietiia," 10–14.

74. R. Ben-Doiv, "Moi prazdnik," in Daikhes, *Bar-Mitsvo*, 53.

75. On the early standardization of the bar mitzvah ritual, see Marcus, *Rituals of Childhood*, 118–24.

76. Gutman, "Jewish Medieval Marriage," 48, 50. For that matter, the shattering of a glass was also an innovation dating back to the late Middle Ages. Initially the glass was thrown against the wall of the synagogue.

77. Lowenstein, "Religious Practice," 148.

78. Snyder, *Building a Public Judaism*, 75, 111–12.

79. According to the *Zeitschrift für Demographie und Statistik der Juden*, in 1905 there were 31,667 Jews who belonged to one of the "important" Berlin *Gemeinden*. In that same year, there were 600 religious weddings in Berlin. See *Zeitschrift für Demographie und Statistik der Juden* 4.5 (1908): 76. In 1905 there were 98,893 Jews in Berlin (see Segal, "Bevölkerungsbewegung der Juden," 61). If we take the German marriage rate for Jews in 1905 (7.12 per 1,000; *Zeitschrift für Demographie und Statistik der Juden* 8.11 [1912]: 166) and apply it to the Jewish population of Berlin, we arrive at 704 Jewish marriages that year.

80. Neither memoir literature nor the Jewish press of the time suggests a debate about the location of religious weddings. Both sources are silent about the possibly contested nature of the choice.

81. Lowenstein, "Religious Practice," 148.

82. Snyder, *Building a Public Judaism*, 75, 301; M. A. Kaplan, "Religious Practices," 241; Cohen, *Jewish Icons*.

83. For instance, the Jewish Student Association of Berlin held at least one meeting at the Germania-Sälen and rented out for this purpose the Hochzeitssaal of the venue. Invitation for a gathering on February 25, 1908, from the Jüdische Studenten-Versammlung, Central Zionist Archives, Jerusalem, A11/17/4, unnumbered document.

84. *Berliner Vereinsbote* (January 10, 1896): 2.

85. Henriette Hirsch, "Erinnerungen an meine Jugend," Leo Baeck Institute/ Jüdisches Museum Berlin, MM38, p. 74.

86. Joseph Gallinger, "Erinnerungen," Leo Baeck Institute/Jüdisches Museum Berlin, MM 26, p. 12. Joseph married in a hotel in Frankfurt am Main.

87. Rewald, "Der Preis des Überlebens," 199.

88. Besser interview, in Herzberg, *Überleben heißt Erinnern*, 235–38. The building is now an Orthodox synagogue, but it had once been a Bnai Brith lodge, later a *Volksschule*, and after Kristallnacht a prayer space for Reform and liberal Jews.

89. Besser interview, in Herzberg, *Überleben heißt Erinnern*, 235–38.

90. Posner, *Through a Boy's Eyes*, 21. Regarding Kurt's second wife's religiosity and insistence on keeping a kosher kitchen, see Posner, *Through a Boy's Eyes*, 22, 26. References on page 30 seem to suggest a far laxer level of observance; apparently, she would mix meat and milk together at the same meal (a definite transgression of Jewish law).

91. Schieb, *Nachricht von Chotzen*, 81.

92. The unnamed groom (!) worked in Zak's bank (and was presumably a member of the extended Gintsburg family). Gintsburg offers scant biographical details.

Born in Moligev, her family moved to St. Petersburg, but dates are few and the overwhelming majority of the people mentioned in the memoir are important musicians and acquaintances of Zak's. Gintsburg, *Vospominaniia ionosti*, 24.

93. The legal differences between France and Russia, however, caused problems for marriage and divorce cases of Russian Jews, a topic that was mentioned repeatedly in the press for well over a decade. See "Le divorce israélite et la loi russe," *Archives Israélites* (March 14, 1912): 84; "Le divorce en France des israélites russes," *Archives Israélites* (January 2, 1913): 4–5; "Le divorce des israélites russes en France," *Archives Israélites* (February 27, 1913): 69; and Lion, "Le mariage des israélites russes," 70.

94. Günzburg, "My Father," 251.

95. "Nouvelles diverses," *Archives Israélites* (January 31, 1901): 39.

96. Dubnova-Erlich, *Bread and Matzoh*, 76.

97. Dubnow, *Kniga zhizni*, 1: 167.

98. Dubnova-Erlich, *Bread and Matzoh*, 164.

99. Vygodskaia, *Story of a Life*, 134.

100. Vygodskaia, *Story of a Life*, 139.

101. Vygodskaia, *Story of a Life*, 142–43.

102. "Dekret o svobode sovesti, tserkovnykh i religioznykh obshchestvakh," issued on January 20, 1918, according to the old calendar. The decree extended to Soviet Ukraine in 1919 and Belorussia in 1920.

103. Rothenberg, *Jewish Religion*, 111–12.

104. Commissariat of Interior Affairs (NKVD), No. 149, April 7, 1924, quoted in Rothenberg, *Jewish Religion*, 112.

105. Rothenberg, *Jewish Religion*, 113.

106. Spiegel, *Through Fire and Water*, 104–8, 112–14.

107. An acronym for the Bsesoiuznyi Leninskii Kommunistichestii Soiuz Molodezhi (All-Union Leninist Young Communist League), a political youth organization.

108. Rothenberg, *Jewish Religion*, 113–14; Altshuler, *Soviet Jewry*, 64.

109. Applications pour le mariage à domicile: "Il ne pourra être accordé d'autorisation de mariage à domicile que dans les cas suivants: 1ᵉ Deuil récent dans l'une des deux familles, par suite de la mort du père, de la mère ou de l'un des plus proches parents de l'un des deux époux; 2ᵉ Maladie grave du père ou de la mère de l'un des deux époux; 3ᵉ Mariage *in extremis*. Pour tout autre cas, une Commission, spécialement nommée par le Consistoire, est chargée d'accorder ou de refuser l'autorisation demandée. La redevance consistoriale dûe pour les mariages à domicile, exceptionnellement autorisés, est fixée par la Commission," Archives du Consistoire, Paris, GG 43, unnumbered document.

110. Announcement in *Archives Israélites* (January 17, 1901): 19.

111. See the 1895–1896 fee schedule for a Jewish marriage ceremony in *L'annuaire des Archives Israélites* 12 (1895–1896): 65, 68–69. Only in 1925–1926 did the prices increase and the options change slightly; see *L'annuaire des Archives Israélites* 42 (1925–1926): 55, 118.

112. Prague, "Contre la laïcisation," 169–71.

113. And certain restaurants made clear their ability and willingness to cater to the latter portion of the wedding festivities. See the ad for the kosher Grand Restaurant Vve [veuve] Dreyfus in Paris that advertised its large space, which could seat 150 people. The restaurant's ad specifically notes its ability to cater for "weddings and banquets." See *Univers Israélite* (September 28, 1900): 62.

114. Letter dated May 15, 1911, Meaux, Archives du Consistoire, Paris, GG43, unnumbered document.

115. *Univers Israélite* (October 22, 1920): 152.

116. Burns, *Dreyfus*, 84–85.

117. "Nouvelles diverses," *Univers Israélite* (June 1, 1895): 560–61. The article also reminds the reader of the standards of a traditional Jewish wedding. Both the bride and the groom had comparable *yihus*, coming as they did from powerful financial families.

118. For example, see "Un grand mariage," *Archives Israélites* (March 21, 1905): 70.

119. "Un grand mariage," 118.

120. "Nouvelles diverses," *Univers Israélite* (July 1, 1889): 640–41. For other examples, see "Nouvelles diverses," *Univers Israélite* (January 1, 1890): 242–43; "Nouvelles diverses," *Univers Israélite* (March 1, 1890): 376; and "Nouvelles diverses," *Univers Israélite* (June 1, 1895): 562.

121. "Une cérémonie nuptiale: Mariage Cahen-Hayem," *Archives Israélites* (February 27, 1902): 68–70.

122. To give a sense of the scope of the activities, between 1899, the year of its founding, and 1927, the CBIP housed 1,749 women and provided work to 6,807. *Univers Israélite* (August 26, 1927): 614 ff. For information on R's marriage in 1930 (the marriage mentioned in the text), see Minutes from meeting of Toît Familial, La Fondation CASIP-COJASOR, Paris, ser. 2B10, p. 41.

123. Although a number of articles bemoaned the fact that the number of Jewish couples who chose to marry only in a civil service was growing, the number of religious weddings performed in France, even into the post-Shoah period, remained relatively high (certainly in comparison to Berlin and St. Petersburg). Prague, "Contre la laïcisation," 169–71; Prague, "Mariages mixtes," 25–26.

124. Halachically, Judaism also distinguishes between major and minor holidays—ones on which you can do some or most forms of work (e.g., Hanukkah, Tu b-Shvat) and others where work is explicitly forbidden (e.g., Shavuot, Rosh Hashanah, Yom Kippur).

125. For example, Sukkot (Festival of Booths), a central pilgrimage festival when the Temple in Jerusalem still stood, today has receded in relative importance for many Jews (the Passover seder is far more universally celebrated today than Sukkot).

126. Perry, "Private Life of the Nation," 51.

127. Richarz, "Der jüdische Weihnachtsbaum," 282; M. A. Meyer, *Response to Modernity*, 190.

128. Wolff, "Hanoukka-Noël," 461–63.

129. Guesnet, "Chanukah."

130. For example, see Aizenshtadt, "Khanuka"; and Don-Yehiya, "Hanukkah," 5. Although the focus is on Zionism in the Yishuv and later in the State of Israel, François Guesnet does make reference to Zionist thinkers from Europe (Guesnet, "Chanukah," 237).

131. Guesnet, "Chanukah," 227–45.

132. Guesnet, "Chanukah," 230.

133. S. Z. Luria, writer for the Zionist Russian-language newspaper *Razsviet*, and Abraham Tenenboym were the instigators of this ball. Gelber, "Reshit tnuat," 46–47, 52–53.

134. *Razsviet* (February 22, 1907): 35.

135. *Razsviet* (March 7, 1910): 49. The event was technically held on Shushan Purim, the date chosen for walled cities. Pavlovoi Hall was not a restaurant or a hotel but, like the Noble Assembly, a meeting hall used for associational gatherings and musical and theatrical events. Although the advertisement placed in the Russian Zionist newspaper *Razsviet* makes no mention of the physical address of the hall, therefore suggesting its fame and popularity among readers, other sources allow us to determine that Pavlovoi Hall was located at Troitskaia Ulitsa 13 (now Ulitsa Rubinshteina), less than half a kilometer from Nevskii Prospekt. See www.citywalls.ru/house1182.html (accessed February 27, 2017).

136. Announcements, *Novyi Voskhod* 5.7 (February 20, 1914): 27.

137. Announcements, *Budushchnost'* 1.1 (January 7, 1900): 5. Other organizations held children's celebrations for the holiday. The Heder Ivriia held a gathering that included the recitation of poems and singing, along with a fruit treat. See "Obshchinnia zhizn'," *Razsviet* (January 31, 1910): 36.

138. Cohn-Sherbok, *Introduction to Zionism*, 60; Abramov, *Perpetual Dilemma*, 65, 72.

139. *Univers Israélite*, December 11, 1896, 380–382.

140. Liudvipol', "Khanuka," 1293–96.

141. L. L., "Nouvelles diverses," *Univers Israélite* (March 26, 1897): 23–24.

142. The dance was preceded by a concert with artists from the opera. "Nouvelles diverses," *Univers Israélite* (March 18, 1898): 825.

143. Czerny, "L'association des étudiants russes."

144. A number of the youth organizations discussed in Chapter 3 used the opportunities afforded to them by having a captive audience to expose children to festivals and holidays. For example, the OSE camp held Purim celebrations in 1937; see *Revue OSÉ* (March 1937): 26–27.

145. Central Zionist Archives, Jerusalem, A11/17/5, unnumbered document.

146. *Jüdische Rundschau* (December 12, 1902): 81; *Jüdische Rundschau* (December 19, 1902): 91. The Imperial is located not far from where the Jewish museum of Berlin is located today.

147. We need to be cautious with our estimation of participants in such an event;

after all, Berlin's Zionist population was decidedly small compared to Jews who subscribed to other political movements. *Jüdische Rundschau* (January 2, 1903): 5.

148. *Jüdische Rundschau* (January 2, 1903): 7.

149. Central Zionist Archives, Jerusalem, A11/17/4, unnumbered document.

150. *Jüdische Rundschau* (March 13, 1903): 97.

151. *Jüdische Rundschau* (February 20, 1903): 59–60. These were repeat events. See Central Zionist Archives, Jerusalem, A11/17/5.

152. *Jüdische Rundschau* (February 20, 1903): 59–60.

153. Invitation card from the Jüdisch-nationale Frauenvereinigung, Central Zionist Archives, Jerusalem, A11/21, unnumbered document.

154. *Monatsschrift der Berliner Logen* 6.12 (March 1927): 237.

155. Auerbach, "Chanukkah und der Orden," front page.

156. The ad is printed but mislabeled in Hofmeester, *Jewish Workers*, 268.

157. "Carnet des sociétés," *Univers Israélite* (October 18, 1929): 89.

158. Green, *Pletzl of Paris*, 58.

159. London was the first city to witness such an event in 1888. The London ball began on Erev Yom Kippur and continued well into the night. Guests were invited, for the price of 1 shilling, to indulge in a good meal, which would be followed by singing, dancing, and a number of lectures and recitations. The following year, a similar ball was held in New York, and in the years thereafter Yom Kippur balls spread across the United States among Jewish anarchists. One of the final Yom Kippur balls appears to have been held in Montreal in 1905. See Margolis, "Tempest in Three Teapots."

160. For an example of the negative reaction that the Yom Kippur ball received in the Jewish press in Paris, see R. T., "Le banquet de kippour," *Univers Israélite* (October 19, 1900): 133–36.

161. R. T., "Le banquet de kippour," 133–36.

162. *Univers Israélite* (September 18, 1908): 22.

163. Scholem, *Berlin to Jerusalem*, 11.

164. Gronemann, *Sammy Gronemann*, 211.

165. Shternshis, *Soviet and Kosher*, 20–27.

166. Rothenberg, *Jewish Religion*, 75.

167. Shternshis, *Soviet and Kosher*, 35.

168. Shternshis, *Soviet and Kosher*, 27–35. Anna Shternshis does note that alternative Passover seders were held and that families did hold seders that were emptied of religious meaning, but she gives no further details as to their location.

NOTES TO CHAPTER 5

1. Dwork, *Children with a Star*, xi. Dwork estimates that only 11% of European Jewish children alive in 1939 survived the Holocaust. Similarly, a report by the Joint Distribution Committee from January 1946 cited the French humanitarian Justin Godard's postwar estimate that of the 1.2 million Jewish children living in Europe (outside the Soviet Union) in 1939, only 150,000 survived. See Leon Shapiro, "Jew-

ish Children in Liberated Europe: Their Needs and the JDC Child Care Work," American Jewish Joint Distribution Committee Archives, JER44-52_029_0583, p. 1. However, both statements are less straightforward than they might first appear. One of the many challenges in studying the history of children is in the very definition of what constitutes a child: someone under 18 years of age? or someone under 12? In the same report, Shapiro regularly cites statistics according to which children are defined as those under the age of 15, though he acknowledges that many of the numbers probably include those over 15 as well. See Shapiro, "Jewish Children in Liberated Europe," 2–4.

2. Hazan, *Les orphelins*, 71. Those who survived and those who would be born after the Holocaust thus became a high priority; various organizations worked to address the material and spiritual recovery of young Jews.

3. Michael Lipka, "The Continuing Decline of Europe's Jewish Population," Pew Research Center, February 9, 2015, www.pewresearch.org/fact-tank/2015/02/09/europes-jewish-population/ (accessed July 30, 2015). Lipka's statistics are based on the research of Italian Israeli demographer Sergio DellaPergola. Such population statistics are necessarily estimates. Arthur Ruppin estimated the European Jewish population in 1939 at 9.2 million; cited in Mendes-Flohr and Reinharz, *Jew in the Modern World*, 881.

4. Mandel, "Genocide and Nationalism," 198.

5. Atina Grossmann states that of the 8,000 members of the Berlin Jewish community in 1946, 5,500 of them were married to a non-Jewish spouse. See Grossmann, "Survivors Were Few," 317, 323.

6. Brenner, *After the Holocaust*, 42. Privileged marriages included partnerships in which the woman was Jewish, the man was not Jewish, and there were either no children or the children were raised as non-Jews; and partnerships in which the man was Jewish, the woman was not Jewish, and the children were raised as non-Jews. Nonprivileged marriages were those in which the man was Jewish and the couple had no children, marriages in which one partner was Jewish and the children were raised as Jews, or marriages in which the non-Jewish partner had converted to Judaism. B. Meyer, *Jüdische Mischlinge*, 30.

7. Brenner, *After the Holocaust*, 42.

8. The community that remained was tiny, with somewhere between 6,000 and 8,000 Jews in West and East Berlin around 1949, 80% of which were German Jews. Geller, *Jews in Post-Holocaust Germany*, 77. For additional information on East Berlin, see R. Gay, *Safe Among the Germans*, 222; and Timm, "Ein ambivalentes Verhältnis," 18. According to Michael Brenner, in 1949 Eastern European Jews represented 29.6% of the population, and in 1952 returnees from abroad to Berlin made up a little more than 10% of the population. Brenner, *After the Holocaust*, 45, 60.

9. Atina Grossmann writes, "By 1950, Jewish aid organizations curtailed their programs in Berlin; declaring that 'if Jews in small or larger groups choose to continue to live among the people who are responsible for the slaughter of six millions

of their brothers, that is their affair.' The burden was placed on the small numbers of Jews, both native German or Eastern European, who remained in the land of the murderers" (Grossmann, "Survivors Were Few," 335).

10. Brenner, *After the Holocaust*, 72. On some of the financial benefits that Jews in East Berlin enjoyed, see Kirchner, "Ein schönes Finale," 144–45. On the generally tough conditions, see Einhorn, "Gender," 706. Rabbi Nathan Peter Levinson, among others, describes the hardships of the Berlin Jewish community after the war. See Letter from Rabbi Levinson to Mr. G. of the Reform Congregation Keneseth Israel in Philadelphia, April 1 (no year given but ca. early 1950s), Zentralarchiv zur Erforschung der Geschichte der Juden in Deutschland, Heidelberg, B2/19, Nr. 2, Buchstaben G–J.

11. Unsigned two-page description of the Jewish community, August 8, 1954, Landesarchiv Berlin, B Rep. 002, Nr. 8642/2. See also Galinski, "New Beginning," 101. Galinski lists the three synagogues: the Joachimstaler Synagogue, the Pestalozzi Synagogue, and the Fränkelufer Synagogue. During the High Holidays in September 1945, there were five semifunctioning synagogues, all in various states of disrepair, including the Rykestrasse Synagogue and the Levetzowstrasse Synagogue. See R. Gay, *Safe Among the Germans*, 161. The fate of various Berlin synagogues under the Nazis differed. Some were destroyed during Kristallnacht, such as the synagogue on Fasanenstrasse. Others were used for entirely different purposes; the Rykestrasse Synagogue, for example, was used as a storage space.

12. On the kosher butcher on Eberswalderstrasse, see Landesarchiv Berlin, C Rep. 104, Nr. 63, Bl. 93; and Archiv des Centrum Judaicum, Berlin, 5B1, Nr. 71, Bl. 18, 21, 57; 5B1, Nr. 73, Bl. 3; and personal archive 6.6 (Erich and Nelly Cohn), Nr. 13, Bl. 1 recto/verso, 3, 4 recto/verso.

13. In the eastern sector, returnees initially had priority in housing, "and many were immediately incorporated into high-status political, cultural, and administrative work" (Borneman, "Identifying German Jews," 5).

14. A. Nachama, "From 1945 to the Present," 232. On the Gemeindehaus, see Landesarchiv Berlin, B Rep. 002, Nr. 9788, pp. 121, 184, and an unnumbered pamphlet concerning the fifth anniversary celebrations of the Jewish Gemeindehaus, dated September/October 1964.

15. *Jewish Chronicle Travel Guide*, 140; *Jewish Travel Guide*, 141.

16. Weinberg, "Dealing with Survivor Youth," 188.

17. Levinson had studied under Rabbi Leo Baeck in Berlin. Brenner, *After the Holocaust*, 69, 110.

18. Levinson, *Ein Ort ist*, 107.

19. On West German politics toward Israel, see Herf, *Divided Memory*.

20. According to Rabbi Levinson, the early beginnings of this organization were still fraught with prejudice. See Levinson, "Functions of a Rabbi," 109–10.

21. Invitation to the exhibition "Alt-Neuland-Israel," June 1954, Landesarchiv Berlin, B Rep. 002, Nr. 4872.

22. *Der Weg: Zeitschrift für Fragen des Judentums* (November 21, 1952): front page,

reports of the founding of WIZO in Berlin. See Landesarchiv Berlin, E Rep. 200-22, Nr. 78.

23. Alpern, "Ich habe hier nichts zugelegt," 30.

24. www.kempinski.com/en/berlin/hotel-bristol/press-room/history/ (accessed July 30, 2015).

25. Even publications for Jewish children in Germany reflected this. Consider *Schalom: Zeitschrift des Jugendzentrums der Jüdische Gemeinde zu Berlin.*

26. Kauders, "Money," 62.

27. Brenner, *After the Holocaust,* 66–67.

28. On the Association Brith Rischonim—Union of Old Zionists, see Landesarchiv Berlin, B Rep. 042, Nr. 39895.

29. Levinson, *Ein Ort ist,* 109.

30. Letter from Rabbi Levinson to Mr. G. of the Reform Congregation Keneseth Israel in Philadelphia, April 1 (no year given but ca. early 1950s), Zentralarchiv zur Erforschung der Geschichte der Juden in Deutschland, Heidelberg, B2/19, Nr. 2, Buchstaben G–J. Levinson was clearly trying to speak "American" in his letter, styling his concerns according to two issues that would have found particular resonance with that audience, namely, the cold war and concern over mixed marriage. I am grateful to Marion A. Kaplan for pointing this out at the conference "The Experiences of Modern European Jews: National, Transnational, and Comparative Perspectives," New York University, March 2012.

31. The return to Judaism was expressed in other ways as well. One note placed in *Der Weg* announced the *brit milah* of three sons in 1946; unlikely to have been a case of triplets, the announcement suggests that the ceremony had not been carried out during the Nazi era, when circumcising the boys could have endangered them profoundly. See *Der Weg* (November 1, 1946): 8.

32. Levinson, *Ein Ort ist,* 125.

33. Unsigned two-page report about the community, August 13, 1954, Landesarchiv Berlin, B Rep. 002, Nr. 8642/2.

34. Although the first Jewish summer camps in post-Shoah Berlin catered to Jewish children from all sectors of the city, because the communities were divided, the task fell to communities on the two sides of the border. In East Germany the union of Jewish communities (Verband jüdischer Gemeinden) organized summer camps for the children, though it would appear that the impetus for these camps came from outside Berlin. Announcement for annual summer camp organized by the Verband jüdischer Gemeinden, *Jüdische Gemeinde von Groß-Berlin: Nachrichtenblatt* (April 1962): 8.

35. Zentralarchiv zur Erforschung der Geschichte der Juden in Deutschland, Heidelberg, B.2/19, Nr. 3. See especially the letters by A., J., K., and M.

36. Unsigned two-page letter to the American Hotel Service, August 13, 1954, Landesarchiv Berlin, B Rep. 002, Nr. 8642/2, unnumbered pages.

37. *Für unsere Mitglieder* (March 1961), Landesarchiv Berlin, E Rep. 200-22, Nr. 42.

38. *Für unsere Mitglieder* (September 1960): 6.

39. *Für unsere Mitglieder* (March 1961), Landesarchiv Berlin, E Rep. 200-22, Nr. 42.

40. Borneman, "Identifying German Jews," 5–6. The central administration of the Jewish community was located in the eastern sector, though two other branch offices existed in the city: one on Joachimstalerstrasse and the other in the Jewish hospital on Iranischestrasse (in the French sector). Levinson, *Ein Ort ist*, 108.

41. Epstein, *Last Revolutionaries*, 139–54.

42. "West emigrants," those who had fled to England or Mexico, for instance, during the Nazi era. See Herf, *Divided Memory*.

43. Kantorowicz, *Deutsches Tagebuch*, 2: 16.

44. The Jewish Gemeinden were searched; Julius Meyer (the chairman of the Jewish community in the eastern sector) was arrested; other community leaders fled to West Berlin in January 1953; and the Berlin rabbi living and serving in the West, Nathan Peter Levinson, publicly and vocally urged Jews in East Germany to move to the West, an act that cost him his job. Borneman, "Identifying German Jews," 6; Levinson, "Berlin Jewish Community"; Levinson, *Ein Ort ist*, 135–36.

45. Borneman, "Identifying German Jews," 6. Barbara Honigmann speaks of this from the perspective of her parents' choice; see B. Honigmann, *Ein Kapitel*, 123–24.

46. By 1976 there were only 728 members. We must remember that these figures reflect only those Jews who belonged to the *religious* community. The number of those persecuted by the Nazis and living in East Germany was much higher. Timm, "Ein ambivalentes Verhältnis," 18–19. Timm notes that in 1978 there were 4,000 people living in East Berlin who had been persecuted by the Nazis because of "race." At the same time, the Jewish community of East Berlin had 340 registered members. For membership figures, including a breakdown by gender and age, see Landesarchiv Berlin, C Rep. 104, Nr. 63, p. 108.

47. Transcript concerning the Jewish community of "Groß-Berlin" (i.e., East Berlin), December 1961, Die Bundesbeauftragte für die Unterlagen des Staatssicherheitsdienstes der ehemaligen Deutschen Demokratischen Republik, Berlin, AOPı 1843/64, Bendit, Riesenburger, Part 1, Bl. 60.

48. Hartewig, "Die Loyalitätsfrage," 48–62; Hartewig, "Eine dritte Identität," 292–302.

49. At the same time, however, expressions of nationalist Jewish self-identification were taboo. Consider the case of "E.," Die Bundesbeauftragte für die Unterlagen des Staatssicherheitsdienstes der ehemaligen Deutschen Demokratischen Republik, Berlin, BVDresden, AOP 2222/84, "Zionist," Bd. 1.

50. Timm, "Die ambivalentes Verhältnis," 19. On subsidies, see, for instance, a note stamped by the Magistrat von Groß-Berlin Referat Kirchenfragen regarding the financial support of the Jewish community. It relates that there had been a meeting on May 2, 1958, at which 85,000 DM were transferred to the Jewish community for construction work and religious administration. Landesarchiv Berlin, C Rep. 104, Nr. 620, p. 79. There is some logic in the East German decision to

accept a religiously Jewish identity while denying an ethnic one, if we consider the Nazi legacy. Eager to reject all hints of racial prejudice, an ethnic Jewish identity seemed anathema. Yet, also desirous not to further subject Jews to persecution as Jews, for most of the East German era religious expressions, subject to heavy surveillance, were more acceptable.

51. For instance, Peter Kirchner, the chairman of the Jüdische Gemeinde von Berlin (Ost), was an informant for the Stasi, where he was known as IM [inoffizieller Mitarbeiter, i.e., unofficial informant] Burg. See Emde and Wolffsohn, "DDR."

52. On academic discussions held in the synagogue, see Kirchner, "Ein schönes Finale," 161–62. For invitations to other events, including a "lecture evening" with song and music on November 1, 1956, at 7:30 p.m. and an invitation for a concert and lecture by Rabbi Riesenburger on Sunday, December 9, 1956, at 4 p.m., see Landesarchiv Berlin, B Rep. 002, Nr. 8642/2.

53. *Nachrichtenblatt der Jüdischen Gemeinde von Groß-Berlin und des Verbandes der Jüdischen Gemeinde in der Deutschen Demokratischen Republik* (August 1961): 5.

54. See invitation for *Gedenkfeier* of the East Berlin Jewish community to take place on November 6, 1954, Landesarchiv Berlin, B Rep. 002, Nr. 8642/2.

55. Boris Sapir, "Central Europe." On the process by which Jews were progressively lowered in their relative importance as victims and survivors of Nazi persecution, seen as passive victims of fascism instead of active fighters against fascism, see the discussion in Geller, *Jews in Post-Holocaust Germany*, 98–106.

56. P. Honigmann, "Nur noch lebendes Museumsstück," 150.

57. B. Honigmann, *Ein Kapitel*, 120–21. Unfortunately, little information about this club is available.

58. Hilberg, *Destruction*, 670; Poznanski, *Être juif*, 705.

59. Hyman, *Jews of Modern France*, 164; Weinberg, "Reconstruction," 168.

60. "Mayer Acts in Case of Jewish Orphans," *New York Times* (February 27, 1953): 3; Giniger, "Boys Flying to a New Home," 12.

61. In France the Nazis and their French collaborators had killed about 27% of the total adult Jewish population, whereas 13.8% of Jewish children had met a similar fate. Wieviorka, "Éléments," 159. There is a growing literature on the experiences of Jewish children in France after the war. See, for example, Doron, *Jewish Youth*; and Hobson Faure, "Shaping Children's Lives."

62. Hazan, *Les orphelins*, 71.

63. Weinberg, "Reconstruction," 172.

64. These included the Conseil représentatif des institutions juives de France (CRIF), founded in 1944 by members of the French Jewish resistance; the Comité juif d'action sociale et de reconstruction (COJASOR), founded in 1945; and the Fonds social juif unifié (FSJU), created in 1950. See Sussman, "Changing Lands," 259, 264–65. On the COJASOR, see also "COJASOR 1945–1955: Dix années d'action sociale" (Paris, 1955), Archives de l'Alliance Israélite Universelle, Paris, AP1/46. The brochure notes that much of its efforts were directed at helping Jews from other countries, not just from France.

65. Poznanski, *Être juif*, 676–79; Wieviorka, "Éléments," 160–64, 176–78.

66. Mandel, "Genocide and Nationalism," 199.

67. Robin, *Les juifs de Paris*, 95.

68. According to much of the historiography on this demographic explosion and post-Shoah French Jewish history, the French Jewish community after the Shoah was "saved" by the influx of "traditional" Jews from the Maghreb. One cannot and should not downplay the role that these hundreds of thousands of migrants had on the French Jewish community. At the same time, it would be wrong to overlook the foundations established by the Jewish community of France before their arrival. On the arrival of Jews from the Maghreb, see Benbassa, *Histoire des juifs*, 275–76; and Grynberg, "Après la tourmente," 269–73. Most Algerian Jews came in 1962 or after; they accounted for 140,000 individuals. The migration of Jews from Tunisia and Morocco between 1956 and 1962 brought 65,000 people. See Sussman, "Changing Lands," 1.

69. Belleville is located in the 19th, 20th, and parts of the 10th and 11th arrondissements.

70. Hyman, *Jews of Modern France*, 119.

71. Simon and Tapia, *Le Belleville*, 57–58.

72. Yet, both because of the timing and the nature of the community, I am unable to address in fullness these critical and fascinating changes to French Judaism and the Jewish community of France. For details into this community's history in France, see Abitbol and Astro, "Integration of North African Jews."

73. *Journal de la Communauté* (February 8, 1952): 8.

74. See the variety of monthly bulletins collected in Archives de l'Alliance Israélite Universelle, Paris, AP 1/29.

75. On the growing popularity and visibility of Zionism in Paris, see the following examples: (1) The sporting Club Maccabi de Paris held a "Grand Bal de nuit" at the Hotel Continental on November 15, 1952. The evening combined jazz music, food, and a raffle and took place in a hotel that had long been popular among Jewish groups in the city. Ticket to the ball, Archives de l'Alliance Israélite Universelle, Paris, AP 1/51, unnumbered file. On the hotel's popularity, see Chapter 1. (2) The Sephardi section of the Union sioniste de France held their annual *grande fête* in 1953 at the exclusive Hotel George V (today the Four Seasons) on Saturday, February 21. The organization boasted that the evening would feature "the best dance-orchestras." Ticket to the ball, Archives de l'Alliance Israélite Universelle, Paris, AP 1/81, unnumbered pages. (3) In February 1958 the same group held another similar party at the same hotel, featuring the orchestras of Claude Bolling and Don Diego and "Israeli star" Sarah Rubine. "L'an 10 de l'État d'Israël," letter to Edmond Maurice Lévy, Archives de l'Alliance Israélite Universelle, Paris, AP 1/81. (4) The same organization held educational lectures promoting their political cause. These included talks on "Mendelssohn and the Problem of Assimilation" and "The Zionist Movement in Israel and the World." "L'an 10 de l'État d'Israël," letter to Edmond Maurice Lévy; and unnumbered and blank invitation issued by the Union sioniste to the talk about Mendelssohn, both held in Archives de l'Alliance Israélite Univer-

selle, Paris, AP 1/81. (5) Like the Union sioniste de France, the Organisation sioniste de France held a Blue and White ball on Sunday, January 15, 1956, from 3 p.m. until midnight at the Hotel George V. Ticket to the ball, Archives de l'Alliance Israélite Universelle, Paris, AP 1/51, unnumbered file.

76. "Un grand gala," *Journal des Communautés* (September 18, 1953): n.p.

77. Six-page brochure in French and Yiddish published by the Comité national des colonies de vacances en Israël in 1954, Archives de l'Alliance Israélite Universelle, Paris, AP 1/51.

78. Although *The Jewish Chronicle Travel Guide* recommended two kosher restaurants, Eden (36, Boulevard Bonne Nouvelle, in the 10th arrondissement) and Carmel (33, rue des Rosiers, in the Pletzl, in the 3rd arrondissement), the city did offer more. *Jewish Chronicle Travel Guide*, 135.

79. Raczymow, *Avant le déluge*, 16–17.

80. Raczymow, *Avant le déluge*, 17.

81. In 1948 the first vice president of the CBIP wrote a report on the organization's activities and specifically thanked Grand Rabbi Kaplan for his help in aiding the children of Paris through the *colonies de vacances*. See "Rapport de M. P. G., 1er Vice-Président," La Fondation CASIP-COJASOR, Paris, 2B12: CBIP (1948–), p. 8. Grand Rabbi Kaplan had called on the CBIP to donate a significant sum of money so that children could participate in a summer camp in the Black Forest. See Minutes of meeting, June 22, 1948, La Fondation CASIP-COJASOR, Paris, 2B12: CBIP (1948–), pp. 22–23.

82. Considering the challenges faced by families who attempted to reunite with children hidden by Christian institutions during the Shoah and the experiences of some of the children who were converted during the time, religious tensions remained a concern and motivation for the continued existence of Jewish summer camps. The *Journal de la Communauté* reported that a study presented to the Assises du judaïsme français regarding the danger of Jewish children converting had directly resulted in one Jewish organization opening a "Colonie de Vacances." *Journal de la Communauté* (July 14, 1950): 9.

83. Weinberg, "Reconstruction," 173.

84. The OPEJ, with its origins in the Shoah and mandate to protect and save Jewish children, ran Jewish summer camps that promoted general and Jewish education in addition to offering time for rest and fresh air. "Les vacances des enfants de l'OPEJ," *Journal de la Communauté* (September 22, 1950): 4.

85. A. S., "Plusieurs milliers d'enfants juifs sont eu leurs vacances," *La Terre Retrouvée: Revue Bi-Mensuelle de la Vie Juive en France, en Israël et dans le Monde* (September 1, 1950): 9.

86. Musnik, "Nos colonies de vacances," 6–7.

87. The CBIP was founded in 1809 by the Consistoire. See, for example, "Rapport de M. Pierre Geismar, 1er Vice-Président," La Fondation CASIP-COJASOR, Paris, 2B12: CBIP (1948–), p. 8; and Séance plénière du mardi 22 juin 1948, La Fondation CASIP-COJASOR, Paris, 2B12: CBIP (1948–), pp. 22–23.

88. "Les moniteurs de nos colonies de vacances," *Journal des Communautés* (March 22, 1957): 10.

89. André Bernhein, "Un rapport sur des rapports," June 28, 1948, Archives du Consistoire, Paris, B138, p. 2.

90. "Le Consistoire de Paris et les jeunes," *Journal de la Communauté* (June 22, 1951): 8. See also Kisler-Rosenwald, "La communauté vue par les jeunes," 5.

91. Menahem, "Raison d'être," 9.

92. "Une semaine aux Centre des Jeunes," *Journal des Communautés* (May 23, 1958): 4.

93. Séance Plénière of the CBIP, June 20, 1952, La Fondation CASIP-COJASOR, Paris, 2B12: CBIP (1948), p. 92. Other children's and youth clubs were created, such as the Union scolaire et clubs israélites, which had the goal of "grouping together Jewish youth of all 'tendencies,' to inculcate within them a pride in their past, to support them in the future, and to give them confidence in their future." It was no surprise that the group openly stated that, to accomplish this aim, they would need "to create the largest number possible of permanent meeting centers." Invitation for a *sauterie* on Sunday, February 8, 1948, Archives de l'Alliance Israélite Universelle, Paris, AP 1/29. See also Gourevitch, "Réflexions," 3.

94. "Pour une maison des jeunes," *Journal des Communautés* (March 11, 1955): 3. For more information, see Meeting notes, November 5, 1951, La Fondation CASIP-COJASOR, Paris, 2B12: CBIP (1948), pp. 82–83; inserted letter by Rabbi Paul Bauer (rabbin de l'Association consistoriale israélite de Paris, attaché au Temple de la rue Buffault) regarding the Maison d'étudiants, November 10, 1952, La Fondation CASIP-COJASOR, Paris, 2B12: CBIP (1948); La Fondation CASIP-COJASOR, Paris, Fonds Guy Patin; La Fondation CASIP-COJASOR, Paris, Fonds Toît Familial, I.2: Statuts; and La Fondation CASIP-COJASOR, Paris, Fonds Toît Familial, II.5: Animation culturelle.

95. Meeting notes, November 5, 1951, La Fondation CASIP-COJASOR, Paris, 2B12: CBIP (1948), pp. 82–83; inserted letter by Rabbi Paul Bauer, November 10, 1952, La Fondation CASIP-COJASOR, Paris, 2B12: CBIP (1948); "La Maison d'étudiants: Le Toît Familial," n.d., La Fondation CASIP-COJASOR, Paris, Fonds Guy Patin.

96. "La Maison d'étudiants: Le Toît Familial," n.d., La Fondation CASIP-COJASOR, Paris, Fonds Guy Patin.

97. La Fondation CASIP-COJASOR, Paris, Fonds Toît Familial, I.2: Statuts, unnumbered documents.

98. Notes on the Cine Club Guy Patin, La Fondation CASIP-COJASOR, Paris, Fonds Toît Familial, II.5: Animation culturelle; copies of various journals, including the *Petit Patiniste* from 1956 and the *Guy-Patin Observateur* from 1957, La Fondation CASIP-COJASOR, Paris, Fonds Guy Patin.

99. I am struck by Pierre Birnbaum's article "Grégoire, Dreyfus, and Drancy," in which Birnbaum points to the general forgetfulness about the war and, in particular, French participation in the Holocaust as well as the general disinterest in Zion-

ism. He overlooks early commemoration and instead points to the Six-Day War of 1967 as the turning point in French Jewish consciousness and also highlights the immigration of North African Sephardi Jews as another contributing factor in changing Jewish self-understanding. See Birnbaum, "Grégoire, Dreyfus, and Drancy." Similarly, Henry Rousso wrote that "it would take thirty years for memory to be rekindled in those Jews who had escaped the genocide" (Rousso, *Vichy Syndrome*, 26).

100. On the debates over the erection of the "Memorial to the Unknown Jewish Martyr," see Wieviorka, "Réflexions," 708.

101. Wieviorka, "Réflexions."

102. Quoted in Wieviorka, "Réflexions," 705 (translation mine).

103. Wieviorka, "Réflexions," 705–6.

104. See the ceremony program, "Temple Victoire, Vendredi 25 Avril, 1958," Archives de l'Alliance Israélite Universelle, Paris, AP 1/79.

105. Annette Wieviorka uses the term *reconciliation* (Wieviorka, "Réflexions," 706). For information about governmental guests, see "Auschwitz," *Journal des Communautés* (May 14, 1954): unnumbered page.

106. Throughout the Soviet era, Jews were recognized as a national minority, and many found work within the party, especially in the early years. Jews were Russian Soviet citizens, individuals before the state. Jewish space could be tolerated so long as it was politically correct. An outstanding example was the Moscow State Yiddish Theater (GOSET), which existed from 1919 until it was closed in 1948. Veidlinger, *Moscow State Yiddish Theater*. More generally, in the Soviet Union, various people shared an ideologically based suspicion of religious belief as it was expressed by Jews and members of other religious groups. Officially, Judaism was, in a way similar to other religions, "attacked in statewide propaganda, which aimed, among other things, to separate Jews from Judaism" (Shternshis, *Soviet and Kosher*, 2). Yet this was not only a top-down process of forced secularization. Jewish communists also participated in the early campaigns against "obscurantism." The goal of these early participants was to create good communist citizens, who were, if anything, Jewish by nationality but not by religion. Shternshis, *Soviet and Kosher*, 9, 14–43.

107. Pinkus, *Soviet Government*, 263. Sovietization did not always mean the destruction of Jewish culture or a full rejection of Judaism, as the existence of Jewish cultural and religious institutions in Poland, Hungary, and East Germany should remind us. In Leningrad, however, no significant communist Jewish organizations were created or maintained, and attitudes toward Judaism were far more antipathetic. Beizer, "Jews of a Soviet Metropolis," 116. Also see Beizer, *Evrei Leningrada*, 346–50, 354.

108. Barber, "Introduction." The end of the war did not mean that the situation in the Soviet Union suddenly became dramatically better. The years 1946 and 1947 were marked by hunger and famine. Some estimates suggest that, among the general population of the Soviet Union between 1946 and 1948, 100 million people were malnourished and 2 million died of hunger. Nevertheless, for political reasons, rationing was officially abolished in 1947. Zubkova, *Russia After the War*, 39–40, 47,

53. On the siege of Leningrad and the famine, see Moskoff, *Bread of Affliction*, esp. ch. 10 ("Death's Dominion: the Siege of Leningrad").

109. Shternshis, *Soviet and Kosher*, 2–3.

110. Ioffe, *Semeinye zapiski*, 62.

111. A Jewish liturgical poem or song recited on Shabbat mornings as part of the *shaharit* services as well as at the Passover seder.

112. Belov, *Ekh hayiti kushi*, 24–25.

113. Belov, *Ekh hayiti kushi*, 25.

114. At the same time, somewhat curiously, a number of Leningrad Jews continued to have their sons circumcised. For example, in the first quarter of 1948, 150 *britot milah* (ritual circumcisions) were performed in Leningrad, including by nonreligious families. Altshuler, *Yahadut b-makhbesh ha-sovieti*, 315. Birth rates for this time period among Jews are hard to come by, so it is difficult to determine the exact proportion of Jews who had their sons circumcised. Also, it is unclear whether the first quarter of 1948 was an aberration or was representative of larger trends.

115. Rabbi K. relates how one student had suffered unpleasant consequences when it was known that he was observant. See Transcript of interview with Rabbi K., June 24, 1987, Hartman Institute, OHD (200) 6, p. 2.

116. Hartman Institute, OHD (200) 6, pp. 2–4.

117. Zeltser, "Establishment," 108.

118. The play's title is translated sometimes as "200,000," "The Jackpot," "The Big Win," or even "The Lottery."

119. Zeltser, "Establishment," 109, 111.

120. Pertsovski, "Nayer Program," 5.

121. Weiner, *Making Sense of War*, 8, 19–20, 21, 195, 197, 200, 207, 208, 215. This is echoed in the work of Zubkova, *Russia After the War*, 16–17, 19. One well-known example of this can be seen in the case of Babi Yar. Babi Yar became a symbol of the Soviet government's refusal to commemorate the suffering of the Jews and the genocide committed against them. The issue came to a head as a result of the poem "Babi Yar" by Evgenii Evtushenko, a non-Jew. See Levin, *Jews in the Soviet Union*, 611–12; and Weiner, *Making Sense of War*, 8, 19–21, 215.

122. The lines are reported in the *Folks-Shtime;* see Pertsovski, "Durkhkuk," 1. Additional information can be found in Zeltser, "Establishment," 109.

123. Gilbert, *Music in the Holocaust*, 70, 72.

124. For example, private apartments were the site for dissident meetings, including those of Jewish dissidents. See Rubenstein, *Soviet Dissidents*, 159. Although somewhat beyond our timeframe, the example of N. (born in 1953) reminds us that vacations could serve as moments for friends to meet. As a child, N. and her mother would visit the home of a friend of her mother, and there, in this environment, N. was exposed to Jewish songs and traditions. See Transcript of interview with N., Hartman Institute, OHD (217) 2, p. 7.

125. The Aleph Group assembled several Soviet Jewish artists from Leningrad, who held the first exhibition on November 25, 1975. The exhibition took place

in the apartment of Evgeny Abezhaus. Over the course of six days, twelve artists showed their work, and estimates suggest that 4,000 people attended. A number of the artists of the Aleph Group, an avant-garde movement, had previously (during the early 1970s) shown work in Moscow and Leningrad with official permission. The artists of the Aleph Group presented art with clear and evident Jewish symbolism, which was extremely rare in officially sanctioned artistic expressions. See Genkina, "'Aleph' Group."

126. Genkina, "'Aleph' Group."

127. Zisserman-Brodsky, *Constructing Ethnopolitics.*

NOTES TO EPILOGUE

1. We must recall that, although neither the Soviet Union nor East Germany was a consumerist society, consumption and public leisure did continue to have a place. Restaurants, public eating establishments, cafés, and bars continued to exist and serve the public. Elena Zubkova notes the cafés, snack bars, and beer halls newly opened after the war and how they served the social life of war veterans; see Zubkova, *Russia After the War,* 27.

2. The rate of intermarriage in post-Shoah Berlin must be properly contextualized: A significant proportion of Jews in Berlin survived the Holocaust *because* they were married to non-Jews. This of course skews any statistical analysis of the community after the Shoah, and the relatively high rate of intermarriage gains a different meaning.

3. Today, we can see these modes of community building, celebration, and participation across Western Europe and North America through Jewish summer camps, youth groups, Hillel houses, and Jewish community centers.

4. Gitelman, "Conclusion," 312.

5. Gitelman, "Conclusion," 313.

6. Gitelman, "Conclusion," 316.

Bibliography

ARCHIVAL COLLECTIONS

American Jewish Joint Distribution Committee Archives
1944–1952 Jerusalem Collection

Archiv des Centrum Judaicum, Berlin
1, 75 A Be 2, Nr. 6/1, 280, 282, 285, 286, 307, 309–312, 316–318
1, 75 E, Nr. 423
5B1, Nr. 11, 13, 45, 71, 72, 73, 79, 128, 129, 173, 217, 218, 219, 245–248, 258
Personal Archives: 6.2, Fritz Selbiger; 6.4, Freia Eisner; 6.6, Erich and Nelly Cohn;
  6.7, Denny and Berta Gottlieb; 6.11, Siegfried Sachs

Archives de l'Alliance Israélite Universelle, Paris
Séries F: Documentation d'Isidore Loeb
Séries K: Culte et Consistoire
Séries M: Activités Intellectuelles
Fonds OSE
Archives Modernes: AM O 19b; AM O 19g; AM O 035e; AM O 035g
Personal Archives: AP 1, Edmond Maurice Lévy (1878–1971); AP 21, Benjamin
  Goriély (1898–1986)

Archives du Consistoire Israélite de Paris
Fond B: Divers fonds sur le Consistoire
Fond F: Écoles et cours religieux
Fond G: Cérémonies religieuses
Fond GG: Cérémonies religieuses

Avraham Harman Institute, Oral History Division of the Hebrew University,
Jerusalem
Folders (200) 6; (217) 2; (217) 198; (217) 163

Die Bundesbeauftragte für die Unterlagen des Staatssicherheitsdienstes der ehemaligen
Deutschen Demokratischen Republik, Berlin
AU Untersuchungsvorgang, Nr. 295/52, Archiv Nr. 305/54
BVDresden, AIM 448/58

BVDresden, AOP 2222/84
JGBerlin, AOP 11843/64
MfS 12604/64
MfS 1214/68
MfS HA XVIII, Nr. 11891
ZAIG 1417

Central Archives for the History of the Jewish People, Jerusalem
Folders D/Be 4/157; F Pa/24; F Pa/26; F Pa/28; F Pa/32; F Pa/33; F Pa/58;
    RU 585.12; RU 585.13; RU 1289
Personal Archives: P 1, Simon Dubnow; P 2, Ismar Freund

Central Zionist Archives, Jerusalem
Russia (A. Rafaeli-Zenzipper Collection): F30
Personal Archives: A11, Arthur Hantke; A 135, Sammy Gronemann; A225, Hans Klee;
    A 329, Moses Calvary; A 461, Gustav Krojenker

Centre de Documentation Juive Contemporaine, Paris
Collections CCXVII-8_020; CDV-52a; CDXX-45_001; CDXX-46_002;
    CDXX-39_001; XXI-79/82; XI-12
Fonds CRIF (Conseil représentatif des israélites de France): MDI I.4.2.1–I.4.2.11
Fonds MJS (Le mouvement de jeunesse sioniste en France) et la Commission
    centrale pour l'accueil des enfants: MDXXV, 12, 16, 19, 21
Fonds "Organisation sioniste": MD1–17
Fonds Kaplan: 1–4, 15, 16, 27–29, 44, 45, 61
Archives de M. Alain de Rothschild: MDI-98/99, 137, 139B, 259/261, 264,
    266/267, 273/274

*La Fondation CASIP-COJASOR, Paris (Comité d'action sociale israélite de Paris,
and Comité juif d'action social et de reconstruction)*
Séries 1B: Registres de délibération du CBIP
Séries 2B: Registres de délibérations des commissions et des oeuvres affiliées
Séries 3D: Biens et Tombolas
Fonds Toît Familial

Landesarchiv Berlin
A Pr. Br. Rep. 030 Bln C, Nr. 15
A Pr. Nr. Rep. 030, Nr. 13503
A Rep. 001-02, Nr. 422, 597
A Rep. 010-02, Nr. 1702, 3986, 5197, 7658, 7795
A Rep. 038-01, Nr. 116, 120, 122
B Rep. 002, Nr. 8548, 8642/1+2, 8547, 8643, 4872, 9788, 26202
B Rep. 042, Nr. 28142, 28006, 2897a, 29025, 39895, 47016, 48202
B Rep. 206, Nr. 4260
B Rep. 213, Nr. 1228–1229
C Rep. 101, Nr. 232, 233, 1816

C Rep. 101-04, Nr. 7

C Rep. 104, Nr. 63, 78, 101, 290, 406, 512, 620, 621

C Rep. 118, Nr. 346, 531, 602

C Rep. 120, Nr. 244, 2377, 2381

Personal Archives: E Rep. 200-33, Bleichröder; E Rep. 061-20, Simon;
E Rep. 200-61, Bermann; E Rep. 200-22, Weltlinger; E Rep. 200-32, Lipschitz

Leo Baeck Institute/Jüdisches Museum Berlin
Microfilm Collection: Adolf/Adolph Asch, MM 3; Elizabeth Bab, MM 3; Julius
Bab Collection, MF 475 (reels 1 and 2); Paul Barnay, MM 5; Berlin Jewish
Community Collection, MF 67, 94, 472 (reels 1–3), 587; Käte Dan-Rosen,
MM 17; Mally Dienemann, MM 18, 96; Dora Edinger, MM 21, 96; Helene
Eyck, MM II 41; Ernst Feder, MM 98–101; Joseph Gallinger, MM 26, MF
188; Sammy Gronemann, MM 29; Henriette Hirsch, MM 38; Jacob Jacobson
Collection, MF 447 (reels 26, 28, 30); Johanna Meyer, MF 83, 106; Arthur Stern,
MM 73, 74; Isidor Stern, MM II 11; Valentin Family Collection, MM 104;
Gertrude Weissbluth, MM 80; Doris Zadek, MM 84

Staatsarchiv Hamburg
Polizeibehörde-Kriminalwesen C Jahrgang 1819, Nr. 199

Stiftung Jüdisches Museum Berlin, Historische Sammlung
Personal Collections: Ratheau; Meyer-Salinger; Burchardt; Familie Simon

Zentralarchiv zur Erforschung der Geschichte der Juden in Deutschland, Heidelberg
B2/19, Nr. 1, Buchstaben A–F

B2/19, Nr. 2, Buchstaben G–J

B2/19, Nr. 3, Buchstaben K–M

B2/19, Nr. 4, Buchstaben N–Q

B2/19, Nr. 4, Buchstaben R–S

B2/19, Nr. 4, Buchstaben Sch

B2/19, Nr. 5, Buchstaben St–U

B2/19, Nr. 5, Buchstaben V–Z

NEWSPAPERS, MAGAZINES, AND BULLETINS

Allgemeine Wochenzeitung der Juden in Deutschland (Düsseldorf)

Allgemeine Zeitung des Judentums (Leipzig, Berlin)

Almanach Juif (Paris: La Nouvelle Génération, 1930)

L'annuaire des Archives Israélites (Paris)

Archives Israélites (Paris)

Berliner Allgemeine Wochenzeitung der Juden in Deutschland (Berlin)

Berliner Vereinsbote (Berlin)

Budushchnost' (St. Petersburg)

Esra (Vienna)

Folks-Shtime (Warsaw)

Für unsere Mitglieder (Berlin)
General-Anzeiger für die gesamten Interessen des Judentums (Berlin)
He-avar (Petrograd)
Im Deutschen Reich (Berlin)
Der Israelit (Mainz, Frankfurt am Main)
Israelitisches Familienblatt (Hamburg, Berlin)
Journal de la Communauté (*Journal des Communauté* after 1955) (Paris)
Der Jude (Berlin, Vienna)
Jüdische Gemeinde von Groß-Berlin—Nachrichtenblatt (Berlin)
Die jüdische Presse (Berlin)
Jüdische Rundschau (Berlin)
Jüdische Turn- und Sportzeitung (Berlin)
Menorah (Vienna)
Monatsschrift der Berliner Logen (Berlin)
Der Morgen (Berlin)
Nachrichtenblatt der Jüdischen Gemeinde von Groß-Berlin und des Verbandes der Jüdischen Gemeinde in der Deutschen Demokratischen Republik (Berlin)
Naie Presse (Paris)
Neue jüdische Monatshefte (Berlin)
New York Times (New York)
Novyi Voskhod (St. Petersburg)
Perezhitoe (St. Petersburg)
Popular Science Monthly (New York)
Razsviet (St. Petersburg)
Revue OSÉ: Organe Mensuel de l'Union des Sociétés pour la Protection de la Santé des Populations Juives (Paris)
Schalom: Zeitschrift des Jugendzentrums der Jüdische Gemeinde zu Berlin (Berlin)
Der Schlemiel: Illustriertes jüdisches Witzblatt (Berlin)
Der Shadkhon (Vilna)
La Terre Retrouvée: Revue Bi-Mensuelle de la Vie Juive en France, en Israël et dans le Monde (Paris)
Univers Israélite (Paris)
Voskhod (*Nediel'naia Khronika Voskhoda* between 1882 and 1897; *Khronika Voskhoda* between 1897 and 1899; *Voskhod* thereafter) (St. Petersburg)
Der Weg: Zeitschrift für Fragen des Judentums (Berlin)
Die Welt (Vienna)
YOD (Paris)
Zeitschrift für Demographie und Statistik der Juden (Berlin)

PUBLISHED WORKS

Abitbol, Michel, and Alan Astro. "The Integration of North African Jews in France." *Yale French Studies* 85 (1994): 248–61.
Abramov, S. Zalman. *Perpetual Dilemma: Jewish Religion in the Jewish State.* Cranbury, NJ: Associated University Presses, 1976.

Abramson, Glenda. "Vogel and the City." In Jörg Schulte, Olga Tabachnikova, and Peter Wagstaff (eds.), *The Russian Jewish Diaspora and European Culture, 1917–1937*, 37–54. Leiden: Brill, 2012.

Agnon, S. Y. *A Simple Story*. Trans. Hillel Halkin. New York: Schocken, 1985.

———. *Twenty-One Stories*. Ed. Nahum N. Glatzer. New York: Schocken, 1970.

Aizenshtadt, M. G. "Khanuka." *Razsviet* (December 12, 1910): 9–11.

Alpern, Manfred. "Ich habe hier nichts zugelegt." In Ulrich Eckhardt and Andreas Nachama (eds.), *Jüdische Berliner: Leben nach der Schoa*, 17–35. Berlin: Jaron, 2003.

Altshuler, Mordechai. *Soviet Jewry on the Eve of the Holocaust: A Social and Demographic Profile*. Jerusalem: Center for Research on East European Jewry, 1998.

———. *Yahadut b-mahbesh ha-sovieti: Ben dat l-zehut yehudit b-brit ha-moatsot, 1941–1964*. Jerusalem: Zalman Shazar Center for Jewish History, 2007.

Anderson, Harriet. *Utopian Feminism: Women's Movements in fin-de-siècle Vienna*. New Haven, CT: Yale University Press, 1992.

Ansky, S. *The Enemy at His Pleasure: A Journey Through the Jewish Pale of Settlement During World War I*. Ed. and trans. Joachim Neugroschel. New York: Henry Holt, 2002.

Ariès, Philippe. *Centuries of Childhood*. New York: Vintage, 1962.

Asch, Sholem. *Peterburg: Roman (Ershter Bukh fun "Farn Mabul")*. Buenos Aires: Tsentral-Farband fun Poylishe Yidn in Argentine, 1949.

———. *Three Cities: A Trilogy*. Trans. Willa and Edwin Muir. New York: Putnam, 1943.

Aschheim, Steven E. *Brothers and Strangers: The East European Jew in German and German Jewish Consciousness, 1800–1923*. Madison: University of Wisconsin Press, 1982.

———. "Introduction: Hannah Arendt in Jerusalem." In Steven E. Aschheim (ed.), *Hannah Arendt in Jerusalem*, 1–15. Berkeley: University of California Press, 2001.

L'association "La Colonie Scolaire": De sa fondation à ce jour. Pamphlet. Paris, ca. 1947.

Auerbach, Israel. "Chanukkah und der Orden." *Monatsschrift der Berliner Logen* 7.9 (December 1927): front page.

———. "Sein Junge." *Jüdische Turnzeitung* 2 (1901): 21–26.

Auslander, Leora. *Taste and Power: Furnishing Modern France*. Berkeley: University of California Press, 1996.

Avrutin, Eugene M. "Returning to Judaism After the 1905 Law on Religious Freedom in Tsarist Russia." *Slavic Review* 65.1 (2006): 90–110.

Baader, Benjamin Maria. "Rabbinic Study, Self-Improvement, and Philanthropy: Gender and the Refashioning of Jewish Voluntary Associations in Germany, 1750–1870." In Thomas Adam (ed.), *Philanthropy, Patronage, and Civil Society: Experiences from Germany, Great Britain, and North America*, 163–78. Bloomington: Indiana University Press, 2004.

Baeck, Leo. "Religion und Erziehung." *Der Jude* (1925): 1–10.

Baedeker, Karl. *Berlin and Environs*. Leipzig: Karl Baedeker, 1912.

———. *Paris and Its Environs with Routes from London to Paris*. Leipzig: Karl Baedeker, 1913.

―――. *Russia, with Teheran, Port Arthur, and Peking*. Leipzig: Karl Baedeker, 1914.

Bajohr, Frank. *"Unser Hotel ist judenfrei": Bäder-Antisemitismus im 19. und 20. Jahrhundert*. Frankfurt am Main: Fischer, 2003.

Baker, Cynthia M. *Rebuilding the House of Israel*. Stanford, CA: Stanford University Press, 2002.

Barber, John. "Introduction: Leningrad's Place in the History of Famine." In John Barber and Andrei Dzeniskevich (eds.), *Life and Death in Besieged Leningrad, 1941–44*, 1–12. New York: Palgrave Macmillan, 2005.

Barkai, Avraham. "Between Deutschtum and Judentum: Ideological Controversies Within the Centralverein." In Michael Brenner and Derek J. Penslar (eds.), *In Search of Jewish Community: Jewish Identities in Germany and Austria, 1918–1933*, 74–91. Bloomington: Indiana University Press, 1998.

Baskin, Judith R. "Piety and Female Aspiration in the Memoirs of Pauline Epstein Wengeroff and Bella Rosenfeld Chagall." *Nashim: A Journal of Jewish Women's Studies and Gender Issues* 7 (2004): 65–96.

Batnitzky, Leora. *How Judaism Became a Religion: An Introduction to Modern Jewish Thought*. Princeton, NJ: Princeton University Press, 2011.

Bauer, Rabbi Jules. "La femme et nos traditions religieuses." *Univers Israélite* (April 30, 1897): 170–71.

Beizer, Michael [Mikhail Beizer]. *Evrei Leningrada, 1917–1939: Natsional'naiia zhizn' i sovetizatsiia*. Moscow: Mosty Kul'tury; and Jerusalem: Gesharim, 1999.

―――. "The Jews of a Soviet Metropolis in the Interwar Period: The Case of Leningrad." In Zvi Gitelman and Yaacov Ro'i (eds.), *Revolution, Repression, and Revival: The Soviet Jewish Experience*, 113–30. Lanham, MD: Rowman & Littlefield, 2007.

―――. *The Jews of St. Petersburg: Excursions Through a Noble Past*. Ed. Martin Gilbert. Trans. Michael Sherbourne. Philadelphia: Jewish Publication Society, 1989.

―――. "The Leningrad Jewish Religious Community: From the NEP Through Its Liquidation." *Jews in Eastern Europe* 28 (1995): 16–42.

―――. *Yehude Leningrad: 1917–1939*. Jerusalem: Merkaz Zalman Shazar le-Toldot Yisrael, 1999.

―――. "Zionist Youth Movements in Post-October Petrograd-Leningrad." *Jews in Eastern Europe* 5 (1997): 7–31.

Belov (Elinson), Avraham. *Ekh hayiti kushi*. Trans. Shlomo Even-Shushan. Jerusalem: Avieli, 1990.

Benain, Aline. " 'Bâtissez des maisons et habitez-les' (*Jérémie*, 29, 5): Trouver une place, construire son espace." *Archives Juives* 37.1 (2004): 4–8.

Benbassa, Esther. *Histoire des juifs de France*. Paris: Éditions du Seuil, 1997.

Benjamin, Walter. *Das Passagen-Werk*. Frankfurt am Main: Suhrkamp, 1982.

Bergel-Gronemann, Elfriede. "Über religiöse Erziehung." *Der Jude* (1925): 100–105.

Bergelson, Dovid. *Leben ohne Frühling*. Berlin: Aufbau Taschenbuch, 2000.

―――. *The Shadows of Berlin: The Berlin Stories of Dovid Bergelson*. Trans. Joachim Neugroschel. San Francisco: City Lights Books, 2005.

Berkovitz, Jay R. *Rites and Passages: The Beginnings of Modern Jewish Culture in France, 1650–1860*. Philadelphia: University of Pennsylvania Press, 2004.

————. *The Shaping of Jewish Identity in Nineteenth-Century France*. Detroit: Wayne State University Press, 1989.

Berkowitz, Michael. *The Jewish Self-Image in the West*. New York: New York University Press, 2000.

Bermann, Ch. "L'éducation de nos enfants." *Archives Israélites* (August 25, 1919): 269–70.

Bernfeld, Siegfried. "Das europäische Erziehungsvorbild und die jüdische Gegenwart." *Der Jude* (1918): 383–94.

Bernstein, Leon. *Ershte Shprotsungen (Zichronot)*. Buenos Aires: Yidbukh, 1956.

Biale, David. *Eros and the Jews: From Biblical Israel to Contemporary America*. New York: Basic Books, 1992.

————. "Love, Marriage, and the Modernization of the Jews." In Marc Lee Raphael (ed.), *Approaches to Modern Judaism*, 1–17. Chico, CA: Scholar's Press, 1983.

Biélinky, J. "En faveur de l'enfance et de la jeunesse juive en France." *Révue OSÉ* (August 1937): 24–28.

Birnbaum, Pierre. "Grégoire, Dreyfus, and Drancy and the Rue Copernic: Jews at the Heart of the French Republic." In Pierre Nora (ed.), *Realms of Memory: Rethinking the French Past*, vol. 1, *Conflicts and Divisions*, trans. Arthur Goldhammer, 379–423. New York: Columbia University Press, 1996.

Birnbaum, Pierre, and Ira Katznelson. *Paths of Emancipation: Jews, States, and Citizenship*. Princeton, NJ: Princeton University Press, 2014.

Bloch, Albert "Jugendvereinigungen." *Monats-Bericht der Grossloge für Deutschland* (February 1899): 11.

Bloch, Isaac. *Petit catéchisme israélite*. Paris: Durlacher, 1911.

Bloch, Maurice. "Les colonies scolaires." *Univers Israélite* (October 27, 1899): 181–84.

Böhm, Adolf. "Die neue Erziehung als Weg zur nationalen Wiedergeburt." *Esra* (1919/1920): 60–62.

Bollerey, Franziska. "Setting the Stage for Modernity: The Cosmos of the Coffeehouse." In Christoph Grafe and Franziska Bollerey (eds.), *Cafés and Bars: The Architecture of Public Display*, 44–81. New York: Routledge, 2007.

Borck, Inge. "Ich war nie weg." In Ulrich Eckhardt and Andreas Nachama (eds.), *Jüdische Berliner: Leben nach der Schoa*, 37–63. Berlin: Jaron, 2003.

Borneman, John. "Identifying German Jews." In John Borneman and Jeffrey M. Peck (eds.), *Sojourners: The Return of German Jews and the Question of Identity*, 3–33. Lincoln: University of Nebraska Press, 1995.

Borrero, Mauricio. "Communal Dining and State Cafeterias in Moscow and Petrograd, 1917–1921." In Musya Glants and Joyce Toomre (eds.), *Food in Russian History and Culture*, 162–76. Bloomington: Indiana University Press, 1997.

Borut, Jacob. "Antisemitism in Tourist Facilities in Weimar Germany." *Yad Vashem Studies* 28 (2000): 7–50.

————. "Struggles for Spaces: Where Could Jews Spend Free Time in Nazi Germany?" *Leo Baeck Institute Year Book* 56 (2011): 307–50.

Bourdieu, Pierre. *Distinction: A Social Critique of the Judgement of Taste*. Trans. Richard Nice. Cambridge, MA: Harvard University Press, 1983.

Bovy, Phoebe Matlz. "'It Is Not the Number of Adherents': Jewish Authenticity and Intermarriage Anxiety in Nineteenth-Century France." *Journal of Jewish Identities* 8 (2015): 5–22.

Brauch, Julia, Anna Lipphardt, and Alexandra Nocke (eds.). *Jewish Topographies: Visions of Space, Traditions of Place.* Farnham, UK: Ashgate, 2008.

Brayer, Menachem M. *The Jewish Woman in Rabbinic Literature: A Psychological Perspective.* Brooklyn: Ktav, 1986.

Bredereck, Elke (ed.). *Menschen jüdischer Herkunft: Selbstbilder aus St. Petersburg, Vilnius und Berlin.* Konstanz: Hartung-Gorre, 2004.

Brenner, Michael. *After the Holocaust: Rebuilding Jewish Lives in Postwar Germany.* Trans. Barbara Harshav. Princeton, NJ: Princeton University Press, 1997.

———. "Introduction: Why Jews and Sports." In Michael Brenner and Gideon Reuveni (eds.), *Emancipation Through Muscles: Jews and Sports in Europe,* 1–9. Lincoln: University of Nebraska Press, 2006.

———. *The Renaissance of Jewish Culture in Weimar Germany.* New Haven, CT: Yale University Press, 1996.

———. "Turning Inward: Jewish Youth in Weimar Germany." In Michael Brenner and Derek J. Penslar (eds.), *In Search of Jewish Community: Jewish Identities in Germany and Austria, 1918–1933,* 56–73. Bloomington: Indiana University Press, 1998.

Brod, Max (ed.). *Franz Kafka: Briefe, 1902–1924.* New York: Schocken, 1958.

Bruce, Iris. *Kafka and Cultural Zionism: Dates in Palestine.* Madison: University of Wisconsin Press, 2007.

Bubis, Ignatz, with Peter Sichrovsky. *"Damit bin ich Noch Längst nicht Fertig": Die Autobiographie.* Berlin: Ullstein, 1998.

Buckler, Julie A. *Mapping St. Petersburg: Imperial Text and Cityshape.* Princeton, NJ: Princeton University Press, 2005.

Budde, Gunilla-Friederike. *Auf dem Weg ins Bürgerleben: Kindheit und Erziehung in deutschen und englischen Bürgerfamilien, 1840–1914.* Göttingen: Vandenhoeck & Ruprecht, 1994.

Bunim, Shmuel. "Sur les traces de quelques cafés juifs du Paris des années trente." *Les Cahiers du Judaïsme* 26 (2009): 46–51.

Burin, Erich. "Das Kaffeehausjudentum." *Jüdische Turnzeitung* (May–June, 1910): 74–75.

Burns, Michael. *Dreyfus: A Family Affair, 1789–1945.* New York: Harper Collins, 1991.

Calvary, Moses. "Blau-Weiss: Anmerkungen zum jüdischen Jugendwandern." *Der Jude* (October 1916): 451–57.

———. "Erziehung." *Der Jude* (1920): 123–28.

Caplan, Gregory A. "Germanizing the Jewish Male: Military Masculinity as the Last Stage of Acculturation." In Rainer Liedtke and David Rechter (eds.), *Towards Normality? Acculturation and Modern German Jewry,* 159–84. Tübingen: Mohr Siebeck, 2003.

Caron, Vicki. *Between France and Germany: The Jews of Alsace-Lorraine, 1871–1918.* Stanford, CA: Stanford University Press, 1988.

Caron, Vicki, Uri R. Kaufmann, and Michael Brenner (eds.). *Jewish Emancipation Reconsidered: The French and German Models.* Tübingen: Mohr Siebeck, 2003.

Casey, Edward S. "How to Get from Space to Place in a Fairly Short Stretch of Time: Phenomenological Prolegomena." In Steven Feld and Keith H. Basso (eds.), *Senses of Place*, 13–52. Santa Fe: School of American Research Press, 1996.

Cérémonie de l'initiation religieuse instituée par M. le Grand-Rabbin de Paris: Programme des connaissances religieuses exigées pour être admis à l'initiation. Paris: Alcan-Lévy, 1892.

Charnow, Sally. "French-Jewish Identity in the Wake of the Dreyfus Affair, 1898–1931: The Story of Edmond Fleg." In Maya Balakirsky Katz (ed.), *Revising Dreyfus*, 61–78. Leiden: Brill, 2013.

Clark, Katerina. *Petersburg, Crucible of Cultural Revolution.* Cambridge, MA: Harvard University Press, 1995.

Cohen, Richard I. *Jewish Icons: Art and Society in Modern Europe.* Berkeley: University of California Press, 1998.

———. "Nostalgia and 'Return to the Ghetto': A Cultural Phenomenon in Western and Central Europe." In Jonathan Frankel and Steven J. Zipperstein (eds.), *Assimilation and Community: The Jews in Nineteenth-Century Europe*, 130–55. Cambridge, UK: Cambridge University Press, 1992.

Cohn-Sherbok, Dan. *Introduction to Zionism and Israel: From Ideology to History.* London: CIP Group, 2012.

Confino, Alon, and Rudy Koshar. "Regimes of Consumer Culture: New Narratives in Twentieth Century German History." *German History* 19.2 (2001): 135–61.

Czerny, Boris. "L'association des étudiants russes de Paris." *Cahiers du Monde Russe* 48.1 (2007): 5–22.

Daikhes, M. (ed.) *Bar-Mitsvo: Literaturno-khudozhestvennyi sbornik dlia evreiskoi sem'i i shkoly.* St. Petersburg: Gutzats, 1914.

Daniel, Ute. *Arbeiterfrauen in der Kriegsgesellschaft: Beruf, Familie und Politik im Ersten Weltkrieg.* Göttingen: Vandenhoeck & Ruprecht, 1989.

Davidovitch, Nadav, and Rakefet Zalashik. "'Air, Sun, Water': Ideology and Activities of OZE During the Interwar Period." *Dynamis* 28 (2008): 127–49.

Débry, Rabbi Simon. *Catéchisme à l'usage de la jeunesse israélite.* Paris: Léon Kaan, 1906.

Decter, Moshe. "Status of the Jews in the Soviet Union." *Foreign Affairs: An American Quarterly Review* (January 1963). www.foreignaffairs.com/articles/russian-federation/1963-01-01/status-jews-soviet-union (accessed January 2, 2018).

Derenbourg, Joseph. *Livre de versets, ou première instruction religieuse.* Paris, 1844.

Dickinson, Edward Ross. "The Men's Christian Morality Movement in Germany, 1880–1914: Some Reflections on Politics, Sex, and Sexual Politics." *Journal of Modern History* 75.1 (2003): 59–110.

Dix années de Colonie Scolaire, 1926–1936. Paris: Société Parisienne d'Impressions, ca. 1936.

Dobbelaere, Karel. *Secularization: An Analysis at Three Levels.* Brussels: PIE–Peter Lang, 2002.

Döblin, Alfred. *Berlin: Alexanderplatz*. Berlin: S. Fischer, 1929.

Don-Yehiya, Eliezer. "Hanukkah and the Myth of the Maccabees in Zionist Ideology and in Israeli Society." *Jewish Journal of Sociology* 34 (1992): 5–24.

Döpp, Suska. *Jüdische Jugendbewegung in Köln 1906 bis 1938*. Münster: Lit, 1997.

Doron, Daniella. *Jewish Youth and Identity in Postwar France: Rebuilding Family and Nation*. Bloomington: Indiana University Press, 2015.

Downs, Laura Lee. *Childhood in the Promised Land: Working Class Movements and the Colonies de Vacances in France, 1880–1960*. Durham, NC: Duke University Press, 2002.

Dreyfous, Ferdinand. *De l'hystérie alcoolique*. Paris: Adrien Delahaye, 1888.

———. *Essai sur les symptomes protubérantiels de la méningite tuberculeuse*. Paris: Adrien Delahaye, 1879.

Dubin, Lois C. "Jewish Women, Marriage Law, and Emancipation: A Civil Divorce in Late-Eighteenth-Century Trieste." *Jewish Social Studies* 13 (2007): 65–92.

Dubnova-Erlich, Sophie. *Bread and Matzoh*. Trans. Alan Shaw. Tenafly, NJ: Hermitage, 2005.

Dubnow, Simon M. *Kniga zhizni: Vospominaniia i razmyshleniia*, vol. 1. Riga: Jaunatnas Gramata, 1934.

Dwork, Deborah. *Children with a Star: Jewish Youth in Nazi Europe*. New Haven, CT: Yale University Press, 1993.

Eckhardt, Ulrich, and Andreas Nachama (eds.). *Jüdische Berliner: Leben nach der Schoa*. Berlin: Jaron, 2003.

Edmondson, Linda Harriet. *Feminism in Russia, 1900–1917*. London: Heinemann Educational Books, 1984.

Efron, John. "The 'Kaftanjude' and the 'Kaffeehausjude': Two Models of Jewish Insanity—A Discussion of Causes and Cures Among German-Jewish Psychiatrists." *Leo Baeck Institute Yearbook* 37 (1992): 169–88.

Ehrenburg, Ilja (Ilya). "Briefe aus dem Café: Deutschland im Jahre 1922." In Ilja Ehrenburg and Hans Ruoff, *Visum der Zeit*, 29–41. Leipzig: Paul List, 1929.

———. *Viza vremeni*. Leningrad: Izdatelstvo pisatelei, 1933.

Einhorn, Barbara. "Gender, Nation, Landscape, and Identity in Narratives of Exile and Return." *Women's Studies International Forum* 23 (2000): 701–13.

Eisen, George. "Zionism, Nationalism, and the Emergence of the Jüdische Turnerschaft." *Leo Baeck Institute Yearbook* 28 (1983): 247–62.

Eliav, Mordechai. *Jüdische Erziehung in Deutschland im Zeitalter der Aufklärung und der Emanzipation*. Trans. Maike Strobel. Münster: Waxmann, 2001 [1960].

Ellis, Markman. *The Coffee House: A Cultural History*. London: Weidenfeld & Nicolson, 2004.

Emde, Heiner, and Michael Wolffsohn. "DDR—Der goldener Fußtritt." *Focus Magazin* 45 (1997). www.focus.de/politik/deutschland/ddr-der-goldene-fusstritt_aid_168711.html (accessed January 2, 2018).

Emmons, Terence. "Russia's Banquet Campaign." *California Slavic Studies* 10 (1977): 45–86.

Endelman, Todd M. "Introduction: Comparing Jewish Societies." In Todd M.

Endelman (ed.), *Comparing Jewish Societies*, 1–21. Ann Arbor: University of Michigan Press, 2000.

Engelstein, Laura. *The Keys to Happiness: Sex and the Search for Modernity in Fin-de-Siècle Russia*. Ithaca, NY: Cornell University Press, 1992.

Epstein, Catherine. *The Last Revolutionaries: German Communists and Their Century*. Cambridge, MA: Harvard University Press, 2003.

Eschelbacher, Max. "Mischehen." *Ost und West* 17.3/4 (1917): 73–88.

Estraikh, Gennady. "Vilna on the Spree: Yiddish in Weimar Berlin." *Aschkenas: Zeitschrift für Geschichte und Kultur der Juden* 16 (2006): 103–27.

Etkes, Immanuel. "Marriage and Torah Study Among the *Lomdim* in Lithuania in the Nineteenth Century." In David Kramer (ed.), *The Jewish Family: Metaphor and Memory*, 153–78. Oxford, UK: Oxford University Press, 1989.

Faguet, Emile. "Les pères et les enfants, hier et aujourd'hui." *Univers Israélite* (February 24, 1911): 741–46.

Farago, Uri. "The Influence of a Jewish Summer Camp's Social Climate on the Camper's Identity." Ph.D. diss., Brandeis University, 1972.

Feiner, Shmuel. *The Origins of Jewish Secularization in Eighteenth-Century Europe*. Trans. Chaya Naor. Philadelphia: University of Pennsylvania Press, 2011.

———. "The Pseudo-Enlightenment and the Question of Jewish Modernization." *Jewish Social Studies* 3 (1996): 62–88.

Fishberg, Maurice. "The Jews: A Study of Race and Environment." *Popular Science Monthly* 69 (November 1906): 441–50.

Fitch, Noel Riley, and Andrew Midgley. *The Grand Literary Cafés of Europe*. London: New Holland, 2006.

Fitzpatrick, Sheila. *Everyday Stalinism: Ordinary Life in Extraordinary Times—Soviet Russia in the 1930s*. Oxford, UK: Oxford University Press, 1999.

Fleg, Edmond. "Scoutisme et vie juive." *Univers Israélite* (June 27, 1930): 357–58.

Föllmer, Moritz. *Individuality and Modernity in Berlin*. Cambridge, UK: Cambridge University Press, 2013.

Fonrobert, Charlotte Elisheva, and Vered Shemtov. "Introduction: Jewish Conceptions and Practices of Space." *Jewish Social Studies* 11 (2005): 1–8.

Foucault, Michel. "Of Other Spaces." Trans. Jay Miskowiec. *Diacritics* 16.1 (1986): 22–27.

Frankel, Jonathan. *Crisis, Revolution, and Russian Jews*. Cambridge, UK: Cambridge University Press, 2009.

Freeze, ChaeRan Y. *Jewish Marriage and Divorce in Imperial Russia*. Hanover, NH: University Press of New England, 2002.

Freimark, Joseph. "Die jüdische Frau und das jüdische Haus." *Menorah* 5.8 (1927): 489–90.

Frevert, Ute. *Emotions in History: Lost and Found*. Budapest: Central European University Press, 2011.

Galinski, Heinz. "New Beginning of Jewish Life in Berlin." In Michael Brenner, *After the Holocaust: Rebuilding Jewish Lives in Postwar Germany*, trans. Barbara Harshav, 100–102. Princeton, NJ: Princeton University Press, 1997.

Gamzon, Denise R. *Mémoires.* Jerusalem, 1997.

Gassenschmidt, Christoph. *Jewish Liberal Politics in Tsarist Russia, 1900–14.* London: Macmillan, 1995.

Gay, Peter. *My German Question: Growing Up in Nazi Berlin.* New Haven, CT: Yale University Press, 1998.

Gay, Ruth. *Safe Among the Germans: Liberated Jews After World War II.* New Haven, CT: Yale University Press, 2002.

Gebhardt, Miriam. *Das Familiengedächtnis: Erinnerung im deutsch-jüdischen Bürgertum 1890 bis 1932.* Stuttgart: Franz Steiner, 1999.

Gelber, N. M. "Reshit tnuat ha-studentim ha-tsionim b-rusia b-shanim 1882–1891." *He-avar* 2 (1954): 46–60.

Geller, Jay Howard. *Jews in Post-Holocaust Germany, 1945–1953.* Cambridge, UK: Cambridge University Press, 2005.

Genkina, Marina. "The 'Aleph' Group." *Jewish Art* 21–22 (1995–1996): 168–82.

Gesellschaft OSE. *Die Entstehung der Gesellschaft OSE und ihre ersten Maßnahmen.* Berlin: Sinaburg, 1925.

Gessen, Valery. "The Jewish University of Petrograd." *East European Jewish Affairs* 22 (1992): 73–79.

Gilbert, Shirli. *Music in the Holocaust: Confronting Life in the Nazi Ghettos and Camps.* Oxford, UK: Oxford University Press, 2005.

Gillermann, Sharon. "The Crisis of the Jewish Family in Weimar Germany: Social Conditions and Cultural Representations." In Michael Brenner and Derek J. Penslar (eds.), *In Search of Jewish Community: Jewish Identities in Germany and Austria, 1918–1933,* 176–99. Bloomington: Indiana University Press, 1998.

———. "Samson in Vienna: The Theatrics of Jewish Masculinity." *Jewish Social Studies* 9 (2003): 65–98.

Gilman, Sander. "Introduction: The Frontier as a Model for Jewish History." In Sander Gilman and Milton Shain (eds.), *Jewries at the Frontier: Accommodation, Identity, Conflict,* 1–25. Urbana: University of Illinois Press, 1999.

Giniger, Henry. "Finaly Boys Flying to a New Home in Israel; Aunt Gives up Charges Against Catholics." *New York Times* (July 26, 1953): 12.

Gintsburg, Evgeniia Isidorovna. *Vospominaniia ionosti.* Paris: Val, 1937.

Gitelman, Zvi. "Conclusion." In Zvi Gitelman (ed.), *Religion or Ethnicity? Jewish Identities in Evolution,* 303–22. New Brunswick, NJ: Rutgers University Press, 2009.

Gleason, Mona. "Avoiding the Agency Trap: Caveats for Historians of Children, Youth, and Education." *History of Education* 45 (2016): 446–59.

Gluck, Mary. "The Budapest Coffee House and the Making of 'Jewish Modernity' at the Fin de Siècle." *Journal of the History of Ideas* 74.2 (2013): 289–306.

———. "The Budapest Flâneur: Urban Modernity, Popular Culture, and the 'Jewish Question' in Fin-de-Siècle Hungary." *Jewish Social Studies* 10 (2004): 1–22.

Goldhammer, Leo. "Die Mischehe: Eine Gefahr für das jüdische Volk." *Menorah* 5–6 (May 1930): 279–84.

Goldman, Wendy Z. *Women, the State, and Revolution Soviet Family Policy and Social Life, 1917–1936.* Cambridge, UK: Cambridge University Press, 1993.

Goldmann, Nahum. *The Jewish Paradox*. New York: Fred Jordan Books, 1978.

Goldstein, Dara. "Gastronomic Reforms Under Peter the Great: Towards a Cultural History of Russian Food." *Jahrbücher für Geschichte Osteuropas* 48 (2000): 481–510.

Gourevitch, E. "Réflexions sur l'éducation religieuse." *Journal de la Communauté* (August 11, 1950): 3.

Gousseff, Catherine. "Les juifs russes en France: Profil et évolution d'une collectivité." *Archives Juives* 34 (2001–2002): 4–16.

Grafe, Christopher. "Café Bauer." In Christopher Grafe and Franziska Bollery (eds.), *Cafés and Bars: The Architecture of Public Display*, 118–23. New York: Routledge, 2006.

Grazia, Victoria de, with Ellen Furlough (eds.). *The Sex of Things: Gender and Consumption in Historical Perspective*. Berkeley: University of California Press, 1996.

Green, Nancy L. "The Modern Jewish Diaspora: East European Jews in New York, London, and Paris." In Todd M. Endelman (ed.), *Comparing Jewish Societies*, 113–34. Ann Arbor: University of Michigan Press, 2000.

———. *The Pletzl of Paris: Jewish Immigrant Workers in the Belle Époque*. New York: Holmes & Meier, 1986.

Greenbaum, Alfred Abraham. *Jewish Scholarship and Scholarly Institutions in Soviet Russia, 1918–1953*. Jerusalem: Jerusalem Center for Research and Documentation of East European Jewry, Hebrew University, 1978.

Gregor, Neil, Nils Roemer, and Mark Roseman (eds.). *German History from the Margins*. Bloomington: Indiana University Press, 2006.

Grévy, Jérôme. "Les cafés républicains de Paris au début de la Troisième République: Étude de sociabilité politique." *Revue d'Histoire Moderne et Contemporaine* 50 (2003): 52–72.

Gronemann, Sammy. *Sammy Gronemann: Erinnerungen*. Ed. Joachim Schlör. Berlin: Philo, 2002.

Grossmann, Atina. " 'The Survivors Were Few and the Dead Were Many': Jewish Identity and Memory in Occupied Berlin." In Marion Kaplan and Beate Meyer (eds.), *Jüdische Welten: Juden in Deutschland vom 18. Jahrhundert bis in die Gegenwart*, 317–35. Göttingen: Wallstein, 2005.

Grunberger, Richard. *The 12-Year Reich: A Social History of Nazi Germany, 1933–1945*. New York: Da Capo Press, 1995 [1971].

Grünfeld, M. "Über Barmitzwah-Vorbereitungen." *Israelitisches Familienblatt* (October 10, 1907): 9–10.

Grynberg, Anne. "Après la tourmente." In Jean-Jacques Becker and Annette Wieviorka (eds.), *Les juifs de France: De la Révolution française à nos jours*, 249–86. Paris: Éditions Liana Levi, 1998.

Guesnet, François. "Chanukah and Its Function in the Invention of a Jewish-Heroic Tradition in Early Zionism, 1880–1900." In Michael Berkowitz (ed.), *Nationalism, Zionism, and Ethnic Mobilization of the Jews in 1900 and Beyond*, 227–45. Leiden: Brill, 2004.

Günzburg, Sophie. "My Father, Baron David." In Lucy S. Dawidowicz (ed.), *The Golden Tradition*, 248–56. New York: Holt, Rinehart & Winston, 1967.

Gutman, Joseph. "Jewish Medieval Marriage Customs in Art: Creativity and Adaptation." In David Kramer (ed.), *The Jewish Family: Metaphor and Memory*, 47–62. Oxford, UK: Oxford University Press, 1989.

Habermas, Jürgen. *The Structural Transformation of the Public Sphere: An Inquiry into a Category of Bourgeois Society*. Trans. Thomas Burger. Cambridge, MA: MIT Press, 1989.

Haine, W. Scott. *The World of the Paris Café: Sociability Among the French Working Class, 1789–1914*. Baltimore: Johns Hopkins University Press, 1996.

Hartewig, Karin. "Eine dritte Identität? Jüdische Kommunisten in der Gründergeneration der DDR." In Elke Scherstjanoi (ed.), *"Provisorium für längstens ein Jahr": Protokoll des Kolloqiums—die Gründung der DDR*, 292–302. Berlin: Akademie, 1993.

———. "Die Loyalitätsfrage: Jüdische Kommunisten in der DDR." In Moshe Zuckermann (ed.), *Zwischen Politik und Kultur: Juden in der DDR*, 48–62. Göttingen: Wallstein, 2002.

Harvey, David. "From Space to Place and Back Again: Reflections on the Condition of Postmodernity." In Jon Bird, Barry Curtis, Tim Putnam, and Lisa Tickner (eds.), *Mapping the Futures: Local Cultures, Global Change*, 3–29. London: Routledge, 1993.

———. *Paris, Capital of Modernity*. London: Routledge, 2006.

Haus, Jeffrey. *Challenges of Equality: Judaism, State, and Education in Nineteenth-Century France*. Detroit: Wayne State University Press, 2009.

Hazan, Katy. "Du heder aux écoles actuelles: L'éducation juive, reflet d'un destin collectif." *Archives Juives* 35 (2002): 4–25.

———. *Les orphelins de la Shoah: Les maisons de l'espoir (1944–1960)*. Paris: Les Belles Lettres, 2000.

Heidegger, Martin. "Building, Dwelling, Thinking." In Martin Heidegger, *Poetry, Language, Thought*, trans. Albert Hofstadter, 143–59. New York: Harper Perennial Modern Classics, 2001.

Heilman, Samuel C., and Menachem M. Friedman. *The Rebbe: The Life and Afterlife of Menachem Mendel Schneerson*. Princeton, NJ: Princeton University Press, 2010.

Heinemann, Jeremiah. *Profession de foi pour les israélites par demandes et réponses, à l'usage de ceux qui donnent la confirmation*. Vienna: George Ueberreuter, 1813. Originally published as *Religions-Bekenntniss für Israeliten in Fragen und Antworten* (Vienna: G. Ueberreuter, 1813).

Heinze, Andrew R. *Adapting to Abundance: Jewish Immigrants, Mass Consumption, and the Search for American Identity*. New York: Columbia University Press, 1990.

Herf, Jeffrey. *Divided Memory: The Nazi Past in the Two Germanys*. Cambridge, MA: Harvard University Press, 1997.

Herrmann, Ulrich. "Familie, Kindheit, Jugend." In Christa Berg (ed.), *Handbuch der deutschen Bildungsgeschichte*, Band IV, *1870–1918: Von der Reichsgründung bis zum Ende des Ersten Weltkriegs*, 69–96. Munich: C. H. Beck, 1991.

———. "Pädagogisches Denken und Anfänge der Reformpädagogik." In Christa

Berg (ed.), *Handbuch der deutschen Bildungsgeschichte*, Band IV, *1870–1918: Von der Reichsgründung bis zum Ende des Ersten Weltkriegs*, 97–133. Munich: C. H. Beck, 1991.

Hertz, Deborah S. *How Jews Became Germans: The History of Conversion and Assimilation in Berlin*. New Haven, CT: Yale University Press, 2007.

Herz, Manuel. "Institutionalized Experiment: The Politics of 'Jewish Architecture' in Germany." *Jewish Social Studies* 11 (2005): 58–66.

Herzberg, Wolfgang. *Überleben heißt Erinnern: Lebensgeschichten deutscher Juden*. Berlin: Aufbau, 1990.

Herzfeld, H. "Kameraden und die Jüdische Sportplatzgesellschaft Berlin." *Im Deutschen Reich* 26 (October 1920): 317–18.

Heschel, Susannah. *Abraham Geiger and the Jewish Jesus*. Chicago: University of Chicago Press, 1998.

Hessler, Julie. *A Social History of Soviet Trade: Trade Policy, Retail Practices, and Consumption, 1917–1953*. Princeton, NJ: Princeton University Press, 2004.

Hetkamp, Jutta. *Ausgewählte Interviews von Ehemaligen der Jüdischen Jugendbewegung in Deutschland von 1913–1933*. Münster: Lit, 1994.

———. *Die jüdische Jugendbewegung in Deutschland von 1913–1933*, Band 1. Münster: Lit, 1994.

Heywood, Colin. *A History of Childhood: Children and Childhood in the West from Medieval to Modern Times*. Cambridge, UK: Polity Press, 2001.

Hilberg, Raul. *The Destruction of the European Jews*. New York: Harper & Row, 1961.

Hilker-Siebenhaar, Carolin. *Wegweiser durch das jüdische Berlin: Geschichte und Gegenwart*. Berlin: Nicolai, 1987.

Hirsch, Salli. "Jüdische Erziehung." *Jüdische Turn- und Sportzeitung* (February 1919): 3–6.

Hirsch, Samson Raphael. "Religion Allied to Progress." In *Rabbi Samson Raphael Hirsch, Judaism Eternal: Selected Essays from the Writings of Rabbi Samson Raphael Hirsch*, trans. and annot. I. Grunfeld, 2: 224–44. London: Soncino Press, 1959.

Hirschfeld, Robert. "Ordensgedanke und Religionsunterricht." *Monatsschrift der Berliner Logen. U.O.B.B.* 7.9 (December 1927), 166.

Hobson Faure, Laura. "Shaping Children's Lives: American Jewish Aid in Post–World War II France." In Zvi Jonathan Kaplan and Nadia Malinovich (eds.), *The Jews of Modern France: Images and Identities*, 173–93. Leiden: Brill, 2016.

Hödl, Klaus. "The Turning to History of Viennese Jews." *Journal of Modern Jewish Studies* 3 (2004): 17–32.

———. "Der Zionismus als 'Therapie': Zionistische Strategien zur Bekämpfung des Antisemitismus." *Zeitgeschichte* 24 (1997): 49–61.

Hofmeester, Karin. *Jewish Workers and the Labor Movement: A Comparative Study of Amsterdam, London, and Paris, 1870–1914*. Burlington, VT: Ashgate, 2004.

Hofmeister, Alexis. *Selbstorganisation und Bürgerlichkeit: Jüdisches Vereinswesen in Odessa um 1900*. Göttingen: Vandenhoeck & Ruprecht, 2007.

Honigmann, Barbara. *Ein Kapitel aus meinem Leben*. Munich: Carl Hanser, 2004.

Honigmann, Peter. "Nur noch lebendes Museumsstück? Über das Problem, in der DDR ein Jude zu sein." *Tribüne* 24 (1985): 146–51.

Höppner, Solvejg. "'Ostjude ist jeder, der nach mir kommt . . .': Jüdische Einwanderer in Sachsen im Kaiserreich und in der Weimarer Republik." In Werner Bramke and Ulrich Heß (eds.), *Wirtschaft und Gesellschaft in Sachsen im 20. Jahrhundert*, 343–69. Leipzig: Leipziger Universitätsverlag, 1998.

Horowitz, Brian. *Empire Jews: Jewish Nationalism and Acculturation in 19th- and Early 20th-Century Russia*. Bloomington, IN: Slavica, 2009.

————. *Jewish Philanthropy and Enlightenment in Late-Tsarist Russia*. Seattle: University of Washington Press, 2009.

Hyman, Paula E. *From Dreyfus to Vichy: The Remaking of French Jewry, 1906–1939*. New York: Columbia University Press, 1979.

————. "Introduction." In Puah Rakovsky, *My Life as a Radical Jewish Woman: Memoirs of a Zionist Feminist in Poland*, 1–19. Bloomington: Indiana University Press, 2002.

————. "Introduction: Perspectives on the Evolving Jewish Family." In Steven M. Cohen and Paula E. Hyman (eds.), *The Jewish Family: Myths and Reality*, 3–13. New York: Holmes & Meier, 1986.

————. "Jewish Fertility in Nineteenth Century France." In Paul Ritterband (ed.), *Modern Jewish Fertility*, 78–93. Leiden: Brill, 1981.

————. *The Jews of Modern France*. Berkeley: University of California Press, 1998.

————. "The Modern Jewish Family: Image and Reality." In David Kramer (ed.), *The Jewish Family: Metaphor and Memory*, 179–93. Oxford, UK: Oxford University Press, 1989.

————. "Two Models of Modernization: Jewish Women in the German and Russian Empires." *Studies in Contemporary Jewry* 16 (2000): 39–53.

Im Hof, Ulrich. *Das Gesellige Jahrhundert: Gesellschaft und Gesellschaften im Zeitalter der Aufklärung*. Munich: C. H. Beck, 1982.

Ioffe, Berta. *Semeinye zapiski*. Haifa: B. D. Ioffe, 2003.

Isaac, M. "La libre-pensée et le mariage religieux dans le judaisme." *Archives Israélites* (April 4, 1907): 108–9.

Izrael', Kh. "Russko-evreiskaia uchashchaiasia molodezh' v Germanii." *Novyi Voskhod* (January 23, 1914): 11–14.

Jacobs, Jack. *Bundist Counterculture in Interwar Poland*. Syracuse, NY: Syracuse University Press, 2009.

The Jewish Chronicle Travel Guide, 1955. London: Jewish Chronicle Publications, 1955.

The Jewish Travel Guide, 1960. London: Jewish Chronicle Publications, 1960.

Joskowicz, Ari, and Ethan Katz. "Introduction: Rethinking Jews and Secularism." In Ari Joskowicz and Ethan Katz (eds.), *Secularism in Question: Jews and Judaism in Modern Times*, 1–21. Philadelphia: University of Pennsylvania Press, 2015.

Kafka, Franz. *Letter to His Father*. New York: Schocken, 1966.

Kantorowicz, Alfred. *Deutsches Tagebuch*, vol. 2. Munich: Kindler, 1961.

Kaplan, Marion. "Apprenticeships in Work and Love: Jewish Youth Growing Up in Imperial Germany." In Lauren B. Strauss and Michael Brenner (eds.), *Mediating*

Modernity: Challenges and Trends in the Jewish Encounter with the Modern World, 224–46. Detroit: Wayne State University, 2008.

———. "'Based on Love': The Courtship of Hendele and Jochanan, 1803–1804." In Marion Kaplan and Beate Meyer (eds.), *Jüdische Welten: Juden in Deutschland vom 18. Jahrhundert bis in die Gegenwart*, 86–107. Hamburg: Wallstein, 2005.

———. *Between Dignity and Despair: Jewish Life in Nazi Germany*. Oxford, UK: Oxford University Press, 1999.

———. "For Love or Marriage: Jewish Marriage Strategies." In Marion Kaplan, *The Making of the Jewish Middle Class: Women, Family, and Identity in Imperial Germany*, 85–116. Oxford, UK: Oxford University Press, 1991.

———. "For Love or Money: The Marriage Strategies of Jews in Imperial Germany." *Leo Baeck Institute Yearbook* 28 (1983): 263–300.

———. *The Making of the Jewish Middle Class: Women, Family, and Identity in Imperial Germany*. Oxford, UK: Oxford University Press, 1991.

———. "Redefining Judaism in Imperial Germany: Practices, Mentalities, and Communities." *Jewish Social Studies* 9.1 (2002): 1–33.

———. "Religious Practices, Mentalities, and Community." In Marion A. Kaplan (ed.), *Jewish Daily Life in Germany, 1618–1945*, 235–51. Oxford, UK: Oxford University Press, 2005.

Kaplan, Zvi Jonathan. "The Thorny Area of Marriage: Rabbinic Efforts to Harmonize Jewish and French Law in Nineteenth-Century France." *Jewish Social Studies* 13 (2007): 59–72.

Kassow, Samuel D. *Who Will Write Our History? Emanuel Ringelblum, the Warsaw Ghetto, and the Oyneg Shabes Archive*. Bloomington: Indiana University Press, 2007.

Katz, Jacob. "Nisuim v-haye ishut b-motsae yame ha-benayim." *Tsion* 10 (1944/1945): 21–54.

———. *Tradition and Crisis: Jewish Society at the End of the Middle Ages*. Trans. Bernard Dov Cooperman. Syracuse, NY: Syracuse University Press, 2000.

Kauders, Anthony D. "Money Makes the Jew Go Round: West German Jewry and the Search for Flexibility." In Gideon Reuveni and Sarah Wobick-Segev (eds.), *The Economy in Jewish History: New Perspectives on the Interrelationship Between Ethnicity and Economic Life*, 62–76. New York: Berghahn Books, 2011.

Kelly, Catriona. *St Petersburg: Shadows of the Past*. New Haven, CT: Yale University Press, 2014.

Kesten, Hermann. *Dichter im Café*. Vienna: K. Desch, 1959.

Khmel'nitskaia, Irina. "Eda davno minuvshikh dnei." *Moskovskaia Promyshlennaia Gazeta* 36.201 (September 19–25, 2002).

———. "Restorannaia zhizn'." *Moskovskaya Promyshlennaia Gazeta* 50.215 (December 26, 2002–January 1, 2003).

———. "Stolichnyi dosug v nachala XX veka: Peterburg i Moskva." Ph.D. diss., Moscow State University, 2004.

Kirchner, Peter. "Ein schönes Finale." In Ulrich Eckhardt and Andreas Nachama (eds.), *Jüdische Berliner: Leben nach der Schoa*, 141–68. Berlin: Jaron, 2003.

Kisler-Rosenwald, A. "La communauté vue par les jeunes." *Journal de la Communauté* (June 27, 1952): 5.

Kleinmann, Yvonne. *Neue Orte—Neue Menschen: Jüdische Lebensformen in St. Petersburg und Moskau im 19. Jahrhundert.* Göttingen: Vandenhoeck & Ruprecht, 2006.

Knörzer, Heidi (ed.). *Expériences croisées: Les juifs de France et d'Allemagne aux XIXe et XXe siècles.* Paris: Éditions de l'éclat, 2010.

————. "Hippolyte Prague, rédacteur en chef des Archives israélites (Paris, 16 novembre 1856–Paris, fin décembre 1935)." *Archives Juives* 1 (2010): 140–43.

Kobrin, Rebecca, and Adam Teller (eds.). *Purchasing Power: The Economics of Modern Jewish History.* Philadelphia: University of Pennsylvania Press, 2015.

Königseder, Angelika. *Flucht nach Berlin: Jüdische Displaced Persons, 1945–1948.* Berlin: Metropol, 1998.

Krinsky, Carol Herselle. *Synagogues of Europe: Architecture, History, Meaning.* Mineola, NY: Courier Dover, 1985.

Kümper, Michal, Barbara Rösch, Ulrike Schneider, and Helen Thein (eds.). *Makom: Orte und Räume im Judentum: Real—Abstrakt—Imaginär.* Hildesheim: Georg Olms, 2007.

Lasker-Schüler, Else. *Else Lasker-Schüler: Gesammelte Werke.* Ed. Friedhelm Kemp. Frankfurt am Main: Suhrkamp, 1996.

Lässig, Simone. *Jüdische Wege ins Bürgertum: Kulturelles Kapital und sozialer Aufstieg im 19. Jahrhundert.* Göttingen: Vandenhoeck & Ruprecht, 2004.

Lazare, Lucien. "Educational, Rescue, and Guerilla Operations of the Jewish Youth Movements in France, 1940–1944." In Asher Cohen and Yehoyakim Cochavi (eds.), *Zionist Youth Movements in the Shoah,* 173–83. New York: Peter Lang, 1995.

Lee, Daniel. *Pétain's Jewish Children: French Jewish Youth and the Vichy Regime, 1940–1942.* Oxford, UK: Oxford University Press, 2014.

Lefebvre, Henri. *The Production of Space.* Trans. Donald Nicholson-Smith. Cambridge, MA: Wiley-Blackwell, 1991.

Leff, Lisa Moses. *Sacred Bonds of Solidarity: The Rise of Jewish Internationalism in Nineteenth-Century France.* Stanford, CA: Stanford University Press, 2006.

Lehman, Marjorie. "The Gendered Rhetoric of Sukkah Observance." *Jewish Quarterly Review* 96 (2006): 306–35.

Lehnert, Salomon. "Jüdische Volksarbeit." *Der Jude* 1.2 (1916): 104–11.

Leibovitch, Ketty. *La moitié de beaucoup: Regards sur une enfance.* Geneva: Éditions du Tricorne, 2004.

Lempa, Heikki. "The Spa: Emotional Economy and Social Classes in Nineteenth-Century Pyrmont." *Central European History* 35 (2002): 37–73.

Lerner, Paul. *The Consuming Temple: Jews, Department Stores, and the Consumer Revolution in Germany, 1880–1940.* Ithaca, NY: Cornell University Press, 2015.

Levanda, Lev Osipovich. "Starinnie evreiskie svadebnie obichai." *Perezhitoe* 3 (1911): 103–35.

Levin, Nora. *The Jews in the Soviet Union Since 1917: Paradox of Survival.* New York: New York University Press, 1988.

Levinson, Nathan Peter. "The Berlin Jewish Community: Letter to the Editor." *Commentary Magazine* (July 1, 1954). www.commentarymagazine.com/articles/the-berlin-jewish-community/ (accessed January 3, 2018).

———. *Ein Ort ist, mit wem du bist: Lebensstationen eines Rabbiners.* Berlin: Edition Hentrich, 1996.

———. "The Functions of a Rabbi in Postwar Germany." In Michael Brenner, *After the Holocaust: Rebuilding Jewish Lives in Postwar Germany*, 107–10. Princeton, NJ: Princeton University Press, 1997.

Lévy, Louis. "Les femmes d'Israël." *Univers Israélite* (November 30, 1900): 329–33.

———. "L'Union Scolaire." *Univers Israélite* (March 5, 1897): 755–58.

Lévy, Monique. "Juda Lubetski, rabbin." *Archives Juives* 34 (2001–2002): 128–30.

Lichtenstein, J. "Notre sabbat et nos enfants." *Univers Israélite* (September 30, 1932): 23–24.

Lilienblum, Moshe Leib. *Katavim otobiografiim*, vol. 1. Jerusalem: Bialik Institute, 1970.

Lion, Thérèse "Le mariage des israélites russes en France." *Archives Israélites* (May 3, 1923): 70.

Lipphardt, Anna, Julia Brauch, and Alexandra Nocke. "Exploring Jewish Space: An Approach." In Julia Brauch, Anna Lipphardt, and Alexandra Nocke (eds.), *Jewish Topographies: Visions of Space, Traditions of Place*, 1–23. Burlington, VA: Ashgate, 2008.

Lippman, Gert. *A Link in the Chain: Biographical Notes.* Sydney: Star Printery, 1990.

Liudvipol', A. "'Khanuka' i parizhskikh palestinofilov," *Nediel'naia Khronika Voskhoda* (December 8, 1896): 1293–96.

Lowenstein, Steven M. *The Berlin Jewish Community: Enlightenment, Family, and Crisis, 1770–1830.* New York: Oxford University Press, 1994.

———. "Jewish Intermarriage and Conversion in Germany and Austria." *Modern Judaism* 25 (2005): 23–61.

———. "Religious Practice and Mentality." In Marion A. Kaplan (ed.), *Jewish Daily Life in Germany, 1618–1945*, 93–171. Oxford, UK: Oxford University Press, 2005.

Magnus, Shulamit S. "Kol Isha: Women and Pauline Wengeroff's Writing of an Age." *Nashim* 7 (2004): 28–64.

———. "Sins of Youth, Guilt of a Grandmother: M. L. Lilienblum, Pauline Wengeroff, and the Telling of Jewish Modernity in Eastern Europe." *Polin* 18 (2005): 87–120.

Malinovich, Nadia. *French and Jewish: Culture and the Politics of Identity in Early Twentieth-Century France.* Oxford, UK: Littman Library of Jewish Civilization, 2008.

Mandel, Maud. "Genocide and Nationalism: The Changing Nature of Jewish Politics in Post–World War II France." In Zvi Gitelman (ed.), *The Emergence of Modern Jewish Politics: Bundism and Zionism in Eastern Europe*, 197–219. Pittsburgh: University of Pittsburgh Press, 2003.

Mann, Barbara. *A Place in History: Modernism, Tel Aviv, and the Creation of Jewish Urban Space*. Stanford, CA: Stanford University Press, 2006.

Mann, Vivian B. *A Tale of Two Cities: Jewish Life in Frankfurt and Istanbul, 1750–1870*. New York: Jewish Museum, 1982.

Manuel, Albert. "L'initiation a cent ans." *Journal de la Communauté* (June 27, 1952): 4.

Maoz, Eiyahu. "The Werkleute." *Leo Baeck Institute Year Book* 4.1 (1959): 154–82.

Marcus, Ivan G. *Rituals of Childhood: Jewish Acculturation in Medieval Europe*. New Haven, CT: Yale University Press, 1996.

Margolis, Rebecca E. "A Tempest in Three Teapots: Yom Kippur Balls in London, New York, and Montreal." *Canadian Jewish Studies* 9 (2001): 38–84.

Matt, Susan J., and Peter N. Stearns. "Introduction." In Susan J. Matt and Peter N. Stearns (eds.), *Doing Emotions History*, 1–13. Urbana: University of Illinois Press, 2014.

Matthäus, Jürgen (ed.), with Emil Kerenji, Jan Lambertz, and Leah Wolfson. *Jewish Responses to Persecution*, vol. 3, *1941–1942*. Plymouth, UK: Altamira Press, 2013.

Maurer, Trude. "From Everyday Life to a State of Emergency: Jews in Weimar and Nazi Germany." In Marion A. Kaplan (ed.), *Jewish Daily Life in Germany, 1618–1945*, 271–373. Oxford, UK: Oxford University Press, 2005.

———. *Ostjuden in Deutschland, 1918–1933*. Hamburg: Hans Christian, 1986.

———. "Partnersuche und Lebensplanung: Heiratsannoncen als quelle für die Sozial- und Mentalitätsgeschichte der Juden in Deutschland." In Alice Jankowski, Peter Freimark, and Ina S. Lorenz (eds.), *Juden in Deutschland: Emanzipation, Integration, Verfolgung und Vernichtung—25 Jahre Institut für die Geschichte der Deutschen Juden Hamburg*, 344–74. Hamburg: Hans Christians, 1991.

Mayer, Adolph. "Referat." *Monats-Bericht der Grossloge für Deutschland* (April 1891): 3.

Mayer, M. *Instructions morales et religieuses*. Paris: Durlacher & Blum, 1885.

Mayer, Paul Yogi. "Deutsche Juden und Sport: Ihre Leistungen—ihr Schicksal." *Menora* 5 (1994): 287–311.

McReynolds, Louise. *Russia at Play: Leisure Activities at the End of the Tsarist Era*. Ithaca, NY: Cornell University Press, 2002.

Menahem, Freddy. "Raison d'être au centre des jeunes." *Journal des Communautés* (December 9, 1955): 9.

Mendes-Flohr, Paul, and Jehuda Reinharz. *The Jew in the Modern World: A Documentary History*, 3rd ed. Oxford, UK: Oxford University Press, 2011.

Meyer, Beate. *"Jüdische Mischlinge": Rassenpolitik und Verfolgungserfahrung, 1933–1945*. Munich: Dölling und Galitz, 2002.

———. "The Mixed Marriage: A Guarantee of Survival or a Reflection of German Society During the Nazi Regime?" In David Bankier (ed.), *Probing the Depths of German Antisemitism: German Society and the Persecution of the Jews, 1933–1941*, 54–77. New York: Berghahn Books, 2000.

Meyer, Michael A. "*Gemeinschaft* Within *Gemeinde*: Religious Ferment in Weimar Liberal Judaism." In Michael Brenner and Derek J. Penslar (eds.), *In Search of Jewish Community: Jewish Identities in Germany and Austria, 1918–1933*, 15–35. Bloomington: Indiana University Press, 1998.

———. "'How Awesome Is This Place!' The Reconceptualization of the Synagogue in Nineteenth-Century Germany." *Leo Baeck Institute Year Book* 41 (1996): 51–63.

———. "Jewish Communities in Transition." In Michael A. Meyer and Michael Brenner (eds.), *German-Jewish History in Modern Times: Emancipation and Acculturation, 1780–1871*, 90–127. New York: Columbia University Press, 1997.

———. *Response to Modernity: A History of the Reform Movement in Judaism.* Oxford, UK: Oxford University Press, 1988.

Michel, Alain. *Les Éclaireurs israélites de France pendant la seconde guerre mondiale.* Paris: Édition des EIF, 1984.

———. *Juifs, français, et scouts: L'histoire des E.I. de 1923 aux années 80.* Jerusalem: Éditions Elkana, 2003.

———. "Qu'est-ce qu'un scout juif? L'éducation juive chez les Éclaireurs israélites de France, de 1923 au début des années 1950." *Archives Juives* 38 (2005): 77–101.

Michlin, Gilbert. *Aucun intérêt au point de vue national: La grande illusion d'une famille juive en France.* Paris: Albin Michel, 2001.

Miller, Uri. "Maccabi Russia in a General Historical Context." In George Eisen, Hayim Kaufman, and Manfred Lämmer (eds.), *Sport and Physical Education in Jewish History*, 116–25. Netanya: Wingate Institute, 2003.

Miron, Guy. "'Lately, Almost Constantly, Everything Seems Small to Me': The Lived Space of German Jews Under the Nazi Regime." *Jewish Social Studies* 20 (2013): 121–49.

Mogilevskii, Solomon. *Prozhitoe i perezhitoe.* Leningrad and Jerusalem: Mishmeret Shalom, 1997.

Moskoff, William. *The Bread of Affliction: The Food Supply in the USSR During World War II.* Cambridge, UK: Cambridge University Press, 1990.

Moss, Kenneth. *Jewish Renaissance in the Russian Revolution.* Cambridge, MA: Harvard University Press, 2009.

Mosse, George L. *German Jews Beyond Judaism.* Bloomington: Indiana University Press, 1985.

———. "Max Nordau, Liberalism, and the New Jew." *Journal of Contemporary History* 27.4 (1992): 565–81.

———. "Nationalism and Respectability: Normal and Abnormal Sexuality in the Nineteenth Century." *Journal of Contemporary History* 17 (1982): 221–46.

Murav, Harriet. *Music from a Speeding Train: Jewish Literature in Post-Revolution Russia.* Stanford, CA: Stanford University Press, 2011.

Musnik, Roland. "Nos colonies de vacances donnent à l'enfant le goût d'un Judaïsme vivant." *Terre Retrouvée* (October 1, 1955): 6–7.

Nachama, Andreas. "From 1945 to the Present." In Andreas Nachama, Julius H. Schoeps, and Hermann Simon (eds.), *Jews in Berlin.* Trans. Michael S. Cullen and Allison Brown, 221–44. Berlin: Henschel, 2001.

Nachama, Lili. "In der Arche Noah." In Ulrich Eckhardt and Andreas Nachama (eds.), *Jüdische Berliner: Leben nach der Schoa*, 169–87. Berlin: Jaron, 2003.

Nagen, M. "Vecher evreiskoi muzyki v Peterburgie." *Razsviet* (January 17, 1910): 25–26.

Nash, Stanley. *In Search of Hebraism: Shai Hurwitz and His Polemics in the Hebrew Press*. Leiden: Brill, 1980.

———. "Tmunot m-hug sochare ha-ivrit b-berlin, 1900–1914." *Association of Jewish Studies Review* 3 (1978): 1–26.

Nathans, Benjamin. *Beyond the Pale: The Jewish Encounter with Late Imperial Russia*. Berkeley: University of California Press, 2002.

———. "Mythologies and Realities of Jewish Life in Prerevolutionary St. Petersburg." *Studies in Contemporary Jewry* 15 (1999): 107–48.

Nord, Philip. *The Republican Movement: Struggles for Democracy in Nineteenth-Century France*. Cambridge, MA: Harvard University Press, 1995.

Osokina, Elena. *Our Daily Bread: Socialist Distribution and the Art of Survival in Stalin's Russia, 1927–1941*. Trans. Kate Transchel. Armonk, NY: M. E. Sharpe, 2001 [1999].

Ostwald, Hans. "Berlin Coffeehouses." In Iain Boyd Whyte and David Frisby (eds.), *Metropolis Berlin: 1880–1940*, 183–87. Berkeley: University of California Press, 2012.

Parush, Iris. *Reading Jewish Women: Marginality and Modernization in Nineteenth-Century Eastern European Jewish Society*. Trans. Saadya Sternberg. Hanover, NH: University Press of New England, 2004.

———. "Women Readers as Agents of Social Change Among Eastern European Jews in the Late Nineteenth Century." *Gender and History* 9 (1997): 60–82.

Pereferkovich, N. "Bar-Mitsva." *Voskhod* (February 19, 1900): 22–25.

Perry, Joseph B. "The Private Life of the Nation: Christmas and the Invention of Modern Germany." Ph.D. diss., University of Illinois, Urbana-Champaign, 2001.

Pertsovski, I. "Durkhkuk fun Yidisher kunst-tetikeyt in Leningrad." *Folks-Shtime* (April 15, 1958): 1.

———. "Nayer program fun Leningrader Yidishn muzik-ansambl." *Folks-Shtime* (April 26, 1958): 5.

Petras, Renate. *Das Café Bauer in Berlin*. Berlin: Verlag für Bauwesen, 1994.

Pfister, Gertrud. "Die Rolle der jüdischen Frauen in der Turn- und Sportbewegung (1900–1933)." *Stadion* 15.1 (1989): 65–89.

Philippe, Béatrice. *Les juifs à Paris à la Belle Époque*. Paris: Albin Michel, 1992.

Pickus, Keith H. *Constructing Modern Identities: Jewish University Students in Germany, 1815–1914*. Detroit: Wayne State University Press, 1999.

Pinkus, Benjamin. *The Soviet Government and the Jews, 1948–1967: A Documented Study*. Cambridge, UK: Cambridge University Press, 1984.

Pinsker, Shachar. "Between the 'House of Study' and the Coffeehouse: The Central European Café as a Site for Hebrew and Yiddish Modernism." In Charlotte Ashby, Tag Gronberg, and Simon Shaw-Miller (eds.), *The Viennese Café and Fin-de-Siècle Culture*, 78–97. New York: Berghahn Books, 2013.

———. "The Urban Literary Café and the Geography of Hebrew and Yiddish Modernism in Europe." In Mark Wollaeger and Matt Eatough (eds.), *The Oxford Handbook of Global Modernisms*, 433–58. Oxford, UK: Oxford University Press, 2012.

Poliakov, Alexander. "Serebrianyi samovar: vospominaniia." In Alexander Poliakov, *Sem'ia Poliakovykh*, ed. Larisa Vasil'eva, 11–130. Moscow: Atlantida, 1995.

Posner, Louis. *Through a Boy's Eyes: The Turbulent Years, 1926–1945*. Santa Ana, CA: Seven Locks Press, 2000.

Poznanski, Renée. *Être juif en France pendant la seconde guerre mondiale*. Paris: Hachette, 1994.

Prague, H. "Après Simchat Tora: De l'enseignement religieux." *Archives Israélites* (October 10, 1912): 321–23.

——. "Le caractère familial du culte israélite." *Archives Israélites* (October 15, 1908): 329–30.

——. "Ce qui manque au Paris israélite." *Archives Israélites* (December 10, 1908): 393–95.

——. "Contre la décadence." *Archives Israélites* (January 21, 1897): 17–19.

——. "Contre la laïcisation des mariages israélites." *Archives Israélites* (May 30, 1907): 169–71.

——. "Contre les mariages mixtes." *Archives Israélites* (November 17, 1910): 365.

——. "Le culte des parents et le respect de la religion." *Archives Israélites* (August 4, 1910): 241–42.

——. "Défendons notre jeunesse." *Archives Israélites* (February 8, 1912): 41–43.

——. "De l'instruction religieuse." *Archives Israélites* (May 27, 1920): 93.

——. "Des actes!" *Archives Israélites* (March 31, 1910): 97–98.

——. "Le devoir des parents." *Archives Israélites* (September 5, 1907): 282–84.

——. "La marée monte des mariages mixtes." *Archives Israélites* (May 22, 1919): 93–94.

——. "Mariages mixtes." *Archives Israélites* (January 23, 1902): 25–26.

——. "Nos jeunes israélites." *Archives Israélites* (December 26, 1912): 409–11.

——. "Religion et famille." *Archives Israélites* (August 13, 1925): 129–130.

——. "Le rôle de la femme dans la régénération religieuse." *Archives Israélites* (March 20, 1910): 73–75.

——. "Toujours les mariages mixtes." *Archives Israélites* (March 11, 1909): 74.

——. "Une dangereuse innovation." *Archives Israélites* (June 20, 1907): 193–95.

Prestel, Claudia T. "Die Jüdische Familie in der Krise: Symptome und Debatten." In Kirsten Heinsohn and Stefanie Schüler-Springorum (eds.), *Deutsch-jüdische Geschichte als Geschlechtergeschichte: Studien zum 19. und 20. Jahrhundert*, 105–22. Göttingen: Wallstein, 2006.

Pulzer, Peter. *Jews and the German State: The Political History of a Minority, 1848–1933*. Detroit: Wayne State University Press, 2003.

Raczymow, Henri. *Avant le déluge: Belleville années 1950*. Paris: Phileas Fogg, 2005.

Rakovsky, Puah. *My Life as a Radical Jewish Woman: Memoirs of a Zionist Feminist in Poland*. Bloomington: Indiana University Press, 2002.

Reagin, Nancy R. *A German Women's Movement: Class and Gender in Hanover, 1880–1933*. Chapel Hill: University of North Carolina Press, 1995.

Rearick, Charles. *Paris Dreams, Paris Memories: The City and Its Mystique*. Stanford, CA: Stanford University Press, 2011.

Reinharz, Jehuda (ed.). *Dokumente zur Geschichte des deutschen Zionismus, 1882–1933*. Tübingen: Mohr Siebeck, 1981.

Reuveni, Gideon. *Reading Germany: Reading Culture and Consumer Culture in Germany Before 1933*. New York: Berghahn Books, 2005.

Rewald, Ilse. "Der Preis des Überlebens." In Ulrich Eckhardt and Andreas Nachama (eds.), *Jüdische Berliner: Leben nach der Schoa*, 189–207. Berlin: Jaron, 2003.

Richarz, Monika. "Der jüdische Weihnachtsbaum: Familie und Säkularisierung im deutschen Judentum des 19. Jahrhunderts." In Michael Grüttner, Rüdiger Hachtmann, and Heinz-Gerhard Haupt (eds.), *Geschichte und Emanzipation: Festschrift für Reinhard Rürup*, 275–89. Frankfurt am Main: Campus, 1999.

Rieker, Yvonne. *Kindheiten: Identitätsmuster im deutsch-jüdischen Bürgertum und unter ostjüdischen Einwanderern, 1871–1933*. Hildesheim: Georg Olms, 1997.

Roberts, Mary Louise. "Gender, Consumption, and Commodity Culture." *American Historical Review* 103 (1998): 817–44.

Robin, Michel. *Les juifs de Paris: Démographie—économie—culture*. Paris: Éditions A. et J. Picard, 1952.

Rodinson, Maxime. *Souvenirs d'un marginal*. Paris: Fayard, 2005.

Roemer, Nils. "The City of Worms in Modern Jewish Traveling Cultures of Remembrance." *Jewish Social Studies* 11 (2005): 67–91.

Rosengart, Laurence. "Les maisons de l'OSE: Parcours d'une enfance fragmentée." In Martine Lemalet (ed.), *Au secours des enfants du siècle: Regards croisés sur l'OSE*. Menil-sur-L'Estrée: Nil Éditions, 1993.

Rössner, Michael (ed.). *Literarische Kaffeehäuser, Kaffeehausliteraten*. Vienna: Böhlau, 1999.

Roth, Joseph. *The Wandering Jews*. Trans. Michael Hofmann. New York: Norton, 2001.

Roth, Norman. *Daily Life of the Jews in the Middle Ages*. Westport, CT: Greenwood Press, 2005.

Rothenberg, Joshua. *The Jewish Religion in the Soviet Union*. New York: Ktav, 1971.

Rousso, Henry. *The Vichy Syndrome: History and Memory in France Since 1944*. Trans. Arthur Goldhammer. Cambridge, MA: Harvard University Press, 1996.

Rozenblit, Marsha. "Jewish Courtship and Marriage in 1920s Vienna." *AJS Perspectives* (spring 2013): 26–27.

Rubenstein, Joshua. *Soviet Dissidents: Their Struggle for Human Rights*. Boston: Beacon Press, 1985 [1980].

Ruppin, Arthur. *The Jews in the Modern World*. London: Macmillan, 1934.

———. "Die Mischehe." *Zeitschrift für Demographie und Statistik der Juden* 4.2 (1908): 17–23.

———. *Soziologie der Juden: Zweiter Band—Der Kampf der Juden um ihre Zukunft*. Berlin: Jüdischer, 1931.

Salzberger, Georg. "Die jüdisch-christliche Mischehe." *Der Morgen* 5.1 (1929): 18–30.

Samuel, Vivette. *Sauver les enfants*. Paris: Liana Levi, 1995.

Sapir, Boris. "Central Europe." *American Jewish Year Book* 62 (1961): 253–81.

Schatzker, Chaim. *Jüdische Jugend im zweiten Kaiserreich*. Frankfurt am Main: Peter Lang, 1988.

———. "The Special Character of the Jewish Youth Movement." In Asher Cohen and Yehoyakim Cochavi (eds.), *Zionist Youth Movements During the Shoah*, trans. Ted Gorelick, 19–31. New York: Peter Lang, 1995.

Schieb, Barbara. *Nachricht von Chotzen: "Wer immer hofft, stirbt singend."* Berlin: Edition Hentrich, 2000.

Schlögel, Karl. *Petersburg: Das Laboratorium der Moderne, 1909–1921.* Munich: Carl Hanser, 2002.

Schlör, Joachim. *Das Ich der Stadt: Debatten über Judentum und Urbanität, 1822–1938.* Göttingen: Vandenhoeck & Ruprecht, 2005.

Schmelz, U. O. "Die Demographische Entwicklung der Juden in Deutschland von der Mitte des 19. Jahrhunderts bis 1933." *Leo Baeck Institute Bulletin* 83 (1989): 15–62.

Schochat, Asriel. *Der Ursprung der jüdischen Aufklärung in Deutschland.* Trans. Wolfgang Jeremias. Frankfurt: Campus, 2000. [Originally published as Azriel Shohat, *Im hilufe tkufot* (Jerusalem: Dvir, 1960).]

Scholem, Gershom. *From Berlin to Jerusalem: Memories of My Youth.* New York: Schocken, 1980.

Schorestène, E. "Les mariages israélites il y a 50 années." *Univers Israélite* (June 1, 1890): 572–76.

Schwartz, Rabbi Isaac. "Education morale" (reprinted sermon). *Univers Israélite* (December 11, 1896): 382–84.

Schwartz, Vanessa. *Spectacular Realities: Early Mass Culture in Fin de Siècle France.* Berkeley: University of California Press, 1998.

Segal, Jacob "Bevölkerungsbewegung der Juden in Berlin." *Zeitschrift für Demographie und Statistik der Juden* 12.7–9 (1916): 57–78.

Seidman, Naomi. *The Marriage Plot, Or, How Jews Fell in Love with Love, and with Literature.* Stanford, CA: Stanford University Press, 2016.

Shabi, M., and W. El Ansari. "Youth Perceptions of Identity: Participant Profile of a Summer Camp in the United Kingdom." *Journal of Progressive Judaism* 13 (1999): 51–66.

Sharfman, Glenn R. "Between Identities: The German-Jewish Youth Movement Blau-Weiss, 1912–26." In Michael Berkowitz, Susan Tananbaum, and Sam Bloom (eds.), *Forging Modern Jewish Identities: Public Faces and Private Struggles*, 192–228. London: Vallentine Mitchell, 2003.

Shneer, David. *Yiddish and the Creation of Soviet Jewish Culture, 1918–1930.* Cambridge, UK: Cambridge University Press, 2004.

Sholem Aleichem (Scholem Alejchem). *Marienbad: Kein Roman, sondern eine ziemlich verwickelte Geschichte . . .* Trans. Salcia Landmann. Munich: Deutscher Taschenverlag, 1972 [1911].

———. *Tevye's Daughters.* Trans. Frances Butwin. New York: Crown, 1949.

Shorter, Edward. *The Making of the Modern Family.* New York: Basic Books, 1975.

Shternshis, Anna. "Choosing a Spouse in the USSR: Gender Differences and the Ethnic Jewish Factor." *Jews in Russia and Eastern Europe* 2 (2003): 5–30.

———. *Soviet and Kosher: Jewish Popular Culture in the Soviet Union, 1923–1939.* Bloomington: Indiana University Press, 2006.

Shtif, N. "Di tsen-yorike geshikhte fun 'OZE.'" *Folks-Gezunt* (September–October, 1923): 4–5.

Simmel, Georg. "The Metropolis and Mental Life." In Georg Simmel, *The Sociology of Georg Simmel*, ed. Kurt Wolff, 409–24. Glencoe, IL: Free Press, 1950.

Simon, Patrick, and Claudia Tapia. *Le Belleville des juifs tunisiens.* Paris: Éditions Autrement, 1998.

Singermann, Felix. *Die "Lippmann-Tausz" Synagoge und das Rabbinerhaus der "Lipschütz."* Berlin: Itzkowski, 1920.

Slutsky, Yehuda. *Ha-itonut ha-yehudit-rusit be-rashit ha-meah ha-esrim.* Tel Aviv: Tel Aviv University, Diaspora Research Institute, 1978.

Smith, Alison K. "Eating Out in Imperial Russia: Class, Nationality, and Dining Before the Great Reforms." *Slavic Review* 65 (2006): 747–68.

Snyder, Saskia Coenen. *Building a Public Judaism: Synagogues and Jewish Identity in Nineteenth-Century Europe.* Cambridge, MA: Harvard University Press, 2013.

Soja, Edward. *Thirdspace: Journeys to Los Angeles and Other Real-and-Imagined Places.* Cambridge, MA: Blackwell, 1996.

Sorkin, David. "Enlightenment and Emancipation: German Jewry's Formative Age in Comparative Perspective." In Todd M. Endelman (ed.), *Comparing Jewish Societies*, 89–112. Ann Arbor: University of Michigan Press, 2000.

———. *The Transformation of German Jewry, 1780–1840.* Oxford, UK: Oxford University Press, 1987.

Spiegel, Alexander S. *A Life in Storm.* Jerusalem: M. Neuman, 1953.

———. *Through Fire and Water: Three Generations.* Tel Aviv: Achdut, 1959.

Stanislawski, Michael. *For Whom Do I Toil? Judah Leib Gordon and the Crisis of Russian Jewry.* Oxford, UK: Oxford University Press, 1988.

Stearns, Peter N. "Challenges in the History of Childhood." *Journal of the History of Childhood and Youth* 1 (2008): 35–42.

———. "Modern Patterns in Emotions History." In Susan J. Matt and Peter N. Stearns (eds.), *Doing Emotions History*, 17–40. Urbana: University of Illinois Press, 2014.

Stein, Sarah Abrevaya. *Making Jews Modern: The Yiddish and Ladino Press in the Russian and Ottoman Empires.* Bloomington: Indiana University Press, 2004.

———. *Plumes: Ostrich Feathers, Jews, and a Lost World of Global Commerce.* New Haven, CT: Yale University Press, 2010.

Steinberg, Mark D. *Petersburg: Fin de Siècle.* New Haven, CT: Yale University Press, 2011.

Stern, Erich. "Über die Bedeutung religiöser Formen für die Erziehung." *Der Morgen* (1928): 433–44.

Stern, William. *Anfänge der Reifezeit: Ein Knabentagebuch in psychologischer Bearbeitung*, 2nd ed. Leipzig: Quelle & Meyer, 1929 [1925].

Stites, Richard. *Russian Popular Culture: Entertainment and Society Since 1900.* Cambridge, UK: Cambridge University Press, 1992.

———. *The Women's Liberation Movement in Russia: Feminism, Nihilism, and Bolshevism, 1860–1930.* Princeton, NJ: Princeton University Press, 1978.

Stoltzfus, Nathan. "The Limits of Policy: Social Protection of Intermarried German Jews in Nazi Germany." In Robert Gellately and Nathan Stoltzfus (eds.), *Social Outsiders in Nazi Germany*, 117–44. Princeton, NJ: Princeton University Press, 2001.

Stone, Lawrence. *The Family, Sex, and Marriage in England, 1500–1800*. New York: Harper & Row, 1977.

Strasser, Susan, Charles McGovern, and Matthias Judt (eds.). *Getting and Spending: European and American Consumer Societies in the Twentieth Century*. Cambridge, UK: Cambridge University Press, 1998.

Strauss, Herbert A. *In the Eye of the Storm: Growing Up Jewish in Germany, 1918–1943—A Memoir*. New York: Fordham University Press, 1999.

———. "The *Jugendverband*: A Social and Intellectual History." *Leo Baeck Institute Year Book* 6 (1961): 206–35.

Strauss, Lotte. *Over the Green Hill: A German Jewish Memoir, 1913–1943*. New York: Fordham University Press, 1999.

Strauss, Rachel. *Wir lebten in Deutschland: Erinnerungen einer Deutschen Jüdin, 1880–1933*. Stuttgart: Deutsche Verlags-Anstalt, 1961.

Sussman, Sarah Beth. "Changing Lands, Changing Identities: The Migration of Algerian Jewry to France, 1954–1967." Ph.D. diss., Stanford University, 2002.

Sutcliffe, Adam. "Anxieties of Distinctiveness: Walter Sombart's *The Jews and Modern Capitalism* and the Politics of Jewish Economic History." In Rebecca Kobrin and Adam Teller (eds.), *Purchasing Power: The Economics of Modern Jewish History*, 238–58. Philadelphia: University of Pennsylvania Press, 2015.

Tänzer, A. *Die Mischehe in Religion, Geschichte und Statistik der Juden*. Berlin: Louis Lamm, 1913.

Teitel, Jacob. *Aus meiner Lebensarbeit: Erinnerungen eines jüdischen Richters im alten Rußland*. Teetz: Hentrich & Hentrich, 1999.

Tichauer, Horst. "Wer sind wir?" In Ulrich Eckhardt and Andreas Nachama (eds.), *Jüdische Berliner: Leben nach der Schoa*, 249–72. Berlin: Jaron, 2003.

Tiersten, Lisa. *Marianne in the Market: Envisioning Consumer Society in Fin-de-Siècle France*. Berkeley: University of California Press, 2001.

Timm, Angelika. "Ein ambivalentes Verhältnis: Juden in der DDR und der Staat Israel." In Moshe Zuckermann (ed.), *Zwischen Politik und Kultur: Juden in der DDR*, 17–33. Göttingen: Wallstein, 2002.

Tomaschewsky, Johanna. "Mädchenerziehung." *Jüdische Turn- und Sportzeitung* (February 1919): 6–10.

Triendl-Zadoff, Mirjam. *Nächstes Jahr in Marienbad: Gegenwelten jüdischer Kulturen der Moderne*. Göttingen: Vandenhoeck & Ruprecht, 2007.

Tsherikover, E. (Elias or Elye). "M-yerushat mishpaha patriarkalit." *He-avar* 1 (1918): 117–30.

Tysler, I. "Evreiskii gimnasticheskii kruzhok v Petrogradie (1914–1917 gg.)." *Makkabi* 1.2–3 (1917–1918): 39–42.

Urbah, Marianne. "Le mariage des Juifs devant le droit français (1896–1967): Sa celebration." *Archives Juives* 17 (1981): 50–64.

Ury, Scott. *Barricades and Banners: The Revolution of 1905 and the Transformation of Warsaw Jewry.* Stanford, CA: Stanford University Press, 2012.

Valensi, Lucette. "Multicultural Visions: The Cultural Tapestry of the Jews of North Africa." In David Biale (ed.), *Cultures of the Jews,* vol. 3, *Modern Encounters,* 165–209. New York: Schocken, 2002.

Valensi, Lucette, and Nathan Wachtel. *Jewish Memories.* Berkeley: University of California Press, 1991.

Van Rahden, Till. "Intermarriages, the 'New Woman,' and the Situational Ethnicity of Breslau Jews from the 1870s to the 1920s." *Leo Baeck Institute Year Book* 46 (2001): 125–50.

Veidlinger, Jeffrey. "Jewish Cultural Associations in the Aftermath of 1905." In Stefani Hoffman and Ezra Mendelsohn (eds.), *The Revolution of 1905 and Russia's Jews,* 199–211. Philadelphia: University of Pennsylvania Press, 2008.

———. *Jewish Public Culture in the Late Russian Empire.* Bloomington: Indiana University Press, 2009.

———. *The Moscow State Yiddish Theater: Jewish Culture on the Soviet Stage.* Bloomington: Indiana University Press, 2000.

Vogel, David. *Married Life.* Trans. Dalya Bilu. Milford, CT: Toby Press, 2007.

Vogt, Stefan. *Subalterne Positionierungen: Der deutsche Zionismus im Feld des Nationalismus in Deutschland 1890–1933.* Göttingen: Wallstein, 2016.

Volkov, Shulamit. "German-Jews Between Fulfillment and Dissolution: The Individual and the Community." In Michael Brenner and Derek J. Penslar (eds.), *In Search of Jewish Community: Jewish Identities in Germany and Austria, 1918–1933,* 1–14. Bloomington: Indiana University Press, 1998.

Vygodskaia, Anna Pavlovna. *Istoriia odnoi zhizni.* Riga: Dzive un Kultura, 1938.

———. *The Story of a Life: Memoirs of a Young Jewish Woman in the Russian Empire.* Trans. and ed. Eugene M. Avrutim and Robert H. Greene. DeKalb: Northern Illinois University Press, 2012.

Waal, Edmund de. *The Hare with Amber Eyes: A Family's Century of Art and Loss.* New York: Farrar, Straus & Giroux, 2010.

Walk, Joseph (ed.). *Das Sonderrecht für die Juden im NS-Staat: Eine Sammlung der gesetzlichen Maßnahmen und Richtlinien—Inhalt und Bedeutung.* Heidelberg: C. F. Müller Juristischer, 1981.

Wasserman, Henry (ed.). *Shaye: Early Writings of Prof. Yeshayahu Leibowitz and His Wife, Grete.* Jerusalem: Carmel, 2010.

Wassermann, Ch. "Beobachtungen an jüdischen Ferienkolonisten." *Zeitschrift für Demographie und Statistik der Juden* (May 1907): 79.

Webber, Andrew J. *Berlin in the Twentieth Century: A Cultural Topography.* Cambridge, UK: Cambridge University Press, 2008.

Weil, Patrick. "De l'affaire Dreyfus à l'occupation." In Jean-Jacques Becker and Annette Wieviorka (eds.), *Les juifs de France: De la révolution française à nos jours,* 103–68. Paris: Éditions Liana Levi, 1998.

Weill, E. "De l'enseignement religieux: Lettre au rédacteur en chef." *Archives Israélites* (January 20, 1910): 19–20.

Weinberg, David H. "Dealing with Survivor Youth in West European Jewish Communities After the War." In Suzanne Bardgett, David Cesarani, Jessica Reinisch, and Johannes-Dieter Steinert (eds.), *Survivors of Nazi Persecution in Europe After the Second World War*, 181–97. London: Vallentine Mitchell, 2010.

———. *Les juifs à Paris de 1933 à 1939*. Paris: Calman-Lévy, 1974.

———. "The Reconstruction of the French Jewish Community After World War II." In Yisrael Gutman and Avital Saf (ed.), *She'erit Hapletah, 1944–1948: Rehabilitation and Political Struggle*, 168–86. Jerusalem: Yad Vashem, 1990.

Weiner, Amir. *Making Sense of War: The Second World War and the Fate of the Bolshevik Revolution*. Princeton, NJ: Princeton University Press, 2001.

Weinstein, Roni. *Marriage Rituals Italian style: A Historical Anthropological Perspective on Early Modern Italian Jews*. Trans. Batya Stein. Leiden: Brill, 2004.

Weitzman, Steven. "From Feasts into Mourning: The Violence of Early Jewish Festivals." *Journal of Religion* 79 (1999): 545–65.

Wengeroff, Pauline. *Memoiren einer Grossmutter: Bilder aus der Kulturgeschichte der Juden Russlands im 19. Jahrhundert*, 2nd ed. Berlin: M. Poppelauer, 1913.

Wiese, Christian. "Modern Antisemitism and Jewish Responses in Germany and France, 1880–1914." In Michael Brenner, Vicki Caron, and Uri R. Kaufmann (eds.), *Jewish Emancipation Reconsidered: The French and German Models*, 129–53. Tübingen: Mohr Siebeck, 2003.

Wieviorka, Annette. "Éléments pour servir à l'histoire des maisons d'enfants de l'OSE dans l'après-guerre." In Martine Lemalet (ed.), *Au secours des enfants du siècle: Regards croisés sur l'OSE*. Menil-sur-L'Estrée: Nil Éditions, 1993.

———. "Réflexions sur une commémoration." *Annales: Économies, Sociétés, Civilisations* 48 (1993): 703–14.

Wildman, Daniel. *Der veränderbare Körper: jüdische Turner, Männlichkeit und das Wiedergewinnen von Geschichte in Deutschland um 1900*. Tübingen: Mohr Siebeck, 2009.

Williams, Rosalind H. *Dream Worlds: Mass Consumption in Late Nineteenth-Century France*. Berkeley: University of California Press, 1982.

Wobick-Segev, Sarah E. "Buying, Selling, Being, Drinking; Or, How the Coffeehouse Became a Site for the Consumption of New Jewish Identities." In Gideon Reuveni and Sarah Wobick-Segev (eds.), *Speculation and Exchange: New Approaches to the Economy in Jewish History*, 115–34. New York: Berghahn Books, 2011.

———. "German-Jewish Spatial Cultures: Consuming and Refashioning Jewish Belonging in Berlin, 1890–1910." In Nils Roemer and Gideon Reuveni (eds.), *Jewish Longings and Belongings in Modern European Consumer Culture*, 39–60. Leiden: Brill, 2010.

Wolff, Mathieu. "Hanoukka-Noël." *Univers Israélite* (December 23, 1910): 461–63.

———. "Première communion—bar mitsva—initiation." *Univers Israélite* (May 12, 1911): 268.

———. "Propos sabbatique: Féminisme juif." *Univers Israélite* (November 9, 1900): 232–33.

Wolski, B. "L'activité de la Colonie Scolaire." *Almanach Juif,* 9–23. Paris: La Nouvelle Génération, 1931.

Wormser, Georges "L'initiation religieuse: Mise au point." *Journal de la Communauté* (April 25, 1952): 8.

Yeykelis, Igor. "Odessa Maccabi, 1917–20: The Development of Sport and Physical Culture in Odessa's Jewish Community." *East European Jewish Affairs* 28 (1998–1999): 83–101.

Zeltser, Arkadii. "The Establishment of a Jewish Musical and Dramatic Group in Leningrad in 1958." *Jews in Eastern Europe* 47–48.1–2 (2002): 105–24.

Zimmermann, Moshe. "Muscle Jews Versus Nervous Jews." In Michael Brenner and Gideon Reuveni (eds.), *Emancipation Through Muscles: Jews and Sports in Europe,* 13–26. Lincoln: University of Nebraska Press, 2006.

————. "Zwischen Selbstbehauptung und Diskriminierung: Deutsch-Jüdische Turn- und Sportzeitungen." In Michael Nagel (ed.), *Zwischen Selbstbehauptung und Verfolgung: Deutsch-jüdische Zeitungen und Zeitschriften von der Aufklärung bis zum Nationalsozialismus,* 295–317. Hildesheim: Georg Olms, 2002.

Zisserman-Brodsky, Dina. *Constructing Ethnopolitics in the Soviet Union: Samizdat, Deprivation, and the Rise of Ethnic Nationalism.* New York: Palgrave Macmillan, 2003.

Zubkova, Elena. *Russia After the War: Hopes, Illusions, and Disappointments, 1945–1957.* Trans. Hugh Ragsdale. Armonk, NY: M. E. Sharpe, 1998.

Zweig, Arnold. *The Face of East European Jewry.* Ed. and trans. Noah Isenberg. Berkeley: University of California Press, 2004.

Index

STANFORD STUDIES IN JEWISH HISTORY AND CULTUR

David Biale and Sarah Abrevaya Stein, Editors

This series features novel approaches to examining the Jewish past in the form of innovative work that brings the field into productive dialogue with the newest scholarly concepts and methods. Open to a range of disiplinary and interdisciplinary approaches from history to cultural studies, this series publishes exceptional scholarship balanced by an accessible tone that illustrates histories of difference and addresses issues of current urgency. Books in this list push the boundaries of Jewish Studies and speak compellingly to a wide audience of scholars and students.

For a complete listing of titles in this series, visit the Stanford University Press website, www.sup.org.